W0036181

Advance Praise

Father Camille Bulcke was an exceptional missionary who devoted his entire life to serving Hindi. Buckle's lifelong association with *Ramcharitmanas* and its remarkable creator, Tulsidas, brought some of the finest writings on the genesis and development of *Ramkatha*. As a distinguished lexicographer, Bulcke compiled an excellent English–Hindi dictionary, which is very useful even after so many decades. This book offers a fascinating account of Bulcke's life, his times and his contribution to India and the Hindi world.

Emmanuel Baxla
Director, Fr Camille Bulcke Research Centre, St Xavier's College, Ranchi
Translator of Bulcke's English–Hindi dictionary into Hindi–English dictionary

After my arrival in India in 1965, I lived in the same house (Manresa) as Father Bulcke's in Ranchi, and he directed me in my study of Hindi and Sanskrit. Once a week we went for a 20-kilometre cycle ride, regularly overtaken by dangerous trucks. He told me he would cycle in the middle of the road: 'You still have a longer life to live than me.' This *snehi*, loving and humane Father Bulcke emerges beautifully in this book, as much as the great scholar and the ascetic Jesuit. The backdrop descriptions of his native Flanders, his Allahabad *maika* and the Ranchi guru-ship are most interesting. His hearing impairment made his life at times lonely, but he found a firm footing in spirituality, both Christian and Rama-oriented, although some may argue that the juxtaposition of Christ and Tulsidas as the idols of Bulcke*ji* is too simplistic. The synthesis of Bulcke*ji*'s life in the conclusion is a remarkable piece of balanced scholarship.

Winand M. Callewaert
Emeritus Professor, Centre for Advanced India–EU Studies,
Katholieke Universiteit Leuven (KU Leuven)
Renowned Sanskrit scholar and author with over two dozen books on Bhakti literature

This critical biography of the remarkable Camille Bulcke is both an appreciative assessment of his extraordinary contributions to Ramayana scholarship, lexicography and inter-religious understanding and a nuanced appraisal of his complex and at times contradictory motivations as a devout Catholic missionary, born-again Indian and scholar and votary of Tulsidas, who served his adopted nation and its people with wholehearted devotion. In the polarised and politicised climate of twenty-first-century India, Baba Bulcke's unflinching commitment to active *prem*—for *desh*, *bhasha*, *samskriti* and *log*—transcending religious and class barriers, is inspiring even in its imperfections.

Philip Lutgendorf

Emeritus Professor of Hindi and Modern Indian Studies, University of Iowa
Author of *The Life of a Text: Performing the Rāmcaritmānas of Tulsidas*; translator of
The Epic of Ram (7 volumes, 1991)

This is a lovely book. It reveals, layer by layer, the profound forms of knowledge and respect that can connect people of very different religious traditions, through examining the life of Camille Bulcke, a Flemish Jesuit and scholar sent to India in the 1930s as a missionary, but whose embrace of Hindi and respect for Hinduism and the work of Tulsidas on *Ramcharitmanas* were transformative for both Indian and European audiences. Ravi Dutt Bajpai and Swati Parashar have not only provided a penetrating biography of this priest, his love for the Hindu saint and poet Tulsidas and the limitations of his cosmology, but have also brought the reader into the linguistic, theological, poetic and methodological forms that engage and enliven connections across worlds. The divinities must be pleased.

Cecelia M. Lynch

Professor, Political Science, School of Social Sciences, University of California, Irvine

Amidst the turbulence of today's world, where uncertainty looms large, the solace and enlightenment drawn from history are invaluable. Father Camille Bulcke emerges as a beacon from not-so-distant times, his life a testament to the virtues of compassionate transgression and intellectual endeavour. Hailing from Belgium, this Jesuit missionary transcended boundaries as a noted Indologist and *Ramkatha* exponent, leaving behind a legacy rich in social understanding. In an era marked by entrenched ideologies, figures like Father Bulcke are scarce. Their commitment to dialogue and understanding stands in stark contrast to prevailing hardline positions. Bajpai and Parashar's book pays fitting tribute to Father Bulcke, capturing the essence of his mission: fostering harmony amidst cultural diversity and divergent belief systems.

Priyankar Upadhyay

UNESCO Chair for Peace and Intercultural Understanding Professor, Banaras Hindu University, Varanasi Global Fellow, Peace Research Institute Oslo (PRIO)

A portrait of a charming man and engaged scholar who was a bundle of contradictions – devoted to Tulsidas but also to the idea that Christianity is the only path to salvation. His approach to Hindu texts and ideas has a lot to do with the Christianising of modern Hinduism.

Ruth Vanita

Author of *Love's Rite* (2005), *Memory of Light* (2020) and *The Dharma of Justice in the Sanskrit Epics* (2021)

Camille Bulcke

This is the first English biography of the Belgian Jesuit, Padma Bhushan recipient and renowned scholar of Hindi, Awadhi and Sanskrit: Father Camille Bulcke (1909–1982). Father Bulcke came to India when it was still a British colony, found spiritual inspiration in the life and compositions of the great Indian poet Goswami Tulsidas, and emerged as one of the renowned exponents of the *Ramkatha* (The Story of Rama) and the Hindi language. This book attempts to read and critically examine his life, while also analysing his writings on comparative religious studies. In doing so, it provides a brief overview of the world of Hindi literature and its development in postcolonial India through the contributions of Father Bulcke, and highlights the cultural and religious encounters between the West and the East, Europe and India, Christianity and Hinduism.

Ravi Dutt Bajpai is an author and visiting researcher at the School of Global Studies, University of Gothenburg, Sweden. He is the co-author (with Harivansh) of *Chandra Shekhar: The Last Icon of Ideological Politics* (2019) and author of *Civilization-States of China and India: Reshaping the World Order* (2024).

Swati Parashar is Professor in Peace and Development at the School of Global Studies, University of Gothenburg, Sweden. She is the author of *Women and Militant Wars: The Politics of Injury* (2014), co-author of *Ripping, Cutting, Stitching: Feminist Knowledge Destruction and Creation in Global Politics* (2023) and co-editor of *Revisiting Gendered States: Feminist Imaginings of the State in International Relations* (2018).

Camille Bulcke

The Jesuit Exponent of *Ramkatha*

Ravi Dutt Bajpai
Swati Parashar

CAMBRIDGE
UNIVERSITY PRESS

Shaftesbury Road, Cambridge CB2 8EA, United Kingdom

One Liberty Plaza, 20th Floor, New York, NY 10006, USA

477 Williamstown Road, Port Melbourne, VIC 3207, Australia

314–321, 3rd Floor, Plot 3, Splendor Forum, Jasola District Centre, New Delhi – 110025, India

103 Penang Road, #05–06/07, Visioncrest Commercial, Singapore 238467

Cambridge University Press is part of Cambridge University Press & Assessment, a department of the University of Cambridge.

We share the University's mission to contribute to society through the pursuit of education, learning and research at the highest international levels of excellence.

www.cambridge.org
Information on this title: www.cambridge.org/9781108838122

© Ravi Dutt Bajpai and Swati Parashar 2024

This publication is in copyright. Subject to statutory exception and to the provisions of relevant collective licensing agreements, no reproduction of any part may take place without the written permission of Cambridge University Press & Assessment

First published 2024

Printed in India by Avantika Printers Pvt. Ltd.

A catalogue record for this publication is available from the British Library

ISBN 978-1-108-83812-2 Hardback

Cambridge University Press & Assessment has no responsibility for the persistence or accuracy of URLs for external or third-party internet websites referred to in this publication, and does not guarantee that any content on such websites is, or will remain, accurate or appropriate.

The inspiration for this book comes from Father Camille Bulcke's Christ and Goswami Tulsidas' Rama, both of whom are the finest examples of the human-divine, inspiring the most outstanding and universally recognised standards of public welfare, personal integrity, ethical living, moral values, and love and compassion for all humans.

One was an 'avatar' of God, a humble king who embraced the hardship of exile as self-sacrifice and devotion to his family, and later ruled over his kingdom with great sense of love and justice for all his subjects. The other was the 'son of God', an ordinary shepherd who embraced the suffering of people, extending compassion, generosity and kindness to all.

We dedicate this book to seekers of knowledge and the divine in every tradition who work to mitigate differences among humans based on gender, race, ethnicity, religion, creed and caste – and who teach that empathy, compassion and justice are the only redemption for humanity.

For even the Son of Man did not come to be served, but to serve, and to give his life as a ransom for many.

—Mark 10:45, Bible

परहित सरिस धरम नहिं भाई।
पर पीड़ा सम नहिं अधमाई॥

There is no better *dharma* (religious duty) than benevolence; nothing more sinful than malevolence towards others.

—Goswami Tulsidas, *Ramcharitmanas*

Contents

Figures

Foreword

Of the numerous scholars of Hindi among the British administrators and European missionaries who came to India over the last two hundred years – most notably John Gilchrist, George Grierson, F. W. Keay and Edwin Greaves – and lately among the post-colonial 'South Asianists', only Camille Bulcke seems to have the distinction of becoming a household name in the extensive Hindi-speaking areas of the country.

That is because one can find in countless Hindi homes a copy of his *Angreji–Hindi Kosh* (English–Hindi Dictionary), first published in 1968, in its third revised edition by 1981, and reprinted altogether 19 times already by 1991 when I belatedly acquired my copy. As Bulcke explained in his preface, he intended it for the use of those who already had English but wished to learn Hindi (like himself) and hoped that it might prove useful 'also to those whose mother tongue is Hindi, especially those engaged in translation work' (like myself). But he also added a third category of people to whom this work might be of help: 'Indian students who wish to improve their knowledge of English'. One may suspect that it is this last category which has benefitted the most from Bulcke's triple-function dictionary, for it nicely supplements or even supersedes the usual English–English dictionaries, where the explanation given is, for many early learners, nearly as challenging as the words they look up.

Bulcke also provided the correct pronunciation of each word in the Devanagari script, which is incomparably more phonetic than the Roman script. Moreover, he cut out the frills which needlessly complicate the life of a language learner. For example, the title of his work has for its first word not the English word 'English' but the Hindi word 'Angreji', which is here spelt not as 'Angrezi' with a *z* but as 'Angreji' with a *j*, the common pronunciation of the word without the non-native sound *z*. Bulcke had obviously learnt his Hindi well enough to know what is indigenous to it and what is not (Bulcke 1968, vii). Here and there he also indicated a personal predilection as when he defined 'Christianity' as not only 'Isai dharm', which is common usage (following the Arabic name for Jesus which is common among Muslims), but alternatively also as 'Khreest dharm' or 'Khreestiyata', which are unmediated approximations of the name 'Christ' though hardly commonly used (Bulcke 1968, 106).

Ramkatha and Christian Faith

The status of this dictionary as Bulcke's best-known work is ironic and illustrates the vagaries of fortune and fame for his life's work was not this useful pedagogical device but a scholarly treatise which was unprecedented in Hindi in terms of scope, ambition and erudition. This magnum opus of his was titled *Ramkatha: Utpatti Aur Vikas* (The Rama Story: Its Origin and Development, 1950). It was the outcome of his doctoral dissertation, undertaken at the University of Allahabad and completed in a period of just over two years from 1947 to 1949. The research that Bucke conducted for it was as original as it was extensive, for he ranged beyond Hindi over other major Indian languages, beginning with Sanskrit and the Vedas, down to the languages of South-East Asia. His erudition looks highly impressive even now and was in his own pre-internet age simply phenomenal.

   This was just the beginning of a long and rich scholarly career in which Bulcke produced a large number and variety of works. Besides these two outstanding works, he authored and edited several works centred on his favourite Hindi poet, Tulsidas, and on Hindi and its propagation as a national language, a cause of which he was a dedicated champion. On the other hand, he produced an even larger number of books rendering into Hindi several key Christian texts, including a Hindi translation of the New Testament under the title *Naya Vidhan*. He created an immensely popular account of the life of Christ in which he hit upon the innovative idea of amalgamating the four different Gospels into one; this was published in English as *The Saviour* and in his own Hindi version as *Muktidata*. (Incidentally, this self-translation seems to elide the theological question that someone who saves souls from damnation, as in Christian belief, may be thought to perform a function quite different from someone who grants liberation, *mukti*, to souls from the cycle of rebirth, but such are the ever-present perils of translation.) Bulcke also produced a Hindi version of the psalter, and in his last years he undertook a new translation of the Old Testament, which he had nearly completed when he passed away at the age of 73. Indeed, as in the case of *The Saviour*, all these translations may be studied for the ways in which Bulcke sought to achieve theological and cultural equivalence between the source language and the target language.

Altogether, of the 29 books or booklets that Bulcke published in Hindi and English, 9 were related to Hindi language and literature, 19 were on Christian themes, and 1, titled *Hindi Christian Names*, could be classed under either category. Of the 65 articles he wrote, those in English were often about some aspect or the other of the story of Rama while those in Hindi provided authoritative information about Christian subjects. And of the 85 chapters or entries in books that he published, as many as 76 were contributions to a single publication, *Hindi Vishvakosh* (Hindi Encyclopaedia, 1965), mostly on Christian figures or themes: from 'Abraham', 'Archbishop' and 'Augustine' to 'Jesuit', 'Tritva' (the Trinity) and 'Vatican'.

But in a double distinction, the same Hindi encyclopaedia also invited Bulcke to contribute entries on 'Ramkatha', 'Ramkavya' and 'Rambhakti'! This was perhaps the unique achievement of Bulcke: to be honoured equally as an expert with an encyclopaedic and authentic knowledge of Christianity, which was the faith he lived by, and as an expert on the Hindu cult of devotion to Rama, which was the subject of his dedicated lifelong scholarship. This may seem to some readers like a paradox, but Bulcke's life and works are a living testimony that one can lead a doubly worthy life at two distinct levels. He stood between two religious faiths, languages and cultures as a bridge, promoting mutual understanding between them not only literally as a dictionary does or even a translation, but also at a deeper cultural and religious level as only a true and sympathetic interpreter can. Born in Belgium and brought up and educated there as an engineer, he decided in his youth to turn a new leaf to lead a life of an exile and a missionary in a strange far-away land. His life is thus as fascinating as it is challenging to comprehend and interpret.

This Biography

The authors of this first-ever biography of Bulcke, Ravi Dutt Bajpai and Swati Parashar, thus had their work cut out for them, and it would be immediately clear to any reader that they have conceptualised and executed their task with assiduous erudition and scrupulous objectivity. In this full and fair account, they provide a wealth of information about the life of Bulcke while also analysing several of his major works as they proceed. And they finally arrive at conclusions which are the more persuasive for being appreciative and unremitting at the same time.

Among other things, Bajpai and Parashar offer an especially sensitive and nuanced discussion of a vexed question as to where precisely Bulcke stood vis-à-vis Christianity and Hinduism. They show how Bulcke believed that Tulsidas' Rama is not a historical figure and that Tulsidas himself nowhere claimed this to be the case. On the question of the 'authenticity' of the Hindu gods, Bajpai and Parashar tell us, Bulcke 'embraced the standard approach of a civilising mission'. A cardinal difference here, in Bulcke's view, was that the Hindu gods did not suffer for the sins of humanity as Jesus did in Christian belief. Bulcke also held that some Hindus who believed that all religions were the same were mistaken for, as he put it, 'one of us is wrong' (see pages 217 and 223). Altogether, this biography presents a clear, coherent and consolidated account of Bulcke's long and productive life in the many locations where his quest took him. In doing so, it supersedes all previous accounts of Bulcke, which were often memoirs based on partial personal knowledge or a discussion of any one particular phase of his life or work.

Of these, the foremost is *Dr Bulcke Smriti Granth* (Dr Bulcke Commemoration Volume, 1987), edited by Dineshwar Prasad and Shravan Kumar Goswami, a voluminous tribute which in its 440 pages comprises 98 contributions. These include memoirs of Bulcke as a man, assessments of his published works, learned essays providing information about his motherland, Belgium, accounts of his arena of action in and around Ranchi in the state now named Jharkhand, and a final section of miscellaneous essays. Another similar volume is *Father Camille Bulcke: Bharteeyata Ke Prakash Punj* (Father Camille Bulcke: A Beacon Light of Indianness, 2015); it was commissioned by the Indian Council for Cultural Relations and edited by Suresh Rituparna. By arrangement with the editors of the former volume, this collection reprinted several of its essays so that these might have a wider circulation now while also including many other contributions which were new or collected from different sources. Most valuably perhaps, it includes a 20-page interview given by Bulcke in 1976 to Dineshwar Prasad, in which he candidly answered many questions regarding Christianity vis-à-vis Hinduism, and a selection of nine essays written in Hindi by Bulcke. To these two primary sources may be added a more popular and often overlooked source, a one-hour documentary film titled *Baba Bulcke*, made by the government-owned Rajya Sabha TV channel in the series *Virasat* (Heritage) and anchored and narrated by Rajesh Badal in 2017. A special feature of this film is the inclusion of several clips of Bulcke speaking in Hindi; he may sound slightly accented but is always meticulously correct (Rajya Sabha TV 2017).

The present biography by Bajpai and Parashar goes beyond all these previous accounts not only in being more substantial, consecutive and authoritative but also in several other respects. To mention first the most obvious difference, while the aforementioned sources, including the documentary film, are all in Hindi, this book is in English and thus addresses a different and potentially wider readership. It also follows a different scholarly protocol by being objective and critical rather than adulatory as memoirs in Hindi tend to be. It is critical not in the sense of being carping or nitpicking but in assessing Bulcke and his contribution in an unbiased and impartial manner. In the process, Bajpai and Parashar present a new portrait of Bulcke, warts and all, which is the more attractive because it is more realistic and credible. In situating Bulcke 'as a product of specific times' (see page 18), the biography facilitates, paradoxically, a better understanding of the man on our own terms and in our own times now.

Issues and Future Directions

As if not content with setting up through this biography a scholarly monument to Bulcke, Bajpai and Parashar raise questions at various points in their narrative which may signal new directions for future scholars of Bulcke. A few of these, which may be thought to be particularly significant, are briefly highlighted as follows.

The first such question concerns the very heart of the matter. What precisely was it that attracted Bulcke to India, to *Ramkatha* and to the poet Tulsidas, whose *bhakta*, or devotee, he professed himself to be, just as Tulsidas was a *bhakta* of Rama? Bulcke himself often cited a couplet from Tulsidas' *Ramcharitmanas*, which he first read in Belgium in a German translation, as having caused for him an epiphany and inspired his love for Tulsidas even before he arrived in India. This couplet, beginning 'धन्य जनम जगतीतल तासू', is aptly cited in this biography as many as three times in different places (see pages 56, 64 and 107). But it may be suggested that in its original context of Rama's banishment by his father, Dashratha, this couplet perhaps does not sound particularly felicitous or pious for though Rama happily obeys his father and says in the couplet that he feels blessed for doing so and thus being a cause of happiness to his father, the father himself is far from happy. As depicted by Tulsidas, he has been coerced by the queen Kaikeyi to banish Rama against his own will and in fact dies shortly afterwards

of regret and grief. (There might have been a deep psychological reason as to why
Bulcke liked these lines for he and his father never derived much joy from each
other, but this can be nothing more than a surmise.) Bulcke never got around
to writing a whole book on Tulsidas which might have shed more light on this
matter, though he nurtured that ambition till his last years. In the situation,
all that Bulcke ever said about Tulsidas in different places needs to be closely
collated to account for his devotion to the poet.

A corollary of this, for which Bulcke himself was not as responsible as are
some of his overzealous Indian admirers, is the widespread misunderstanding
that Bulcke was himself a Rama *bhakt*, a devotee of Rama. Throughout the
numerous tributes to Bulcke paid by his friends and admirers in the Hindi
literary sphere, this belief is casually purveyed as being the undisputed truth,
including by the anchor of the aforementioned documentary on Bulcke. Even
the poet Harivansh Rai Bachchan seems to subscribe to this wishful view in a
poem he wrote as a tribute to Bulcke, which is given a place of honour in both
the commemoration volumes mentioned earlier by being printed (in his own
handwriting) immediately after the title page. He wrote: 'Isai sanskar liye bhi /
Pujya hue tumko Shri Rama' (You grew up adhering to the Christian faith / Yet
Shri Rama was for you an object of worship). Among a host of over-pious and
over-eager Hindi admirers, the poet and novelist Agyeya stands out as clearly
stating that Bulcke's erudite study of *Ramkatha* is 'a shining example not of his
Rama-bhakti but rather of his love of scholarship and his dedication to research
work' (quoted in Rituparna 2015, p. 64).

To their credit, Bajpai and Parashar do not subscribe to this widely prevalent
fallacy and are not ready to convert Bulcke to Hinduism or to deify him! But
perhaps a further philosophical discussion is called for on how Bulcke could
worship a worshipper (Tulsidas) without worshipping what that worshipper
worshipped (Rama). On the other hand, Bajpai and Parashar note that Tulsidas
does not figure prominently at all in Bulcke's great study of *Ramkatha* as does
Valmiki, and they call it an 'anomaly' or even a 'contradiction' (see page 105). But
a partial explanation for this may lie in the fact that though Bulcke had initially
set out to write his dissertation on the subject 'Tulsi Ki Rambhakti' (Tulsi's
Devotion to Rama), the introductory chapters on the origin of the Rama story
of Valmiki and numerous other sources prior to the rise of the Bhakti movement
grew so voluminous in themselves that Bulcke had in fact to stop there and give
his dissertation a revised title: 'Ramkatha Ki Utpatti Aur Vikas' (The Rama
Story: Its Origin and Development).

In his preface to the first edition of his book *Ramkatha: Utpatti Aur Vikas*, Bulcke readily admitted that his work remained incomplete. He promised that in a subsequent volume, he would focus on the development of Rama *bhakti*, basing his study especially on the Rama-centred literature in Hindi (*visheshkar Hindi Ram-sahitya*). He said he would publish it 'within a year or two' and would go on after that to undertake further comparative studies encompassing both the *katha* and the *bhakti* in Hindi (Bulcke 2020 [1950], pp. 19–20). But his priorities obviously changed after he returned to Ranchi in 1950 to take up his pastoral duties, and the next few works he published were all to do with the propagation of the Christian gospel.

Incidentally, it may also need to be conclusively established whether Bulcke functioned only as what was called an 'educational missionary' or whether he also ventured into the 'field' – that is, among the local Indian people to seek to convert them to Christianity – as many of his colleagues and predecessors in the Jesuit mission in Ranchi had done for decades before him. These included Bulcke's fellow Belgian, Father Constant Lievens, who had in the late nineteenth century converted the local tribals by tens of thousands, bringing virtually 'a whole people to Catholicism' (see pages 56; 236–237; see also the entry on Lievens on the website of 'Ranchi Jesuits', https://www.ranjesu.org/biographypub/view/6). Bulcke often said that Allahabad was his *maika* (mother's home, where he had grown up) while Ranchi was his *sasural* (in-laws' home, where he lived after getting married – only metaphorically of course). This pregnant phrase needs to be unpacked fully to disclose all its connotations, and never mind the complete omission of Belgium in this two-part formulation. Bulcke spent five years in Allahabad, from 1945 to 1950, and thereafter 33 years in Ranchi, from 1950 until his death in 1983, and though Allahabad glowed bright in his memory, it was Ranchi which was his *karma bhumi*, or arena of action.

Finally, the life and works of Bulcke provide a fertile subject for a sustained comparative study between Christianity and Hinduism in theological as well as literary terms. Such a book was published by a younger contemporary of Bulcke, Roger Hooker, a Protestant missionary who lived in Agra, Bareilly, Varanasi and Allahabad from 1965 to 1978 (the last being the place where Bulcke had lived too) and acquired, like Bulcke, high competence in Hindi and Sanskrit. Though he focused in his dissertation not on a medieval Bhakti poet but on a (then) living Hindi writer mentioned earlier, a comparative theological focus was at the heart of his book, titled *The Quest of Ajneya: A Christian Theological Appraisal of the Search of Meaning in His Three Hindi Novels* (1998).

A point of departure for such a discussion of Bulcke may be found in Kesri Kumar's essay in the commemoration volume, in which he suggested that Bulcke's work on *Ramkatha*, though highly laudable, is conditioned 'by a Christian vision and a colonial approach'. Bulcke's erudite treatment of a large number of versions of the Rama story and of the differences between them may also be thought to be comparable to some later radical scholarship along similar lines, especially the essay 'Three Hundred Ramayanas' by A. K. Ramanujan, collected by Paula Richman with other similar studies in her *Many Ramayanas: The Diversity of a Narrative Tradition in South Asia* (1991).

With regard specifically to Tulsidas, there are many comparative possibilities to explore. In chapter 4 of this biography, the longest chapter in the book, Bajpai and Parashar provide an illuminating commentary of their own on the selections made by Bulcke from Tulsidas' *Ramcharitmanas* in his *Manas Kaumudi* (An Exposition of the *Ramcharitmanas*), in which Bulcke provided footnotes but no commentary. It may be worth exploring what broad criteria or predilections lay behind the choice of passages in this anthology, perhaps by comparing Bulcke's selections with any other selections made in his own times, or indeed made more recently by Rupert Snell, a secular Western scholar, in his *Reading the Ramcharitmanas* (2022).

If Bajpai and Parashar had not already accomplished so much in their biography, these hints and suggestions of themes to explore in future studies of Bulcke may possibly not have arisen. They have laid a solid foundation of Bulcke studies on which a grand edifice of many dimensions can gradually be erected. As well done as this biography is, it is valuable also beyond itself in indicating in one way or another how much more can be done. All readers of this work will be enlightened as well as stimulated by it.

Harish Trivedi
University of Delhi
Delhi, April 2024

Acknowledgements

स्वान्तःसुखाय तुलसी रघुनाथ गाथा
भाषानिबन्धमतिमञ्जुलमातनोति॥

Swantah sukhaya Tulsi Raghunath gatha
Bhasha nibandh mati manjul matnoti

Tulsidas wrote the *Ramcharitmanas* not for greater glories, but for his personal satisfaction, for the joy that he felt such work would bring him. That spirit of Tulsidas and his devotee (also the subject of this biography) are what inspired us to undertake this ambitious project – documenting the life of an extraordinary personality who not only traversed diverse geographies and sociocultural contexts, between Belgium and India, but also made many inward journeys balancing his Christian missionary life with his devotion to Tulsidas and the *Ramkatha*. The Covid-19 pandemic and several other personal situations delayed this project, and we are so pleased that it will see the light of day.

This book is spiritually owned by everyone who has contributed in any way to make it a reality. Our heartfelt thanks to St Xavier's College, Ranchi; Xavier Institute of Social Sciences, Ranchi; the Camille Bulcke Research Centre, Ranchi; and Manresa House, Ranchi, for supporting this project and giving us access to their rich libraries and resources. A very special thanks to Father Emmanuel Baxla, director of the Camille Bulcke Research Centre, Ranchi, who gave us abundant time, guidance and material during the writing of this book, and to Father Emmanuel Barla, the former principal of St Xavier's College, Ranchi, who first enabled our access to the library at Manresa House. Mridula

Prasad, the head of the Department of Hindi, Ram Lakhan Singh Yadav College, Ranchi, shared some valuable anecdotes, memories and material from the personal archives of her father, the late Dineshwar Prasad. He was a long-term friend and associate of Father Camille Bulcke, and we are very grateful to have gained access to both their writings through the generosity of Mridula Prasad.

We benefitted from conversations, exchanges and interviews with a large number of people who either attended the reburial ceremony of Father Bulcke's mortal remains in Ranchi in March 2018 or with whom we connected through recommendations from different sources. We are grateful to each one of them for giving us time and sharing their thoughts.

Jagdeep Hembrom and Anju Toppo helped us in the initial stages, by drawing our attention to the writings of Father Bulcke and, by connecting us to people who provided information and insights. We are very grateful to Rohit Ranjan Toppo for converting the pictures to the high resolution required for publication. Bajpai would like to thank his students of the Department of History, St Xavier's College, Ranchi, who provided delightful distractions in between gruelling writing schedules. He would also like to thank his colleague, Nisha Singh, for her support and encouragement during the writing of the book. Parashar would like to acknowledge her friend Prabha Rani for being a source of emotional support during periods of ill health and for always believing in her capabilities in moments of self-doubt. We are grateful to Qudsiya Ahmed at Cambridge University Press who encouraged us to undertake this project and worked with us during the initial submission of the book proposal. We have also received great support from Anwesha Rana and Koyena Roy at the Press, constantly renegotiating deadlines, especially during the Covid-19 pandemic and through personal bereavement. The meticulous copyeditors, Priyanka Das and Semanti Basu, ensured that the manuscript is qualitatively improved.

We would like to thank Ruth Vanita and Philip Lutgendorf for proofreading the manuscript so carefully despite being such busy scholars and for engaging with the text, giving us valuable feedback to sharpen the arguments and providing wonderful endorsements. Thanks are also due to Winand Callewaert, Cecelia Lynch, Priyankar Upadhyay and Father Emmanuel Baxla for their generous reading of the text and kind endorsements. We are deeply honoured and delighted to have Harish Trivedi write the foreword to this book. He not only agreed instantly but also encouraged us with generous words, and his wisdom not just in the foreword but throughout his interactions with us. We were so fortunate to have connected with these scholars through this book!

All mistakes and shortcomings remain ours alone, and we hope, dear readers, that the book will provide some insights into the life of an extraordinary Jesuit Indologist, whose story deserved to be told long time ago. Many other stories about Father Bulcke need to reach us from sources closer to him than we can ever claim to be, and ours will not be the only or even remotely authoritative voice. We will rest assured that we made an honest, albeit imperfect, attempt in bringing Father Bulcke's story to all those who wish to understand his life and mission and are seeking knowledge and inspiration from his works to address the angst, violence and also hope of contemporary times.

1

⅋

Camille Bulcke

A New Horizon of Indology

Against the 'Current'

On a train from Calcutta (Howrah) to Allahabad, a tall, lanky European with blue eyes and an auburn beard, clad in the white robe of a Christian priest, sat, immersed in a book. In India, during the 1960s and 1970s, the train-running schedule had enough stoppages at major stations to allow a thorough inspection and recharge–refuel of the engines. At the Asansol station, the train took that extra halt; the European priest put his book down and got off the train to stretch his long limbs. Upon his return to the seat, he found the gentleman sitting next to him reading his book; his fellow passenger wore an expression of sheer amazement as he flipped through the pages. Seeing that the book's owner was back, the gentleman hurriedly put the book back and blurted, 'I did not know that you knew Hindi' (Ponette 1987, p. 69). The European priest nodded his head in affirmation, and the two started talking; it soon became apparent that the foreigner-looking clergyman was exceptionally proficient in Hindi. The two talked non-stop for several hours until the train reached Allahabad. As the tall priest prepared to leave the train, his fellow passenger said, 'What a loss for me; I missed the chance to converse with you in Hindi for the first three hours of our journey between Calcutta and Asansol' (ibid.). As the two passengers bid adieu, the one on the platform started walking towards the exit door of the Allahabad railway station. He was Reverend Father Camille Bulcke, also known as Baba Bulcke by then.

Camille's[1] appearance, dress and demeanour all marked him as a foreigner, yet his sense of belonging to India held great significance for him throughout his life. He spent most of his life in Ranchi, Jharkhand (erstwhile Bihar), where he taught Hindi and Sanskrit at St Xavier's College. Manresa House, the residential compound of the Jesuits in Ranchi, proudly displays his statue in his white priestly robe. In more recent times, St Xavier's College has installed a bust of the legendary Christian priest on its premises, with his favourite words from the *Ramcharitmanas* (Divine Lake of Ram's Deeds) inscribed underneath.[2] The road outside the college is named after him, and his English–Hindi *shabdkosh* (dictionary) is still popular and found in most homes and offices. And yet, as long-time residents of Ranchi in Jharkhand, we were always surprised that not much was known in the public domain about his life. Who was this enigmatic European Jesuit, and why should we be interested in the life and works of Father Camille Bulcke?

Camille found his religious calling during his university days in Belgium, trained as a Christian evangelist, came to India on missionary work, discovered Hindi literature and through it realised *bhakti* (devotion) through various renditions of the Ramayana, and especially the *Ramcharitmanas*. Camille journeyed to and within India when travel was fraught with dangers, not just during the 'passage to India' but more so during the 'passage through India'. Natural calamities, diseases and starvation were all too frequent in early- to mid-twentieth-century India. In this journey, the Jesuit Camille Bulcke transgressed the ecclesiastical, sectarian and religious divide and transformed himself into Baba Bulcke, a leading exponent of Hindi, the Ramayana and the *Ramcharitmanas*.

In recent times, identity politics has taken a strong parochial turn, and divisions based on race, caste, creed, religion and language are continuously amplified for political benefits. The growing hostility among different societies has moved the United Nations to organise a 'Dialogue of Civilisations' to foster greater affinity and understanding among different civilisations (United Nations Alliance of Civilizations 2006). In times like this, it is pertinent to recall that a foreign Christian monk raised and trained in a different cultural milieu travelled to India, imbibed its civilisational attributes and devoted his life to enriching both the civilisations (European and Indian) through his words, deeds and literary feats. His scholarship nurtured Indian 'local' traditions, languages, literary cultures and expressions of faith and devotion. Indeed, he created an impressive corpus of literature and left behind an enduring legacy of scholarship synthesising two different traditions and cultures.

Few of the older generation who knew Father Bulcke remain to tell his story, in fragments, and their narratives are impacted by contemporary politics and polarised religious identities. The Church and its missionary activities are increasingly being scrutinised for incentivised and widespread conversions and appropriation of local cultures and traditions, while the figure of Rama and his life story in the *Ramcharitmanas* have become an important part of the Hindu nationalist narrative and the revival of Indian (Hindu) civilisational ethos. Religious traditions that originated outside the Indian subcontinent are seen as foreign and only invested in acquiring converts, at the cost of preserving indigenous traditions and culture. In such a deeply distrustful, masculinised and polarised public discourse, telling the story of Father Bulcke constitutes a political act to disrupt emotional chest-thumping and shallow understanding of the past that masquerade as commonplace wisdom and lived experiences, and that have normalised a disconnect from complex and plural histories and coexistence of diverse thoughts and syncretic traditions. How, then, should we locate him in his time and context and understand his works within the template of Christian missionary activities in India in the nineteenth and twentieth centuries?

Christianity has had a complex place in India's historical and cultural milieu. On the one hand, modernity, social reforms and cultural transformation addressing caste, race and ethnic inequalities have been attributed to its direct impact; on the other, colonial conquests and imperial projects globally were inextricably linked to the spread of Christianity. Stephen Charles Neill, missionary bishop and scholar, argued, 'It is no accident that the "great century" of the expansion of the Christian Church was also the great century of European expansion' (Neill 1954, pp. 35–42). The historian S. Gopal provides a critical assessment of Christianity's role in the imperial domination: 'Christianity did not make the empire Christian, but the empire made Christianity political. It was, above all else, the religion of the white race' (Gopal 1989, p. 3). Christianity's link with race and colonialism made it a powerful political force in the nineteenth and twentieth centuries. The missionaries made the spread of Christianity part of the Western civilisational mission, which included the spread of European thought. Some of the early works undertaken by missionaries were to counter what they erroneously and disparagingly considered the iniquitous superstition and irrationality of indigenous faiths and to establish the superiority of Christian beliefs and practices (Frick 1926). They were invested in studying other religious traditions, not because they believed 'there might be grains of truth in them but to combat them better' (Gopal 1989, p. 4). It is here that we think Camille's scholarly legacy is not just outstanding, but also well intentioned to study Indian literary texts, languages and religious traditions, to engage with them at a deeper level, enrich them with his own contributions and facilitate a culture of mutual learning and intellectual exchanges.

Christian Missionaries in India: Histories and Perspectives

Popular historical analysis claims that the arrival of Christian missionaries in India took place in three different phases. The first phase is linked to the origin of Christianity itself in India, which has been the subject of controversy among historians owing to the absence of documentary evidence. The Christian message is claimed to have been brought to India by Saint Thomas and Saint Bartholomew, two Apostles of Jesus Christ (Moffett 2005a, 2005b). Saint Thomas' mission in India mainly used Syriac as the language of ritual and scripture, and he is mentioned in the Syrian works, and his followers are referred to as the followers of the ancient Syrian Church of Malabar (Brown 1982; Jeyaraj 2019, p. 143). However, most of these claims appear more as traditional knowledge than historical facts. Christianity first arrived via the trans-oceanic network in South India and Goa, mainly through the seaports, which at one time carried on a flourishing trade with Western Asia and beyond. Christianity, in South India, was not a single unit but instead comprised of three streams: the Syrian, the Roman Catholic and the Protestant, each with a distinct character of its own.

One of the earliest recorded migrations of Christians via Persia is traced to the year 345 CE when a convoy of a Jerusalem merchant named Thomas brought 'a bishop from Edessa, accompanied by Presbyters and deacons, and by a company of men and women, youths and maidens from Jerusalem, Bagdad and Nineveh' (Richter 1908, p. 30). The arrival of these Christians was welcomed by local Christians, and the ruler granted important privileges, which is seen as 'the beginning of a flourishing epoch in the history of the Malabar Church' (ibid.). This was not a singular event. In fact, several waves of refugees escaped to the western shores of India to evade persecution. These Thomas Christians on the western coast of India, despite their foreign origins, had merged into the sociocultural milieu of the society, adopting all the customs and mores of the local non-Christian population. Most of the people converted by the Apostle were high-caste Hindus, and their day-to-day lives continued to resemble very closely to that of the Brahmins.

The Roman Catholics referred to most Christians of the East as 'Nestorian'[3], a mark of ecclesiastical and geographical distinction instead of major theological differences (Frykenberg 2008, p. 103). For almost 1,000 years, the period from 600 CE until the arrival of the Portuguese ships, the rise of Islamic power from Spain to Sindh put 'a curtain of darkness and incomprehension descended between the Christians of the West and their counterparts in the East' (ibid., pp. 116–117). There are very few exceptions to this total disconnect, including the travels of Marco Polo and the Franciscan John of Monte Corvino to the western coast of India (Richter 1908, pp. 42–43). However, this tenuous link between the Western and Eastern Christians soon underwent a metamorphosis with the landing of the Portuguese ships on Indian shores at Calicut in May 1498 (ibid., p. 44).[4]

The landing of the Portuguese marks the advent of a new epoch, an epoch of the Roman Catholic Mission in India (ibid.). This second phase of the arrival of the Christian missionaries in India, thus, begins with the arrival of Vasco da Gama in Calicut on 14 May 1498 (Subrahmanyam 1998). This officially marks the advent of state-sponsored Christianity and missionary activities in India. It heralded a new phase not only for the Church in India but also in the cultural contacts between India and Europe. The Portuguese Church is credited with sending Christian missionaries to the court of the Mughal emperor Akbar and later on for establishing a church in Lahore in 1595 (Coward 1993, pp. 1–2).

A series of Portuguese kings 'deemed it their most sacred duty, together with colonial conquest and exploitation, to plant Christianity – ofcourse [sic] of the Romish type – in the newly discovered and inestimably vast regions' (Richter 1908, p. 44). In the second Portuguese fleet for India, 'under Cabral in 1500, hosts of monks destined for missionary service were dispatched, and by nearly every ship bound thither after that their numbers were augmented' (ibid.). The rise of Portuguese power in Goa and some of the coastal parts of India also unleashed the more militant form of Christendom of the Padroado Real.[5] By the 1530s, Goa became the centre of an ecclesiastical hierarchy and of a religious colonial empire, and the local Hindus bore the brunt of the religious zeal of the Portuguese, who ordered the destruction of Hindu temples and prevented the Hindus from observing their religious festivals (Xavier and Županov 2015, pp. 122–127; Henn 2014, pp. 42–46).

The Thomas Christians in the Malabar region faced the wrath of the Padroado Real and the religious zeal of enforcing Portuguese Christianity on the local Indian Christians (Vu Thanh 2019). The Malabar Syrian Christians were seen as heretics by the new colonial masters, and despite the resistance of Thomas Christians, the Portuguese enforced their command (Županov 2005b). The Portuguese did not have much respect for local customs and, in their evangelisation, tried to replace both the indigenised Christianity and Indian cultural values with their European values and sensibilities. The Thomas Christians had lived among the Hindus and Buddhists for centuries and had never challenged the prevalent social and cultural order. Indeed, the European colonial powers changed the narrative of Christianity in India through their aggressive proselytisation and by imposing foreign (European) social norms and cultural values. The complete disregard for Indian traditions and way of life then led to resentment and resistance from the Indians.

> In the eyes of the Hindus, Christianity was the religion of the 'franks or parangis', the term used to denote especially the Portuguese but also any kind of European. It was not a complimentary term, it suggested meat-eating, wine-drinking, loose-living, arrogate persons, whose manners were so far removed from Indian propriety that social intercourse with them was unthinkable. (Firth 1998, p. 111)

The majority of contemporary writings (including Camille's own) on the history of Christianity in India tend to trace the roots back to the first century and Saint Thomas (C. Bulcke 2009, p. 110; Kavunkal 2008, p. 29). The same group of Thomas Christians faced unceasing persecution with the arrival of colonial Christianity, while the rest of the population was faced with aggressive proselytisation. Colonialism and the Christian mission were closely allied to each other since the arrival of the Portuguese. While the operational means may have differed from one colonial power to another, this alliance remained strong. During British colonisation, except for a few years of hiatus, this association was again on full display and with renewed vigour (Neill 1984a).

The third and the most decisive phase of Christianity in India begins with the arrival of the British East India Company, although most historical narrations of the Company's activities underplay its role in missionary activities. The Company's Charter of 1698 included the following clause: '[T]he chaplains in the factories are to study the vernacular language, the better to enable them to instruct the Gentoos, that shall be the servants or slaves of the same Company, or of their agents, in the Protestant religion' (Tisdall 1901, p. 100). Quite interestingly, most historical accounts focusing on the spread of Christianity refer to the battle of Plassey in 1757 as the pivotal moment, after which the Company actively supported missionary activities. One can argue that the state patronage of Christian missionary activities continued until Indian independence in 1947.

Missionary work in India is a subject of intense debate; at one level, it represents the 'missionary zeal' of do-gooders, while it also has all the connotations of colonialism and the 'civilising mission'. To cite one such instance, while trying to comprehend the religious tension that sparked off the Indian Rebellion of 1857 – an event which would eventually lead to the end of the East India Company rule in South Asia – the colonial historian John William Kaye pointed out that there were amongst the European officers of the Bengal army many 'earnest minded and zealous Christians' who used to seriously think of saving the souls of the indigenous people by teaching them from the Bible (Kaye 1896, p. 261). Kaye claimed that such officers 'went about with the order-book in one hand and the Bible in the other; and thus they did a great and grievous wrong to the Government they professed to serve' (ibid., p. 262). Clare Anderson has pointed out in a similar context that it was, thus, little wonder that many Indians regarded missionaries as the religious arm of the Company (Anderson 2007). Arguably, the aggressive missionary work under the patronage of the Company suffered a significant blow in the immediate aftermath of the Rebellion of 1857. However, contrary to the popular belief of the time, the colonial government never really pursued the proselytisation policy, not officially at least (Copland 2006). As Kim Wagner reminds us, missionaries were only allowed, albeit reluctantly, to operate in India after 1813 and other foreign churches after 1833. The colonial authorities were particularly concerned that proselytisation might provoke and alienate the sepoys and did their bit to curb this (Wagner 2017, pp. 51–56).

However, missionaries from America and Europe, especially Belgium and Ireland, kept visiting India under the patronage of the British Crown. The missionary contribution to social reforms that addressed some of the harshest social, cultural and religious practices cannot be discounted, while at the same time, the missionaries themselves were not free from structural violence and institutional exploitation (Chandra 2016, p. 84). It was in this context that Camille (and others, like Constant Lievens, before him) came to India to spread the word of the gospel and bring people to the path of Christ, but this encounter with India and Indians changed their worldview and forged an unexpected and complex relationship with the country they adopted as their 'home'. In this intimate encounter, both – the missionaries and the local people – were transformed, and the Christianity that took root had its own distinct Indian character.

This encounter continues to occur even today in different contexts and is not without problems and contestations that are unsettling for both sides. The larger Hindu majoritarian nationalist impulse has not fully grasped the role and impact of the Church and the contribution of the minority Christians in different parts of India, and an acrimonious relationship has emerged centring the debate on incentivised conversions especially of vulnerable people. Behind this acrimony is also a latent curiosity and quiet admiration for missionary work that has enabled some of the most remarkable and long-lasting contributions in the field of education and healthcare, led by various Jesuit missions in some of the remotest parts of the country. We have witnessed this first-hand in our city, Ranchi, which was 'home' to the protagonist of our story.

Camille Bulcke and His Mission

A Jesuit from Belgium with a love for Christ in his heart and committed to spreading the gospel travelled all the way to India in 1935. George V of Britain was the sovereign of undivided colonial India (that also included Pakistan and Bangladesh at that time). The Government of India Act, 1935, had just been legislated by the Parliament of the United Kingdom as a measure to address the demands for sovereignty and self-rule by Indian nationalists. At a time of great turmoil and with the country at the cusp of major political and social changes, India welcomed this Jesuit who would, among other things, make it his anti-colonial mission to promote Indian languages and literary traditions. The young priest, only 26 years of age, would not only make India his home and permanent resting place, but would also become one of the leading exponents of its rich cultural and spiritual heritage, a renowned scholar of its myths, traditions and epics, thereby bridging the gap between the East and the West. That personality was Father Camille Bulcke (1 September 1909–17 August 1982), and this book is a modest attempt at documenting his life story and literary contributions.

Camille came to India when it was still a British colony but died in independent India, having proudly embraced his Indian citizenship and 'Indian-ness'. He came to spread the teachings of Christ and not only found spiritual inspiration in Goswami Tulsidas, a poet-saint of medieval India, but also became one of the most well-informed exponents of the *Ramkatha* (The Story of Rama). He spent most of his life in present-day Jharkhand serving the Christian Church and the local people and wrote several insightful commentaries on the works of Tulsidas and the many tellings of the Ramayana, one of the two great Indian epics, in different parts of South and South-East Asia. He documented the development of the different Ramayana stories much before A. K. Ramanujan's *Three Hundred Ramayanas: Five Examples and Three Thoughts on Translation* was published in 1991.

He devoted his life to the development of the Hindi language that he learnt in India (even earning a doctorate in it from the University of Allahabad) and translated many key texts in Hindi. He was an extraordinary lexicographer, and his English-to-Hindi *shabdkosh* is still used in all government offices and institutions. His long-time collaborator and friend, Dineshwar Prasad, mentions how Camille wasted no time getting to his Hindi lessons at the St Ignatius School in Gumla, where he could be found sitting on the last bench with his own students to develop fluency in the language. Soon, he mastered Brij Bhasha as well as Awadhi, adding to the five European languages and Sanskrit, which he spoke with great ease. As a Christian missionary committed to spreading the gospel, he also developed an interesting model of synthesis and coexistence, working among the tribals and non-tribals of Jharkhand (erstwhile undivided Bihar). He delivered powerful sermons on the life of Christ and his teachings, and also offered extraordinary scholarly insights on the *Ramcharitmanas* and other sacred Hindu texts.

Affectionately also called Baba Bulcke, Camille's humanitarian activities are still remembered by those whose lives he touched, many of them non-Christians. He was an eminent educator with advanced pedagogical focus on the teaching of Indian languages such as Hindi and Sanskrit. In March 2018, his remains were brought back from Delhi to Jharkhand after 36 years and buried on the premises of Ranchi's St Xavier's College, where he was once the founding head of the Department of Hindi and Sanskrit. The ceremony of the reburial of his remains was attended by thousands of citizens of all religious persuasions, including prominent Hindu, Muslim and Christian leaders in Jharkhand. It was a reminder of the great significance of his life and works in these times of aggressive assertion of identity and masculinity, in the backdrop of a cultural renaissance and civilisational revival.

India, as a secular republic, is a strong proponent of equality of all religions and that the state should not champion any one religion. However, inter- and intra-religious harmony in the country has always been fraught with conflicts, selective and narrow understanding of history and other challenges. A Camille Bulcke in contemporary India would invite disapproval and even contempt from condescending and aggressive Christian missionaries, as well as the proponents of Hindu majoritarian nationalism, focused on Indic civilisational glories. Camille would be caught between the proverbial rock and hard place; his fellow evangelists would suspect him of reneging on his Christian pledge to spread the gospel of Christ, while Hindu hardliners would accuse him of appropriating their most popular deity, Rama, and the works of Tulsidas for proselytising Christianity. However, was it any different during his time? How should we read and interpret his mission, his works and his legacy?

This book explores some of these complex questions about his life and literary contributions and fills an important gap since there is no biography of Father Bulcke (or Baba Bulcke as he was popularly known) available in the public domain. His long-term collaborator and, on occasion, co-author, the late Dineshwar Prasad of Ranchi University, authored several essays and a book offering one of the most insightful life sketches of Father Bulcke in Hindi. However, a comprehensive story of his life has been long overdue. It is in this context that we want to offer to our readers our version of the life story of Father Camille Bulcke, the Jesuit priest from Belgium, who left an enduring legacy in post-colonial India as a teacher-scholar and as an Indologist who became a leading exponent of the *Ramkatha*, the story of Rama, especially as retold by Tulsidas, the literary genius of the Indian Bhakti tradition, in his *Ramcharitmanas* (Feys 1988, pp. 206–207).

Methodological Challenges

Writing a biography of any renowned personality is a challenge even under the best of circumstances; if the subject is not around, hails from foreign shores, leaves no family and direct descendants and has lived a life mostly devoted to archives, translations and other scholarly pursuits, the challenges increase manifold. Attempting the biography of Father Camille Bulcke comes with all these challenges; fortunately, he had shared detailed information about his origins, family, childhood and early youth, documented by his friends and associates, which came in very handy for our project. Moreover, he was a scholarly figure and not a recluse or hermit; he interacted with friends, associates, students and their families as an indulging parent, showering them with his incessant love, affection and beneficence. Thus, he left behind a large pool of people who have cherished memories of their beloved Baba Bulcke, and these individuals became a veritable source of first-hand information on Camille, the person, the padre and the patron.

Our pursuit for information for this biography indeed was helped by sharing our hometown, Ranchi, with Camille. This town was his 'home' too for the longest period of his life in India. It is here that he lived and preached among the faithful and wrote all his important scholarly works. The various communities in Ranchi sustained and nurtured his quest for knowledge and humanitarianism and also gave him some long-lasting friendships. He was an enigmatic figure, a familiar sight in his white priestly robe with the rosary, and often covering great distances on his bicycle, in a town which was still not fully urbanised and modern amenities had not unleashed a drastic pace of life where people found no time to greet their neighbours. The inspiration and information for this biography have come mainly from our physical and intellectual 'location' in Ranchi and mainly from four different sources:

(a) Camille's own writings, interviews and notes about his personal and family life;

(b) the written memoirs, reminisces and commemorative articles from Camille's friends, family and associates;

(c) travelogues, diaries, personal notes and anecdotes shared by those who interacted with him; and

(d) our interviews and exchanges with individuals associated with Camille, who spent time with him or interacted with him on different occasions.

Having spent a great deal of our lives in Jharkhand, we have witnessed the impact and influence of Camille's work in different walks of life. The English–Hindi dictionary he compiled continues to be a lifeline in government institutions that require Hindi language skills. His educational and humanitarian work among the tribals is well remembered; the Church and the Jesuit mission also recognise his contributions to Christianity, and his students remember him as a fountain of knowledge with an extraordinary dedication to Hindi, not found even in native speakers. He encouraged and inspired everyone to treat learning their own languages as a serious post-colonial mission.

In 1974, Camille was awarded the Padma Bhushan, India's third highest civilian honour, for his contributions to education and Hindi scholarship, and yet there is a lack of resources documenting his life and works. In that itself, we think the book fills an important gap, although numerous books have been published on Jesuit missionaries in India by the missions and churches themselves (Bauman and Voss Roberts 2021). These books are theologically inclined and highlight (often uncritically) the work of the missions and certain well-known Jesuits. Many would qualify as written from the Church's perspective and could also be considered religious propaganda. We hope to have also brought to this biography our experiences of living in many different countries (India, Singapore, the United Kingdom, Ireland, Australia, the United States and Sweden) and having interacted closely with scholars of Hinduism and Christianity and Christian missionaries in Jharkhand, as well as our abiding interest in and understanding of the *Ramkatha*, especially the *Ramcharitmanas*. We are both bilingual and can read and write Hindi fluently, which allowed us access to Camille's scholarly works in Hindi without dependence on a translator. We have translated all the text from original Hindi sources unless it is attributed to other authors. Given the limitations of the English vocabulary, translations of Sanskrit, Hindi and Awadhi can never capture the true essence of the original text. Moreover, there are no corresponding English synonyms for the fundamental concepts of Hindu cosmology.

Outline of the Book

From Belgium to India: Inner and Outer Journeys

Born in a small village named Ramskapelle, in West Flanders, Belgium, on 1 September 1909, Camille Bulcke would remind people that it was preordained even before his birth that he be associated with the Indian deity Rama. His was from a wealthy landowning family who lost practically everything due to his grandfather's profligate habits; his father then had to live with his in-laws in the village of Lissewege. Camille's early childhood was spent in rustic settings in a deeply religious family; his father was a disciplinarian but kind-hearted, while his mother was very docile and affectionate and sang Flemish folk songs to him. Camille was deeply attached to his mother and would often get emotional talking about his mother. As an exceptionally bright student, Camille cleared his engineering entrance exam, and he was the first person from his village to get into university. At the engineering college, he encountered the politics of language and the hegemony of French over his mother tongue, Flemish. He soon emerged as one of the student leaders challenging the imposition of French.

Camille planned to complete his education and start a normal household life, but the universe had other designs. One day during the vacations in his first year at the engineering college, Camille was all alone at home reading a book; suddenly, a bright light flashed on the page of the book, and he realised that very moment that he would become a monk. Since that day, he was withdrawn and became an introvert. Upon his return to college, he started learning Latin at the Jesuit seminary, given that the knowledge of Greek and Latin was compulsory for aspirants of any religious training. After his final-year exams, he announced his decision to become a monk to his parents; both were shocked. His mother wept, and his father looked pensive but accepted it as God's will. Camille formally joined the religious training in 1930, first at Drongen, a town nearby, and later at Valkenburg in the Netherlands. During this training, he developed a great affinity for German poetry, especially of Goethe, Heine and Rilke. He completed his Master of Arts (MA) degree in Philosophy, securing 90 per cent marks, and it was here that the writer in Camille took shape.

In 1934, the newly anointed Brother Camille came to a fork in his life; he was offered to stay in his motherland or take overseas assignments. Camille chose the second option and wished to be sent to India, reaching Ranchi in November 1935. Initially, he was sent to St Joseph's College in Darjeeling as a physics and chemistry teacher; however, the weather did not suit him, and he returned to Ranchi. In 1937, he was sent to teach mathematics at St Ignatius School in Gumla. This chapter traces the inner transformations in Camille while living with his family and during his student days in Belgium, his decision to become a Jesuit missionary and subsequently his life-changing journey to India as a young missionary.

A Scholar-Priest in the Making

Camille had begun learning Hindi since his arrival in India, and at the school in Gumla, where he taught math, he used to sit on the last bench with the students during Hindi classes. An exceptional learner, he developed proficiency not only in Hindi and its dialects, but he also developed great love for the writings of Tulsidas and yearned to acquire more profound knowledge of Hindi and Sanskrit. The Church authorities recognised Camille's felicity with Indian languages and, in 1938, sent him to Pandit Badri Dutt Shastri at Sitagarh (Hazaribagh) for further learning. Within a few months, Camille was so proficient in Hindi that his teacher, Pandit Shastri, designated him a 'walking dictionary'. Thus began his lifetime association with Hindi; it paved the way for his extraordinary contribution to Hindi literature.

In January 1939, Camille arrived at St Mary's Theologate, Kurseong, and spent the next four years completing his higher learning of theology. As part of his MA degree in Theology, he completed a dissertation, *The Theism of the Nyaya-Vaisesika*,[6] under the guidance of the renowned Indologist Reverend Joseph Bayart. This was later published as a book by the Oriental Institute, Calcutta (C. Bulcke, 1947). He also wrote the life of Jesus Christ based on the New Testament and published it as a book titled *The Saviour*. The Hindi translation of the book as *Muktidata* was published in 1940, illustrating Camille's command over Hindi. The same year, he completed the exam of *visharad* (bachelor's degree) in Hindi, organised by the Hindi Sahitya Sammelan, Prayag (Allahabad).

In 1941, he was ordained as Father Camille Bulcke, and he spent the next two years in Kodaikanal to complete his training. Upon his return to Ranchi, he enrolled as a private student at the University of Calcutta and received his Bachelor of Arts (BA) degree in Hindi and Sanskrit. In 1945, he went to meet the head of the Hindi department of the University of Allahabad, Dhirendra Verma, to seek admission to the MA degree. To assess Camille's proficiency in Hindi, Verma gave him two verses from the *Vinaya Patrika* (The Petition to Rama), one of Tulsidas' literary works, to analyse. A profoundly impressed Verma then granted him admission, which changed Camille's life (C. Bulcke 2015 [1976], p. 331).

Camille completed his MA in 1945 and then registered for his PhD in Hindi on 'Rama Bhakti Ka Vikas'. In 1949, Camille was awarded the D. Phil. on the thesis 'Ramkatha: Utpatti Aur Vikas'. In those times, only English-language theses were accepted by the University of Allahabad; therefore,

Camille sought and received special permission from the vice chancellor of the university to submit his thesis in Hindi (Parashar 2016). He returned to Ranchi in 1950 and was appointed the head of the Hindi and Sanskrit department of St Xavier's College. Thus began the glorious academic life of the Hindi scholar, Father Bulcke, and this chapter documents his various scholarly pursuits and contributions.

From Christ Bhakti to Tulsidas' Rama Bhakti

Camille appeared as an enigma to several people, who found in him a dedicated, ordained Christian priest, but with much devotion to Tulsidas and Rama *bhakti*. He was convinced that Christ, Hindi and Tulsidas constituted the three chief elements of his life of devotion, and rather than opposing each other, they were closely intertwined. He did not see any contradiction between faith and learning, for he believed that religious faith was not a matter of arguments, and he drew inspiration, peace and joy from the teachings of Christ. His mother was a devout Christian lady who inculcated piety in him as a child, and Camille credited his decision to become a monk to his religious upbringing. His parents consented to his decision to take up religious duty, and he never saw his mother again after leaving for India in 1935. Later, he read the passage in the *Ramcharitmanas* where Sumitra tells her son, Laxman, 'Only that woman is a mother in this world, whose son is God's votary, else she better be childless' (C. Bulcke 2010, p. 134). Camille was reminded of his own mother and her sacrifices whenever he read these words attributed to the character of Sumitra.

It was in 1938 that Camille read, for the first time, the entire *Ramcharitmanas* and the *Vinaya Patrika*. He developed a strong religious, emotional and literary attachment to Tulsidas (C. Bulcke 2009, p. 14). He used to explain that while Tulsi's god was Rama and his was Christ, he found some similarities in their devotional approaches, and yet he lamented that he lacked Tulsidas' steadfastness. This chapter explores Camille's devotion to Tulsidas and his deep engagements with and critical insights into the latter's life and works.

Contributions to Indology and Scholarly Legacy

In an essay, 'The Faith of a Christian: Devotion to Hindi and to Tulsi' (2009), Camille wrote, 'When I arrived in India in 1935, I was surprised and troubled when I realised that many educated people were unaware of their cultural traditions and considered it a matter of pride to speak in English. I resolved that my duty would be to master the language of the people' (C. Bulcke 2010, p. 136). His biggest contribution was to raise awareness about the lack of pride, ownership and dignity in using Hindi in India. He compiled *A Technical English–Hindi Glossary of General Culture*; this dictionary became very popular and had two quick editions. The success motivated him to compile a complete English–Hindi dictionary: *Angreji–Hindi Kosh*. His English–Hindi dictionary is one of the mandatory references for learners and experts of both languages and translators.

About his fascination with Tulsidas and the *Ramcharitmanas*, Camille wrote, 'You may wonder what attraction could Tulsidas have for a foreigner and a Christian. It is no doubt partly a personal equation, possibly a matter of irrational love. But this is not the whole or the main factor. The real truth is that Tulsidās is so great a poet as to transcend the barriers of time, country and religion: he is a poet of all humanity' (ibid., p. 141). As a devout Christian, Camille could not accept the Rama of Tulsidas as God, yet he had an unwavering commitment to Tulsidas and his devotional approach. Camille believed that the narration of Rama's legend by Tulsidas was uniquely heartwarming. It had such a delicate admixture of art and idealism that no lover of literature could remain untouched. He found that 'the Bhakti cult so well propounded by Tulsidās in his works, the ideals that he has placed before his readers in such simple but lively language, and his deeply-held philosophy of wilful and complete submission to the will of the Almighty would appeal to anybody who has any claims to be called religious and God-fearing' (C. Bulcke 2009, p. 76).

He published his PhD thesis in the form of a book titled *Rama Katha: Utpatti Aur Vikas* (The Genesis and Development of the Rama Story), which gained rapid popularity and ran into several editions. His other books, such as *The Ramayana of Hinduism: A Course by Letters*, *Ramkatha Aur Tulsidas* (The Rama Story and Tulsidas) and *Manas Kaumudi* (An Exposition of the Ramcharitmanas) are considered milestones of scholarly writings on the Ramayana and Tulsidas. This chapter documents his contributions to the study of the *Ramkatha* and Tulsidas, his skills as a lexicographer and his scholarly insights on Indology. It also analyses his politics and especially his views on Indian secularism and way of life.

The Man and His Mission: A Critical Appraisal

Camille epitomised the idea of India, an abode not just for learning, knowledge and wisdom, but a place open and accommodating of all the contradictions, divergences and inconsistencies. It pained him if anyone doubted the loyalty of Indian Christians to India or their commitment to the Indian ethos. He claimed, 'We Christians are taught to be patriotic to our nation. We are instructed that without being sincere to our nation, we cannot be sincere to God' (ibid., p. 111). He argued that the lack of knowledge about the make-up of Indian Christianity and the contribution of Indian Christians towards the nation-building efforts in India have led to distrust between Christians and other communities.

Camille believed that the Indian ethos of tolerance, its liberal and assimilatory nature of pluralism, was not rooted only in its constitution. Instead, the Indian social milieu nurtured it based on the ancient culture of welcoming other beliefs, religions and traditions. For him, the virtues of Indian-ness – its eternal, universal values – stemmed from not only the Hindu religion but also the ancient cultural norms of non-aggression towards other faiths. He avowed that the traditional Indian beliefs were so tolerant that Christianity could well become a part of it. He considered himself a fine example of such harmony between Christianity and Indian-ness, and this chapter critically reflects on that 'secular', 'Indian' legacy. This concluding assessment examines his relationship with and the impact of his work on different constituencies that include Jharkhand and the Adivasis, the ecclesiastical community, his friends and critics in the Hindi literary world, the constitution and Indian nationhood, and, finally, us, as authors, admirers and critics who tell his story.

Our Hope…

Writing a biography is always challenging; it becomes all the more arduous for academy-trained social scientists, juggling their innate subjectivities and biases with the mandate of offering something distanced, worthwhile and analytical. Objectivity in the social sciences and humanities, as is widely understood and used, is neither possible nor desirable. In most cases, the biographer does not choose the subject; instead, it is the opposite. The life of that individual character compels the biographer to write about the protagonist one chooses. We definitely feel that Father Bulcke's personality and contributions compelled us to ensure that his story reaches a wider audience. On the one hand, a biography may succeed in emerging as an inferior type of history; on the other, it may become an unreserved hagiography. Our attempt is not to provide the definite narrative of Camille Bulcke's life; instead, we examine our subject in multiple and different associations to the ecclesiastical, literary and the wider social, political and cultural worlds he inhabited. We do not even aspire to offer the most objective and distanced account of Camille's life; at best, we attempt to provide, hopefully, an engaging, enriching and critical story of one man who was a missionary, littérateur, lexicographer, translator, teacher, Indologist, a *Ramakatha* exponent and one of the most compassionate yet most tenacious Hindi activists in post-colonial India.

There is an inherent contradiction here that we would like to be upfront about. Readers will wonder why we chose to write this biography in English – the language that Camille opposed as he considered it a colonial imposition. Would not a biography in Hindi be a far more befitting tribute to a man who worked for the status and glory of Hindi all his life? While we are convinced that we will be undertaking that task in the near future and retelling his story in Hindi, which is also our native language, we believe that an English-language biography will deliver his message and works to a wider non-Hindi-speaking audience, even outside India. Language is a powerful medium through which multiple stories are communicated, and we would be very pleased to see Flemish and French versions of this biography as well.

We also want to remind the readers that this book is about Father Camille Bulcke and not a historical account of the role of missionaries and Christianity in India on which several scholarly works are available. We have provided only a brief history of Christianity in India in this chapter to contextualise Camille's travel to the Indian shores and his learnings and unlearnings in a society where religion was part of everyday life, part of the national movement and anti-colonial resistance, part of the story of the 1947 partition and the subsequent post-colonial nation-building. This is a story about how Camille, the Belgian missionary, the foreigner, the white European and the Christian priest navigated a multi-religious, multi-lingual, multi-ethnic India and its social and cultural milieu equipped with his personal convictions, scholarly pursuits and humanitarian activities.

We wish to emphasise that Camille was a product of specific times and contexts when gender, race and caste-sensitive language and discourses were not always prevalent. Colonialism and Orientalism shaped political vocabularies, public discourses and private utterances. We have analysed his works for what they represented and conveyed and not for what they did not. We have tried to focus on the meanings and methods he drew from and insisted on, and not so much on how to read his works in these times when we are equipped with different vocabularies and sensibilities. This courtesy should be extended to everyone who wrote, worked, preached, resisted or was an activist within the context of their life and times. To apply modern standards and contemporary sensibilities to assess people's lives and works from a different era would be both unfair and unproductive. In chapter 4, we have discussed at length Camille's defence of Tulsidas with reference to the latter's derogatory references to women and problematic views on caste hierarchies. Camille learnt from Tulsidas, and we learnt from Camille's context-based understanding and empathetic reading of Tulsidas.

This is a compelling story for our times, with all its complexities and shades of grey. In these times when we lack genuine leaders, cultural risk-takers and guiding lights, it becomes important to explore the lives of these inspiring and influential figures from our past with such rich legacies and contributions to the making of post-colonial India. Camille Bulcke was one such personality whose life story this book attempts to capture, with all its nuances, in the hope that it would be accessible, both for informed academics and general audiences. We leave the readers to judge for themselves as we claim neither expertise on, nor any exclusive or extraordinary insights into his life. We humbly share here what we have witnessed and learnt and what has stayed with us, puzzled us, inspired us, niggled us, cheered us and filled us with both despair and hope.

Notes

1. We use Camille Bulcke's first name throughout this biography – as it feels intimate and right – but occasionally also refer to him as Father Bulcke. He was addressed as Baba Bulcke, Father Bulcke, Father, and so on, but 'Camille' to us captures his relationship with all the people he was associated and interacted with, including his family in Belgium. We were also inspired by John Dugdale's rationale that biographers may choose to use the first name of their protagonists 'to portray a human being rather than relate the history of a monument' (Dugdale 2015).

2. The verse reads, 'परहित सरिस धरम नहिं भाई । पर पीड़ा सम नहिं अधमाई ।' (There is no better dharma [religious duty] than benevolence; nothing more sinful than malevolence towards others.)

3. Nestorianism, a Christian sect that originated in Asia Minor and Syria, stresses the independence of the divine and human natures of Christ and, in effect, suggests that they are two persons loosely united. This schismatic sect was formed in the fifth century CE by Nestorius, the archbishop of Constantinople. It asks for an explanation of Christ's dual nature, both divine and human, existing together in Christ.

4. There is widespread contestation among different records on the actual date of the landing of Vasco da Gama at Calicut.

5. The concept of Padroado Real started in 1455 CE, when the Pope handed over the spiritual jurisdiction and missionary work of the newly discovered territories in Asia and the Americas to the Portuguese–Spanish Crown.

6. Nyaya and Vaisesika represent two different schools of Indian philosophy. Nyaya is primarily a system of logic and dialectics, while Vaisesika refers to the atomic theory and deals with physics and metaphysics (C. Bulcke 1947, pp. 1–2).

2

ೞ൞

From Belgium to India

Inner and Outer Journeys

Belgium: A Brief Historical Context

To understand Camille's childhood and youth in Belgium, it is imperative to have an overview of the political, social and cultural milieu of that time and some of the historical processes that shaped them. While Belgium was not considered a major European power, it held an enormous influence in Europe and Africa in the nineteenth and twentieth centuries. Carved out of the Netherlands, Belgium emerged as an independent state in 1830 and was a small country of 30,000 square kilometres; its 'population was divided between often antagonistic French-speaking Walloons and the Dutch speakers of the Flanders region, alongside a small German community' (Aldrich and Stucki 2022, p. 430). The birth of Belgium as a new nation-state in 1830 reflected the two interrelated trends of the modernisation of state apparatus such as law, institutions and bureaucracy and the quest for ethno-nationalism.

Like the rest of Europe, this trend of modernisation also marked strains between the state and the Roman Catholic Church and growing tensions between autocracy and democratic principles. Coupled with these political churnings, Belgium also witnessed major social and economic changes; capitalist industrial production advanced rapidly, changing the fundamental nature of the agrarian and cottage-industry-based economy. Remarkably, while Belgium stood out as a champion of liberalism and as the world's second industrial nation, the socio-economic disparities were rampant. Karl Marx found refuge in Brussels between 1845 and 1848 and wrote the *Communist Manifesto* during his stay, calling Belgium an archetype bourgeoisie state. In

Das Capital, Marx presented Belgium as the 'paradise of continental Liberalism' against 'the paradise of capitalists' (Vanthemsche and Peuter 2023, p. 249).

The population of Belgium remained devoutly and almost exclusively Catholic; the region was seen as 'a bastion of the Counter-Reformation' (ibid., p. 6). For the first 50 years, the Belgian parliament was dominated by the Catholics, facilitating the expansion of the Catholic Church and its morals over the society. Liberals were another significant political group who sought an end to religious domination in the state and society. The church overcame the opposition of the liberals to regain domination over the education system, holding a monopoly on primary education while controlling secondary and university education. In the early 1880s, the liberals sought to break the Catholic Church's educational monopoly. This move made the church far more powerful as a regulator of society and a dominant political force (Witte, Craeybeckx and Meynen 2009, p. 90).

The march of modern capitalism led to severe spatial and social disruptions. The nation saw a population boom, from 3.7 million in 1831 to 6.7 million in 1900. Such a massive population surge marked unprecedented urbanisation: 'While only 18 percent of the population lived in cities of at least 5,000 inhabitants in 1800, this was the case for 57 percent in 1910' (Vanthemsche and Peuter 2023, p. 250). Even at the beginning of the twentieth century, Belgium's industrial working class faced severe hardships with low wages and long working hours. Belgium's political system, exalted as exemplary in the first half of the nineteenth century, gradually lost that distinction; in the early 1890s, less than 10 per cent of adult males had suffrage (ibid., pp. 283–285). To subvert the growing clamour for general male suffrage, the Belgian elites introduced 'proportional representation – almost a première in European history' to perpetuate their dominance over the political system. However, at the beginning of the twentieth century, the rise of the Socialist Party challenged the Catholics and Liberals, and the regional divide based on language and culture soon became a division along political ideologies. In very simplistic terms, Flanders 'was the Catholic Party's stronghold, and the French-speaking part of Belgium became the electoral bastion of the Socialists' (ibid.)

Belgium started as a constitutional monarchy, and Leopold I took the reins in 1831; his familial links with other European royalties and his astute diplomacy enabled Belgium to successfully negotiate several international crises that shook nineteenth-century Europe. Despite severe economic hardships, most migration was within Belgium or adjacent countries. Few Belgian businessmen and scientists ventured to non-European countries, except the 'Catholic missionaries preaching the Gospel in "heathen" countries' (ibid., p. 258). The Belgian state always followed a policy of neutrality and stayed off the power politics of other major European powers. At the international level, Leopold I deployed family relations with other European royals; and his diplomacy to use neutrality in amplifying Belgium's impact on the global scene yielded benefits. However, unlike the other European powers, such as the Netherlands, France and Britain, Belgium had no colonies. From 1840 onwards, Leopold I endeavoured to procure offshore colonies for Belgium; the ambitions were realised in 1885 by his successor, Leopold II, who seized African territories in the Congo Free State (Aldrich and Stucki 2022, p. 431). This colony was 'seventy-seven times the size of Belgium', and within a short time, 'significant political, business and missionary interests had become rooted in Leopold's colony and, along with the king himself, were reaping the benefits' (ibid.).

The Congo Free State remained Leopold II's personal property until 1908, when it was recognised as a Belgian colony. 'Colonialism was more popular among the Walloons than the Flemish, yet the Flemish city of Antwerp was, in terms of business, shipping and general engagement, Belgium's "colonial capital"' (ibid.). Surprisingly, unlike France or the United Kingdom, there was little opposition within Belgium towards colonial practices. After 1908, this 'civilising mission was a strictly national undertaking, it had to be defended against any foreign interference' (Vanthemsche 2012, p. 47). The Belgian Congo 'rapidly began to occupy a prime position in official patriotic discourse', and between 1908 and 1940, 'attention was above all focused on the establishment and the deepening of Belgian colonial order in the Congo' (ibid.). Under Belgian control, in the 1920s, the Congo emerged as one of the world's largest suppliers of 'industrial diamonds, copper, tin, uranium, gold, palm oil, and cotton' (Vanthemsche and Peuter 2023, p. 287). In the 'interwar period onwards, the authorities started to expand primary schools, extend medical help throughout the country (essentially realised through religious missions)' (ibid.). Although Belgium's imperialism left one of the most grotesque trails of destruction and exploitation in the Congo, it remained at the margins of the Belgian public discourse for a long time (Stanard 2019).

The two linguistic regions based on Flemish (a Dutch dialect)-speaking Flanders and French-speaking Walloons were quite distinct in earlier times, but rapid urbanisation and industrialisation saw a greater number of Flemish speakers migrate to the more prosperous Walloon areas. French was the official language in Belgian public services and administrative life and a marker of social hierarchy. Elites such as the landlords, industrialists, rich traders 'and even the petty bourgeoisie spoke French to differentiate themselves from common people using a Flemish dialect, an idiom they considered obscure and unfit for civilised persons' (Vanthemsche and Peuter 2023, p. 7). In the late nineteenth century and the first half of the twentieth century, 'social, political, and cultural discrimination against the Flemish population generated the "Flemish movement"' (ibid.). The Flemish movement gradually achieved 'equality, before the law and in public life, of the Flemish language (meanwhile standardised into "correct" Dutch)' (ibid.).

Belgium's neutrality implied that it stayed clear of the rivalry among the French, British and Germans for domination and kept these powers at equidistance. Given its unprecedented trade and industrial production levels, by 1880 Belgium enjoyed excellence in the international arena. Belgian universities and technical colleges attracted many international students, and newly emerging nations sought its legal and administrative expertise. Its religious missions attained global presence; the 'Belgian Jesuits, Franciscans, Scheutists, etc., evangelized parts of India, the Philippines, North America, Mongolia and, of course, the Congo' (ibid., p. 288). However, the outbreak of the First World War in 1914 dragged Belgium into the conflict, and it faced the full fury of the invading German troops. The Allied forces came to the defence of Belgium, yet 'tens of thousands of soldiers from Great Britain, Australia, New Zealand, and other places lost their lives in Flanders' fields' (ibid.). While the four years, 1914–1918, were very painful, Belgium witnessed unprecedented patriotic fervour and eventually emerged victorious. The post-war period saw electoral reforms, the adoption of 'one man, one vote' and the rise of Flemish political representation that sought to preserve their language and culture. It was in this context that Camille spent the formative years of his life in Flanders, in Belgium, resisting the hegemony of the French language and culture and fighting for the dignity and autonomy of the Flemish language and way of life. Camille later carried these values of resistance to India, taking up the cause of popularising Hindi over the colonial language of English.

Birth and Childhood

Like all the big, bountiful and beneficent rivers that originate from a small place, Camille too started his life in a small village, Ramskapelle, in West

Flanders, Belgium, where he was born on 1 September 1909. Narrating his own life story, Camille would jocularly mention that given that his birthplace had 'Ram' prefixed to its name, it was preordained that he would devote his life to studying the story of Rama. However, he would also clarify that the word 'Ram' has a different meaning in his mother tongue, Flemish. His first name Camille is often compared to a flower with a similar name, camellia, while one of the more popular meanings has a religious connotation as 'the helper to the priest'. Indeed, as we traverse Camille's life, it would appear that he epitomised the literal meaning as an effervescent flower of intellect and as one of the most renowned helpers to Christian and Hindu priests with his enormous corpus of literary work that he made available to them. Remarkably, a homophone 'Kamil' also exists in Urdu, and its synonyms include 'full', 'complete', 'plenary', 'accomplished', 'dexterous', 'expert', 'perfect man', 'miraculous saint' and 'ascetic', among several others, and one could use any of these meanings to describe him (Ghosh 2015, p. 132).

Camille's forefathers were big landowners living in Ramskapelle for many generations; his grandfather, Philippus Bulcke (b. 17 January 1817), was also a landowner like his forefathers. However, unlike his predecessors, Philippus Bulcke did not believe in accumulating wealth but in spending and enjoying it. As Camille recalled, his grandfather used to go to church early in the morning and then would spend his time idling away in different inns. Although his grandfather was not an alcoholic, his profligacy led to the sale of his entire landed property, and he became bankrupt at the end of his life. After he died in 1902, his two sons, Camille Josephe and Adolf Francis, struggled for their livelihood for several years (D. Prasad 1987, p. 3). These two young men from the Bulcke household were married during the decline of the family's prestige and growing financial crisis.

Adolf married Maria Gheyle, and in 1909 Adolf and Maria had their first child. According to the local custom, the firstborn girl child would be named after the maternal grandmother while the boy would get his paternal grandfather's name. Since the grandfather was no more, as per the local custom, the child was given his eldest paternal uncle's name, Camille (Saxena 2017, p. 73). Baby Camille was born prematurely – at seven months – and was so weak that no one expected him to survive. His mother, Maria, anxious about the newborn's survival, wept incessantly after his birth. Fortunately, from the fourth day, his condition began to improve, and it seemed that the infant might survive (D. Prasad 1987, p. 4). When Camille was barely three months old, the Bulcke family's only remaining property, their home, was sold. His uncle, Camille, shifted to a neighbouring village, Heist, while his parents moved to a village named Lissewege, which was also his mother's ancestral home. The two senior Bulcke siblings were starkly different: Camille's uncle was a man of this world and quite astute and tactful. He started a timber business, and in no time, his business was thriving, and he became a rich man. Uncle Camille set up a vast warehouse in the port of Zeebrugge, near Lissewege, where many logs of different types of wood were stored. The work of sawing wood was done in the factory; around a hundred and fifty employees worked at unloading the timber from the ships, stacking it, loading it onto the wagons and sawing it in the factory. While the business was already flourishing, the end of the First World War delivered an unexpected windfall to the timber business. The war had brought widespread destruction of buildings, churches and houses, and their reconstruction and repair led to an unprecedented demand for timber, making Camille's uncle very wealthy.

Uncle Camille then constructed a big house in the village of Heist and also owned some hotels. For the newly rich people eager to flaunt their upward social mobility or keen to join the elite class, it implied the adoption of the French language, culture and etiquette. His uncle's family consisted of his aunt and a cousin, and despite their Flemish origins, the whole family conducted their domestic conversations in French while French manners governed all the family interactions. As a child, Camille was much loved by his uncle's family, his female cousin was of the same age, and the kids were great friends. He stayed in the large mansion with his uncle and was overwhelmed by their affection, though he found their lifestyle quite repelling. Even at that young age, Camille was convinced that he found his parents' religious disposition and simplicity much to his liking (Raghuvansh 1961, p. 209).

Adolf was the antithesis of his elder brother, and Camille described his father as a tall, robust, disciplined and serious man who was very religious. He wrote, 'The more I consider his [father's] character, the more I am impressed by him' (C. Bulcke 2015 [1976], p. 325). Moreover, Camille believed that the firmness in his father's nature came as a reaction to his grandfather's disorderly life. As a householder with family responsibilities, Adolf realised that his duty was to earn a living and provide for the family. However, he also earned wealth in this world, keeping in mind the hereafter, and was a morally upright man who always followed, what he considered, the most ethical path. Adolf considered profiteering through business deals as unholy, and while he agreed to work as an employee in his brother's business, he did not become a business partner. Camille always said that while his uncle was keen to have his father as a partner in his international timber business, his father flatly declined and agreed to work only as his paid employee (ibid.).

Before the First World War, Adolf worked as a manager in his elder brother's sawmill, and after the war, he again joined his brother's factory as a manager. Adolf knew the secret of the immense wealth he got from the wood business. As Camille recounted, his father knew that the wood bought at much lower prices and stored for some time was sold at three to four times its original price to Norway and Sweden. 'As an idealist man, my father refused to partner in such blatant profiteering, and for that reason, I have great reverence for him' (Bulcke cited in Saxena 2017, p. 74). He admired his father's strong character; he never got angry and never got into a fit of rage, yet the people working under him were quite intimidated by him. His father embodied the human values of a deeply religious person; however, he was not someone who indulged in the arts, literature, poetry and any kind of sentimentality. Adolf always had a special regard and affection for Camille as his firstborn, and Camille believed that he inherited the firmness of resolve, tenacity for arduous work and contentedness from his father.

Among all the people, Camille's mother had the most defining influence in shaping her son's character, innate sensibilities, religious piety and humane values. Born as Maria Gheyle in 1890 to Philippus Gheyle and Rosalie in the village of Lissewege, she was married in 1908 to Camille's father, Adolf. She was as religious as her husband, and unlike him, she was slightly built and was a very sensitive, emotional and compassionate woman. She was keenly interested in literature and was particularly fond of poetry and folk songs, and she sang Flemish folk songs and read Flemish poetry to her children. His mother's aesthetic indulgences introduced Camille to the beauty and aesthetics of the Flemish language and its folk literature. This introduction inculcated in him great love and respect for one's mother tongue throughout his life, ultimately resulting in his strong advocacy for Hindi in India.

Camille's mother, Maria, was very kind and sympathetic, and whenever someone fell ill, she would offer every possible help and assistance. In case of any death in the village, she would visit the family of the diseased, consoling and assisting with the last rites. She was warm and friendly and treated everyone with the same love and respect regardless of their social or economic status. Her affable nature made her very popular in the village, and everyone respected her. Camille's love for literature and his tendency to meet all kinds of people as equals and with ease came from his mother, while his faith in religion was derived from both his parents. Maria was very affectionate to all her four children: Camille; his younger brother Julien; his sister, Gabrielle; and the youngest, Robert. However, she had a special bond with Camille since he was her firstborn. His mother always believed that given his premature birth and delicate health, Camille survived only through divine mercy, and she always thanked Jesus for saving him. In fact, baby Camille did not speak until his younger brother Julien, who was born a year after him, started to speak. At the age of three, Camille joined the local convent and excelled in memorising and reciting poetry; when people praised his eloquence to his mother, she would say that he started to speak only after his younger brother, and maybe he was making up for all the silence of those early days (J. Bulcke 1987, p. 65).

Camille's earliest memory from his childhood was from the days of the First World War in 1914. As a five-year-old boy, one morning he witnessed the British cavalry passing through his village to fight the Germans (C. Bulcke 2015 [1976]). At the beginning of the war, Camille's village had organised a public meeting where he recited a poem denouncing the war:

> It's a cruel time as the fury of war burns all around
> As if to let the rivers of human blood run abound[1]

In August 1914, Camille's father, Adolf, was called to mandatory military service during the war, leaving Maria alone to look after the four children; the youngest child, Robert, was just 18 months old. It was a hard time for the family; apart from grave risks to the father's life, the Bulcke family was without the only earning member. Within a few months of his departure, the family learned that Adolf had been captured in Holland and was taken as a prisoner of war. It was a terrifying time for the villagers of Lissewege, especially the women who were left to look after the children and provide for the family's needs. For some time, the tall and burly German army soldiers stayed in the village, and the villagers were suspicious and fearful; mothers rounded up the children in the evenings and locked them inside their houses. Several different armies crossed through Lissewege; however, he did not remember any complaints about the behaviour of those German soldiers (Raghuvansh 1961, pp. 208–209). One of Camille's most reassuring memories from these traumatic times was that of the local priest, who would often visit the Bulcke family and offer his sympathies and console them. The priest's kindness and loving words had a lasting impact on his mind (ibid.).

One cannot even imagine the family's hardships when their father was taken as a prisoner of war. However, through the trauma Camille realised that despite her slight frame and sensitive nature, his mother showed extraordinary tenacity and resilience, never revealing her anxieties to the children. Paying tribute to his mother, he later wrote, 'I saw my mother's solitary struggle for nearly five years, through which she endeavoured to provide for a safe and nurturing home to her four children' (Saxena 2015, p. 157). Scared of her own mortality, she confided in her eldest, though only five-year-old, son; she told Camille where gold was kept in the family home. The knowledge of this confidential information and watching his mother suddenly made him feel he had rushed from childhood into adulthood (Saxena 2017, p. 25).

The end of the German occupation led to unbridled euphoria among the residents of the village. Suddenly it seemed as if the atmosphere of fear, despair and depression had disappeared, and the light of hope and joy had spread. The children were especially delighted because they would now enjoy complete freedom to go to school and play (Raghuvansh 1961, p. 209). Camille's father was released after the armistice and was to return home by February 1919. His maternal grandfather was also staying with them, and his grandfather and mother were awake the whole night waiting for his father's return. He recalled that the next morning, 'when father arrived – grandfather was at the door and announced, "Mary, he is here", sharing the happy news with his daughter in great relief and joy' (Saxena 2017, p. 25).

Camille often narrated a very poignant incident – that whenever they, as naughty children, used to trouble their mother, she used to threaten them by saying,

> 'When father returns, he will mete out proper punishment to all of you.' I still remember seeing our father climbing the stairs that morning, and all of us, the little kids, hid behind the bed. When he went behind the bed looking for us, we were petrified, but our little brother, who thought he was the most innocent, came forward and said, 'Father, I am Robert.' Then we also came out to greet our father. (C. Bulcke 2015 [1976], p. 326).

Camille recounted his father's homecoming, when he saw his tough mother suddenly break down and cry, as one of the most moving experiences of his life. He understood how much pain and suffering his mother had endured silently and bravely (Saxena 2017, p. 25).

After five years since the brutal war took him away, Camille's father returned to reconnect with his own children. A couple of days later, as Camille returned from school, his father was still disoriented and could not recognise him. He called out to his wife, 'Mary, look, some boy has come', and Camille's mother snapped 'Don't you recognise your own son?' (ibid., p. 26) His father sat still as if he had committed a grave mistake while his mother's face was covered in tears. Camille and his siblings witnessed some of the most devastating effects of the war on human relations, family and social life in those few years. However, the children were delighted to have their father back; and Camille noticed more affection and kindness in his mother's behaviour as her anxieties and struggles had ended (Raghuvansh 1961, p. 209).

Camille always considered his mother his most beloved person on earth; his affection and admiration also led him to adopt some of her teachings and habits. One such habit was letter writing; he used to write to his mother regularly regardless of whether he was studying in high school or university, whether he was training in theology or working for his PhD or writing his scholarly books in India. His closest friend from his days at the University of Allahabad, Raghuvansh, mentioned that Camille never delayed writing to his mother for he knew that his anxious mother would always wait for his letters eagerly (ibid., pp. 139–140). He was aware that she used to read his letters several times and keep them in chronological order in a cupboard. For his mother, these letters were the only material connection with her beloved son. In the same cupboard, she kept all of Camille's books, writings and pictures, and maintained this collection not just as a museum but as a shrine. Although she could not read even a word of Camille's rather copious Hindi writings, she would tenderly hold these creations of her son as if she were holding Camille himself (ibid., p. 215). His mother never showed her sorrow for not having her son with her; instead, he came to know of these poignant details from his sister, Gabrielle. Inspired by his mother, he followed the practice of writing letters to all his friends and associates, especially after visiting them. He said, 'If I stayed with friends or relatives during my childhood, my mother instructed me to write to them to thank them for their hospitality and to inform them of my safe arrival' (Saxena 2015, p. 153).

Camille was very proud that he came from a village; in fact, his perception of life, community living, selfless service, and living a simple, frugal and yet very fulfilling life came from his upbringing in a small Belgian village. He always cherished his love for the village ambience, its people and its distinct cultural traditions. He claimed that, like millions of Indians, he too was brought up in a village and used to recite the following poem:

We who were born
In country places
Far from cities
And shifting faces
We have a birthright
No man can sell
And a secret joy
No man can tell. (Bulcke cited in Prasad 2002, p. 18)[2]

Camille's affection for his village, Lissewege, and its lifestyle was reflected in his writing and interpersonal interactions. As a young man in 1933, he wrote an outstanding essay in German depicting his village, its people and culture. He believed that there was nothing beautiful or romantic about his village, even if it was on the banks of a small river that very leisurely carried its turbid waters towards its destination, the North Sea (C. Bulcke 1987, p. 15). However, his love for the village came from its residents' unwavering faith in the Christian way of life. It preserved their childlike innocence, which saw no conflict between God and the world, between nature and God's grace. The villagers lived a life animated by faith, and in their humble hearts, they accepted God's will and bore the sorrows silently and patiently. All the days of their lives were spent in the company of God and in the belief that their difficulties were absorbed in God because the cross of Christ was a living reality for them. Faith did not mean a complete surrender with bowed heads and rosaries like neophytes making an unusual display of devotion. They were not mystics; instead, they had rustic manners and unsophisticated tastes by urban standards, yet they were full of innocence, honesty and faith (C. Bulcke 1987, p. 17).

In his interview with his long-time friend and collaborator, Dineshwar Prasad, Camille described Lissewege as an ancient village that, even during his childhood, had a big population of around two and a half thousand, and it was so wide that it took almost two hours on foot to reach from one end to the other. The village had a mixed economy; there were landowners, farmers and labourers, who worked in the only factory in the village (C. Bulcke 2015 [1976], p. 324). The longest road of the village ran along the river; the older single-storey houses, some of them barely six-feet high, were on this street, and the poorest people lived in them. Another road that cut it straight and led to the historic cathedral was commonly known as the 'Prosperous Road' and had some of the most modern architecture occupied by more affluent and wealthier people (ibid.). However, most people lived by the unpaved tracks or trails by the agricultural fields and meadows, in harmony with nature for generations.

Camille most fondly remembered the large chunks of farms, gardens and vast swathes of natural habitation around his village. He believed that the villagers loved the earth even more than their non-Christian ancestors, a belief that he perhaps carried all his life in India as he served the ecclesiastical community with uncritical devotion. They loved living amidst nature – they loved the flowers, birds, trees and meadows, the fields they tilled and the animals they worked with. Camille's maternal uncle was a landowner, and as a child, he used to visit his uncle's farm and get fresh milk to drink. The harvest time in the village was a lot of fun and his village upbringing instilled in him a love of nature and a fondness for the open environment. He found this aplenty in Jharkhand, in India, when he made that his home for his missionary and scholarly activities.

The other natural attraction of the village was its proximity to the sea; Lissewege was located in the low-lying areas near the North Sea, and the land on which his village stood was reclaimed from the sea by building a wall with huge stones. The wall was only two miles away from Camille's childhood home, and loud roars could be heard as the sea collided with the enormous stones of the wall (Raghuvansh 1961, p. 189). He walked on that stone wall or cycled against the fierce westerly wind for miles as one of his enjoyable activities during his childhood. On occasions, the westerly wind would blow so strongly that Camille and his young companions had to crawl along the walled road. The ferocity of the westerly wind made all the trees on the coast of his country bend towards one side (ibid.). For the residents of the areas around Lissewege, the sea was the source of all their romantic fantasies; one could see the beautiful landscape along the sea and the kaleidoscope of colours across the sky, with the changing of the tide along with the phases of the moon. During the high tide, the ocean water flowed over the road, and people from all over the country congregated in beach hotels for entertainment. This was a festive time, and so many people assembled along the sea-facing streets that it was impossible to cross the road.

A great formative experience that shaped Camille's own perspectives was the community life and the emotional well-being of his village, where people shared not only their meagre resources but also their happiness, achievements, sorrows and failures with others. He explained in his writings that the villagers in Lissewege were one united family where everyone believed in the same God, everyone prayed together in the same church (C. Bulcke 2009, p. 144). Every senior citizen was familiar with every family's circumstances and knew the villagers by their names. Even children could quickly tell you who lived in a particular house. Nothing could be kept under wraps, and if someone fought with their wife or if a love affair blossomed, the whole village got to know about it (ibid.). The village celebrated each birth and mourned every death together; the whole village would assemble in the church and gather in the cemetery at the time of burial. When an animal was slaughtered at someone's place to cook meat, some part of it was shared with the neighbours and relatives. Camille insisted that it was the shared living of the villagers that made life so complete, fulfilling and beautiful.

The nostalgia of innocent childhood in his little Belgian village persisted all his life, as he yearned for the green fields, those fences and enclosures where he used to search for birds' nests, the groves where he plucked fruits, the small rivers in which he swam and which froze in the winter. If sacred and fond memories protect a person in perilous circumstances, then the memories of the people in his village in Belgium and its surroundings brought him happiness all his life. He tried to recreate those memories throughout his life in India, especially in the rural environment of Jharkhand.

Camille's own religiosity and unwavering faith in Christianity were also nurtured in the religious surroundings of his childhood. Religion was one of the most prominent aspects of the Belgian social milieu; not only was the Bulcke household deeply religious, but their village proudly claimed to host one of the most renowned and historical pilgrimage centres of Christianity. Lissewege is home to the great thirteenth-century church of the Virgin Mary, famous throughout Europe for its artistry, miracle stories and tall and flat tower. Churches with flat towers of such height are exclusive to this part of Europe and are representative of the early Gothic-style architecture. According to the local legend, in medieval times, some fishermen miraculously found a statue of the Virgin Mary while casting their nets in one of the numerous water wells; the church was built at the same place. The cathedral, now known as the Our Lady of the Visitation Church of Lissewege, was originally constructed between 1225 and 1270 AD, while the tower was built later, between 1250 and 1270 AD. Even in those days, while the village of Lissewege was of modest size, the church was prominent and well-known around the region for Christian pilgrims who visited it on their way to Santiago de Compostela in Spain. The donations of these pilgrims primarily funded the construction of this church.

The original statue was lost during a fire in 1586, and the repair started in the year 1624 when a new wooden statue was placed. The same statue has been the centre of attraction for several thousand pilgrims even after almost 500 years (Clarysse 1987, p. 195). The transept, choir and pulpit were restored gradually. In 1652, Wairam Romboudt, a local carpenter, created the root screen and the organ closet, while the organ mechanics were created in 1808 by a local artist, Karel Van Peteghem. Six bells have been placed inside its tower, of which three are made of bronze and three of iron. The bronze bells are from after the Second World War, installed in place of the three old bells, which were removed for some other purpose during the war. The heaviest of the three iron bells is from around 1869, weighing about 1603 kilograms. There is confusion about the exact number of stairs in the tower; however, they are certainly more than 250 (ibid.). As a child, Camille enthusiastically participated in the annual procession of the Virgin Mary held in the village. He used to attend this church early in the morning to assist in the altar service, and this practice had instilled in him a tender devotion to the mother of Jesus since his childhood (C. Bulcke 2015 [1976], p. 324).

The other major historical attraction in the village is the Ter Doest Abbey; it was founded in 1106 by the Benedictines of Saint-Riquier (near Abbeville). However, the abbey did not attract any real monastic community, and the Benedictine bishop transferred it to the Cistercians in 1174–1175 (Nuytten 2005, p. 60). Twelve monks and three lay brothers were sent to Lissewege to establish a Cistercian abbey, which grew into a major monastery by the thirteenth century and acquired large agricultural and forest land (van Acker 2021). Around 1280, a monumental barn was added that has survived almost unchanged, although the roof construction dates from the fourteenth century. Mostly made of Oak wood, the barn is approximately 54 metres long and 20 metres wide, with a ridge height of approximately 16.5 metres (Nuytten 2005, p. 61). At its peak, the community consisted of 120 monks and lay brothers. However, by the sixteenth century, growing religious dissent between the Catholics and the Protestants led to tensions and a lack of monks for its upkeep. While not much is left of the abbey, the historical barn has survived unscathed (Clarysse 1987, p. 195).

In his description of Lissewege, Camille designated these two monuments: the Church of Our Lady and the barn of Ter Doest Abbey as historically significant and with whom was associated some of his best childhood memories in the land of his birth (C. Bulcke 1987, p. 6). Remarkably, in its abstraction, Camille found the unwavering faith of his fellow villagers as exemplary, and even in the material manifestations, his two examples were related to Christianity.

Early Influences and Hobbies

Apart from his own mother, Gertrude, the Mother Superior of the village, had the greatest influence on Camille. She was the head of the convent in the village where he went for primary education at the age of three, and Camille had a lifelong and utmost reverence towards her since his childhood. An extraordinary personality who had become a legend in her lifetime, Camille considered the Mother Superior as the second tower of Lissewege's cathedral. She epitomised a life full of piety and was always there to provide selfless service to the entire community. More than being a bright and engaged religious worker, she was incomparably brave and would never tolerate injustice, even at grave personal risks. During the First World War, two dozen German cavalrymen entered their village on horseback and started roaming around with guns drawn in search of the Belgian soldiers who were hiding. The villagers were terrified and feared for their safety; most had shut their doors. As the German horsemen arrived near the convent, Mother Gertrude, without fear for her life, faced them and shouted, 'Kine soldat' (No soldier here); immediately, the German soldiers retreated and left the village (C. Bulcke 2015 [1976], p. 325).

Mother Gertrude had been headmistress of the convent of Lissewege for 50 years and knew everyone in the village. Camille was her favourite student; he joined the kindergarten at the convent as a three-year-old boy and was proficient in memorising and reciting poems. Mother Gertrude taught him a poem about the war; he used to recite it so well that she used to take him from one class to another to recite it. He was the best student during his primary schooling, although he was two to three years younger than his classmates (J. Bulcke 1987, p. 65). On the day of his baptism, she told a five-year-old Camille, 'Ask God for the boon of becoming a monk' (D. Prasad 1987, p. 6). He always remembered Mother Gertrude as one of his first inspirations from early childhood to adolescence. He never forgot to mention her courage in defiantly standing up to the German soldiers and her resolute piety and selfless service to others. From his childhood days, he also fondly remembered his family friends who were men in the art world. Among them were Brother Ildephonse, a novelist and musician, and Brems, a painter (ibid., p. 6).

As a child growing up in the picturesque rural settings of Belgium, Camille was influenced by the natural beauty of his village and the social milieu of the villagers. He was fortunate to develop a circle of affectionate friends and reliable companions since childhood. He was very much into sports and loved football; along with his friends, he established the first Lissewege football team from the village. During his childhood, there was no separate playground in the village, so he used to play on the road or near the dam of the canal. He used to play as the forward in this team and participated in several local matches (J. Bulcke 1987, p. 65). He also took up boxing; he could not only take the hit but could also hit the opponent (ibid.). Camille also loved sprinting, especially with his long legs; he could run large distances and would run from one village to another to attend student meetings while his companions cycled. Some of his other interests included a love for literature, acting and sports. Until then he performed many roles in Shakespeare's plays and would enthusiastically accompany other students to faraway towns to perform (Raghuvansh 1961, p. 209).

Camille was fond of wearing fashionable clothes; whenever new clothes were to be stitched, he would go to the shop with his mother and meticulously select from the available samples. All four children in the Bulcke family received pocket money every Sunday; while the other children usually bought sweets, Camille would save the money and buy fashionable clothes and shoes of his choice (J. Bulcke 1987, p. 66). He probably had not imagined then that his later life would be spent in a padre's robe and fashion would be the last thing on his mind. It was not that he disliked sweets; rather, he loved chocolates. Whenever he was given a choice of something with bread at the time of refreshments, he would always choose chocolate. To get rid of this habit, once his father forced him to eat chocolate with potatoes at mealtime; undaunted, Camille savoured the bizarre combination with great relish (ibid.).

During his childhood, Camille used to go to church every day to help the priest who served at the altar. Once, a man was on his deathbed, so at the end of the church service, the priest asked Camille to accompany him to the dying man's house. That person's house was half an hour away from the village. At the doorsteps of the sick man's house, Camile heard the loud moaning, and frightened, he ran away, leaving the lamp and the bell on the ground. The priest had no option but to carry the lamp and the bell back to the church. The next day as preparations were on for the burial of the deceased in the church, the priest wanted to prevent Camille from participating. Camille, however, was adamant about being a part of this service and kept interfering until the priest lost his temper and was ready to thrash this little helper. Luckily, Camille sensed the potential danger and decided to run away (J. Bulcke 1987, p. 65). While the sick man and his moaning were too much for little Camille, he did not want to miss out on the important burial service. The priest, meanwhile, had other ideas after having observed him at the sick man's house!

While Camille was still in school, some Jesuits visited Lissewege looking for potential candidates to join their society. Mother Gertrude sent a message for Camille to see the Jesuits; however, the young boy had no intention of joining any order or becoming a monk, so he ran away from school. No sooner did his fellow students know of this, they started to tease him, addressing him as 'Father'. Camille failed to see the humour and was ready to punch anyone giving him this unwanted reverence (ibid., p. 66). Little did he know then that he would go on to make outstanding contributions to the ecclesiastical world and gain tremendous fame and reverence as Father Bulcke in his later life.

One of the most profound experiences for Camille during his childhood occurred when he was about 10 years old. A 20-year-old girl from the neighbourhood named Miriam died of tuberculosis. She was a tall, beautiful girl and used to participate in the local drama. Camille knew the girl well, and sometimes she would play with him. His mother asked him to accompany her in paying last respects to Miriam. Scared and trembling, he entered the room where her body was kept. It was delightful spring weather, and the sun's rays entered the room through the closed window. The dead girl was lying completely still, and she looked the same as before. She was lying in the white clothes that used to adorn her when she carried the idol of the Virgin Mary in religious processions. To him, the dead girl looked serene and beautiful, and it appeared as if she was blushing a bit because Camille was looking at her face with his downcast eyes.

He did not understand it then, but he was keen to stay with the dead girl, and when his mother asked him to leave after offering prayers, he pleaded,

'Mother, let me stay here. I will stay here.' His mother was surprised and asked, 'Why?' Camille replied, 'I will watch her; she looks so beautiful' (Raghuvansh 1961, p. 158). Upon hearing his reply, his concerned mother held his hand tightly while she walked him home. Later, when Camille's mother narrated this incident to Miriam's mother, she was pleasantly surprised to hear that the boy wished to spend time with her deceased daughter while everyone else who visited that day was in a hurry to return after praying (ibid.). Recalling this incident, Camille wrote,

> I asked my mother to let me stay longer in the room; I sat down to watch the girl in complete peace. I felt as if I was at home. A silent grief came over me, a grief I was not entirely aware of because of the untimely death. I was much calmer that day than on other days. I do not remember what I thought that day, but afterwards, I often thought that she was a human being like me, that I would die someday, and that we all have the same fate in this world. The seed of renunciation was probably sown on the same day. (C. Bulcke 2009, pp. 146–147)

Camille was a quick learner, and from Mother Gertrude's convent, he went to the local municipal school; the headmaster of his middle school was the father of his classmate and friend, Remo (D. Prasad 1987, p. 6). He excelled in his studies, and since there were no high schools in Lissewege, he had to look for admission at schools in the neighbouring town. The closest major town to Lissewege was Bruges, also known as the Venice of the North, because of its beauty (C. Bulcke 2015 [1976]). Admission to high schools was not easily possible for every student, but with his academic brilliance, he faced no difficulty; and in 1921, he joined the St Francis Xavier School in Bruges, where he continued to study till 1928 (D. Prasad 1987, p. 6). On school days, he used to take a train early morning from Lissewege and had to leave the house by half past six to go to the station. The station was about half an hour away from the village, and on several days he had to run to the station because he used to get up late. However, he used to sleep till noon on the initial days of the long holidays (J. Bulcke 1987, p. 66).

In high school, he focused on studying science, though his special interest was mathematics. Due to his humility, pleasant disposition and intellectual intensity, he became the school's favourite, loved by his teachers and classmates (D. Prasad 1987, p. 6). He used to take an active part in the students' group during the long vacations. The group used to go from village to village and enact dramas; fond of acting, Camille played in several of Shakespeare's dramas. He performed leading roles in these plays and was undaunted by the long monologues (J. Bulcke 1987, p. 66). Apart from his love for science and mathematics in high school, Camille was equally keen on literature and poetry; he learnt German and read Rilke and Goethe.[3] Shakespeare was one of his favourite authors right from his childhood, when he started reading translations of his plays and acted in several of them. He memorised the entire text of Hamlet and was convinced that the analysis of the human heart found in Shakespeare's writings is rare elsewhere (C. Bulcke 2015 [1976]).

The renowned Flemish poet Guido Gezelle was Camille's idol; Gezelle not only wrote exceptional poetry, but, more significantly, he wrote in Flemish and was an ordained Catholic priest. As a teacher in Roeselare, in Belgium, Gezelle was in charge of the students from England,[4] where he 'developed an unrelenting campaign among his pupils to recruit missionaries' (Vincent 2016, p. 3). In 1861, writing to the famous Dutch writer J. A. Alberdingk Thijm, Gezelle said that 'the latter could not imagine how Flemish youth was burning to realise the papal ideal of conversion "as far as the four corners of the globe"' (ibid.). Camille was greatly inspired by Gezelle's writing, piety and endeavour to spread the gospel. It is also worth reiterating that Camille was deeply touched by the kindness of the local priest who visited them during his childhood while his father was taken as a prisoner of war. He also found the work of Constant Lievens, a Flemish missionary who went to India and achieved phenomenal success in spreading the gospel, truly inspiring (Clarysse 1985).

In his adolescence, Camille started writing poetry, but once a teacher laughed at his work, he was terribly discouraged and gave up writing poetry altogether (ibid.). At the high school in Bruges, Camille became acutely aware of the discrimination against the Flemish-speaking population and French hegemony in all the higher echelons of society (C. Bulcke 2015 [1976]). He wrote, 'The agitation of the protagonists of Flemish language began to gather momentum after the First World War, and during my student days, for the sake of my mother tongue and Flemish culture, I took an active part in the fight for the suppression of French in the public and social life of the northern part of Belgium' (C. Bulcke 2010, p. 135).

Camille was excellent with his academics and sports and even had great acting skills; however, when it came to working on home maintenance or other domestic chores, he was found wanting. He probably had neither the flair nor the requisite dexterity for such artisanship for any such assignment at home. Instead of thinking about how best to accomplish it, Camille would start calculating how many hours it would take to complete the work. Once the children were asked to put wooden pegs in the backyard, the lower part of each peg had to be painted in bitumen before hammering it into the ground. His brother Julien remembered that while he applied bitumen only to the pegs, Camille was so unwieldy that he blackened both his hands (J. Bulcke 1987, p. 66).

Camille fared exceptionally well in his high school; despite his daily commute, he stood first in every class and passed the high school examination in 1928 with very high marks (D. Prasad 2002, p. 10). Even before completing his high school studies, he had decided that he would study engineering at Louvain University because, at that time, the engineering entrance exam was considered the most challenging. However, he appeared in the entrance exam solely based on his studies in high school and passed with very high marks (C. Bulcke 2015 [1976]). In fact, his own family did not believe that a 19-year-old Camille, based on his school education alone, could pass such a complex exam. Once he cleared the exam, he was feted by the whole village since no one from Lissewege had managed to pass high school and get admission to the renowned Louvain University.

Before his departure to Louvain to commence his engineering degree, Camille went to see Mother Gertrude to seek her blessing. She said to him rather affectionately, 'Why do you study so much? You have to become a priest' (D. Prasad 2002, p. 10). He did not understand the import of those words at that time, as he was getting ready to join Louvain University. He had a clear map of his future in his mind: he wanted to become an engineer and live the life of an ordinary householder (ibid., p. 11). K. L. Devriendt, Camille's friend from the St Francis Xavier School, Bruges, also joined Louvain University in 1928. Camille joined the university to become a mining engineer, while Devriendt planned to study chemistry. Apart from pursuing higher education, Camille and Devriendt went to Louvain as both believed that university was not only a place to earn a degree but also a place to make life meaningful as a human being and as a Flemish citizen. They believed that their objectives could only be accomplished in Louvain (Devriendt 1987, p. 78).

University Life, Student Activism, Renunciation

Located 150 kilometres south-east of Lissewege, Louvain University is Belgium's oldest and biggest university. On 9 December 1425, Pope Martin

V founded the Studia Generalia at Louvain to fulfil a threefold mission: 'the advancement of science, the education of youth, and the creation of a centre of cultural and social influence for the promotion of peace and tranquillity, the essential elements of a Christian order' (Strakhovsky 1939, p. 179). In September 1426, at the time of inauguration, Louvain was one of the few comprehensive universities offering instructions in civil law, canon law, medicine and the arts. Theology was added to the curriculum later in 1426, and the medium of instruction was Latin. In the period of Reformation, Louvain supported 'the old religious concepts' and along with 'Cologne, Louvain was the first institution of learning to condemn the teachings of Martin Luther' (ibid.). The university continued to flourish until the 1560s, when the recurring wars, floods, droughts and pandemics pushed it into near extinction (Callewaert 1987, p. 197). The university was revived at the beginning of the seventeenth century only to face its biggest challenge with the French takeover of these territories in 1794 (Woitrin 1998, p. 72). It was shut down in 1797, and there were no academic activities for the next 20 years, with most of its precious holdings being either destroyed or auctioned off (Callewaert 1987, p. 197). In 1817, King William I of the Netherlands reopened it as the State University of Leuven, which was meant to be impartial; however, on the initiative of the Belgian bishops, it became a Catholic institution again in 1834 (McRae 1983, pp. 20–21).

During the First World War, Louvain University was systematically looted and burned. After the war, the library was rebuilt with German and American assistance and was inaugurated in 1928. However, at the beginning of the Second World War, in 1940, the library was burnt again, and many old manuscripts were destroyed (Callewaert 1987, p. 198). Even after its revival under the Dutch regime, the use of French as the official language continued a decision that eventually triggered a full-blown political struggle between the Flemish-speaking students and the university administration. When Camille joined the university in 1928, like most of his young Flemish and Catholic contemporaries, he took a keen interest in the struggle for the cultural and political sphere of Flanders (Devriendt 1987, p. 78).

Even from a very young age, Camille was well aware of the ongoing language dispute in Belgium; his own language, Flemish, was popular in the north, while French was prevalent in the south. However, the French language dominated the country in the administration, the army and at the school and university levels; additionally, in the north, the educated people derived a sense of pride in speaking French and embracing French culture (C.

Bulcke 2010, p. 135). To ordinary Flemish speakers, French was the language of the colonisers; not only did it have official patronage, but it was also regarded as a mark of upward mobility and the language of choice among the elites and the parvenus of the Flemish society. In his extended family, while Camille's parents were keen to preserve and promote the Flemish language and culture, his wealthy uncle readily adopted the French language and culture to promote his business interests (D. Prasad 1987, p. 4). He had little respect for those in the Flemish society who had embraced the French language and cultural practices (Saxena 2017, p. 29).

The movement to defend the rights and dignity of the Flemish people gained renewed momentum at the end of the First World War. During his school and university days, he actively participated in the agitation to defend his mother tongue and Flemish culture (C. Bulcke 2009, p. 115). At Louvain University, while studying for his engineering degree, Camille emerged as a prominent leader of the young Flemish and Catholic students and was fondly referred to as the 'soldier of Flemish culture' by his peers (Saxena 2017, p. 30). The Flemish students used to make a pilgrimage to the Basilica of Our Lady located in the town of Scherpenheuvel. The legend of a miraculous old wooden statue of Mother Mary, dating back to the fourteenth century, is at the heart of this pilgrimage church. Camille used to accompany other Flemish students on their overnight trip to Scherpenheuvel; on some occasions, he would undertake the pilgrimage all alone (Devriendt 1987, p. 79).

Camille also participated in political campaigns to demand the protection of the political and cultural rights of the Flemish people. Interestingly, the more the Belgian government suppressed the Flemish movement, the more convinced Camille was that the government was an obstacle to the Flemish people's social, cultural and material development. He was an enthusiastic participant in literary and cultural activities and engaged in several literary and intellectual campaigns to preserve the Flemish language and culture, even during his engineering days.

On several occasions, despite his dedication towards his studies, Camille would miss his lectures to participate in Flemish literary events and other political campaigns opposing the imposition of French. He joined the protest organised by the Flemish people against the Belgian king during the royal visit to Louvain. On one occasion, a French-speaking professor was hired at Louvain University; he accompanied a group of Flemish students who went to the vice chancellor's residence to register their disapproval. He and his friends invented a novel way to protest against the use of French; they would start singing loudly any Flemish song whenever a teacher delivered a lecture in French to his class (D. Prasad 2002, p. 11).

Camille's enthusiastic support for the Flemish movement was not based on a dreamy romantic idealism or some parochial nationalism; instead, he viewed his participation in this campaign as a service to his fellow Flemish people (Devriendt 1987, pp. 78–79). He realised that to accomplish its hegemonic ambitions, the materially superior French resorted to the cultural colonisation of the Flemish people. Later, as he gradually leaned towards more spiritual pursuits, he also realised the narrow political aims of the Flemish movement and how parochial nationalism subsumed the movement's broader social and cultural purposes. His friend Devriendt believed that Camille would have emerged as a prominent leader of the Flemish movement had he stayed on with his worldly pursuits (ibid.). Camille always viewed his participation in the pro-Flemish movement as a challenge to the hegemonic colonial practices, a vision that later inspired his entire life's work in India.

Years later, recalling his time at Louvain University, Camille said that most of his time was spent in academic pursuits, and he never went to watch movies. Apart from his studies, he pursued one hobby in sports – of playing football regularly. However, his foremost commitment was to the student movements to restore the honour of the Flemish language, and in that he was recognised as a prominent student leader of the Flemish movement among his peers and other activists at Louvain (C. Bulcke 2015 [1976]).

The other aspect of Camille's intellectual development at Louvain University was his deeper engagement with religion and theology. Along with the study of science as a tangible and rational subject, he developed a greater interest in the abstract and intangible aspects of spirituality. He grew pensive and used to reflect a lot on theological arguments, and he also consulted his religious mentor about these deliberations. He put forth the doubts of his mind, the confusion of faith and his religious ideas before his religious godfather[5] (Raghuvansh 1961, pp. 210–211). The religious godfather would then try to resolve his doubts or explain the theological arguments through the holy life of Jesus. Such discussions inculcated great interest and appreciation for the Christian way of life and love for Jesus in Camille (ibid.). He was determined to complete his mining engineering degree and then pursue gainful employment to fulfil his parents' dreams and restore the Bulcke family's prestige in the community.

Some moments come up unexpectedly and suddenly change the direction of one's life. Camille's entire life transformed in one such moment. He had come home to Lissewege from Louvain to prepare for the final exam of his first-year engineering degree. One evening after playing football, he returned to an empty home as the family members had gone out. Making the best use of this solitude to prepare for his upcoming exam, He was reading a book in his study. Suddenly lightning flashed on the page of the book, and in that supernatural moment Camille realised that he was to renounce the world and become a monk (C. Bulcke 2015 [1976]). He put the book away and broke down because the beautiful image of the future that he had so assiduously carved was shattered in that extraordinary moment of reckoning (D. Prasad 1987, p. 7). However, he had had enough spiritual experiences and developed sacred wisdom to understand that it was the call of his Lord, and he was obligated to accept it (ibid.). He gathered himself with great difficulty, handed over the house keys to the neighbours and went for a long walk to the seashore. He returned home very late and felt so heavy and depressed that he did not speak to anyone for three days.

Everyone in the family was surprised to see a usually jovial and cheerful Camille in a grim and pensive mood; however, they did not dare ask him anything. He spent many days at home, always withdrawn from the rest of the world and agonising throughout his preparatory leave at Lissewege. Later he returned to Louvain to take the exam, and, despite his preoccupation and mental agony, he passed the exam with very high marks and enrolled for the second year (ibid.).

In those days, the knowledge of Latin was mandatory to become a priest; hence, Camille decided to learn Latin and went twice a week to the Jesuits Seminary in Louvain to study the language (D. Prasad 2002, p. 12). His Latin teacher at the seminary was Father Salzman, who was among the world-renowned Christian ethics and theology teachers. He revealed his decision to renounce the world and become a Christian priest only to his closest friend, Devriendt, at Louvain University. Camille informed him that by the end of the academic session, he would join the novitiate and asked his friend to keep it a secret as he still had to resolve several issues. Camille had to complete his engineering exams and also needed to take the exams in Latin (Devriendt 1987, p. 78). While the news of Camille's decision to become a Christian priest shocked Devriendt, he was even more stunned to know that Camille would leave Flanders and go to serve the mission in India (ibid.).

Camille also confided in his spiritual mentor, the godfather, about his resolve to enter the holy life of Christ. His godfather praised Camille's resolution but also advised him to think and understand the implications of such a critical decision with a calm mind (Raghuvansh 1961, p. 211). Like a sincere and concerned guide, the godfather also instructed him about the challenges on this path and reminded him of his worldly duties. He also gave him books to study and to make an informed decision based on all the different perspectives. However, once the godfather saw Camille's firm determination, he finally gave his consent for him to enter the Society of Jesus. That day brought immense satisfaction and unbounded inner happiness to Camille (ibid.).

He cleared his second-year engineering exams with flying colours; and having attained the requisite educational qualifications to be a mining engineer, he returned home to Lissewege. The entire family was overjoyed to see their favourite child at the cusp of excellent material success. Meanwhile, he agonised over how best to tell his parents about his heartbreaking decision to become a priest; he took several days to gather enough courage to break this news to them (D. Prasad 2002, p. 12). One evening in January 1930, while all the other family members went out to watch a play, Camille ensured that only his parents stayed home and informed them about his decision to renounce worldly pursuits and become a priest (C. Bulcke 2015 [1976]). His mother broke down and then, gathering herself, said, 'I consider myself blessed.' His usually taciturn father said, 'It would be nice if you stayed here, though I have no objection' (ibid.).

At night he heard his mother saying to his father, 'I had an inkling that he would go.' His father, always reserved, said nothing but 'yes' with a sigh. Twenty-five years later, recollecting this moment, Camille said that maybe he did not comprehend the solemnity of this talk between his parents. However, after so many years, he could better understand their sorrow (Raghuvansh 1961, pp. 211–212). The ordination of boys to priesthood is celebrated with joy in Belgian Catholic families. Likewise, there was rejoicing and celebration in his family, but he understood that his mother's heart was grieving inside, and she looked glum. Moreover, she was anxious that since Camille had resolved to enter the Jesuit order with the vow to go to India, she would never be able to see her eldest and her most beloved child again (ibid.).

Camille was quite aware that his decision to become a priest equally shocked his relatives, friends and acquaintances, especially in Louvain.

During his university days, he was a prominent face of several organisations of the Flemish movement. He recalled, 'The election of their new office-bearers was about to take place, and I was sure to be elected among them because of my popularity' (C. Bulcke 2015 [1976]). However, destiny had something else stored for him. Devriendt, his friend, wrote to him: 'This information of yours has caused an explosion in Louvain' (ibid.). Camille's entire family and relatives were shocked; his uncle, who had come to see him off, wept all the way to the railway station. It looked as if his uncle was deeply saddened to see his nephew rejecting the splendour he had cultivated throughout his life (ibid.).

The one person who saw Camille's development at Louvain University from very close quarters was Devriendt; in his writings, he narrated his observations of this transformational process. Camille never had any doubts about his calling which affirmed his life's mission. Devriendt believed that the decision to renounce the worldly and embrace the spiritual life was not easy for Camille. In fact, this decision triggered a lot of sorrow and doubt in the beginning, and it required intense introspection, immense self-reflection, indomitable courage and brutal honesty (Devriendt 1987, pp. 79–80). As a brilliant student, an incomparable cultural protagonist of the Flemish people and an emerging leader, Camille during his time at Louvain could develop his personality in what was both a challenging and a nurturing environment. The outstanding intellectual and scholarly environment based on the long and lofty intellectual traditions inspired profound learning, while the inimical environment based on language hegemony warranted persistent defiance. He successfully negotiated the two aspects of his student life and became a gifted engineer and a gritty language warrior, which prepared him for the challenges of priesthood in his later life (ibid.).

Only later, Devriendt discovered that Saint Paul was Camille's idol during his early life, even before he joined Louvain University. Camille drew inspiration from Saint Paul's life, which was devoted to spreading the message of Christ to all the known nations and non-Jews of his time (ibid.). Saint Paul worked to spread the gospel for he had nothing but immense love for God and men. As a parting gift, Camille presented Devriendt a booklet of the letters of Saint Paul with a message: 'May your life journey be successful and beautiful' (ibid.). Devriendt believed that this gift was not just a testimony of their friendship, but, more pertinently, it represented a spiritual gift from his dear friend, now on the path of God. Moreover, the message was more of a reflection of Camille's own life and his way of telling Devriendt that the epistles of Saint Paul contained the secret of his decision to join the Jesuits' order. His decision to join the Jesuits was driven by his assessment that the men in this society embodied the spirit of Saint Paul, especially in the work of evangelisation (ibid.).

On 23 September 1930, Camille left Lissewege to join the Jesuits novitiate at Drongen, near the city of Ghent in Belgium, and stayed there for the next two years (D. Prasad 1987, p. 7). From there, he went to the monastery at Valkenburg near the Netherland–Germany border to study Philosophy for the next three years. At the Drongen novitiate, he had the option of travelling home to Lissewege and meeting his family, thus maintaining a sense of normalcy. Once he completed the novitiate, he was again asked if he would like to stay in Belgium or would still insist on going to India. Camille remained firm in his determination to go to India, which was his condition for joining the Society of Jesus (Raghuvansh 1961, p. 212). With this reaffirmation, he established the future course of his life and also informed his parents that, eventually, he would leave Belgium and Europe.

Upon completing his two-year tenure at the Drongen novitiate and the Valkenburg monastery where he studied Philosophy, he was back to Louvain University to study physics, particularly Albert Einstein's theory of relativity. From Valkenburg and Louvain, Camille could visit his family and join them on specific occasions. Once it was decided that he had to leave for India, he had around two weeks to spend at home and finally take leave of his family, friends and relatives. When he got home, he could sense the gloom around him, and the grief and sorrow in the hearts of his loved ones; and yet given the auspiciousness of his journey and the sanctity of his work, everyone was being stoic (Raghuvansh 1961, pp. 212–213). He was astonished to see his mother's self-restraint; she would do all the work and help him with travel preparations with a pleasant smile. She did not want to dampen his spirits by revealing her emotions and endured such a challenging situation with aplomb. In a few days, Camille's uncle, aunt and cousin came to stay with them, allowing his mother to hide behind several relatives and a busy household (ibid.).

Eventually, the day of his departure arrived, and Camille had already forbidden any of his relatives to accompany him to the nearby town of Bruges except his cousin. The scene at the time of his leaving home was very moving.

Everyone in his family was making every effort to bid him a cheerful goodbye despite the sadness. He understood that while his mother was feeling unbearable pain, she was still trying to do everything to the best of her ability for the welfare of her child (ibid.). He was determined to keep the facade of normalcy despite the churning of emotions within him, and on the face of it, he was happily taking leave of everyone. His father kept a very sombre face and camouflaged his emotions behind a serious exterior. His mother stood at the door of the house, and Camille kissed her hand as part of his goodbye; for a moment, he felt his emotions would overpower him. However, his mother kept calm and recited a prayer for his safe and happy journey. It was only after reaching India that he came to know through his younger sister Gabrielle's letter that his mother could not bear to see her beloved son leave forever and fell unconscious (D. Prasad 1987, p. 8).

While sitting alone in the train, it dawned on him that he was leaving his country and his relatives probably forever. He could see from the galloping train all that he was leaving behind: the green pastures, the lush fields and the lovely villages and towns of the country. His eyes welled up once he realised that he would never see his beautiful motherland, and the path of God was taking him to unknown and far-off shores. An elderly lady was travelling in the same compartment; she was attentive to him ever since he boarded the train. The lady probably understood the situation and had tears in her eyes while she kept looking at him. Suddenly, Camille was reminded of his mother and her agony, forcing him to hide his tears in his handkerchief (Raghuvansh 1961, p. 214). What he did not know then was that he would never be able to meet his mother again.

Camille left Belgium on 20 October 1935 to take the voyage from Antwerp to far-off India; it was the first step to realising his cherished dream of serving the mission of Christian life. Before his departure, he had collected substantial information about India's history, geography, climate, culture and literature; yet he always admitted learning a lot more through his interactions with his fellow passengers on his long journey. During the 17-day-long sea voyage, he made friends with several Indians on board; however, more than the conversation, he was instinctively drawn to the language his Indian co-passengers used to converse among themselves (Saxena 2017, p. 35). He arrived in Bombay on 6 November 1935. Despite his meticulous research, methodical homework and multifaceted training, nothing had prepared him for the onward journey that would keep him busy for the rest of his life.

Notes

1. Translated by the authors.
2. Translated by the authors.
2. Rainer Maria Rilke (1875–1926) was an Austrian poet known for his lyrically potent work in German. Johann Wolfgang von Goethe (1749–1832) was one of the most celebrated German poets of the modern era.
3. The young Gezelle, educated for priesthood in the predominantly Catholic West Flanders of the nineteenth century, was exposed very early to the continental idea, then prevalent, that England was a country to which missionaries should be sent. For that matter, many of the buildings in the medieval city of his birth, Bruges, bore witness to the history of English Catholicism (Vincent 2016, p. 2).
4. We found references to his religious godfather in the writings of his friend, Raghuvansh, but we were unable to ascertain his name. However, Camille referred to him a few times as someone who guided him in moments of doubt.

3

❀

A Scholar-Priest in the Making

The Linguaphile Activist

The celebrated Hindi poet Mahadevi Verma claimed that a monk does not need to be a scholar or an author. However, should the three qualities of spiritual practice, scholarship and literary craft blend, such a synthesis is sublime and sacred (M. Verma 1987, p. 32). For Verma, Camille, her dear younger brother, embodied this rare confluence. This chapter explores his progression from a young engineering student into Father Bulcke, the world-renowned scholar on the *Ramkatha*, Hindi literature and Indology. Rama's story in the *Ramcharitmanas*, written by the celebrated Indian poet from the Bhakti era, Tulsidas, is considered a literary masterpiece and one of the most popular versions of the Ramayana in India. Tulsidas believed that the narration of Rama's story (in Awadhi, a north Indian vernacular language), undertaken purely for his own personal happiness, would ultimately bring him *moksha*,[1] the highest spiritual goal in the teachings of Hinduism. Camille always referred to Tulsidas as his idol; propitiously, one may argue that by working on the genesis and the development of the Rama story, much like what Tulsidas wished for himself, Camille also strove for his intellectual *moksha*.

He was proud of his linguistic heritage; he loved his native Flemish language, while the society around him considered embracing French as the mark of upward mobility. His deep emotional bond with his mother tongue inspired him to become one of the leading activists in the political movement to adopt Flemish as a medium of academic, institutional and official language. As a protagonist of the Flemish language, he was greatly inspired by the

Flemish writer Guido Gezelle; in fact, Gezelle was one of the first serious intellectual and theological influences on Camille's life. As a linguaphile, Camille was not against the French language per se; his opposition was directed against the imposition of a language as part of a colonial project to erase the local language and culture. His early brush with the French cultural and linguistic hegemony and his belief that language is the custodian of the cultural essence of any society eventually shaped the future course of his life, and his scholarship and activism in India.

Influence of Guido Gezelle and the Struggle for Flemish

For Camille, the call to spread the word of God and his desire to serve humanity were identical. It led him to an arduous path that mandated unflinching devotion and unwavering commitment to a much higher ideal. Appropriately, it inspired him to undertake several inner and outer journeys to prepare himself for a much loftier goal; indeed, the two voyages were mutually reinforcing, thereby making his life an extraordinary saga of the 'pilgrim's progress'. As discussed previously, instead of cherishing the honour of becoming the first engineer from his village, he joined the Jesuit order at the Drongen novitiate in Belgium in 1930; upon completing a two-year-long training, he took the vow of lifelong austerity, celibacy and obedience to the ecclesiastical community. He then joined the Jesuit monastery at Valkenburg in the Netherlands, the most venerable training centre for German Catholics. It was renowned for its religious and spiritual training and rigorous scholarly pursuits across Europe. Valkenburg was indeed the place that allowed his spiritual and intellectual curiosity to blossom; it enabled him to expand his intellectual horizons and dive into the vast ocean of languages and literature. However, to explore Camille's intellectual progress, it is imperative to further trace his journey since his student days at Louvain University in 1928.

It would not be an exaggeration to claim that Guido Gezelle was one of the first serious intellectual influences on Camille's scholarly development. One can find several affinities between Guido Gezelle and Camille Bulcke. Both were from the West Flanders region, both were nature lovers, and both came from middle-class families entrenched in Christian religious beliefs. Gezelle, born in Bruges in 1830, inherited the love of nature from his gardener father and a deep reverence for Christian values from his mother. Gezelle's school education was interrupted, given his poor health and family's financial precarity; eventually, he completed his education at the Minor Seminary, Roeselare. It was here that he nurtured his love for languages, learning Greek, Latin, French and English, and also started writing poetry. Much to his dismay, Gezelle also realised the elite's disdain for his mother tongue, the Flemish language, and pledged to restore Flemish to its place of pride.

Remarkably, by the time Gezelle finished his school education, he was clear about his life's mission: to dedicate himself to the revival and restoration of the Flemish language. However, he was unsure whether he could serve this mission as a worldly man or as a man devoted to the service of God. He sought parental guidance to get some wise counsel; Gezelle's father wrote to him, '[L]eave yourself in the hands of God much like the soft clay in the hands of the potter' (Quiren 1987, p. 212). Gezelle then decided to join the Major Seminary of Bruges to become a priest, where he spent the next six years studying philosophy, theology and languages. Upon completing his religious training, Gezelle joined the Minor Seminary of Bruges and progressed through different roles, starting as a teacher and then going on to serve as a parish priest and eventually as the curate of an Anglo-Belgian seminary. However, apart from writing exceptional lyrical poetry, Gezelle was 'very active as a philologist and folklorist, a journalist, an editor of periodicals and as a translator, of Longfellow's The Song of Hiawatha among other things' (Deleu 1999, p. 100).

As a teacher, priest and poet, Gezelle inspired a generation of young intellectuals to embrace Flemish cultural nationalism, which saw 'the language as the deposit and the protector of the Christian Flemish soul' (Deprez and Vos 1998, p. 9). Remarkably, for Gezelle, the Flemish language represented the traditional ways of life; he considered the march of modernity and the rapid rise of the industrial society as a threat to Flemish identity as an agrarian society. Moreover, Gezelle imagined Flemish as the language of the Catholics in the Southern Netherlands and Belgium while standard Dutch as the language of the Protestant North (ibid.). Gezelle wrote all his poetry in the traditional form of Flemish; he described it as a pure form of Flemish and 'as the work of a free Fleming and a confirmed Catholic poet' (Couttenier 1998, p. 58).

Through his prolific writing, Gezelle emerged as the torchbearer for a literary and linguistic work identified as the West Flemish School. Gezelle introduced a distinctive Flemish style of writing by borrowing generously the words, phrases, idioms and expressions that he had discovered through his intensive and lifelong study of the ancient West Flemish dialect. Jozef Deleu argues that 'in his poetry, Gezelle created a language all his own. And that is a gift only great artists have' (Deleu 1999, p. 101). He is celebrated as 'the most innovative and original Flemish poet between 1680 and 1880', and in contrast to 'his contemporaries, his romantic and religious nature lyrics have a strikingly personal and natural character' (Couttenier 2016, p. 1). As his student and later collaborator Hugo Verriest posited, 'Guido Gezelle is the soul of Flanders' (cited in Roosbroeck 1919, p. 21).

Gezelle's prolific poetic range spanned nature, the Flemish landscape, his reminisce of childhood and his religious, devotional, and spiritual contemplations. However, he 'also wrote a small number of idealistic and nationalist texts, which were to exert great influence on subsequent generations of students' (Couttenier 1998, p. 57). In his poetry, Gezelle repeatedly propagated that the Flemish nation is a distinct sociocultural-political entity. As someone who revered the Flemish language and adored poetry, it was natural that Camille would be deeply inspired by Gezelle's phenomenal work and his participation in the sociocultural campaigns for the Flemish-speaking people. Even from a very young age, he was aware of the ongoing language dispute in Belgium; his own language, Flemish, was popular in the north, while French was prevalent in the south. In his extended family, while his parents were keen to preserve and promote the Flemish language and culture, his wealthy uncle readily adopted the French language and culture to promote his business interests (Prasad and Goswami 1987, p. 4). He had little patience and respect for those in Flemish society who had embraced the French language and cultural practices (Saxena 2017, p. 29).

The movement to defend the rights and dignity of the Flemish people gained renewed momentum at the end of the First World War. During his school and university days, Camille actively participated in the agitation to defend his mother tongue and Flemish culture (C. Bulcke 2009, p. 115). On several occasions, he would miss his lectures to participate in literary events and agitational activities; yet he always managed to clear his exams. Camille's enthusiastic support for the Flemish movement was not based on dreamy romantic idealism or some parochial nationalism; instead, he viewed his participation in this campaign as a service to his fellow Flemish people (Devriendt 1987, pp. 78–79). He realised that to accomplish their hegemonic ambitions, the materially superior French resorted to the cultural colonisation of the Flemish people and that had to be opposed. He introduced the same model of opposition to the dominance of the English language in postcolonial India, promoting Hindi even in missionary activities.

The Early Inspirations

Constant Lievens

At Valkenburg, the linguaphile in Camille found the most benign environment, acquired exceptional proficiency in Greek and Latin and gained mastery over the German language to speak and write it like a native. In fact, several of his colleagues took him to be a native German, given his chaste pronunciation and vocabulary. His first two writings are essays in German titled *Mein Dorf* (My Village) and *Die Universalität der Menschheit* (The Universality of Humankind). Although these essays were only intended to hone his German writing skills, Dineshwar Prasad, a renowned Hindi writer, considered them exceptional pieces of writing that mark the advent of the litterateur in him. During his stay at Valkenburg, Camille immersed himself in the poetic works of Goethe, Heine and Rilke and was so taken in by Rilke's wizardry that he could recite most of his poetry extempore.

As part of the religious training, all the scholastics were expected to complete three years of study of philosophy. However, with his Bachelor's degree in Engineering, Camille received special approval to complete his degree in two years (C. Bulcke 2015 [1976], p. 328). During the pursuit of his MA degree in Philosophy, he studied major philosophers, including Aristotle and Socrates. Through his earlier self-study and prior engagements with spiritual and philosophical pursuits, along with the outstanding guidance of his teachers, he managed to score 90 per cent marks in his exam at the Gregorian University of Rome. It was a level of academic excellence not achieved easily while observing all the protocols of the seminary and undergoing the exacting schedule of his religious training. Camille's contemporaries, including his intellectual and spiritual mentors, were astonished at the incredible feat of mastering some of the most profound wisdom so naturally and with such exceptional clarity. His academic success came from his traits that were to be his innate nature: to live an austere life, observe strict self-discipline and labour for constant intellectual and spiritual growth to undertake arduous scholarly work of excellent quality.

In 1934, having completed his training at Valkenburg, Camille returned to the Louvain seminary; he was offered two options: either to undertake missionary work at home or to serve in a foreign country. He conveyed his resolve to go to India for missionary work. It was not a decision made lightly;

instead, it was based on two major and enduring intellectual and spiritual influences. These were Father Constant Lievens and Goswami Tulsidas. They could be considered the bedrocks of Camille's spiritual and intellectual edifice, or the two riverbanks through which his river of life flowed. Lievens, a Jesuit, is considered the 'greatest missionary since St. Francis Xavier' on account of his 'sensational apostolate in Chhota Nagpur' (Froerer 2018, p. 79). He remains one of the most well known and controversial figures in the history of Christian missionaries in Jharkhand. With his knowledge of customary laws and legal processes, he took on the British who usurped tribal land and, in a short duration, converted a large number of Chhota Nagpur tribals to Christianity.

Like Camille, Lievens was from the West Flanders region, born in 1856. At the age of 11, he had lost his mother and worked on the family farm tending to cattle and two horses, a skill that would stand him in good stead in the latter part of his life. His father and teachers encouraged him to join the Society of Jesus in 1878, and he was sent to India in 1880. He was ordained as a priest in 1883, and after teaching at St Xavier's College in Calcutta for the next two years, in 1885 he was assigned to the Chhota Nagpur mission (in present-day Jharkhand state) (Tete 1993; Namboodiry 1995). As a language enthusiast and linguist, Lievens was a trailblazer for his successors. While at Calcutta, he trained to become a fluent speaker of English, Hindi and Bengali; and upon reaching Chhota Nagpur, he set out to master the dialects of the three major tribes: the Mundas, the Oraons and the Kharias (Fitzgerald 1943, p. 455; S. Kumar 1990).

As soon as Lievens began his missionary work in Chhota Nagpur, a local police officer advised the young priest that 'to convert the natives, the only way was to undertake the defence of their interests, especially in connection with their rights regarding land tenure and landlord services' (K. Sahay 1968, p. 925). The tribal people faced tremendous hardships and exploitation apart from losing their land and livelihood; they were forced to render unpaid labour (*begari*) to the landlords, moneylenders and local administration (Tete 1993). Lievens soon realised that in order 'to save souls the only way would be to struggle for justice' (van Exem 1988, p. 82). Therefore, instead of focusing on spiritual or otherworldly matters, he concentrated on material and critical problems and invested his energies in studying local customs, laws and colonial justice systems (Tete 1984). He took to counselling the 'tribal people on legal matters and urged them to refuse illegal demands from the landlords or to pay rent without receipts' (Froerer 2018, pp. 79–80).

Lieven's childhood work with horse-keeping allowed him to ride on horseback to the remotest and most inaccessible corners of the Chhota Nagpur plateau. He led an ongoing campaign to file complaints and seek redressal before the colonial judiciary, and almost on every occasion, he got a reprieve for local tribal people (Fitzgerald 1943, p. 456). The Catholic mission also propagated 'other kinds of non-evangelical activities, such as education, medical services, famine relief, and cooperative banking societies' (Froerer 2018, p. 80). It is no wonder that gradually a large population decided to embrace Christianity, and 'by 1889, Lievens had succeeded in converting around 75,000 tribal people' (ibid.).

Apart from his relentless campaign for justice and dignity for the tribal people, Lievens used his exceptional literary gifts to leave behind a rich legacy of literary works. These include the translations of 'St. Luke's Gospel and Schuster's Bible history; short lives of the Blessed Virgin, St. Francis Xavier and St. Peter Claver' (Fitzgerald 1943, p. 457). He also compiled a book of hymns consisting of 'Catholic adaptations of native songs and original compositions in Hindi' and two books in Kurukh, the language of the Oraons:[2] 'The Book of Baptism and The Book of Communion' (ibid.). His hectic schedule and constant travels led to serious health issues. He left for Belgium in 1892, hoping to return to India and carry out his ongoing missionary work; a year later, he died in Louvain. Camille was greatly inspired by the exemplary accomplishments of Lievens and was keen to continue the unfinished tasks of his illustrious compatriot within the tribal communities of Chhota Nagpur.

The Bhakti Movement and Tulsidas

The other significant influence on Camille was Tulsidas; he was going through a book on world literature and read the German translation of certain portions of the *Ramcharitmanas* and was captivated by the poetic genius of the Indian poet. In one of the couplets, Tulsidas described the bond between father and son as follows: 'The birth in this world of one whose qualities fill the heart of his sire with heavenly bliss is a great good fortune. All the four achievements of this world – dharma, artha, kama and moksha – are within the palm of the one who loves his parents like life itself' (C. Bulcke 2010, p. 140).[3] In all his studies and readings of literature in other languages, Camille had never come across such an exquisite and profound rendering of the relationship between father and son. He recalled, 'Enchanted, I read these lines over and over again. They felt like sweet music. Invisible strings tugged at my heart' (ibid.). Later, he described that he was deeply moved by the depth and tenderness of such a representation and 'a niche in my heart was reserved for Tulsidas' (ibid.).

More than an intellectual curiosity, it stirred his spiritual yearning to learn about India and its literature. Camille's fascination with this sensitive portrayal of the bond between father and son was not strange; it emerged from his deep reverence for the Christian faith and the Trinity doctrine: the Father in Heaven, his son, Jesus, and the Holy Spirit as three identities in one Godhead. He always acknowledged that this particular verse of Tulsidas changed his life and led him to decide that India was going to be his place of work, the *karma bhumi* (Saxena 2017, p. 42). Indeed, one verse triggered the most spiritually enriching and intellectually fruitful association between Tulsidas' poetry and Camille's scholarly quest. Like Tulsidas in the fifteenth century, Camille, in the twentieth century, sought spiritual enlightenment, not as a personal goal but to bring out the divine consciousness and spiritual advancement of fellow human beings. They did this at different times, in different contexts and by adopting different ways.

In the Middle Ages, India grappled with many severe crises prompted by widespread sociocultural decay, the collapse of prevailing political structures, feudalism, obscurantism and excessive ritualism. Indeed, the challenge to prevailing orthodoxy, draconian and discriminatory social order and extractive religious practices did not emerge from a formal, organised group but under the Bhakti movement, an umbrella of religious, social and cultural reforms across the Indic civilisational and cultural space. It was a renaissance led by some individuals with exceptional literary competencies who sought a personal union with the divine and, in the process, shattered the existing sociocultural configuration. Initially started in south India by poet-saints between the seventh and the tenth centuries, it reached north India with the help of saint Ramanuja in the eleventh century. The Bhakti movement is not one singular mode of thought; it comprises several different streams of beliefs and practices. Some of the most eminent poet-saints in the north of India include Ramananda, Chaitanya, Kabir, Guru Nanak, Dadu Dayal, Mirabai, Tulsidas and Surdas, among several others (Shukla 1929; Sharma 1987). Almost every Bhakti poet embraced the Hindu epics and Upanishads (the treatise on the Vedas), and they 'derived many of their doctrines, terms, images, and anti-discrimination ideas' from these religious texts (Vanita 2022, p. 225).

The Bhakti movement in India witnessed some of the most prolific writings in Indian literature, and Tulsidas continues to figure as one of the most prominent and popular littérateurs of that era (Sharma 1987). Apart from his poetic genius in writing some of the most lyrical poetry in Awadhi, the local dialect of ordinary people, Camille found the unwavering devotion of Tulsidas and abiding faith in his idol, Lord Rama, exemplary, and he attempted to emulate this in his own spiritual progress. It is not far-fetched to claim that in Tulsidas, Camille discovered his intellectual–spiritual anchor, an exemplar whose intellectual pursuits reflected his spiritual pursuits and for whom devotion to the divine led him to produce outstanding literature for the ordinary people in their language. He followed in the footsteps of Tulsidas throughout his life, renouncing the world to seek spiritual progress while working to restore the common person's language to its place of pride through his writings in Hindi.

Preparations for the Missionary Path

To prepare himself for his missionary duties in India, Camille was keen to learn more about the country. However, given the lack of material resources and scarce connectivity, he could not find many people to share their first-hand experiences in India. Undaunted by such constraints, he laboured to find all possible sources to learn more about India, read as much as possible for the next few years and gain considerable knowledge about the land, its people, culture and life. As a mandatory requirement to complete his education, he was supposed to undergo one year of military service after his MA. However, one could take a one-year course in tropical medicine instead of military training to engage in overseas assignments or missionary work. Several Belgian missionaries were sent to Congo, where malaria was common; hence, it was quite helpful for such missionaries to study tropical medicine. It was a propitious opportunity for Camille, who had decided to go to India; and he completed his education in tropical medicine at Louvain University in 1935.

After he had completed all the requisite formal education, the officials at the Louvain seminary informed Camille about his impending travel to India. Instead of simply waiting for his travel arrangements, he decided to use this time to prepare himself for the most significant assignment of his life. Having already completed a substantial part of his religious and academic training in theology and philosophy, he then turned to master the complex concepts in higher mathematics and Einstein's theory of relativity.

At Louvain University, Camille studied Maths and the theory of relativity under the guidance of Georges Lemaître, a Belgian professor and renowned physicist and cosmologist, who was also an ordained priest.

Lemaître was an authority on Einstein's theory of relativity and is considered the first scientist to propose what is now known as the Big Bang Theory (Holder and Mitton 2013, p. 23). On 17 March 1934, Lemaître received the Francqui Prize, the highest Belgian scientific distinction conferred by King Leopold III of Belgium (Lambert et al. 2015, p. 180). Among the three people who proposed Lemaître's name for this prestigious award was Einstein himself. Lemaître considered theology with modern science as two different paths toward truth. He argued that science explores 'the truths related to the physical universe' while theology 'conveys truths conducive of man's salvation' (ibid., p. 212). Most significantly, Lemaître argued that 'these two paths are respectful of one another, but do not intersect' and that 'science has not shaken my faith in religion and religion has never caused me to question the conclusions I reached by scientific methods' (ibid.).

Camille had some of the most outstanding individuals, such as Lemaître, guiding his path and supporting his overall development in the formative stages of his intellectual and spiritual progress. Indeed, his sharp intellect, sensitive heart, affinity for learning and rigorous training in several disciplines under some of the most brilliant minds provided a solid foundation for him to take on much bigger challenges in his later life. He trained to become a qualified engineer, and then turned to spiritual pursuits and gained such proficiency in several languages that he could be considered a native speaker of those languages. Apart from being able to fluently converse in French, Greek, Latin and German, he could read literature and enjoy poetry in these languages. During his training as a Catholic priest, Camille gained expertise in Christian theology and philosophy and then turned to master the latest developments in mathematics and physics. Indeed, he was already a polyglot and a polymath before making the voyage to India and brought his work ethic, intellectual competence, religious piety and devotion to the language of ordinary people to its fruition.

Religious Training in India: 1935–1940

Camille left Belgium on 20 October 1935 to take the voyage from Antwerp to far-off India; it was the first step to realising his long-cherished dream. Before his departure, he had collected substantial information about India's history, geography, climate, culture and literature; yet he recalled learning a lot more through his interactions with his fellow passengers. During the 17-day-long sea voyage, he made friends with several Indians on board; however, more than the conversation, he was instinctively drawn to the language his Indian co-passengers used to converse among themselves (Saxena 2017, p. 35). He landed in Bombay on 6 November 1935; despite his meticulous research, methodical homework and multifaceted training, nothing had prepared him for the cultural shock he experienced upon setting foot on Indian soil. He recalled his first four days in Bombay as startling; the unending stream of people and their colourful clothes all around him left him dazzled; he had never seen such a kaleidoscope of the diversity of clothes and colours, not even during a fair or festival in Europe (ibid.). However, he was dismayed looking at the poverty around the place and was shocked to see many homeless people sleeping in the open air and on the footpath (J. Gupta 1987, p. 63). One of Camille's most incredible first sights in India was cattle roaming freely amid heavy traffic; he was amazed to see a car stop so that a cow could leisurely cross the street. He was aware of the religious sanctity the cow enjoyed among Hindus; yet this bizarre scene inspired the poet in him to humorously exclaim, 'Oh cow, dear mother; Traffic sense isn't your bother' (ibid.).

During the long train journey from Bombay to Ranchi, Camille had first-hand experience of India's diversity, cultural wealth and also abject material poverty. He witnessed some very peculiar behaviour all around him, the constant jostling and shouting among passengers to get into the third-class compartment of the train, while women with fully covered heads and faces walked behind their men like cattle (Saxena 2017, p. 36). Camille thought he had ventured into a different planet upon seeing food items being sold at the stations without any cover or care for hygiene, numerous hawkers constantly bellowing to attract customers, people washing under the tap on the platform and an endless stream of beggars. He was intrigued that each time the train crossed a major river, his co-travellers hailed the river as a deity and threw coins into the water; the amount of food and luggage his co-passengers travelled with astonished him. He had never seen coolies in Europe and could not imagine the passengers not carrying their own luggage. He saw a large number of coolies at the stations in India and wondered about their job and lives. Looking at the volume and the bulk of iron and tin boxes that the passengers carried, Camille thought these people must be moving to another place with all their belongings. Clearly, India was going to be both challenging and exhilarating for the young European missionary.

A poignant journey, which was also one of the most intense and insightful learning experiences, marked Camille's entry into India. At the Ranchi station, he was welcomed by two young Jesuits from the Jesuit society. As a strange coincidence, he landed in India exactly after 100 years since Thomas Babington Macaulay, who made the English language aspirational for the colonised natives and the most important tool of colonialism. Macaulay sought to institutionalise a hierarchy in knowledge production whereby English education was compulsory not only to master modern science but also to impart superior morals to the natives.

On his first passage through Ranchi's streets, Camille realised that to please their British masters, the Indians had embraced the language, the clothes, the customs and the etiquettes of their colonisers. He was surprised to see that most of the signboards at the station, signs in the streets, names of shops and even nameplates at individual homes were all in English. It dawned on him that, like the bourgeoisie in his homeland Belgium who had abandoned Flemish to embrace French, their Indian counterparts had adopted the colonial language while discarding their mother tongue (C. Bulcke 2009, p. 115). He reached Manresa House, the main residential complex of the Jesuits in Ranchi, relieved that his long journey was over. However, this joy was short-lived for the young man, who was used to people doing their own work; he was stunned to see turban-clad waiters serving food in the dining hall as if the people around him could not serve themselves (Saxena 2017, p. 38). Camille had arrived in an India where British colonialism was not just the political and social reality but was manifested in everyday lived experiences and mentalities, even in areas far from the metropoles. His country, Belgium, had acquired colonies in Africa; in contrast, India was a colonised space and had to be understood and navigated as such, with empathy and care.

Learning Hindi

In order to facilitate Camille's acclimatisation to India's warmer weather, the Jesuit Society decided to send him to the cooler climes of Darjeeling in the Himalayan foothills to teach math and science at St Joseph's College. However, instead of finding the Darjeeling weather to his liking, he suffered asthma attacks and stomach infections during his short stay and requested the Jesuit authorities to send him to another place. Eventually, he returned to Ranchi, spent a few months recuperating and then joined St Ignatius School at Gumla, a small town on the outskirts of Ranchi, as a math teacher. At Gumla, Camille started to learn Hindi formally and rather uniquely; instead of learning it in solitude or through personal coaching, he used to sit in the Hindi classes at the same school where he taught mathematics. The young students were amused to find their new math teacher, a tall European, seated on the last bench during the Hindi lessons and listening to every word spoken during the class with rapt attention.

Within the first months since his arrival in India, Camille had understood that to serve the local people he needed to learn Hindi, the prevalent language in north India. He was deeply affected and pained by the hegemony of English, the foreign language imposed by the colonial masters over the local languages and the alacrity with which the Indians had embraced English. For Camille, this was almost a recurrence of what he had experienced in Belgium; the local language, Flemish, was seen as inferior, while the colonial language, French, was considered the mark of status and prestige. He explained later that when he was travelling to India, he had never intended to work for Hindi, but once he saw the antipathy of the elite Indians towards Hindi, he was reminded of his struggle for his mother tongue, and it convinced him to take up the cause of Hindi. Camille, the Jesuit, had taken vows to serve God and not to follow worldly pursuits. Yet this language hegemony of the colonial masters in India affected him deeply, and he decided to learn Hindi, the language of the ordinary people around him, and resolved to restore Hindi to its rightful place of honour (Devriendt 1987, p. 9).

In Camille's own words, 'When I arrived in India in 1935, I was surprised and pained when I realised that many educated people were unaware of their cultural traditions and considered it a matter of pride to speak in English. I resolved that my duty would be to master the people's language' (C. Bulcke 2010, p. 136). Years later, tracing his intellectual evolution, he would identify the year 1935 as the time when he recognised the deep-seated contempt for Hindi among elite Indians and resolved to attain mastery over Hindi as the first major step towards his research in Hindi and on Tulsidas. With that, he created an extraordinary model of resistance to colonialism by inspiring people to take pride in and reclaim the vernacular.

St Ignatius School in Gumla was the preparatory seminary where Camille took the first steps to learn Hindi. Patras Bara, his first Hindi teacher at the school, likened his dedication to learning Hindi and his quest for knowledge to the legendary Saint Ignatius himself. Bara recalled that being a polyglot, Camille paid particular attention to the sound of the Hindi words and very minutely observed the teacher's mannerisms, body language and enunciation. In a small school where most of the students came from tribal communities, Bara took extra care of these students and spent considerable time and energy educating them about proper pronunciation, correct spelling, the rules and conventions of Hindi grammar and the structure of the joint and compound words. Camille attended all the Hindi classes from grades 8 to 11 and was one of the most attentive and assiduous learners. Bara recalled that Camille would be absorbed when he attended his Hindi prose classes; however, whenever Bara taught poetry, particularly the sections from the *Ramcharitmanas*, it would seem that Camille was in a state of trance (Bara 1987, p. 91). According to some legends, poet Tulsidas had the divine *darshan* (view or sight) of his idol, Lord Rama, at the banks of Mandakini River in Chitrakoot. Camille's lifelong friend and collaborator, Dineshwar Prasad, argues that for Camille, Gumla was the Chitrakoot[4] where he met with Tulsidas and became his devotee for life.

Camille started to learn Awadhi and Brij Bhasha to understand better the finer nuances and delicate subtleties of Hindi poetry.[5] It was almost mandatory for him to pick up these two dialects of Hindi given that a large proportion of Tulsidas' work was in Awadhi while another eminent poet, Surdas, wrote in Brij Bhasha. His quest to master Hindi and study Tulsidas' literature also inspired him to make strenuous efforts to learn Sanskrit. However, despite his best efforts and the extra support of his fellow teachers, Camille realised the limits of his intellectual and especially linguistic development at Gumla. To expand the scope and quicken the pace of his learning, he requested the Jesuit Society officials to let him study Hindi and Sanskrit under the tutelage of a learned scholar of these languages. In 1938, he moved to Sitagarh in Hazaribagh (now in Jharkhand) to study Hindi and Sanskrit under the guidance of Pandit Badridutt Shastri. He was fortunate to find an eminent scholar like Shastri, a gold medallist in Sanskrit from the prestigious Banaras Hindu University (Ponette 1987, p. 67). Later, Shastri became the head of the Department of Hindi at the prestigious St Columbus College, Hazaribagh.

Camille turned out to be an extraordinary learner; with his sharp intellect and photographic memory, among all his contemporaries under Shastri's tutelage, he could memorise each word on his first reading. The Hindi students devised an exciting method to quicken learning: During their evening walks, they would carry one of the prescribed texts, *Sevasadan*, a novel by the renowned Hindi writer Munshi Premchand. First, the students would translate one Hindi sentence from the novel into English and then translate it back into Hindi to see how close they could get to the original text. Father Pierre Ponette, a fellow student, recalled that Camille's reverse translation would always match each syllable of the original text (ibid., p. 66). Impressed with the rapid progress of his illustrious student and the ease with which he memorised a whole new vocabulary, Shastri designated Camille as a *chalta-phirta shabdkosh* (walking dictionary).

Camille had resolved to learn Hindi and Sanskrit within a year, for he considered these two languages the path to the heart of the Indian cultural and civilisational heritage. To his great satisfaction during his stay with Shastri, Camille learnt not merely to read and write in Sanskrit, but he also acquired enough expertise to interpret and explain the Sanskrit text of Valmiki's Ramayana and the *Panchatantra*.[6] Under the guidance of Shastri, Camille read two of Tulsidas' greatest works: the *Ramcharitmanas* and the *Vinaya Patrika*. At Sitagarh, he read the original text, including the meaning and context of the memorable couplet on the bond between father and son which he had read in Belgium years ago (C. Bulcke 2015 [1976], p. 330).

धन्य जनमु जगतीतल तासू। पितहि प्रमोदु चरित सुनि जासू॥
चारि पदारथ करतल ताकें। प्रिय पितु मातु प्रान सम जाकें॥

'Blessed is his life upon this earth', he [Rama] said, 'whose father is pleased to hear of his doings. The four rewards of life (viz., religious merit, material riches, sensuous gratification and final beatitude) are within his grasp who loves his parents as he loves his own life. (R. Prasad 1988, p. 278)

Camille maintained that in the year 1938, he made a thorough study of the *Ramcharitmanas* and the *Vinaya Patrika* for the first time in his life and grasped their meaning so lucidly that he could offer scholarly expositions on the two works. The more he contemplated upon the writings of Tulsidas, the more he felt attached to the poet. In his own words, his 'attachment to Tulsidas which started at that time, and has never ceased growing since, was not merely an emotional one; it is deeply related to my literary and religious conviction' (C. Bulcke 2010, p. 137). He conceded that people 'may wonder what attraction Tulsidas could have for a foreigner and a Christian' (ibid., p. 141). To substantiate his attraction beyond a personal equation or irrational love, he asserted, 'Tulsidas is so great a poet as to transcend the barriers of time, country and religion: he is the poet of all humanity' (ibid.). He was enchanted with Tulsidas' choice of simple but lively language and argued that the poet's 'deeply held philosophy of wilful and complete submission to the will of the Almighty would appeal to anybody who has any claims to be called religious and God-fearing' (ibid.).

Tracing his intellectual evolution, Camille would always highlight 1938 as the time when he discovered his devotion to Tulsidas and identified it as the second major step towards his research in Hindi and Tulsidas. He also identified 1938 as the most critical year of his life; he was inundated with several opportunities to work in different places and even join the administrative set-up of the Jesuits in Rome. However, having spent so much of his time and energy learning Hindi, he was not prepared to forego his affection for the language and decided to stay in India and continue serving Hindi, to the best of his abilities (C. Bulcke 2015 [1976], p. 330).

During his stay at Sitagarh, Camille also wrote a Flemish story about a mother's love for her son in medieval times, in Hindi. The wayward son takes to crime and then commits matricide, and as he is rushing to get away, the son stumbles and falls; the mother's heart comes out of her body, hop-skips to the son and asks, 'Oh!! My dear son, are you hurt?' This and other sentiments that he expressed often in his speeches and writings alluded to his own relationship with his mother, who he believed had sacrificed everything and endured enough hardship for her children throughout her life. Thoughts about his mother always remained with him, as he was never able to meet her once he left the shores of Belgium.

During the first four years of his stay in India, Camille had gained considerable proficiency in Hindi and could offer detailed expositions of the works of his favourite Hindi poet, Tulsidas. With his knowledge of Sanskrit and Hindi, he did not need the earlier translations by the Europeans since such translations were implicated in sustaining the hierarchy of the rulers (colonial powers) over the ruled (Indians) (Gallien 2021). Having spent four years in self-learning and teaching at different institutions, it was time for Camille to pursue higher theological studies and spiritual training to complete his religious education and fulfil his missionary mandate.

The Making of an Institution: The Calcutta School of Indology

In January 1939, Camille joined St Mary's Theologate in Kurseong, a small town close to Darjeeling in the foothills of the Himalayas, and stayed there for the next four years until November 1942. St Mary's Theologate was the only educational institute for theological training for the Jesuit order, and the geographical and scholarly environments were particularly conducive to the aspiring clergy who sought to complete their religious education and training towards priesthood. The early Christian missionaries who came to India believed that in a country where religiosity and traditional beliefs reigned supreme, the Christian preachers needed to understand the indigenous spiritual and religious discourses and practices before undertaking effective missionary work. St Mary's Theologate was considered the embodiment of an intellectual initiative to seek convergence between Christianity and the Hindu religious system known as the Bengal School of Indology, or the Calcutta School of Indology.[7]

Ostensibly, while Indology refers to a meticulous study of Indian social, religious and philosophical systems until the nineteenth century, it promotes an Orientalist discourse that 'present[ed] itself as a form of knowledge that is both different from, and superior to, the knowledge that the Orientals have of themselves' (Inden 1986, p. 408). Indeed, the European Christian missionaries also adopted the Orientalist approach – not just to study the Indian religious practices as they are, but to also establish the superiority of Christian beliefs over them. In this context, the Calcutta School of Indology forged a new path and championed an enlightened, nuanced and sensitive study of Indian culture, contrary to the pervasive Orientalist approach of the philosophical and theological systems as preached by the European missionaries.

In order to study Camille's evolution into an eminent Indologist, it is imperative to examine the genesis of Indology, or the European engagement with India's cultural, philosophical and religious knowledge systems. The development of Indology is linked to the need of the Christian missionaries to understand the prevalent religious and cultural practices but with very clear intentions and consequences: first, to dispossess the natives of self-knowledge, intelligence and rationality, and then to supplant the indigenous knowledge and practices with the predominantly European cultural and Christian belief system. Among the Christian missionaries, while the Franciscans preceded the Jesuits, the missionaries from the Society of Jesus occupy a pre-eminent position in the annals of the history of Indology as an intellectual endeavour (Amaladass 1988).

Francis Xavier occupies the most prominent position in spreading Christianity in Asia, specifically in India; he is credited with converting many people in Goa and along the Fishery Coast in Tamil Nadu (Selwyn 2016, p. 105). However, he also deployed certain aggressive tactics to supplant the existing religious and cultural order, especially his campaign against Hindu temples. Writing to his peers, he said,

> When all are baptized I order all the temples of their false gods to be destroyed and all the idols to be broken in pieces. I can give you no idea of the joy I feel in seeing this done, witnessing the destruction of the idols by the very people who but lately adored them. (Xavier cited in Coleridge 1872, p. 281)

Xavier extolled young people who, upon baptism, acquired 'an ardent love for the Divine law, and an extraordinary zeal for learning our [Xavier's] holy religion' (ibid., p. 153). However, he found the repugnance of these newly converted towards idolatry exemplary.

> Their hatred for idolatry is marvellous. They get into feuds with the heathen about it, and whenever their own parents practise it, they reproach them and come off to tell me at once. Whenever I hear of any act of idolatrous worship, I go to the place with a large band of these children, who very soon load the devil with a greater amount of insult and abuse than he has lately received of honor and worship from their parents, relations, and acquaintances. The children run at the idols, upset them, dash them down, break them to pieces, spit on them, trample on them, kick them about, and in short heap on them every possible outrage. (Ibid.)

Xavier also pleaded with João III, the king of Portugal, to establish the Holy Inquisition in the newly acquired Indian territories because many people lived 'according to the Jewish laws, and according to the Mahomedan sect, without any fear of God or shame of the world' (Priolkar 1961, p. 23). While King João III did not act on this advice in 1560, eight years after Xavier's death, the Inquisition was implemented in Goa.

Xavier did not wait for the royal decree but realised that overcoming the language barrier was mandatory for greater assimilation and hired local interpreters to translate 'essential prayers and necessary parts of the catechism book from Portuguese into Tamil' (Henn 2014, p. 65). Although he could not master Tamil during his stay on the Fishery Coast, 'working outside

Goa and away from direct Portuguese administration, Xavier had learnt a most important lesson that would not be forgotten: that the Christianization of Asia was not coeval with "Portugalization"' (Županov 2005a, p. 246). Predictably, Xavier commanded his other European associates to learn local languages since the local interpreters 'were seen as either malicious or simply incapable of translating Christian messages correctly' (Xavier and Županov 2015, p. 213).

Predictably, learning Tamil became a priority for Xavier's successors on the Fishery Coast (Schouten 2018, p. 185). Henry Henriques attained such proficiency that he managed to produce a book on Tamil grammar. However, for the Jesuits, while learning the Indian languages was critical to the spread of Christian beliefs, preserving the European essence of Christianity was paramount; they made all efforts to keep Christianity and their missionary work unblemished from the local cultural or social norms (ibid.). Even Henriques, the most renowned Tamil linguist among the Jesuits, instructed the European missionaries on the Fishery Coast to speak in Tamil among themselves and insisted upon erasing any remnants of the local social or cultural affiliations from the new converts. Henriques mandated the new converts to not only replace their and their children's Tamil names with Christian names, but also instructed them to discard their earlier identity altogether: 'If anybody calls you by your Tamil name, do not respond' (Županov 2005a, p. 233).

The missionaries also realised that simply erasing the external markers of earlier cultural and religious affiliations was necessary but not sufficient; instead, they needed a counter-narrative to obliterate the inherent cultural underpinnings of the recent converts. The construction of such a counter-narrative required authentic and comprehensive knowledge of the Indian religious and cultural system, and among the Indians, the Brahmins, or priests, were seen as the custodians of such knowledge. Xavier had described the Brahmins 'as perverse and wicked a set as can anywhere be found' and lamented that 'if it were not for the opposition of the Brahmins, we should have them all [Indians] embracing the religion of Jesus Christ' (Xavier cited in Coleridge 1872, pp. 158–159). In 1543, Xavier had one and probably the only public discussion through his interpreter with the Brahmins at the Tiruchendur Temple (in Thoothukudi district of Tamil Nadu); later, Xavier claimed all the Brahmins applauded once he finished his statement (Young 1989, p. 72). Remarkably, despite his aversion to the Brahmins, Xavier recognised the social eminence and knowledge of the local religious practices in his limited interactions with them. He apparently reported to his companions in Rome that the Brahmins 'acknowledged the truth of his own positions and admitted the truth of the Christian religion as most harmonious with the best in human nature' (Clooney 2020, p. 81). It is, of course, impossible to verify this claim against the testimony of the Brahmins, and it is perhaps in line with what Xavier wanted his missionary colleagues to believe of his mission in India.

It is pertinent to underline that Xavier considered the Japanese and the Chinese as more civilised and rational and, thus, worthy of true conversion to Christianity (Halbfass 1989, p. 37; Rubiés 2005, p. 251). One of his successors, Alessandro Valignano, described Indians as 'universally contemptible' and argued that genuine conversion was impossible given that 'none of them can be converted through internal motion of spirit or reason' (Xavier and Županov 2015, p. 128; Ross 2019, p. 343). Accordingly, Valignano decided to downgrade 'the inferior civilisation of the brahmins' and 'directed well-trained missionaries like Matteo Ricci away from the Indian hinterland' (Rubiés 2000, p. 9). However, despite his contempt for local traditions, Valignano also recognised the criticality of cultural adaptations and conformity to Japanese customs for the success of missionary activities (Fujitani 2016). His close associate, Matteo Ricci, then inspired the Jesuits in China to dress like Buddhist monks and to embrace 'the lifestyle and etiquette of the Confucian elite of literati and officials' (Standaert 2019, p. 352). Unlike the friendly approach to cultural adaptation in China and Japan, the Jesuits took an offensive approach in India. In Goa, the Jesuits employed the Brahmin converts to steal books from a Brahmin and decode the Hindu sacred books including 'Vyasa's Mahabharata and Namdev's Ananda Purana' (Xavier and Županov 2015, p. 134). These books were used by the Jesuits to publicly refute theological points and 'for preaching and for the instructions of the Goan Brahmans who were compelled to be present at the Sunday catechism classes' (ibid.).[8]

It can be argued that despite their aversion to the Brahmins, the Jesuits realised their utility given their knowledge 'about the religious beliefs and practices of the heathens in India' (ibid., pp. 132–133). Soon these Brahmin informants emerged as the 'building bloc of the Catholic Orientalist anthropology of religion' (ibid.). Indeed, while the Jesuits made dogged efforts to learn about Indian cultural and religious practices, they showed little interest in learning from or adapting to indigenous practices. Moreover, convinced of their moral superiority, the missionaries were indifferent to the perceptions and sensitivities of the local population towards Christianity and the radical social changes that ensued. In 1595, Father Goncalo Fernandez, a Jesuit priest who could speak Tamil, established a church, an elementary school, a dispensary and a house in Madurai (Cronin 1959). However, despite his exemplary life of service and devotion, in the next 11 years he could not attract any new converts from the local Hindu population.

In 1606, Roberto de Nobili, an Italian Jesuit, was sent to help the Madurai mission, and he quickly realised that the locals did not convert to Christianity as they looked down on Christians as impure *paranghi*s.[9] In order to amplify the appeal of Christianity, Nobili, renowned as 'the Renaissance missionary', left the Jesuit residence and 'lived in a hut built in the Brahmin quarters of Madurai dressed as an Indian sannyasi, eating only one meal a day consisting of vegetarian food' (Fernando 2014). Moreover, he 'presented himself first as a nobleman from the West, of the *ksatriya* caste (*varna*)',[10] observed the caste rules, mastered Tamil and learnt Sanskrit (Clooney 2020, p. 37). Nobili's unreserved embrace of pagan practices triggered a major dispute among the Indian Jesuits; eventually, Nobili's theological resourcefulness won the Pope's patronage. Indeed, Nobili's cultural adaptation led to many new converts; however, his most significant contribution was introducing an epistemological distinction to Indology (Amaladass and Clooney 2000; Clooney 2009). Thus, instead of viewing India's social and cultural make-up as one odious monolith, it saw two constituents: 'civility encompassing customs, habits, and rituals' as distinct from 'religion referring principally to the beliefs' (Xavier and Županov 2015, p. 153; Clooney 2017). In many ways, Nobili's model of cultural assimilation became a popular method of winning more converts, and later missions also adopted this mantra.

One of Nobili's famous dictums about Indian society, 'These people have one civil way of life, but multiple religions', emerged as the cardinal principle of Indology (Županov 2001, p. 269). Undoubtedly, Nobili was a pioneer among the European Jesuits, who, on the one hand, 'set no limits to his adaptation to the externals of Indian society, he also conceded no ground on the content of his Catholic faith' (Clooney 2020, p. 37). He consigned any set of indigenous beliefs or religious practices that appeared contradictory to his Christian worldview as superstitions and ignorant. Moreover, in his numerous writings on Indian civility and religion, Nobili could not bring himself to make 'any explicit, positive appreciation of Hindu religiosity per se' and did not make 'any positive comments about Hindu religious texts, doctrines of the divine, ritual practices, and so on' (ibid.).

Nobili's work inspired a new generation of Jesuit scholars such as Constantine Joseph Beschi, Jean Venance Bouchet and Gaston-Laurent Coeurdoux, who made major contributions to anthropology and Indian languages.[11] Remarkably, while all these scholars showed immense 'respect for the great cultures and literature of the East', they sought 'to import a better Western Christianity to Asia' (Clooney 2018, p. 280). However, even for them, 'actual love of an Asian religion was unlikely to be expressed directly or, perhaps, even to be experienced' (ibid.). Apart from their religious undertakings, the Jesuits put in enormous efforts to produce literature and linguistics in Indian languages and an enormous corpus of historical writing about India. Commending the Jesuits for their impartiality to history writing, Jawaharlal Nehru, while describing Akbar, wrote: 'I cannot, however, resist giving you some more quotations from the accounts of the Portuguese Missionaries. Their opinions are of far greater value than those of courtiers' (Nehru 1962, p. 322).

Just as the Jesuits were making impressive gains in India, in 1773 a papal decree ordered the suppression of the Society of Jesus, a clampdown that lasted until 1814 (Casanova and Banchoff 2016, p. 1; Shore 2020).[12] Upon restoration, the society returned to India, and some of the non-Portuguese Jesuits set up the Bengal Mission in 1834, only to close it down in 1846 'facing ill-treatment by the Padroado authorities in Calcutta' (Fernanado 2019). However, in 1859, some Belgian Jesuits returned to Calcutta to revive the Bengal mission; in 1889, they set up St Mary's Theologate in Kurseong. The two institutions, St Xavier's College in Calcutta and St Mary's Theologate in Kurseong, hosted some of the most brilliant Jesuit Indologists and are, accordingly, considered the two sites of the Calcutta School of Indology.

Interestingly, neither William Wallace, acclaimed as the founding father of the Calcutta School of Indology, nor Brahmabandhab Upadhyay, hailed as the original preceptor of Indian Catholicism rooted in Hinduism, was brought up as Jesuit. Upadhyay, a Bengali Hindu scholar, born as Bhavani Charan Banerjee, 'was a disciple of Keshab Chandra Sen and a friend of Vivekananda and Rabindranath Tagore with whom he founded Shantiniketan' (Mattam 1974, p. 192). Upadhyay learned about Christ as the great guru from Keshab Chandra Sen and his uncle Kali Charan Banerji; and in 1891, he was baptised by a Church of England clergyman and, in the same year, became a Roman Catholic. Upadhyay recounted that since conversion, 'my mind has been occupied with the one sole thought of winning over India to the Holy Catholic Church' (ibid.).

For Catholic theologians trained in Thomism,[13] systematic Vedanta represented something similar to Western scholasticism, a resource that could be used just as Saint Thomas had used non-Christian accounts, one which was well suited for expressing Christian monotheism (Ganeri 2007, p. 415). Upadhyay aspired for seamless and comprehensive integration between Vedanta and Thomism and sought to create a Christian monastic community on the traditional Hindu pattern of the ashram (Aleaz 1979; Kanakappally 2020, pp. 55–56). He aimed to construct almost 'exact correspondences between Vedantic ideas and Thomistic ones so that Vedanta in some respects may be seen as a form of crypto-(neo-) Thomism and Samkara as St. Thomas in disguise' (Lipner 2001, p. 188; Ganeri 2007, p. 425). He suggested, 'The Vedanta must be made to do the same service to the Catholic faith in India as was done by the Greek philosophy in Europe. The assimilation of the Vedantic philosophy by the Church should not be opposed on the ground of its containing certain errors' (Animananda 1946, p. 74).

Wallace, an Irish-born Evangelical Anglican missionary, spent seven years between 1889 and 1896 in the Calcutta region. He got disillusioned with the Anglican approach and returned to England, converted to Roman Catholicism, and in 1901 returned to India as a Jesuit missionary (Clooney 2018). Inspired by Upadhyay's ambitions, Wallace sought to divest Christianity from Europeanism, formulate the Christian truth through Vedantic thoughts and hold the Hindu social fabric with respect. Apart from producing some of the most insightful and erudite expositions on the 'Hindoo Philosophy', Wallace was 'instrumental in turning the tide of Catholic attitudes to Hinduism from negativity to positive and reflective engagement with the indigenous spirituality' (Doyle 2006, p. 256). However, his most enduring contribution was to attract some of the most talented Belgian Jesuits to Calcutta and enthuse them to acquire the necessary linguistic tools to undertake a deep study of Hindu texts.

The two prolific Indologists inspired by Wallace's ambitions were the Belgian Jesuits Georges Dandoy and Pierre Johanns, who had come to work as missionaries in Calcutta. In 1922, Dandoy and Johanns, in collaboration with Animananda, a disciple of Upadhayay, established a monthly periodical, *The Light of the East* (Mattam 1974). In very lucid terms, the journal's first editorial asserted its objective: 'What we wish to do is to help India know and understand Jesus. We have no intention of putting out the existing lights. Rather we shall try to show that the best thought of the east is a bud that fully expanded blossoms into Christian thought' (cited in ibid., p. 198). The monthly journal ran for 24 years and is regarded as one of the more innovative periodicals in Indian Church history (Doyle 2006). These journals aimed to fashion 'a reconstructed Catholic theology (in Thomist categories) based on aspects of the exposition of Vedanta' (Robinson 2004, p. 19).

The most articulate Jesuit priest, Pierre Johanns, submitted 137 articles to this journal explaining Vedanta from his Thomist perspective. His writing was later published in four parts. His major work was titled *To Christ through the Vedanta*. He produced 'a thorough explication and analysis of the thinking of the Hindu religious leaders Sankara, Ramanuja, and Vallabha, pointing out what he believed to be the strengths and the weaknesses of each position' (ibid.). In 1938, the scholarly interests of the Jesuits led to the transfer of the journal *Clergy Monthly* from Madras (present-day Chennai) to St Mary's Theologate, Kurseong. This scholarly journal contained many articles on the relationship between Christianity and Hinduism and is still in publication under the name *Vidyajyoti Journal of Theological Reflections*. Other eminent Indologists at this school included Joseph Putz, Joseph Bayart, Jules Volckaert, Robert Antoine, Pierre Fallon and Richard De Smet (Gispert-Sauch 1973; Rukmani 2003). This group of European theologians were quite different from the other Western clergy based in India who 'not only asserted that Christianity was the one true religion, but also believed that Hinduism was inherently false and invaluable' (Beltramini 2016, p. 336). These Christian theologians then endeavoured to find common ground between the two philosophical tenets and seek affinities between the religious precepts.

Theological Education at Kurseong

Upon his arrival at Kurseong, Camille got back into a more formal, specific and structured educational system and the Jesuit learning approach of discipline, diligence and devotion. However, he eased into the strict routine of theological learning and religious practice at Kurseong since he had never lost the practice of rigorous hard work, austere living and resolute piety while teaching at Gumla or learning Hindi at Sitagarh. At Kurseong, Camille devoted special efforts to learning Hebrew, Greek and Sanskrit as the first step towards thoroughly studying the sacred books, the philosophical explanations and theological expositions. Later, he recalled his great fortune to learn under the tutelage of renowned scholars such as Joseph Bayart and Jules Volckaert, the two doyens of the Calcutta School of Indology.

As part of his theological education, Camille submitted a thesis titled 'The Theism of Nyaya–Vaisesika: Its Origin and Early Development' under the guidance of Joseph Bayart, a professor of Indian religions at Kurseong. Camille's choice of subject for the thesis highlights his intellectual prowess and scholarly competence, given that Nyaya–Vaisesika is considered the most sophisticated and insightful perspective among the six schools of Hindu philosophy. Nyaya and Vaisesika represent two different schools of Indian philosophy, yet they are complementary; hence, they are combined. Vaisesika refers to the atomic theory and deals chiefly with physics and metaphysics, while Nyaya is primarily a system of logic and dialectics (C. Bulcke 1947, pp. 1–2). In fact, Maharshi Kanada, whom Camille described as the 'atom-eater, a nickname referring to his atomic theory', is credited with propounding the philosophy of Vaisesika and commands the highest respect among ancient Indian scholars. Kanada is offered the highest eminence in a Sanskrit maxim: 'काणादं पाणिनीयं च सर्वशास्त्रोपकारकम्' (Kanadam Panineeyam cha sarvashatropakarakam), meaning all glory of Sanskrit texts emerges out of the beneficence of Kanada and Panini.[14]

This thesis is one of the definitive examples of Camille's profound admiration for Indian wisdom even at a very early stage of his life. His appreciation for Indian scholarship is reflected throughout his thesis. In the preface, he affirmed, 'Of set purpose I avoided all reference to Western philosophy and have endeavoured, critically yet with sympathy, to propound the system as understood and taught in the school itself, even when its opponents' position has perhaps been misrepresented' (ibid., preface). Indeed, the thesis is replete with some of the most insightful references to the works of Indian scholars, including ancient ones such as Patanjali and Vachaspati Mishra[15] and also Camille's contemporaries such as Mysore Hiriyanna, Surendra Nath Dasgupta, Gopi Nath Kaviraj, Ganga Nath Jha, D. Gurumurti and Satish Chandra Chatterjee. When Camille submitted his dissertation as part of his theological education, it was deemed an insightful and scholarly contribution to the study of an onerous aspect of Indian philosophy. Accordingly, four years since its submission, the thesis was published as a full-fledged book by the Calcutta Oriental Institute.

During his theological training, though Camille had fully immersed himself in the arduous task of elucidating the most challenging aspect of Indian philosophy, he undertook an intense study of the Bible. He started to work on a biography of Jesus Christ based on the Gospels under the guidance of Professor Volckaert. It is important to reiterate that it is never easy to comprehend the Nyaya–Vaisesika school of philosophy; it mandates an uninterrupted and solitary focus to absorb such a complex system. Nevertheless, Camille took on the additional task of narrating the life of Jesus Christ by gleaning his life's intricate and delicate aspects with such finesse so as not to miss any subtle nuances and profound implications. Camille's intellectual pursuits during his stay at Kurseong vividly portray exceptional intellectual competence and his inexhaustible zeal for hard work.

Camille published the biography of Jesus Christ by weaving the story from the four Gospels in the book *The Saviour* in 1942. The four books of the New Testament are known as the Gospels: Matthew, Mark, Luke and John. Each book tells us about the life, ministry, death and resurrection of Jesus Christ (C. Bulcke 1942a). His inspiration to write the book was a well-thought-out attempt to streamline and weave one concise and consistent account from the four diverse narratives presented in the four Gospels. He argued that while the underlying theme of the four Gospels is the same since each of the four authors pursued different objectives and perspectives, they chose to highlight certain sermons and events in their expositions. He sought to incorporate the modern discoveries on time and space with the timeless texts of the four Gospels in his narration. He attempted to stay as close as possible to the original texts, which may have diminished the linguistic flourish; however, he claimed that there was not a single word in the book that was not inspired by the Holy Spirit.

Camille attempted to master two different sets of philosophies, the Nyaya–Vaisesika and the Christian theology, and simultaneously he acquired profound insights into both knowledge systems. Moreover, while he immersed himself in pursuing theological knowledge, he continued with the self-learning of Hindi and Sanskrit. It should come as no surprise that for the rest of his life, he faced no difficulties (or at least outwardly he did not demonstrate any), in managing his devotion to Hindi and his devotion to Jesus Christ and his missionary duties. He translated *The Saviour* from English into Hindi as *Muktidata*. His friend and collaborator Dineshwar Prasad argues that the publication of the Hindi book confirms the level of proficiency Camille had gained in such a short time and in between so many other challenging assignments (D. Prasad 1987, p. 9). *The Saviour* and its Hindi version, *Muktidata*, have gone through several subsequent editions, and the two have sold well over 100,000 copies.

Camille continued to progress with Hindi and Sanskrit, and within a year of reaching Kurseong, in 1940, he successfully cleared the examination of *visharad*, a test conducted by the Hindi Sahitya Sammelan, Prayag. In those times, *visharad* in Hindi was considered an esteemed academic achievement equivalent to a Bachelor's degree from a university. While he was at the theologate, Kaka Kalelkar, an eminent Hindi littérateur, was invited to inaugurate a new library established by the local Marwari community. The organisers of the inauguration ceremony invited Camille to preside over the function, which attracted a large and enthusiastic crowd. Camille made his speech in Hindi; a visibly moved Kalelkar remarked, 'Bulcke Jee has become one of us' (D. Prasad 2002, p. 14). Camille remembered this incident as one of the primary inspirations that firmed his resolve not simply to learn Hindi but to acquire the highest possible education in the language.

Kodaikanal and Manpad

On 21 November 1941, having completed all his training and education, Camille was ordained as a priest, thus progressing from Brother Bulcke to Father Bulcke. He attributed it to God's grace that he managed to take this significant step towards fulfilling his religious duties. In July 1943, the Jesuit authorities sent him to Kodaikanal to complete a nine-month-long spiritual training, including a month of absolute silence (Saxena 2017, p. 39). In Kodaikanal, the seminary was located on a hill where Camille was joined by 14 other spiritual aspirants who received religious and spiritual instructions from their teacher. With this training, he realised he had pledged his life to follow regular but rigorous spiritual practices and also accepted the responsibility to perform religious rituals. As the training period approached its completion, he was filled with anticipation and excitement as he envisaged a life in the service of people after resuming his missionary duties.

Before his return to Ranchi, Camille planned to travel around Tamil Nadu; and among all the places, he was overwhelmed with his pilgrimage to the cave of Saint Francis Xavier in Manpad. He described in detail his train journey to Tiruchendur, where Saint Xavier had the legendary discussion with the Hindu Brahmins in a temple, and then walked to the cave in Manpad where Xavier had spent innumerable hours praying for divine grace, wrote numerous letters and reports and prepared for the campaign to spread the word of the gospel (C. Bulcke 2009, p. 150). As he prepared to leave Manpad, he ruefully noted, 'More than any other place it is at Manpad that a person comes across the truth that the only grief in this world is not being a saint' (ibid., p. 150). This was a true reflection of what Camille aspired as the ultimate goal of being born as a human: to transcend earthly bonds and transgress beyond the limits imposed on humans.

Hindi and Sanskrit Learning: 1943–1950

In 1943, having completed his religious training, the newly ordained Father Camille Bulcke returned to Ranchi: formally to pursue his missionary duties and serve humanity and individually to pursue his life's mission to serve Hindi. Having achieved the religious and organisational credentials, he had no intention of deferring the pursuit of his calling. He was also keen to further pursue his formal Hindi education within the university system as soon as he had passed the *visharad* examination. In 1940, he travelled to several university towns in north India to assess the cultural milieu, intellectual ambience, academic environment and overall literary consciousness to find the most appropriate place to make progress as a Hindi scholar.

Uday Narayan Tiwari, an eminent linguist, recalls meeting Camille in Calcutta in 1940. Camille was preparing for his *visharad* exam and was keen to identify an appropriate university for his higher education in Hindi; Tiwari recommended the University of Allahabad for such academic pursuits (Tiwari 1987, p. 36). Father Ivan A. Extross recalls meeting Camille in 1940 in Allahabad when he was in the town to work out the possibilities of learning Hindi and the prospect of enrolment in the MA programme at the university (Extross 1987, p. 70). As Extross narrates, Camille was not very familiar with Allahabad-based Catholic priests and stayed with one of his acquaintances, B. S. Gilani, the editor of the *Social Order* (ibid.).

In those times, the universities at Kashi (Banaras) and Allahabad were considered the pre-eminent institutions for Hindi scholarship. On his visit to Kashi, Camille met Acharya Ramchandra Shukla, who commended the service rendered to Hindi by the Christian missionaries and was filled with admiration and affection for Camille. From Kashi, he travelled to Allahabad, though he could not get to see Dhirendra Verma, the head of the Department of Hindi at the university. However, in Verma's absence, he met with another Hindi scholar, Ramkumar Verma; impressed with the distinctive cultural milieu of the place, Camille resolved to pursue his MA degree from the University of Allahabad (D. Prasad 1987, p. 9).

In 1943, Camille saw the opportunity to realise his long-cherished ambition of a formal university degree in Hindi on his return to Ranchi.

He wrote a letter expressing his desire to pursue an MA degree at the venerable institution. Camille did not get any reply from Dhirendra Verma; undaunted, he tried to enrol for the BA degree in Hindi and Sanskrit at the University of Calcutta. However, since he already had a Bachelor of Science (BSc) degree, he required special permission from the university's syndicate to appear as a private student for the BA degree examination. In two years, he acquired his BA degree in Sanskrit, History, Hindi and English.

In 1945, having fulfilled all the prerequisites for his MA degree, Camille travelled to Allahabad to present his case to Dhirendra Verma to study at the university. Extross has given a vivid description of the meeting between Camille and Verma since Extross was instrumental in setting up this meeting and accompanied Camille to the Hindi department at the university (Extross 1987, pp. 70–71). 'Dr Verma was a great scholar and did not evince any great interest in the Belgian priest with brown-blue eyes and an auburn beard, for he thought Bulcke was another foreigner enthusiast with fleeting curiosity in India and Hindi' (ibid.). Referring to the earlier letter from Camille, Verma said, 'Last year, I did not respond to your letter since I believe that no foreigner can complete the M.A. degree in Hindi' (C. Bulcke 2015 [1976], p. 331). Verma advised him that as a regular student, 'he was expected to attend the classes regularly and that none of the lectures would offer any explanation in English' (Extross 1987, p. 70). Camille assured him of making the best efforts to keep pace with the lectures to mitigate Verma's worries.

However, Verma was not someone to be moved by sheer perseverance; instead, he wished to evaluate the competence of the prospective student. Upon learning that Camille had a BA degree in Sanskrit and Hindi, Verma picked two verses from Tulsidas' *Vinaya Patrika* and asked him to provide an explication in Hindi. Extross watched Camille pick up the paper and then move to a desk in the corner; for a few minutes, he was immersed in deep thoughts, and then he started to write. In the meantime, Verma continued his conversations with Extross; after a while, Camille placed two handwritten sheets of paper on the desk in front of Verma. Extross describes, 'As Dr Verma was reading these pages, I still remember the interesting changes in the expressions on his face. First, his disinterest turned into interest, and then the interest turned into surprise; finally, the surprise turned into respect' (ibid., p. 71). Finally, Verma said with a smile, 'You would have no problems in the study for M.A. (Hindi)' (ibid.).

Recalling the exact incident, Camille narrated, 'Dr. Dhirendra kept looking at my explanation for a long time as if it was a window through which he could see for miles. He let me get admission into the course' (D. Prasad 2002, p. 14). To facilitate his enrolment, Verma wrote a letter to the registrar of University of Allahabad. More than the fact that Camille convinced Dhirendra Verma, an eminent Hindi scholar, who initially showed very little faith in Camille's competence, is the sheer determination with which he pursued an MA degree in Hindi. He had already gained other academic degrees, including a BSc in Engineering from Louvain University with outstanding marks, and an MA degree in Philosophy with exceptionally high marks. As a scholar, he had already produced an outstanding dissertation on Nyaya–Vaisesika and had authored a book, *The Saviour*, in English with its Hindi translation, *Muktidata*. It would appear extravagant that, at 36, despite his proficiency in several European languages and academic accomplishments, he was still craving another university degree as a full-time student.

However, one must remember that the moment Camille set foot in Ranchi, he was unimpressed with the hegemony of English and resolved to serve Hindi and bring it to the glory it deserved in its own home. Over time, he realised that it was imperative to speak in Hindi to connect with ordinary people directly. Moreover, he understood that to overcome the narrow religious divide, one must establish a conversation in Hindi with the people (D. Prasad 1987, p. 9). To serve Hindi, he would have to study the language not as an amateur or an aficionado but as a conscientious, dedicated and full-time student and go through the official assessment process like a proper examinee (S. Singh 1982, p. 25).

As a student at the University of Allahabad, Camille was in the august company of some of the most illustrious Hindi littérateurs. Some of his classmates and friends went on to become phenomenal authors. In his MA class, his batchmates included Dharmvir Bharati, the pre-eminent poet, author, editor and playwright, and Jagdish Gupta, a distinguished poet and one of the most renowned proponents of Nayi Kavita (Modern Poetry) in Hindi. Raghuvansh, pursuing his PhD, who later became a prominent Hindi littérateur, was Camille's closest friend during his Allahabad days. Raghuvansh suffered from a disability and could not use his hands, so he used to write with his toes with a speed and accuracy that was unattainable to others. He went on to create an extraordinary body of work during his life. An avid cyclist, Camille would ride his bicycle for miles in and around Allahabad with Raghuvansh sitting at the front of the cycle; their close bond remained intact throughout Camille's lifetime (Raghuvansh 1987, p. 55). He joined Parimal, the famed literary circle of Hindi scholars at Allahabad; and as Dharmvir Bharati recalled, the reticent guest to the intense literary debates soon evolved into an honourable member who, despite his few words, made a telling effect on the overall discussions within the group.

Camille was a diligent student during his studies for the MA degree at Allahabad; he followed a strict schedule and worked very hard. In order to build a solid foundation in Hindi, he sought extra help and took tuition from Uma Shankar Shukla, a PhD scholar at the university. Jagdish Gupta recalls that while at Allahabad, Camille developed some problems with his hearing, and in those days, instead of using a hearing aid, he used to sit on the first bench. The teachers at the university liked such a courteous and erudite student, and an eternally polite Camille became a favourite of the staff members. During his studies at Allahabad, he achieved great insights into Indian religious texts; he presented a research paper on the birth story of Hanuman at a conference in the department (J. Gupta 1987, p. 62).

As a student in Allahabad, Camille used to stay at the St Joseph's Seminary, and his neighbour, Extross, remembered that while he used to follow all the routines of the seminary, he worked tirelessly on his studies. On watching him always immersed in his studies, sometimes Extross would distract him so that he could get some rest. It must have been an extraordinary warmth shared between the two priests, given that Extross could infringe upon his friend's study time. Although an exceedingly cordial and gentle person, Camille would not let anyone disrupt his strict schedule (Extross 1987, pp. 70–71). To address some issues with the administration, the students of the University of Allahabad called for a strike; the protestors tried to prevent him from entering his office premises and asked him to join the strike. Camille said rather sternly that the protestors might appeal, but they could not compel others to join the strike. His strong words provoked some of the agitators; he lost his patience and, folding the sleeves of his cassock, roared, 'What do you mean?' The sight of a furious European Christian priest unnerved the protestors who let him pass; remembering the incident, Camille would say, 'As a general rule, those who indulge in unruly behaviour do not have much moral courage' (Saxena 2017, p. 41).

As an avid learner, he was always keen to engage in extended conversations with fellow students, friends and acquaintances in Hindi despite his focus on his studies. This trait allowed him to engage with these people's feelings, interests and aspirations. This capacity to build a warm personal bond made him very popular among the local people, and he was always welcomed in the family homes of his friends, where children would surround him. Camille's friendship was never with one individual or a formal business-like association; instead, he would form a close bond with the entire family. He would emerge as an endearing friend, a doting elder or an affectionate younger person to different members of the same family. He had an exceptional skill for holding a profound discussion on intricate issues about language or literature while simultaneously playing with children (Extross 1987, p. 71).

As a full-time student at the university, he was into the famed Hindi literary circle of Allahabad. Raghuvansh, his dear friend, took him to meet one of the greatest Indian poets, Mahadevi Verma. Camille addressed Verma as *didi*, meaning elder sister. About their affectionate sibling relationship, Verma later wrote,

> Neither do I know nor can I explain how I earned the privilege to become the elder sister of an ascetic monk from an austere Jesuit order who left Belgium, his birthplace, to embrace India as his motherland. However, it is a fact that at very first sight, Father Bulcke did not look like either a foreigner or a stranger to me. It seemed that two of us are siblings collecting shells and conches at the long shores of the vast ocean of knowledge. (M. Verma 1987, p. 31)

Verma was determined to renounce the world and become a Buddhist nun; however, later, she changed her mind and pursued education and social service, though writing was her vocation (M. Verma 2021). Although she never acknowledged it in so many words, one could infer that in Camille, the Christian ascetic with unwavering devotion to his faith and a life dedicated to the service of people, Verma saw a kindred spirit, a younger sibling along the same path of spiritual growth. In fact, before meeting Verma, Camille had learned that she never used to speak in English with anyone, a trait that he could relate to his own sister. He compared this with his childhood experience when the Flemish speakers sought to embrace the French language and culture to appear as modern and elite. Once, to improve their conversational skills, Camille's mother pleaded with her schoolgoing children to speak in French among themselves. His sister defied her mother rather stoutly: 'We are not mules. We shall not speak in French in this house' (C. Bulcke 2009, p. 155).

Since his arrival in India, Camille was distressed to see that, like the Flemish people from his childhood, Indians too considered speaking English and embracing English culture as a matter of pride and a mark of upward mobility. He was delighted to learn that Mahadevi Verma never spoke in English, and in his heart, he put her on the same pedestal where he had placed his self-respecting sister. He greatly admired Verma's profound human sensitivity and intellectual intensity. Moreover, to him, she represented India's genuine self-respect and dignity, a sense of pride that does not seek endorsement from the champions of European modernity, nor does it endorse the obscurantists' idolisation of Indian antiquity (ibid.).

In 1942, Mahadevi Verma took an innovative approach by setting up a *sahityakar sansad* (parliament of littérateur) in Allahabad to institutionalise the literary exchanges among the writers and offer support to them to promote the spread of Hindi. Camille met several prominent Hindi writers in Allahabad at Verma's home or through the *sahityakar sansad*. Maithili Sharan Gupt, the doyen of Hindi poetry, met Camille at Verma's home; Gupt was so fascinated with the Christian priest's affection for Hindi that he hosted Camille at his family home in Chirgaon, in Jhansi, and shared meals with him suspending his strict adherence to Vaishnav kitchen rules (Saxena 2017, p. 41).[16] On the other hand, Camille found in Gupt a very generous, cheerful and jovial person. In his book *Bharat Bharati*, Gupt had depicted Jesus' visit to India.[17] In their interactions, Camille presented some historical evidence contradicting Gupt's account. Gupt was quite remorseful and decided to make the corrections in the subsequent editions. As a deeply religious person, Gupt believed that he had committed an offence against Jesus and wished to atone for it by writing a new poem. Thus, he requested Camille to send him a narration of one of the most poignant events from the Bible. Camille then wrote to Gupt describing the story of the adulterous woman from the Bible, who is saved by the compassion of Jesus. He received a beautiful reply from Gupt, acknowledging his contribution (C. Bulcke 2015 [1976], p. 333).

Camille met other renowned Hindi poets in Allahabad, including the erudite Suryakant Tripathi 'Nirala' whom he found very humble, contrary to popular perceptions. He also met Sumitranandan Pant, whose equanimity and poise Camille likened to being around the Pacific Ocean. He made lifelong friendships with eminent writers, including Ramdhari Singh Dinkar, Harivansh Rai Bachchan, Jainendra Kumar, Ramakrishna Das, Vasudev Sharan Agrawal, Bhagwati Charan Verma, Hazari Prasad Dwivedi and

Shivpujan Sahay, among others. Camille was fascinated with the etiquette and respect among Hindi writers; he recalled that during a meeting of the *sahityakar sansad*, Sumitranandan Pant walked away from the venue since he could not smoke in front of Maithili Sharan Gupt, a senior Hindi writer (ibid.). He held these little things about his Indian friends and colleagues in great esteem and over time developed an understanding and deep respect for Indian values, traditions and social etiquette.

In Allahabad, Camille found a new home in India; he fell in love with the place to the extent that he used to refer to it as his *maika* (bride's native or parental home). In Indian folk traditions, *maika* represents an abode of a pampered, joyous, spontaneous and carefree life of a girl who, in adulthood, finds herself burdened with worldly duties. He said it would not be an exaggeration to call his 'Prayagvaas' (stay in Allahabad)[18] 'the second spring' of his life. He wrote,

> The people at Allahabad embraced me with so much affection and care that I could never forget Prayag on my return to Ranchi. Instead of fading, those memories have become sweeter with each passing day, and the people at Allahabad are as dear to me as the parental home is to a married woman. (C. Bulcke 2009, p. 154)

Likewise, Camille's Allahabad-based adopted elder sister, Mahadevi Verma, echoed these sentiments:

> Camille referred to Allahabad as his parental home (*maika*) while referring to his workplace Ranchi as the home of his in-laws (*sasural*). If he does not visit us for a long time, we worry and wait for him precisely as the people at the parental home wait for their daughters. (M. Verma 1987, p. 31)

As a full-time student at the University of Allahabad, Camille was busy with his education, participated in the usual student activities and was also a part of the social and literary circles. However, he was not oblivious to his responsibilities as a man of religion. Camille started to wear ochre robes during his MA degree at the university, much like the Hindu monks. He believed that if the ochre robe were appropriate for all the other religious men from Hindu, Buddhist and Sufi traditions in India, it would be quite apt for the Christian priests to wear the same colour. Nevertheless, as a matter of practice, while he used to wear the prescribed white robe of the Christian priests most of the time, he tried to look beyond the strict regulation on colour (D. Prasad 1989, p. 24). However, one must not imagine that his sense of duty towards the church, or his faith, ever slackened.

Dharmvir Bharati narrated a remarkable incident when a group of students from the University of Allahabad visited Darbhanga, a town in the Mithila region of Bihar, to participate in the All-India Oriental Conference (Bharati 1987, pp. 57–60). On the first day at the conference, someone informed Camille about a non-functional church in the vicinity, which could not hold Sunday service without any priest. The person requested him to hold the prayer service the next day since he was in the area. On the second day of the conference, which happened to be a Sunday, Bharati accompanied Camille who was dressed in the familiar white cassock, as they took an early morning walk to the old, dilapidated church. Only one local person had come to attend the prayer service; a Maithil Brahmin who was excommunicated from his community for some indiscretion. The poor man faced several ordeals, ultimately finding shelter in the abandoned church where he became the caretaker. Despite his poverty, he had brought candles, incense sticks, flowers and some offerings for the prayer service. Camille changed into the customary clothes to conduct the prayers, and soon the entire empty church reverberated with his invocations. Bharati, who thought of himself as an atheist, noted this incident as one of the most uplifting experiences, when Jesus from Jerusalem had come alive in a decrepit church in distant Mithila. Coincidentally, Rama married Sita from this Mithila region and, even after several centuries, charmed Camille to give up his home and travel across the seven seas to focus on his unique research on the *Ramkatha* (Raghuvansh 1987, pp. 54–55). This incident serves as a necessary indicator that Camille never wavered in his primary duty towards Christ and the Church, and yet he had also opened up his heart to learn about the Ramayana and appreciate the devotion (*bhakti*) towards Rama. This is the spirit that he had carried into his doctoral research in Hindi at the University of Allahabad.

Thesis Writing

As Camille progressed to the second year of his MA degree, Dhirendra Verma enquired if he would be interested in pursuing research in Hindi. He was taken aback and responded, 'Me? Should I undertake research in Hindi?'

Verma offered his assurance in a calm but firm manner that Camille could certainly pursue research in Hindi. However, he needed a formal approval from the Jesuit officials to extend his stay at the University of Allahabad; happily, the Ranchi Jesuits sanctioned two more years for him to complete his research. Once he completed his MA degree, he was to pick an appropriate topic for his doctoral research; Verma suggested a comparative study of the literary works of the poet Surdas in Brij and Gujarati languages as a suitable option. Upon hearing this suggestion, Camille kept quiet out of modesty, but it was as if Verma understood. He spoke with a smile, 'I know you have a much greater fondness for Tulsidas than Sur. Therefore, you may commence your research on Tulsidas under Dr Mataprasad Gupt' (C. Bulcke 2009, p. 14).[19] Tracing his intellectual evolution, Camille referred to Verma's generosity in letting him choose his research topic as the third and final step towards his research in Hindi and Tulsidas.

With the help of Mataprasad Gupt, Camille prepared the outline of his thesis and submitted the research proposal titled 'Tulsi Ki Rambhakti' (Tulsi's Devotion to Rama). As the introduction to his thesis, he intended to discuss the development and evolution of the Rama story through the ages; appropriately, the chapter was titled 'Ramkatha Ka Vikas' (The Development of the Rama Story). As a meticulous researcher, he collected the material on the various traditions and sources of the Rama story; he came across copious but contradictory information on Valmiki, the purported author of the Sanskrit version of the *Ramkatha*. In his research, he identified three distinct recensions of the vulgate[20] Valmiki Ramayana, which he referred to as the southern, Bengal and north-western versions. The discovery of three different recensions was not much of a problem until Camille noticed substantial differences among these versions. He explained that one of the most significant differences lies in the fact that 'each recension has a good number of verses, even long passages and entire cantos which are not to be found in one or, at times even both of the others' (C. Bulcke 2010, p. 43). He also found the differences among the common verses in how they referred to different events or offered different interpretations of the same event. He was fascinated with the story of Valmiki as much as with the *Ramkatha*; as he delved deeper into the Rama story, gathering other sources, it appeared that the entire Indian ethos was immersed in the spirit of Rama.

Camille's thesis advisor, Mataprasad Gupt, was thrilled to see the volume of material collected on the development of the Rama story and asked his student to write on the development of the different aspects of the story. He could not finish even half of the introduction chapter during the first year despite working ceaselessly. However, he had managed to gather an encyclopaedic tome of material on the development of the *Ramkatha* from not just Hindu but also Buddhist and Jain traditions, and not just Indian but also from Central and South-East Asian sources (Saran and Khanna 2018, p. 226). Highly impressed with the originality, the comprehensive volume of information and the remarkable inferences Camille had drawn from, Dhirendra Verma suggested that the thesis should focus exclusively on the development of the *Ramkatha*. Accordingly, Camille changed the title of his thesis to *Ramkatha: Utpatti Aur Vikas* (The Genesis and Development of the Rama-Story).

Camille came across an administrative hurdle no sooner than he had completed writing his thesis; in those times, the official policy mandated that every PhD thesis submitted to any Indian university be written in English. Apparently, given his proficiency in English, it was quite easy for him to prepare his thesis in English. However, as a devoted campaigner for the vernacular, seeking to exalt Hindi to its rightful place of pride, Camille sought permission from the higher authorities at the University of Allahabad to submit his thesis in Hindi. At his request, the then vice-chancellor of the university, Amarnath Jha, made suitable amendments to the rulebook, thereby allowing the submission of the first PhD thesis in Hindi to any Indian university (D. Prasad 1987, p. 10). He, thus, became a trendsetter and after his submission, several Indian universities opened their doors for submission of theses written in modern Indian languages.

In 1949, the University of Allahabad awarded the degree of Doctor of Philosophy (DPhil) to Camille, for his original research work. Looking at the excellent quality of his research, Prakashan Parishad, the publication division of the university, published his thesis as a book titled *Ramkatha: Utpatti Aur Vikas*. Camille's book contained four different parts, and he explored one specific theme of the development and genesis of the Rama story in each part. Camille intended to start his study of the ancient sources of the *Ramkatha* right from the Vedic period. Accordingly, the first part offers an insightful analysis of Vedic literature, Valmiki's Ramayana, the Mahabharata and several Buddhist and Jain texts. In the second part, the book explores the genesis of the *Ramkatha*, whereby Camille traced the earliest references to the Rama story in Pali texts, a meticulous examination of diverse scholarly opinions on the origin of the *Ramkatha*, and a study of different interpolations of Valmiki's Ramayana. In the third part, the book examines the modern account of the *Ramkatha* in different Indian languages, including Sanskrit, Hindi, Tamil, Telugu, Malayalam, Kannada, Bengali and Kashmiri. This section also explored the *Ramkatha* in other Asian nations, including Sri Lanka, Tibet, Khotan, Myanmar, Thailand, Indonesia, India and China. In the last part, the book traces the development of each significant episode of Valmiki's Ramayana and examines its evolution vis-à-vis other sources of the *Ramkatha*. Indeed, the book offers a range that is 'simply astounding and kaleidoscopic' and is the first literary work that highlights 'the immense international popularity of the story and its deep influence on India and South-East Asia' (C. Bulcke 2010, p. vii).

In turning the thesis into a book, Camille received generous help from his thesis supervisor, Mataprasad Gupt. Once again, his dear friend Raghuvansh provided much-needed help with meticulous scrutiny of the entire manuscript. Writing the introduction to the book, Dhirendra Verma offered fulsome praise for Camille, lauding him as an accomplished author who had painstakingly collected almost all of the available material on the *Ramkatha*. Verma described the book as an encyclopaedia on the material related to the Rama story, along with being one of the most scientific, rational and scholarly works of research on the genesis of the *Ramkatha*. Verma upheld the book as a trendsetter and a unique contribution to the literature on the genesis of the *Ramkatha* and claimed it as the only available book of its genre not only in Hindi but in any other Indian or European language (D. Verma 1950, p. 5).

Dineshwar Prasad considered this book as Camille's 'homage to the genius of Valmiki, who gave a definitive form to the story, brought out the enduring ideals and values inherent in it, and raised it to be enviable and everlasting literary heights' (D. Prasad 1987). With the book's publication, Camille 'suddenly shot into fame and within a short period came to be recognised as a great international authority on the subject' (ibid.). However, the new-found prominence, scholarly recognition and celebrity status brought no change in his humility; he was seen in Allahabad carrying the bundles of his newly published book either on his shoulders or on the pillion of his bicycle in order to sell it to interested readers (Saxena 2017, p. 42). Indeed, his book is considered not just essential reading on the development of the *Ramkatha* or Hindi literature; instead, it is one of the classics of Indology (D. Prasad 1987, p. 26).

Upon completing his education at the University of Allahabad, Camille returned to Ranchi in 1950 and joined St Xavier's College as the head of the Department of Hindi and Sanskrit. Indeed, he was back on his home turf, staying at the residential complex of the Jesuits at Manresa House and now equipped with institutional support and individual repute to devote his life to his true calling. He spent the next 32 years of his life in Ranchi – a life studded with extraordinary literary feats, devoted to advancing Hindi and, most importantly, dedicated to serving his fellow human beings. At St Xavier's College, he taught Hindi and Sanskrit from intermediate (freshmen) to the BA (Honours) classes, while also finding time for his remarkable scholarly accomplishments. A conscientious teacher, Camille made extra effort to prepare for his lectures and provide something new, either as a different explanation or by bringing in the latest references to each of his lectures. At the beginning of his teaching career at St Xavier's College, he realised that he struggled to find the appropriate words and phrases during his lectures. He read one complete Hindi novel every week to overcome this vocabulary deficiency for one full year (C. Bulcke 2015 [1976], p. 338).

As a doting teacher, Camille loved his students like his own children and considered it his moral duty to provide for and to protect their interests (Saxena 2017, p. 52).[21] It is no wonder that the young students felt confident enough to share their problems with the kind teacher, and as a man with infinite compassion, he never failed to offer them moral support. His cheerful disposition and quick wit always brought a quick resolution to the students' problems. He believed that on most occasions, it was the lack of candid conversations between the parents and their adolescent children that led to several complications. He believed that all he did was to lend a sympathetic ear and see things from the young people's perspective, and invariably he managed to extend some helpful guidance.

Camille's residence in Manresa House soon became a hub of hectic scholarly activities; students, research scholars and young and aspiring writers seeking his guidance and looking for appropriate references gravitated towards him. He soon recognised the lack of any functional library in Ranchi and started buying books and magazines from his own pocket to help the knowledge seekers. Soon enough, he came to establish a handy library; he was very generous in lending the books; however, he left it to the borrower to list their names and books in the loan register. He realised that people often did not return the books; yet he was averse to rigid regulations and rule enforcement and left it to the individual's conscience to make the right decisions (Saxena 2015, p. 54).

Sharing his knowledge of Hindi was never meant as gainful employment for Camille; instead, it was his life's mission. As a conscientious teacher, he wished to impart knowledge to his students and not just rote learning. He recognised that the Indian education system continued to perpetuate the British colonial-era policy of producing clerks for the empire. As a college teacher, he challenged this practice and sought to reignite his students' love for Hindi and other Indian languages. However, a perceptive Camille soon realised that most of his students were less interested in pursuing knowledge; instead, they were obsessed with scoring high marks in the examination. Gradually, he grew disillusioned with teaching indifferent students; it dawned upon him that he would offer much better service to Hindi through research, studies and other literary activities. In 1960, he wrote to the higher authorities in Rome seeking their permission to be relieved of his teaching responsibilities. The Jesuit authorities relieved him of his regular teaching duties; nevertheless, they insisted that he continue to serve as the head of the Department of Hindi and Sanskrit at St Xavier's College (D. Prasad 1987, p. 11). Camille was happy to relinquish the regular teaching duties, though he never gave up teaching altogether; on occasions, he would teach the *Ramcharitmanas* in the BA (Honours) classes and some Sanskrit classes (Saxena 2017, p. 53).

Since 1950, while being based in Ranchi, and despite his hectic schedule and intermittent health issues, Camille was already working on several of his favourite projects. He was well aware of his limitations as he acknowledged, 'I could not serve my favourite language by writing poetry, stories or novels. I realised that there was no reliable English–Hindi dictionary, and hence, I started to think in this direction. Most of the Christian missionaries had a very limited Hindi vocabulary and for them, I compiled a small dictionary titled *A Technical Hindi–English Glossary*' (C. Bulcke 2015 [1976], p. 338). Camille's dictionary was published in 1955, receiving such widespread acclaim that he was inspired to plan for a comprehensive English–Hindi dictionary. He had gathered extensive information on the *Ramkatha* and planned to incorporate the new material in the next edition of his book. He had also spent much effort discovering and reading more information on his favourite poet, Tulsidas, and wished to write a book on Tulsi's devotion (*bhakti*). Camille had read some of the Hindi translations of the Holy Bible, and he was rather disappointed with them; he felt that their language was such that it might fill someone with contempt for Christianity (ibid., p. 339). He was determined to compose an accurate Hindi translation of the Holy Bible and other prayers and hymns to bring the faith and rituals closer to the local Christians.

Indeed, the decision to move away from teaching should be seen as one of the most momentous decisions of Camille's life, equal to his decision to become a missionary or his resolve to serve in India. Camille's story is incomplete without Tulsidas, who emerged as an anchor to his persona and to his literary and spiritual life; it is indeed a fascinating story of a Christian priest exalting Tulsidas as his idol and trying to emulate him in all aspects of his life. We explore Camille's special bond with the one he referred to as 'my own Tulsi' (*mere apne Tulsi*) and his commentaries on the work of Tulsidas in the next chapter.

Notes

1. Liberation; generally meant to convey the meaning of the deliverance of the soul from recurring births.
2. Fitzgerald (1943) has mentioned the language as Ouraon. It is necessary to point out that Oraon, or Ouraon, refers to a tribe, while the language they speak is Kurukh.
3. 'धन्य जनमु जगतीतल तासू। पितहि प्रमोदु चरित सुनि जासू॥ चारि पदारथ करतल ताकें। प्रिय पितु मातु प्रान सम जाकें॥ ॥' (*Ramcharitmanas*, 'Ayodhyakand', 2.46).
4. Chitrakoot is located in the northern part of the Vindhya mountain range in the Bundelkhand region of Madhya Pradesh. This is the place where Rama, Sita and Lakshmana spent most of their days in exile from Ayodhya. Tulsidas spent a significant part of his life in Chitrakoot, worshipping Rama and craving his *darshan* (sighting). Eventually, it was at Chitrakoot that Tulsidas realised his lifetime dream and had the *darshan* of his beloved deity, Rama.
5. Brij Bhasha, or Braj Bhasha, is a language spoken in the region known as Braj, comprising parts of Uttar Pradesh, Madhya Pradesh, Rajasthan and Haryana. Considered as a western dialect of Hindi, Brij Bhasha is one of the most popular languages for devotional poetry (*bhakti kavya*), particularly on the Hindu deity Krishna. Brij Bhasha is also used in a significant body of work in erotic poetry (*riti kavya*). The prominent literary figures in Brij Bhasha are Surdas, Nand Das, Rahim, Raskhan, Bihari, Dev, Bhushan and Ratnakar. Awadhi is an Indo-Aryan language spoken in northern India and

is grouped under the eastern dialect of Hindi. Awadhi is primarily spoken in Awadh (Oudh) region in the state of Uttar Pradesh in India. The most notable poet of the Awadhi language is Goswami Tulsidas, a medieval saint poet of north India of the Rama *bhakti* branch. Another prominent Awadhi poet is Mailk Mohammad Jayasi, who wrote *Padmavat*.

6. *Panchatantra* literally translates into 'five devices'. It is an ancient Indian collection of interrelated animal fables in verse and prose, arranged within a frame story. The original Sanskrit work, which some scholars believe was composed around the third century BCE, is attributed to Vishnu Sharma.

7. In this case, the Hindu religious system refers to the diverse cosmological practices and beliefs of Indian peoples, which are placed under a broad umbrella of Hinduism. The Hindu belief system emerges from Dharma, or Sanatana Dharma, which is not the same as religion in the Western understanding; instead, it denotes cosmological, ethical, social and legal principles for the proper conduct of individuals, groups, society and the universe.

8. The Mahabharata is one of the two Sanskrit epic poems of ancient India (the other being the Ramayana). The Mahabharata was composed by Vedavyasa. It comprises 10,000 couplets and is an important textual source of Dharma (Hindu moral law) and *itihasa* (history). The epic centres around the struggle for sovereignty between two groups of cousins. The *Ananda Purana* is a compilation of devotional hymns by Namdeva, a Maharashtrian saint, from the first part of the 14th century.

9. The word *paranghi* has a strange history. From the time of the Crusades, the Europeans were known as Franks in Asia. The Chinese referred to the gift of horses from the Pope as 'horses of the Kingdom of Fulang' Farang, or the country of the Franks. In Sanskrit, it is 'Phitanguin', and in Persian it is 'Feringhee'. Babur, in describing the Battle of Panipat in 1526, calls his artillery 'Farangiha'. *Paranghi* is the south Indian version of the word, which had been thought to be particularly appropriate to the Portuguese with their guns and horses. The *paranghi*s were considered polluting, like the members of pariah castes such as Paraiyans and the Pallans (Cronin 1959, p. 43).

10. The Vedic social system arranges society into four occupational divisions (four *varnas*) based on a person's qualities. These are Brahmana, Kshatriya, Vaishya and Shudra. Later on it morphed into a rigid caste system based on birth.

11. Constantine Joseph Beschi (1680–1747) was a linguist, apologist and theologian who showed imaginative mastery in retelling the Christian story in his famed *Tempavani* (The Unfading Garland), which retells the Christian story in an elegant Tamil style and with great originality from the viewpoint of Saint

Joseph. In the works of Jean Venance Bouchet (1655–1732) and Gaston-Laurent Coeurdoux (1691–1779), the missionary agenda is muted, even if Hinduism is inevitably still read through Western and Christian lenses. Bouchet was a Jesuit missionary in south India for over 40 years, largely in the initial decades of the eighteenth century.

12. Pressured by the royal courts of Portugal, France and Spain, Pope Clement XIV suppressed the Society of Jesus, causing Jesuits throughout the world to lose their communities, ministries and properties and often go into exile. Pope Pius VII restored the society on 7 August 1814.

13. Thomism refers to the theology and philosophy of Saint Thomas Aquinas (1224/25–1274), who formulated a synthesis of Aristotelian philosophy and Christian theology. His propositions led to various interpretations, usages and invocations by individuals, religious orders and schools.

14. Maharshi Panini is considered the progenitor of Sanskrit grammar.

15. Patanjali, a sage in ancient India and a renowned expert in Hindu philosophy from the Samkhya school, is thought to have lived during the fourth and fifth centuries CE and compiled several books in Sanskrit. He is credited with compiling the *Yoga Sutras*, a book on the philosophy and practice of yoga. His other major work is the *Mahabhashya*, a classic work on Sanskrit linguistics and grammar that was based on Panini's treatise on Sanskrit grammar. Vachaspati Mishra, born in the ninth century CE in the Mithila region, is considered a colossus among the Indian philosophers. He produced several commentaries on the Nyaya, Mimansa and Sankhya schools of Indian philosophy. He is also credited with producing a commentary on Shankaracharya's *Vedanta Sutras* and Patanjali's *Yoga Sutras*.

16. Vaishnav kitchen rules are traditions that govern food preparation and eating by enforcing strict caste rules.

17. 'Tha Hinduon ka shishya Isa, yeh pata bhi hai chala, Isaiyon ka dharm bhi hai Baudha sanche mein dhala' (It has also been found that Jesus was a disciple of Hindus. Christianity has been moulded in the frame of Buddhism) (Gupt 1912, p. 24).

18. Camille used both 'Allahabad' and 'Prayag' interchangeably to refer to the town.

19. Mataprasad Gupt's special fame in the Hindi world has been as an expert in Tulsidas' poetry and as a major proponent in textual criticism. His book on Tulsidas is considered one of the most authentic works on the Indian poet not only in the field of research but also in the context of criticism. He was a professor in the Department of Hindi at the University of Allahabad.

20. Vulgate refers to a commonly recognised text or version of a text, everyday or informal speech, or the vernacular. Vulgate Bible refers to a Latin version of the Bible authorised and used by the Roman Catholic Church.

21. Camille referred to the Bhagavad Gita, saying he should bear the *yogakshem* of his students. *Yogakshem* means to provide resources to achieve what one aspires and provide protection to what one already possesses.

Figure 1   Portraits of Father Camille Bulcke

Source: Father Camille Bulcke Research Centre, Ranchi.

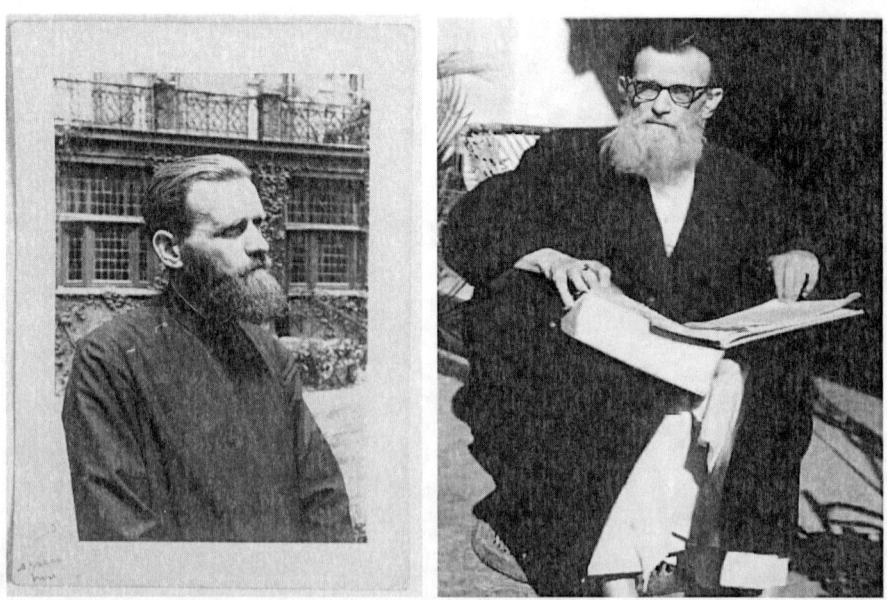

Figure 2   Father Camille Bulcke on the lawns of Manresa House, Ranchi

Source: Father Camille Bulcke Research Centre, Ranchi.

Figure 3   A young Camille Bulcke with his father and other relatives, Belgium, 1956

Source: Father Camille Bulcke Research Centre, Ranchi.

Figure 4   Father Camille Bulcke in his study at Manresa House, Ranchi

Source: Father Camille Bulcke Research Centre, Ranchi.

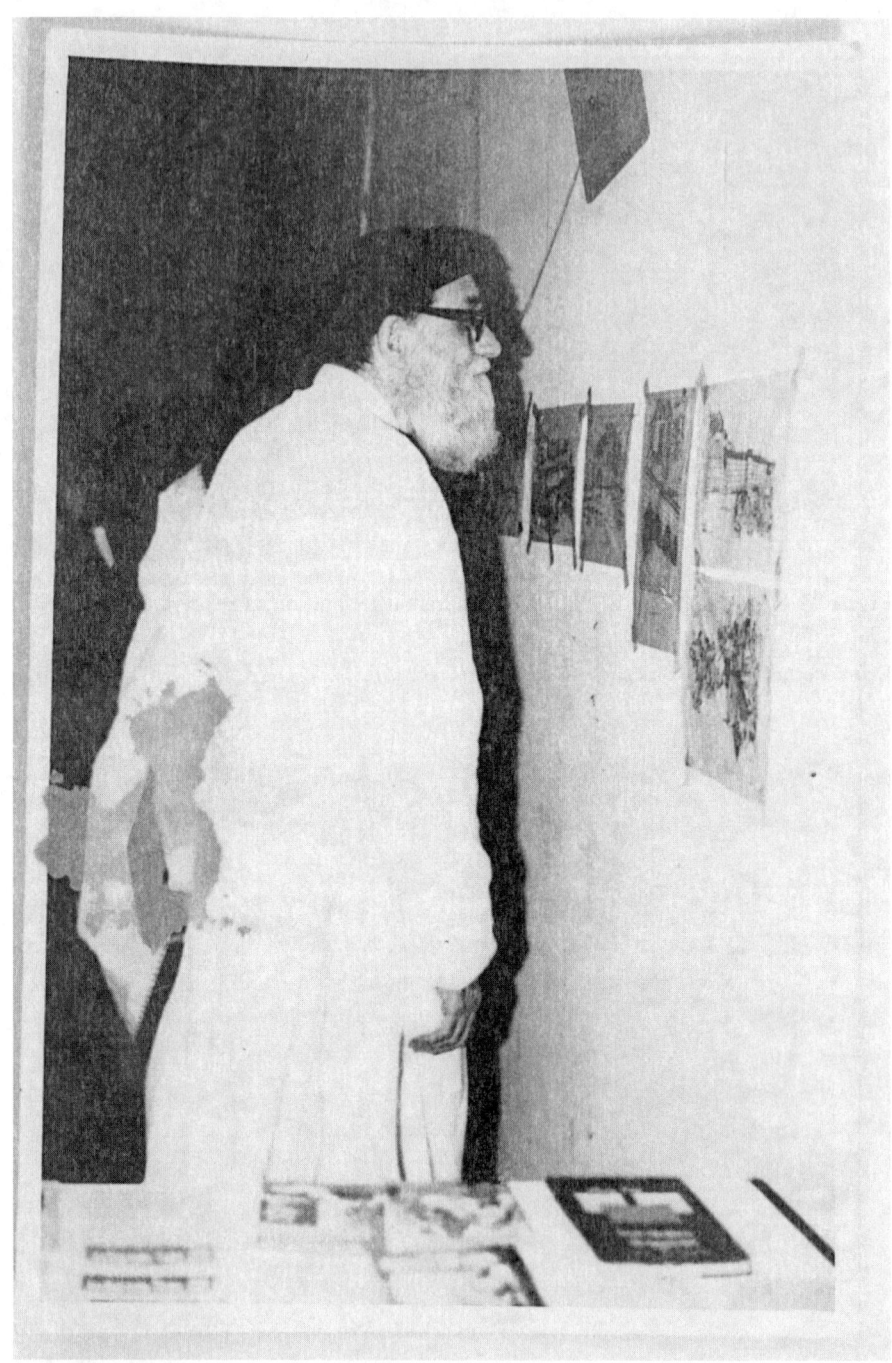

Figure 5 Father Camille Bulcke at an art exhibition
Source: Father Camille Bulcke Research Centre, Ranchi.

Figure 6   Father Camille Bulcke with his university friend K. L. Devriendt
Source: Father Camille Bulcke Research Centre, Ranchi.

Figure 7   Father Camille Bulcke with the Hindi authors Mahadevi Verma and Suryakant Tripathi 'Nirala'
Source: Father Camille Bulcke Research Centre, Ranchi.

Figure 8   Father Camille Bulcke with the Hindi author Radhakrishna, Ranchi
Source: Father Camille Bulcke Research Centre, Ranchi.

Figure 9 Dr Camille Bulcke Hindi Research Library at St Xavier's College, Ranchi
Source: Photograph by the authors.

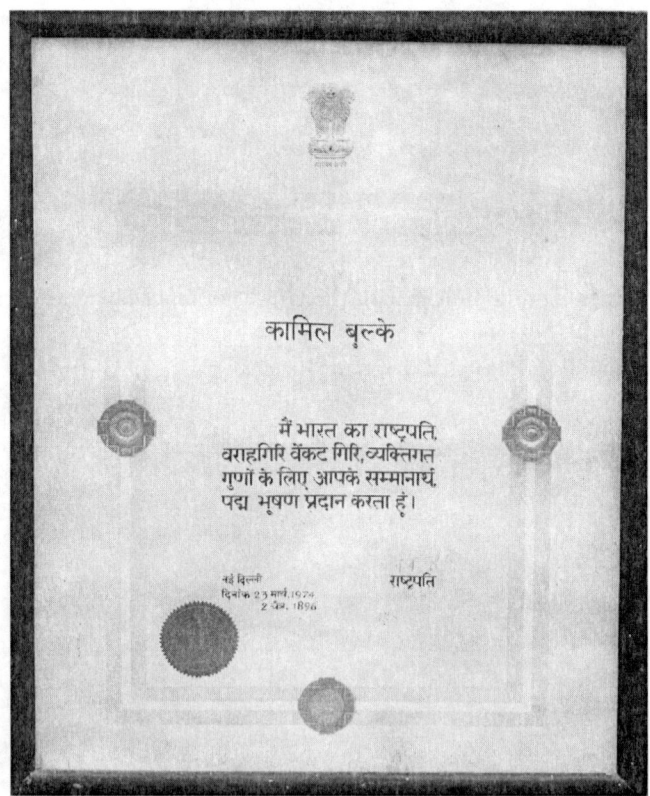

Figure 10 Father Camille Bulcke's Padma Bhushan certificate
Source: Father Camille Bulcke Research Centre, Ranchi.

Figure 11 Father Camille Bulcke's statue at Manresa House, Ranchi

Source: Photograph by the authors.

Figure 12 Prayer ceremony at Father Camille Bulcke's reburial, Ranchi, 2018

Source: Photograph by the authors.

Figure 13 Father Camille Bulcke's reburial procession, Ranchi, 2018
Source: Photograph by the authors.

Figure 14 Father Camille Bulcke's reburial ceremony, Ranchi, 2018

Source: Photograph by the authors.

Figure 15   Father Emmanuel Baxla, the director of the Father Camille Bulcke Research Centre, at Manresa House, Ranchi, 2023

Source: Photograph by the authors.

Figure 16   Father Emmanuel Baxla in Father Camille Bulcke's old room at Manresa House, Ranchi, 2023

Source: Photograph by the authors.

Figure 17   Father Camille Bulcke's bust at St Xavier's College, Ranchi

Source: Photograph by the authors.

4

⚛

From Christ *Bhakti* to Tulsidas' Rama *Bhakti*

Camille's Inspiration and Anchor

During his lifetime, Camille Bulcke appeared to be an enigma, leaving several of his acquaintances nonplussed to see a devout Christian, an ardent missionary and an ordained priest with such inherent and infinite reverence for Tulsidas and his Rama *bhakti*. Indeed, Indian spirituality and religious traditions have attracted a fair share of Westerners, who left their homes to adopt India and embrace its religious and cultural practices. This illustrious list includes luminaries such as Annie Besant (England-born Annie Wood), a renowned Theosophist and a prominent campaigner for Indian independence; Sister Nivedita (Irish-born Margaret Noble), who became the disciple of Swami Vivekananda; Mirra Alfassa, or the 'Mother' of Aurobindo Ashram, Pondicherry; and Mirabehn (Madeleine Slade), a follower of Mahatma Gandhi.[1] Undoubtedly, for these foreigners, India's cultural and spiritual values were the initial attractions, though most of them ended up participating in the independence movement that was pursuing self-respect, self-rule and anti-colonial nationalism. Camille was an exception; he joined the anti-colonial nationalist struggle but not as a political activist. Instead, he participated as a cultural campaigner seeking the respect and restoration of Hindi to its rightful place, by challenging the hegemony of English well beyond the formal end of British colonial rule. Unlike Sister Nivedita, Mirra Alfassa and Mirabehn, Camille came to India as a Christian missionary, and did not have a living person as his guide, mentor or patron; instead, he chose Tulsidas, a sixteenth-century Hindu devotional poet as his anchor.

Tulsidas as the core of Camille's personal, literary and spiritual life is all the more puzzling given that the Indian poet did not figure even remotely in Camille's world when he took the life-changing decision to renounce and become a Christian priest and later to take up missionary work in India. He considered it a divine command to give up worldly affairs and take his priestly vows, drawing inspiration from Father Constant Lievens, the well-known Belgian missionary who served in the Chhota Nagpur region in India.[2] It was only upon reaching India that Camille witnessed the hegemony of the colonial language, English, over the indigenous Indian languages. It reminded him of his own struggle during his student days for his mother tongue, Flemish, in Belgium, and he developed a natural affinity for the local language, Hindi. It was his prior commitment and personal pledge to oppose language hegemony that inspired him to not just take a firm stand for the honour of Hindi, but convinced him to master the language of the people. It was during the very early stages of learning Hindi that Camille discovered Tulsidas, his sublime poetry, the poet's devotion to Lord Rama and his spirit of *lokasangraha*,[3] or universal welfare and universal well-being.

However, despite Camille's oft-expressed adulation for Tulsidas, should one read only *Ramkatha: Utpatti Aur Vikas*, also considered his representative work, an astute or even a casual reader would conclude that the Indian poet is just one of the subsidiary sources to this work. Given Camille's self-proclaimed reverence and professed admiration for Tulsidas, one would imagine that the legendary Indian poet would eclipse all the other raconteurs, poets and writers of the *Ramkatha* in Camille's representative work. However, Camille's most popular contribution to Indology (also his PhD thesis and later book) puts all the limelight on Valmiki's Ramayana, while Tulsidas and his *Ramcharitmanas* are a mere sideshow. It would seem an anomaly that Tulsidas, Camille's most revered figure in all his later works, does not form the core of either his inquiry or his arguments about the *Ramkatha*.

This contradiction is all the more pronounced in the light of Camille's affirmation that his esteem for the *Ramkatha* was but an offshoot of his devotion to the poetic genius of Tulsidas. Therefore, it would be fascinating to explore how he developed such a single-minded and lifelong devotion towards Tulsidas, given that the Indian poet is not a significant presence in Camille's most celebrated work. Camille aimed to pursue his PhD on 'Tulsi's Devotion to Rama' and started to collect material on this topic (C. Bulcke 2009, p. 14). As the first part of his thesis, he intended to gather sources on the origin and genesis of the Rama story. He managed to collect such a broad range of unexplored material on the genesis of the Rama story that his supervisor asked him to develop only this aspect into a complete thesis. Thus, instead of focusing on Tulsidas and his devotion to Rama, Camille ended up exploring only the pre-Tulsidas phase of the development of the Rama story. Subsequent to the publication of his thesis and book, he began to focus exclusively on Tulsidas and his writings.

Camille explained the significance and import of the Indian poet to his life in one of his most popular articles, 'The Faith of a Christian: Devotion to Hindi and to Tulsi'. He narrated that several people seeking inspiration from the Sanskrit quotation 'अव्याहतानुयोगो मुनिजन', meaning that any question can be put to a sadhu, asked him all kinds of personal questions. 'Such as: learned though you are, how is it you have such a strong faith in Christ? Though you are a Christian how do you have such devotion to Tulsi?' (C. Bulcke 2010, p. 134). He was convinced that Christ, Hindi and Tulsidas reigned over his life and regulated his personal, literary and spiritual pursuits. He did not see any contradiction between his faith, the missionary activities and his scholarly work (ibid.). While Camille drew inspiration, peace and joy from the teachings of Christ, he wished to emulate Tulsidas' steadfastness and single-minded devotion to Lord Rama in his own devotion, or *bhakti*, to Christ, which he felt he lacked. This chapter highlights his relationship with Christ and Tulsidas and how he navigated such diverse religious and spiritual paths, unifying them in the process.

The more Camille learned about Tulsidas, the more enamoured he got, and the Indian poet emerged as a pivotal figure in Camille's personal, literary and spiritual pursuits. In this chapter, we look at how Camille developed such a strong and personal bond with an Indian poet who preceded him by some 500 years and explore the three different aspects of this association. In the first section, we explore how Camille's fascination with Tulsidas the littérateur not only led him to master Hindi, Brij Bhasha and Awadhi but also eventually brought about his thesis on the *Ramkatha*. The second section looks at how Camille's devotion to Christ was reinforced by following Tulsidas' devotion to Rama and its core elements. In the third section, we look at how Camille, a Christian missionary, emerged as the most ardent advocate and defender of some of the more problematic aspects of Tulsidas' faith, such as his ideas on the *varna* system, his harsh tone in describing women and his support for some of the traditionalist and conservative approaches to society and religion.

Tulsidas as the Ideal and Idol

Camille exalted Tulsidas as his idol for personal conduct, literary works and spiritual pursuits. He found a great resemblance between his own life and that of Tulsidas in their endeavour to follow the spiritual path through utmost devotion to their chosen deity (*isht devta*) and in their literary activities to express their love for God and humanity. Tulsidas appears as an idol for Camille, as an exemplar or criterion that he tried to live up to. No wonder, then, that Camille turned out to be one of the staunchest defenders of Tulsidas. On occasions, Camille would claim half in jest that it was ordained that he would devote his life to the *Ramkatha* given that he was born in Ramskapelle. To substantiate this claim, Camille posited that if Tulsidas was asked, 'Why is *Ramkatha* the research subject of Father Bulcke?' he would have certainly replied, 'Because God had encouraged him to do so' (C. Bulcke 2009, p. 13). Camille said while he could never dare to contradict his favourite poet, there was no divine communication goading him to 'go to India and do research on Ramkatha'; however, 'God presents such circumstances that we end up taking a specific course in life' (ibid.). As a young man, he was neither acquainted with the Devanagari script nor with its dialect Awadhi when he read the German translations of the following verse.

धन्य जनमु जगतीतल तासू। पितहि प्रमोदु चरित सुनि जासू॥
चारि पदारथ करतल ताकें। प्रिय पितु मातु प्रान सम जाकें॥

The birth in this world of one whose qualities fill the heart of his sire with heavenly bliss is a great good fortune. All the four achievements of this world – dharma, artha, kama and moksha – are within the palm of the hand of one who loves his parents like life itself. (C. Bulcke 2010, p. 140)

Enchanted, Camille read these words over and over again as he was deeply moved, and a niche in his heart was reserved for Tulsidas (ibid.). In 1938, three years since his arrival in India, Camille managed to read the whole text of the *Ramcharitmanas* and the *Vinaya Patrika* of Tulsidas. He believed that his 'attachment to Tulsidas, which started at that time and has never ceased growing since' was not just an emotional bond but one that inspired his 'literary and religious convictions' (ibid., p. 137). Little did he realise when he had read the German translation of Tulsidas' words that he was fated to 'follow this beautiful poet to his native land and taste the nectar of his great epic and sample the divine bliss that is *Ramcharitmanas*, and have the honour of appreciating the beauty of Tulsidas' (ibid., p. 140). Camille not only followed the poet to his native land but also, upon reading his poetry, realised that a wonderland had opened for him, which made an indelible mark on his heart and mind (ibid.).

In his reading of the *Ramcharitmanas*, Camille could identify with certain aspects of the narrative in his own life. His mother was a devout Christian who taught piety to her children from an early age; Camille believed that such an upbringing shaped his decision to become a Christian priest. His parents consented to his decision of renouncing the world; and sadly, he never saw his mother after 1935. Later, while reading the *Ramcharitmanas*, Camille came across the most apt description of his mother's resolve to offer her son in the service of the Lord.

पुत्रवती युवती जग सोई। रघुपति भगतु जासु सुत होई॥
नतरु बाँझ भलि बादि बिआनी। राम बिमुख सुत तें हित जानी॥

In the *Ramcharitmanas*, Tulsidas describes the moment when Lakshmana asked his mother's permission to give up his life at the royal palace and accompany Rama and Sita for their 14-year-long exile. Sumitra, Lakshmana's mother, replies, 'Only that woman is a mother in this world whose son is God's votary, else she better be barren' (ibid., p. 134).[4] Camille felt a strong connection upon reading these lines, and he was reminded of his own mother's resolve to stand by him when she heard that her eldest son had decided to walk on the religious path. Her pride and fortitude seemed like that of Sumitra (ibid.).

The more Camille delved deeper into the literature of Tulsidas, the more he came to identify his inner feelings, aspirations and his literary and religious convictions with the Indian poet. He considered his literary activities as part of his religious observance and claimed his writings and lexicography as something of a service to India. He often stated that 'in this world I have but one desire which is to be able to serve more and more people', and claimed that Tulsidas harboured the very same ambition (ibid., p. 136). To highlight the common aspiration he shared with Tulsidas, he cited one of the verses from the *Vinaya Patrika*.

कबहुंक हौं यहि रहनि रहौगो।
श्री रघुनाथ-कृपाल-कृपा तैं संत सुभाव गहौगो॥
जथा लाभ संतोष सदा काहू सों कछु न चहौगो॥
परहित निरत निरंतर मन क्रम बचन नेम निबहौगो॥

Oh, when shall I, with the grace of God, behave
As an ascetic should
Being satisfied with whatever, I get and desiring
Nothing from anybody. (Ibid.)

Another translation of the above verse is as follows.

When shall I get to lead such a life
With the grace of benevolent Rama (Raghunath),
Will I embrace the behaviour of a saint
Always content with whatever I get, and not desire anything form anyone
Constantly engaged in doing good to others, and observing the rules in
thought, deed and word. (Chhawchharia 2017, p. 575)

Tulsidas' belief in the mission to serve others and his claim that devotion
to God and morality in everyday life were reciprocal and co-constitutive
made Camille idolise the Indian poet. He acknowledged that it was his
devotion to Tulsidas that made him devote 'so many years to *Ramkatha*
literature' (C. Bulcke 2010, p. 137). Tulsidas was also his spiritual mentor,
and Camille affirmed that 'taking Tulsidas by hand, I am moving forward on
the path of my dedicated life' (ibid., pp. 138–139). He saw some similarities
between Tulsidas' devotion to Rama and his own devotion to Christ, though
he conceded rather ruefully that he was not as focused and determined as
Tulsidas. Camille's admiration for Tulsidas may be classified into four broad
themes, such as Tulsidas' use of the common man's language as against
Sanskrit, his idea of literature as part of devotion, his approach to devotion
and his take on the moral and ethical aspects of social life.

Tulsidas' Language of and for the People

Tulsidas chose to write in Awadhi, the language of the common people, instead
of Sanskrit, the preserve of the elite and erudite – something that resonated

with Camille. Like other major dialects from north India, Brij Bhasha and Awadhi too had produced eminent poets. However, most of the traditional religious, philosophical and spiritual texts were available only in Sanskrit. Tulsidas was a great Sanskrit scholar himself and had tremendous reverence for the classical language; yet he decided to write in Awadhi, the regional language of the common people. We want to emphasise that Bhakti poets all over India made this choice of writing in a modern language over Sanskrit, and yet they drew on Sanskrit sources. One among these poets, Tulsidas (like Jnaneswara)[5] also introduced many Sanskrit words, phrases, and Sanskritisms into his poetry. In the very beginning of the *Ramcharitmanas*, in *mangalacharan* (auspicious invocation, or benedictory verses), Tulsidas invokes Sanskrit to affirm his intention of using the common language for this composition. In this verse, he also declares the literary and oral sources on which his composition is based and his purpose for producing this literary text.

नानापुराणनिगमागमसम्मतं यद् रामायणे निगदितं क्वचिदन्यतोऽपि।
स्वान्तःसुखाय तुलसी रघुनाथगाथाभाषानिबन्धमतिमञ्जुलमातनोति॥

In accord with all the Puranas, Nigam (Vedas) and Agama (Tantras), and with what has been recorded in the Ramayana (of Valmiki) and elsewhere. I, Tulsidas, for his own soul's delight, have composed these exceedingly elegant lays of Raghunatha in modern speech. (Sharan 1950; R. Prasad 1988, p. 2)

In the very first seven verses of the *Ramcharitmanas*, in the *mangalacharan*, Tulsidas offers prayers to various deities for an auspicious beginning and the successful completion of his composition which is in Awadhi, the language of the common people in that region. Tulsidas believed that as a devotee, it was the purity of his devotion that mattered far more than any linguistic scholarship or erudition in Sanskrit, as he wrote in his famous collection of couplets called *Dohavali*.

का भाषा का संस्कृत, प्रेम चाहिए साँच।
काम जु आवै कामरी का लै करिए कुमांच॥

What language, what grammar? Only true love and true affection (along with true devotion, true faith and true dedication) is the only

language that is required by a person to sing the divine glories of the
Lord. If one can do with an ordinary blanket, then say, what is the use of
a costly shawl? (Chhawchharia 2015a, p. 524)

Tulsidas was unconventional in his approach to piety, devotion,
religiosity and his literary works, as most of his writings were either in local
dialects Awadhi or Brij Bhasha. He claimed that his true and steadfast love
for Lord Rama was superior to Sanskrit or any poetic skills. He likened the
colloquial language to a blanket as against the costly rug of Sanskrit and the
art of poetry to underline the futility of lofty words or intellectual hyperbole
when simple ideas and common language would connect better with the
masses (Bahadur 1995, p. 114). As a staunch votary for the marginalised or
non-elite languages, Camille was delighted to see Tulsidas' engagement with
the languages beyond the priestly and scholarly pale of Sanskrit.

स्याम सुरभि पय बिसद अति गुनद करहिं सब पान।
गिरा ग्राम्य सिय राम जस गावहिं सुनहिं सुजान॥

The milk of even a dark cow is white and possesses a great medicinal
value and is drunk by all. So do the wise chant and hear the glory of Sita
and Rama even though couched in the vulgar tongue. (Tulsidas 2001,
p. 13)[6]

Tulsidas expressed his gratitude to his predecessors who had produced
lyrical accounts in the praise of God, particularly to sage Valmiki for his
Ramayana, the most outstanding Sanskrit epic narrating the story of Rama.
However, he also offered his homage to the poets who created literature in
Prakrit[7] and other local dialects.

जे प्राकृत कबि परम सयाने। भाषाँ जिन्ह हरि चरित बखाने॥
भए जे अहहिं जे होइहहिं आगें। प्रनवउँ सबहि कपट सब त्यागें॥

Even those poets of supreme wisdom who belong to the Prakrata or
popular class (as opposed to the Sanskrit or the cultured class), who
have narrated the exploits of Sri Hari in the spoken language, including
those who have flourished in the past, those who are still living and
those who are yet to come. (Ibid., p. 16)

Undoubtedly, Tulsidas' reverence for the marginalised or the supposedly inferior but the more popular languages would have found common cause with Camille. However, Camille underlined that the legendary poet realised that his use of colloquial language and his disavowal of the classical poetic traditions would attract ridicule from the elite sections of society. In the very beginning of the *Ramcharitmanas*, Tulsidas declares his choice of language.

भाषा भनिति मोरी मति थोरी। हँसिबो जोग हांसे नहिं खोरी॥

My composition is couched in the popular dialect and my intellect is feeble; hence it is a fit subject for ridicule, and those who laugh shall not incur any blame. (Ibid., p. 11)

सरल कबित कीरति बिमल सोइ आदरहिं सुजान।
सहज बयर बिसराइ रिपु जो सुनि करहिं बखान॥

The wise admire only that poetry which is lucid and portrays a spotless character and which even opponents hear with applause forgetting natural animosity. (Ibid., p. 16)

Camille underlined that the beauty and humility of Tulsidas' poetry is not only that he composed in the local language but also the fact that he never claimed to possess any poetic genius. He cited several verses from the *Ramcharitmanas*, where Tulsidas averred that he did not consider himself a poet.

कबि न होउँ नहिं बचन प्रबीनू। सकल कला सब बिद्या हीनू॥
आखर अरथ अलंकृति नाना। छंद प्रबंध अनेक बिधाना॥
भाव भेद रस भेद अपारा। कबित दोष गुन बिबिध प्रकारा॥
कबित बिबेक एक नहिं मोरें। सत्य कहउँ लिखि कागद कोरें॥

I am no poet, nor am I adept in the art of speech; and am a cipher in all arts and sciences. There are elegant devices of letters, subtleties of meaning, various figures of speech, metrical compositions of different kinds, infinite varieties of motions and sentiments, and all sorts of defects and excellences of verse. I possess no judgement in the art of poesy, I vouch for it on a blank paper. (R. Prasad 1988, p. 10)

Camille argued that contrary to his claim of lacking poetic skills, Tulsidas 'has a supreme felicity of expression, and that is why dozens and dozens of his verses have become proverbs' (C. Bulcke 2010, p. 146). To substantiate his arguments, Camille cited numerous verses from several of Tulsidas' works to highlight the poet's marvellous gift of effortless alliteration and how his verses flow naturally. One of Tulsidas' greatest literary gifts was the ease with which he simplified the Sanskrit terms into the dialect and yet maintained the metrical structure and sonorous harmony of the verse. Camille posited that like Valmiki, Tulsidas is a people's poet; his verse is mellifluous and simpler than prose, and his language is so simple that even an illiterate villager can understand not just the meaning but also the messages in his poetry (C. Bulcke 2009, p. 72). Tulsidas deploys rustic phrases and conversational terms to represent traditional wisdom, complicated philosophical tenets and Sanskrit maxims in his poetry, while 'eternal truths and moral aphorisms abound, but the construction of his verse is never involved' (C. Bulcke 2010, p. 146). The innate beauty and natural mellifluence in his poetry is not his conscious effort or intellectual endeavour, though, as Tulsidas claimed,

अस मानस मानस चख चाही। भइ कबि बुद्धि बिमल अवगाही॥
भयउ हृदयँ आनंद उछाहू। उमगेउ प्रेम प्रमोद प्रबाहू॥
चली सुभग कबिता सरिता सो। राम बिमल जस जल भरिता सो॥

Having seen the said Manasa Lake with the mind's eye and taken a dip in it, the poet's understanding got purged of all its dross. The heart was filled with joy and ecstasy and a torrent of love and rapture welled from it. Then from that lake a stream of beautiful poetry, carrying the water of Rama's fair glory flows out. (R. Prasad 1988, p. 34)

Camille cited this verse quite extensively in his writing on Tulsidas to posit that great poetry is not fashioned in the mind, but emerges from the heart. Poetry from the mind is no more than intellectual gymnastics or literary flourish (C. Bulcke 2009, p. 79).

Undoubtedly, the fact that Tulsidas challenged the hegemony of Sanskrit and flouted the rigid literary norms in his writings were sufficient reasons for Camille to consider him an icon. Moreover, the fact that despite challenging the prevalent hegemony, Tulsidas never appeared arrogant or hostile, instead full of grace and humility, is what Camille found most endearing. Like other literary figures, even Tulsidas battled self-doubt, or what is known as the 'impostor syndrome' in contemporary times; he was worried about the public reception of his poetry.

निज कबित्त केहि लाग न नीका। सरस होउ अथवा अति फीका॥
जे पर भनिति सुनत हरषाहीं। ते बर पुरुष बहुत जग नाहीं॥

Who does not like his own verses, be they delightful or exceedingly insipid? Those good people who are pleased when they hear others' compositions are rare in the world. (R. Prasad 1988, p. 9).

This self-doubt was a reflection of the author's anxiety and his desire to get appreciation from the ordinary people in whose language and for whom he was writing. Tulsidas then asks the wise and saintly people to bestow their blessings on his poetry (C. Bulcke 2009, p. 53).

होहु प्रसन्न देहु बरदानू। साधु समाज भनिति सनमानू॥
जो प्रबंध बुध नहिं आदरहीं। सो श्रम बादि बाल कबि करहीं॥

Be propitious and grant this boon that my song may be honoured in the assemblage of pious souls. A composition which the wise refuse to honour is fruitless labour which only silly poets undertake. (Tulsidas 2001, p. 16)

On the one hand, while Tulsidas was concerned about using language appropriately, his poetry epitomises his innate and infinite compassion for his fellow beings. As Camille explained, 'Tulsi had a particularly sensitive heart. He had nothing but good will for everybody and regarded poetry successful only if it promoted happiness all around' (C. Bulcke 2010, p. 141). Camille argued that most of the Western and Indian scholars of literature and poetics concur that the objective of poetry is not entertainment but to provide constructive knowledge.

कीरति भनिति भूति भलि सोई। सुरसरि सम सब कहँ हित होई॥
राम सुकीरति भनिति भदेसा। असमंजस अस मोहि अँदेसा॥

Of glory, poetry and affluence that alone is blessed that is like the celestial river (Ganga), is conducive to the good of all. The glory of Sri Rama is charming indeed, but my verses are clumsy; such disparity fills me with anxious doubt. (R. Prasad 1998, p. 14; Tulsidas 2001, p. 16)

This is one of the most cited verses of Tulsidas by Camille, to establish the fact that while Tulsidas claims that he composed the *Ramcharitmanas* for his own satisfaction, his composition does not accept 'the principle of art for art's sake, of an aimless art' (C. Bulcke 2010, p. 137). Camille posited that art and literature represent mankind's treasured acquisitions, 'through which man expresses his high deals and profound experiences' (ibid.). While the task of art and literature is to create beauty, for a man of faith, the loftier goal is sublimating earth's finite beauty with infinite beauty. Camille lauded Tulsidas as one of the most exceptional poets who successfully merges the finite earthly beauty with the infinite celestial beauty. As a man of faith, Camille argues that any literature that only addresses the sensory pleasures and one that impedes the spiritual progress of mankind is not authentic literature (C. Bulcke 2009, p. 43).

Camille considered Tulsidas an exemplary poet because in all his writings he attempted to foreground the quest for infinite beauty among people by motivating them to take the rightful path for their own welfare. Camille viewed the constant urging by Tulsidas to seek infinite beauty through devotion to Lord Rama as his commitment to bringing welfare to the common people. Moreover, he considered the promotion of the welfare of the public as the defining characteristic of the exalted literary traditions and accordingly declared Tulsidas as the best representative of such a literary tradition (C. Bulcke 2010, p. 137).

मंगल करनि कलिमल हरनि तुलसी कथा रघुनाथ की।
गति कूर कबिता सरित की ज्यों सरित पावन पाथ की॥
प्रभु सुजस संगति भनिति भलि होइहि सुजन मन भावनी
भव अंग भूति मसान की सुमिरत सुहावनि पावनी॥

The tale of the Lord of Raghus, O, Tulsidas, brings forth blessings and wipes away the impurities of the Kali age (Kaliyug). The course of this stream of my poetry is tortuous like that of holy Ganga. By its association with the auspicious glory of the Lord, my composition will be blessed and will captivate the mind of the virtuous. On the person of Lord Shiva, even the ashes of the cremation-ground appear charming and purify by the very thought. (Tulsidas 2001, p. 13)

In the context of this verse, Camille argued that contrary to Tulsidas' avowal of composing the *Ramcharitmanas* for his own satisfaction, he was in fact driven by the desire to promote welfare and to bring happiness to the masses. He wanted to serve the ordinary people, and hence Tulsidas refrained from composing in Sanskrit and engaged with common parlance (C. Bulcke 2009, p. 53). Moreover, Tulsidas never claimed to have any of the acclaimed poetic skills, and as Camille highlights, he had attributed any literary flair to the divine will (ibid., p. 37).

संभु प्रसाद सुमति हियँ हुलसी। रामचरितमानस कबि तुलसी॥
करइ मनोहर मति अनुहारी। सुजन सुचित सुनि लेहु सुधारी॥

By the grace of Sambhu (Lord Shiva), a blessed idea inspired the mind of Tulsidas, which made him the author of *Ramcharitmanas*. The author has polished his composition to the best of his intellect; yet listen to it with a sympathetic mind, O noble souls, and correct it. (Tulsidas 2001, p. 35)

Camille believes that Tulsidas considered literary talents as a divine gift and decided not to waste it on worldly people, kings, emperors or feudal lords (C. Bulcke 2009, p. 53). Instead, Tulsidas put his poetic faculties to promote the welfare of the common people by writing in a simple language understood by ordinary people (ibid., p. 80).

कीन्हें प्राकृत जन गुन गाना। सिर धुनि गिरा लगत पछिताना॥
हृदय सिंधु मति सीप समाना। स्वाति सारदा कहहिं सुजाना॥

If one recounts the doing of common people, Sarasvati beats her brow and repents her coming. The wise liken the heart of a poet to a sea, his intellect to the shell containing pearls and Sarasvati to the rain that falls under Arcturus' influence. (R. Prasad 1988, p. 12)

Tulsidas did not spend his energy on writing the glories of worldly men and their mundane activities; instead, he devoted all his literary talents to expressing his affection, concern and compassion for his fellow beings. Camille argued that any poet who is filled with kindness and writes for the welfare of common people will not squander their talents on inventing new idioms, innovating ingenious proverbs or devising new literary expressions

(C. Bulcke 2009, p. 80). Furthermore, Camille claimed that Tulsidas 'firmly believed that man attained happiness only if his actions were in accord with the almighty' (C. Bulcke 2010, p. 142). To this purpose, Tulsidas used 'his unusual perception of beauty and extraordinary poetic gifts to awaken and develop love of God in man' (ibid.). Camille believed that the three major attractions for Tulsidas were his choice of local dialect over Sanskrit, his decision to not write a religious treatise or to glorify some rich or powerful patron and his pledge to bring welfare to the common people by propagating devotion to God in the simplest and most elementary forms, as was popularised by the Bhakti movement of those times. Undoubtedly, it was his propagation of the path of devotion for common people in their everyday language that captivated Camille, making the Christian missionary an ardent devotee of the Hindu devotional poet.

Core Ideals of Tulsidas' Devotion

Camille emphasised the devotional approach of Tulsidas as the most important factor that drew him to the great poet. As a religious man, a devotee of Christ and a spiritual seeker, he drew inspiration from Tulsidas' devotional approach for its simplicity, magnanimity and tenacity. As a believer in God, Camille concurred with Tulsidas' view that the ultimate objective of human life on this earth was to attain salvation, despite the doctrinaire differences over the idea of salvation in the Christian and Hindu beliefs (C. Bulcke 2009, p. 77).

बड़ें भाग मानुष तनु पावा। सुर दुर्लभ सब ग्रंथन्हि गावा॥
साधन धाम मोच्छ कर द्वारा। पाइ न जेहिं परलोक सँवारा॥ ॥
सो परत्र दुख पावइ सिर धुनि धुनि पछिताई।
कालहि कर्महि ईस्वरहि मिथ्या दोष लगाइ॥ ॥

It is great good fortune that you have secured a human body, which – as all the scriptures declare – is difficult even for the gods to attain. It is a tabernacle suitable for spiritual endeavours, the gateway to deliverance; and he who receives it and still wins not heaven, reaps torment in the next world and beats his head in vain remorse, wrongly attributing the blame to time, fate and God. (R. Prasad 1988, p. 715)

Tulsidas considered human life as the best form and opportunity to attain the highest form of devotion to Lord Rama. He wrote,

नर तन सम नहिं कवनिउ देही। जीव चराचर जाचत तेही॥
नरक स्वर्ग अपबर्ग निसेनी। ग्यान बिराग भगति सुभ देनी॥

There is no other form as good as the human body, every living creature – whether animate or inanimate – craves for it. It is the ladder that takes the soul either to hell or heaven or to final liberation, and is the bestower of the blessings of wisdom, dispassion and devotion. (R. Prasad 1988, p. 780; Tulsidas 2001, p. 773)

Camille argued that in the *Vinaya Patrika*, too, Tulsidas praises human life but only as a useful form to seek devotion to Lord Rama. The ultimate aim of human life is to achieve salvation, which according to Tulsidas is love and surrender to Rama. There is no purpose of acquiring the human body if one does not develop devotion to and affection for Rama.

जो अनुराग न राम सनेही सों
तौ लह्यो लाहु कहा नर-देही सों

What is the benefit (utility, purpose, fruit) of acquiring a human body if one does not have (or does not develop) affection and endearment for the most affectionate and dearest Lord Sri Rama? (Chhawchharia 2017, p. 645)

Tulsidas never tried to create an immortal poem; instead, he offered an exposition of the glorious pathway of devotion to God as the only way of salvation. As an ardent devotee and a very generous person, he was pained to see common people getting waylaid with complicated yogic practices, confused by various esoteric doctrines and misled by 'the many sects, each with its own ritual and philosophical tenets' (C. Bulcke 2010, p. 146). Camille cited one of Tulsidas' most renowned works, the *Vinaya Patrika*, to highlight what is authentic religion in its simplest form.

बहु मत मुनि पंथ पुराननि जहाँ-तहाँ झगरो सो।
गुरु कह्यो राम-भजन नीको मोहिं लगत राज-डगरो सो॥

The munis (sages) propound many opinions, there are many ways of salvation described in the Puranas and also quite a lot of bickering. My guru told me devotion to Rama is the best way. To me it seems to be the royal road to salvation. (Ibid.)

Tulsidas claimed that this devotional approach (*bhakti marga*), or the surrender to Lord Rama, is the pathway available to everyone and would ensure the salvation of the devotee. He considered salvation as the foremost duty or primary responsibility of everyone born into this world and expounded the idea of devotion (*bhakti*) as the simple, straightforward and easy path towards that objective.

Camille argued that Tulsidas' devotional approach had 'certain characteristics, which made it a truly royal road to God and must have been instrumental in the salvation of missions' (ibid., p. 147). This path offered a direct and affordable path to God; on several occasions, Tulsidas had reiterated this was the easy access to God which even the sages, Vedas and other sacred texts fail to explain. Camille cited the following verses to highlight that for Tulsidas, real devotion meant simple, pure and genuine love for nothing but Lord Rama.

निगम अगम, साहब सुगम, राम साँचिली चाह।
अंबु असन अवलोकियत सुलभ सबै जग माँह॥

The Lord whom even the Vedas cannot grasp, the same Rama is easily accessible to ones with true longing. Just like how nature provides for water and grains for every mortal born into this world. (Bahadur 1997a, p. 10)

Camille underlined that while Tulsidas mentions the other ways of salvation, such as the knowledge approach (*gyana marg*) or through the sacred rituals (*karma marg*) or the practices of other sects, he highlights the great benefits of the devotional approach (C. Bulcke 2010, p. 151). Tulsidas was 'not an eclectic and did not aim at reconciling various religious systems'; however, he has 'unequivocally proclaimed the supremacy and indispensability of bhakti, and stressed the futility of knowledge and religious practices, if one is without bhakti' (ibid.).

ग्यान अगम प्रत्यूह अनेका। साधन कठिन न मन कहुँ टेका॥
करत कष्ट बहु पावइ कोऊ। भक्ति हीन मोहि प्रिय नहिं सोऊ॥

The way of knowledge is difficult to pursue and beset with numerous impediments; its appliances are cumbrous and there is no sure footing for the mind to rest on. There are some who do with infinite trouble attain wisdom, yet, lacking in faith, they fail to win my love. (R. Prasad 1988, p. 716)

Tulsidas posits that only by rigorous mental and intellectual endeavours can one acquire knowledge; the path to wisdom (*gyan*) is extremely difficult because it only provides intellectual stimulation and gives no support to the heart or human emotions. Moreover, despite making such strenuous efforts, only a few achieve erudition, and even among the learned people most are filled with pride and pomposity. Therefore, for a devotee like Tulsidas any intellectual or physical labour that does not seek divine love is not a worthy pursuit (Bahadur 1994, p. 333). Tulsidas warns about the pitfalls along the way for people who seek wisdom as the only path to salvation.

ग्यान पंथ कृपान कै धारा। परत खगेस होइ नहिं बारा॥
जो निर्बिघ्न पंथ निर्बहई। सो कैवल्य परम पद लहई॥

The path of wisdom is like the edge of a sword: one is apt to fall from it very soon, O king of birds. He alone who successfully treads it attains to the supreme state of final emancipation. (Tulsidas 2001, p. 770)

Camille used to quote this verse from Tulsidas to highlight the extreme difficulty in attaining salvation only through the accumulation of knowledge; it is like walking on a razor's edge. Although himself an intellectual and a renowned scholar, Camille found greater affinity with the simple devotion propounded by Tulsidas as an effectual way to seek closeness with the divine and salvation.

वाक्य ज्ञान अत्यंत निपुण, भव पार न पावै कोई।
निशि गृह मध्य दीप की बातन्ह, तम निवृत्त नहीं होई॥

Discussions about religious knowledge, however, clever they may be, will not help anyone to cross the ocean of rebirth. By discussing about light in a dark house, you will not be able to drive away the darkness. (C. Bulcke 2010, p. 152)

Camille used this verse to highlight that in order to propound his devotional approach, Tulsidas did not write a theological treatise but asked people instead to search for God with true longing and genuine love. Like Tulsidas' simple poetry written using the dialect, this devotion too was simple – attainable for everyone with simplicity and sincerity of mind, words and deeds (C. Bulcke 2009, p. 77).

सूधे मन सूधे बचन सूधी सब करतूति।
तुलसी सूधी सकल बिधि रघुबर प्रेम प्रसूति॥

One whose heart is simple, speech is sweet, and actions are gentle and kind – Tulsidas says that such virtuous people will find ways of devotion for Lord Rama's love with ease. (Bahadur 1997a, p. 17)

Camille highlighted that in his *Ramcharitmanas*, Tulsidas showed Lord Rama himself explaining the simplicity of the path of devotion to the people of his kingdom, Ayodhya.

जौं परलोक इहाँ सुख चहहू। सुनि मम बचन हृदयँ दृढ़ गहहू॥
सुलभ सुखद मारग यह भाई। भगति मोरि पुरान श्रुति गाई॥

If you seek happiness here as well as hereafter, listen to my words and imprint them deeply in your heart. The way of devotion to me, my brothers, is an easy and pleasant road, as extolled in the Puranas and Vedas. (R. Prasad 1988, p. 716; Tulsidas 2001, p. 711)

कहहु भगति पथ कवन प्रयासा। जोग न मख जप तप उपवासा।
सरल सुभाव न मन कुटिलाई। जथा लाभ संतोष सदाई॥ ॥

Tell me what pains are involved in treading the path of devotion: it requires neither yoga (mind-control), nor sacrifices, nor japa (muttering of prayers), nor penance, nor fasting. A guileless disposition, a mind free from perversity and absolute contentment with whatever may be got – this is all that is needed. (Tulsidas 2001, p. 711)

Having described the essential elements of devotion, Rama elaborates on the characteristics of his devotee.

बहुत कहउँ का कथा बढ़ाई। एहि आचरन बस्य मैं भाई॥
बैर न बिग्रह आस न त्रासा। सुखमय ताहि सदा सब आसा॥
अनारंभ अनिकेत अमानी। अनघ अरोष दच्छ बिग्यानी॥
प्रीति सदा सज्जन संसर्गा। तृन सम बिषय स्वर्ग अपबर्गा॥
भगति पच्छ हठ नहिं सठताई। दुष्ट तर्क सब दूरि बहाई॥

Lord Rama says, brethren, instead of giving a long disposition on devotion, I narrate the conduct of a man through which I am won over by my devotee. One who has no enmity, has no quarrel with anyone and is devoid of hope and fear, to such a man all quarters are ever full of joy. One who does not start any action for personal gain and is without home, without pride and without sin, free from wrath, clever and wise, ever loving the company of saints and accounting the enjoyments even of heavens as well as final beatitude as no more than a blade of grass, persistent in faith and innocent of folly, giving up all contentious arguments. (R. Prasad 1988, pp. 716–717; Tulsidas 2001, pp. 711–712)

The simplicity of such devotion made the complex rituals, onerous yogic practices, arduous pilgrimages and ornate ceremonies futile to the real purpose of finding love for God. Camille admired Tulsidas' pursuit of love for God as devotion over the ostentatious, symbolic, performative and ritualistic aspects of religiosity.

जोग, जाप, जप, विराग, तप, सुतीरथ-अटत
बाँधिबे को भव-गयन्द रेनु की रजु बटत

Yoga practices, nightly vigils, recitations of sacred formulas, austerities and visiting pilgrimage – all these are as useless, as if one would endeavour to twine a rope with sand, in order to tie up the elephant of rebirth. (C. Bulcke 2010, p. 152)

Indeed, just like one cannot tie an elephant with a rope made of sand particles, it is also impossible to seek deliverance from the world through different practices. Tulsidas defined devotion as genuine love for Lord Rama and argued that this devotion was mandatory to achieve any spiritual progress while the other religious rituals and formalities were mere distractions.

प्रेम भगति जल बिनु रघुराई। अभिअंतर मल कबहुँ न जाई॥

So Raghurai, without the water of living devotion, the inner man cannot be cleansed of defilement. (Ibid., p. 151)

Camille explained that for Tulsidas, the simple and pure devotion to Lord Rama was the panacea and it is easily accessible to all. The overt religiosity or ritualistic performances could not cleanse the accumulated impurities; only the cleansing water of love and devotion could wash them away (R. Prasad, 1988, p. 718).

संजम, जप, तप, नेम, धरम, ब्रत बहु भेषज-समुदाई।
तुलसिदास भव-रोग रामपद-प्रेम-हीन नहिं जाई॥

Tulsidas says that there are many remedies such as self-control, recitation of sacred formulas, austerities, observances, religious practices and vows, but none of them will cure the disease of rebirth, unless there be loving devotion at the feet of Rama (C. Bulcke 2010, p. 152).

नाहिंन आवत आन भरोसो।
यहि कलिकाल सकल साधनतरु है स्रम - फलनि फरो सो॥
तप, तीरथ, उपवास, दान, मख जेहि जो रुचै करो सो।
पायेहि पै जानिबो करम – फल भरि – भरि बेद परोसो॥

I don't have any trust on other means (for attaining liberation) since in this period of misery (Kaliyug), all these means and paths that promise salvation are like the trees that do not bear fruits of exaltation but of mere exertion. According to an individual's likings a person may engage with various rituals and religious practices such as austerities, penance, pilgrimage, charity, fasting, yagya (homa). According to the Vedas, these spiritual paths and auspicious deeds would deliver abundant results only when these rituals are done properly and fully. (Bahadur 1995, p. 99)

In this verse, Tulsidas underlines the fact that while the different religious practices and rituals are approved by the Vedas, in the Kaliyuga these sacred deeds are rendered ineffective. There are two reasons that invalidate the efficacy of the sacred acts; first, in the Kaliyuga, the illusory power, or *maya*, creates obstacles such as attachment to earthly relations and riches (ibid., p. 283). Moreover, in the Kaliyuga, the actual performance of the sacred deeds with the prescribed levels of piety, procedure, perfection and paraphernalia is nearly impossible to attain. Hence, despite all the exertions, these arduous and cumbersome exercises do not deliver the promised benefits.

बलिपूजा चाहत नहीं, चाहत एक प्रीति । सुमिरत ही मानै भलो, पावन सब रीति॥

The Lord does not want or expect anyone to offer any kind of (animal) sacrifices or formality of ritualistic worship to please and honour him, but the only thing that he wants and expects is 'love and affection'. He becomes pleased as soon as one merely remembers him, and in return he purifies that person in all possible ways and frees him from all his worries. (Chhawchharia 2017, p. 356)

जानपनी को गुमान बड़ो, तुलसी के विचार गंवार महा है।
जानकीजीवन जान न जान्यौ तौ जान कहावत जान्यो कहा है॥

'You seem to be very proud of your wisdom', but according to Tulsidas, 'you are a great fool. If you could not realise (the true nature of) Lord Rama, then you have not actually realised anything.' (Chhawchharia 2015b, p. 356)

In this verse, Tusidas censures those self-proclaimed erudite men who use their wisdom to talk about lofty ideals of divine knowledge yet they are engaged in petty worldly gains. Tulsidas asserts that the final objective of 'all knowledge is the revelation of divinity. Divinity is Rama. Therefore, if their knowledge has not revealed Rama, singing his songs and repeating his holy name, what has knowledge taught them?' (Bahadur 1997a, p. 115)

बारि मथें घृत होइ बरु सिकता ते बरु तेल।
बिनु हरि भजन न तव तरिअ यह सिद्धांत अपेल॥

Sooner may ghee be produced by churning water, or oil by crushing sand, than the ocean of worldy existence be traversed without worshipping Hari. This is an irrefutable doctrine. (R. Prasad 1988, p. 783)

ग्यान - बिराग, जोग - जप, तप - मख, जग मुद - मग नहिं थोरे।
राम - प्रेम बिनु नेम जाय जैसे मृग - जल - जलधि - हिलोरे॥

Knowledge, renunciation, yoga (meditation), recitation of sacred mantras, penances and austerities, religious sacrifices and rituals are all prescribed paths to achieve salvation or spiritual liberation. However, without love and affection for the name of Lord Rama, they are mirages; like imagining currents of water on the surface of a hot desert sand. (Chhawchharia 2017, p. 646)

While acknowldging the prevalence and sanction of various rituals and religious practices, Tulsidas asserts that all these are mere optical illusions that do not bring true bliss to its practitioners. Instead, the path of divine enlightenment is having true devotion and genuine affection for Lord Rama.

तुलसी जौं पै राम सों, नाहिन सहज सनेह।
मूंड़ मुड़ायो बादिहीं, भाँड़ भयो तजि गेह॥

Tulsidas argues that if one does not have spontaneous and steadfast love for Lord Rama, there is no purpose of merely shaving the head, wearing the hermit's garb and dwelling in the woods. (Bahadur 1997b, p. 8)

Tulsidas declares that it is futile for one to assume semblances of renunciants such as renouncing worldly life, dwelling in the woods and having their heads shaved if they do not bear true love for Rama in their hearts (ibid., p. 85). He was aware of the various remedies to overcome the spiritual malaise as prescribed in the scriptures and available in traditional wisdom. As Camille underlined, while Tulsidas acknowledged the popular modes of religious and sacred practices such as self-control, chanting of holy mantras, penances, austerities and fasting, he asserted that only love and devotion to the holy feet of Rama would help in removing the attachment to this delusory world. Tulsidas was against the elaborate rituals that had emerged as instruments to fleece human beings. According to Camille, Tulsidas always maintained that in the present epoch, known as the Kaliyuga, only the true devotion to Rama's name would provide salvation (C. Bulcke 1977a, p. 58).

दम दुर्गम, दान दया मखकर्म सुधर्म अधीन सबै धन को।
तप तीरथ साधन जोग बिराग सों होइ नहीं दृढ़ता तन को॥

कलिकाल कराल में, राम कृपालु! यहै अवलंब बड़ो मन को।
तुलसी सब संजम-हीन सबै, एक नाम अधार सदा जन को॥

Indeed, restraint is arduous; while charity, kindness, yagna, religious acts and sacred deeds require wealth. While penance, discipline, pilgrimage, austere yogic practices require great physical and mental strengths. In these vile and harsh times of Kaliyuga, Lord Ram's is the only haven. Tulsidas says when everyone lacks continence, it is only one name that can fend for the saints. (Bahadur 1997b, p. 64)

Tulsidas recognised the popularity of the rituals and religious practices, but he considered them as futile diversions that prevented people from acquiring pure love and, hence, true devotion to God. One may argue that while he could somehow endure these customs despite their superficiality, he could not stand the impostors masquerading as mystics or as godmen. On several occasions, Tulsidas cautioned ordinary people not to fall for the gimmickry or fake religiosity of these charlatans – an advice that would be especially valuable in these times when such people have acquired extraordinary power and popularity in public life. He likened the popularity of such devious people as a sign of moral decay or the period of decay referred to as the Kaliyuga (C. Bulcke 1977a, p. 58).

निराचार जो श्रुति पथ त्यागी। कलिजुग सोइ ग्यानी सो बिरागी॥
जाकें नख अरु जटा बिसाला। सोइ तापस प्रसिद्ध कलिकाला॥
असुभ बेष भूषन धरें भच्छाभच्छ जे खाहिं।
तेइ जोगी तेइ सिद्ध नर पूज्य ते कलिजुग माहिं॥

A reprobate who has abandoned the Vedic ways is a man of wisdom and dispassion in that Kaliyuga, and he who has grown long nails and bound his hair in massive coils is a renowned ascetic in those evil days. Those who clothe themselves in grisly rags and deck themselves in appalling adornments and feed indiscriminately on any kind of food, forbidden or permitted, are ascetics and adepts and object of veneration in that age. (R. Prasad 1988, p. 754)

Tulsidas called his *bhakti marg* a highway because all human beings have the right to walk on it and it needs no special stage of life. Never once did he demean those who lead a householder's life or a worldly person vis-à-vis a hermit or an ascetic; on the contrary, he holds the *grihastha* (ordinary householder) in high esteem. To underline Tulsidas' admiration for ordinary householders over the *sanyasi* (ascetic), Camille cites a verse from the 'Ayodhyakand' of the *Ramcharitmanas*, where Bharata is exalted as an ideal devotee. Tulsidas describes that while Rama, Lakshmana and Sita practise penance in the forest, it is Bharata who rules the kingdom, performs his normal duties and yet observes all the austerities and penances. Comparing the austere lifestyles of Rama and Bharata, Tulsidas gives his verdict in favour of Bharata and claims that 'looking at this matter from both sides, all said that Bharata was in every way worthy of praise' (C. Bulcke, 2010, p. 149).

लखन राम सिय कानन बसहीं। भरतु भवन बसि तप तनु कसहीं॥
दोउ दिसि समुझि कहत सबु लोगू। सब बिधि भरत सराहन जोगू॥

Lakshmana, Sri Rama and Sita dwelt in the forest; Bharata, living at home, mortified his flesh with austerities. After considering both sides, everyone said that Bharata was praiseworthy in every way. (R. Prasad 1988, p. 459)

It is remarkable that Tulsidas considered Bharata's life as a householder superior to the ascetic life of Rama, his supreme deity. He revered and was influenced by the other sacred Hindu texts and earlier renditions of Rama's story. Camille argues that 'it is natural for the *Ramcharitmanas* to have a deep imprint of the *Adhyatma Ramayana*, because during the time of Tulsidas, the *Adhyatma Ramayana* was the most popular devotional text' (C. Bulcke 1977a, p. 82).[8] Yet Tulsidas was prepared to take a contradictory stand even from revered texts like the *Adhyatma Ramayana* to explicate his concept of devotion. The *Adhyatma Ramayana* likened the life of a householder to a blind pit, where a person is engrossed in worldly concerns, children and wife. Indeed, Tulsidas too denounced a life given to sensual pleasures and cautioned against lust, anger, arrogance and greed; he never described the householder's life as a darkened well or a bottomless pit (C. Bulcke 2009, p. 74).

Tulsidas does not mention the most popular Hindu religious text, the Srimad Bhagavad Gita, in his explanation of the superiority of a householder who seeks God while simultaneously sustaining his normal life. Camille made that connection to argue that like the Gita which does not glorify renunciation as the assured path to salvation, Tulsidas too insists that it is the love of the devotee that Lord Rama seeks, not whether he is a householder or a renunciate (C. Bulcke 1977a, p. 78).

जे जन रूखे विषय रस, चिकने राम सनेह। तुलसी ते प्रिय राम को, कानन बसहिं कि गेह।

Tulsidas says that only those who have renounced their attachment to the material gross world of sense objects and a desire or longing for them, and are instead engrossed in enjoying the taste of the nectar of love and devotion for Lord Rama are the ones who are the beloved of the Lord. It does not matter then whether they stay in the forest (as hermits or ascetics) or live as a householder. (Chhawchharia 2015a, p. 61).

घर कीन्हें घर जात है, घर छाँड़े घर जाइ। तुलसी घर-बन-बीच ही, राम प्रेम पुर छाइ।

If one over-indulges in worldly affairs as a householder, he will surely lose his spiritual abode. Conversely, if one is engrossed in the spiritual pursuits, his worldly abode (household and worldly responsibilities) would suffer. Tulsidas advises that a wise man should strive for Lord Rama's affection by balancing the worldly duties of a householder with the spiritual pursuits of a forest-dwelling mendicant. (Chhawchharia 2015a, p. 260)

Tulsidas always placed the life of a householder as the ideal platform to pursue and attain Lord Rama's devotion and affection. Camille argued that Tulsidas' concept of devotion is not for a chosen few but for everyone and particularly for the ordinary householders; to substantiate this claim, he cited Acharya Ramchandra Shukla: 'Blessed is the *Ramcharitmanas*, a beacon of religion in households and blessed is Tulsidas who takes this illumination from door to door' (Shukla 1935, p. 38). Shukla exalts Tulsidas as the beacon of hope for householders who wish to attain spiritual progress along with their daily responsibilities and that too with their defects and human failings. Moreover, Shukla also underlines the fact that Tulsidas did not have any respect for the impostors who feigned to look like a hermit or an ascetic.

नारि मुई गृह सम्पति नासी। मूड़ मुड़ाइ होहिं संन्यासी।

Some people get their heads shaved off to appear like an ascetic once their wife is no more and they have lost their entire property. (Tulsidas 2001, p. 749)

Camille underscored the point that Tulsidas had much greater concern for the salvation of worldly but simple people; he always praised the temperate, balanced and righteous householder over an overzealous hermit or amateurish ascetic. In his *Vinaya Patrika*, Tulsidas goes even further and bluntly states that 'the mind becomes corrupt when one takes sanyasa, just as an unbaked earthen pot gets spoiled when water is poured into it' (C. Bulcke 2010, p. 149).

काम, क्रोध, मद, लोभ, मोह मिलि ग्यान बिराग हरो सो।
बिगरत मन संन्यास लेत, जल नावत आम घरो सो॥

Once worldly desires, lust, anger, vanity, greed and delusion join hands, even the acquired wisdom and progress towards renunciation are lost. Renouncing the householder's life and taking an ascetic's life without due preparation is like pouring water into a half-baked earthen pitcher. The half-baked earthen pot dissolves in water, thereby destroying the pot and losing the water; Tulsidas asserts that without overcoming lust and other weaknesses, the pursuit of an ascetic's life would be counterproductive (Chhawchharia 2017, p. 578).

Moreover, Camille asserted that if one does a comparative analysis of the *Ramcharitmanas* with other narrations of Rama's story in regional languages, one can claim without hesitation that Tulsidas' poetry is the best representative of the tradition of public welfare and benevolence inherent to the *Ramkatha* since ancient times (C. Bulcke 2009, p. 69). Benevolence was an integral part of Tulsidas' path to devotion, and its centrality to the idea of religion, love for the divine made Camille his ardent devotee. What were the core ideas of Tulsidas' devotion that Camille found fascinating and admirable?

On Benevolence

Camille posited that the path to devotion (*bhakti marg*) of Tulsidas 'has several characteristics, which made it a truly royal road to God and must have been instrumental in the salvation of millions' (C. Bulcke 2010, p. 147). For Tulsidas, the two essential constituents of devotion were moral conduct and concern for others' welfare or benefaction; 'he was an uncompromising believer in God, yet he firmly believed that the true measure of love for God is man's behaviour towards man' (ibid., p. 142). The emphasis on moral conduct is the essence of Rama's story since its ancient origins, including in Valmiki's Ramayana; Camille argued that 'some bhakti movements may have neglected this aspect, but it is astonishing to find the same insistence in the very oldest dharma-sutras' (ibid., p. 147).

For Tulsidas, true devotion was not mere sentimentality; instead, it was made up of three constituents: observing ethical and moral conduct, disposing of the duties of a householder and working for the welfare of others. This compassion, benevolence or munificence is an indispensable part of the path of devotion of Tulsidas. Looking at the prevalent social order and the popularity of the wandering mendicants and ascetics in those times, Tulsidas knew that renunciation, or turning one's back to the world, and meditating in solitude were often considered the ideals of a seeker. Tulsidas believed that one need not give up on the world to attain salvation; instead, one should engage with worldly affairs as a conscientious householder and always aspire to bring welfare to others.

In his detailed treatise on Tulsidas' literature, Camille listed several couplets from the *Ramcharitmanas*, *Vinaya Patrika*, *Kavitavali*, *Dohavali* and other works to highlight the significance of benevolence and welfare of others as the core of his devotion.

तदपि करब मैं काजु तुम्हारा। श्रुति कह परम धरम उपकारा॥
पर हित लागि तजइ जो देही। संतत संत प्रसंसहिं तेही॥

However, I shall do your work; for the Vedas say benevolence/charity is the highest virtue. The saints ever praise him who lays down his life in the service of others. (Allchin 1964; Bahadur 1994, p. 24)

This verse from the *Ramcharitmanas* avers that benevolence is the highest ideal and one should be ready to sacrifice one's life for a cause that brings welfare to others. Tulsidas claims that such selfless acts of sacrificing one's life for the welfare of others is lauded in the scriptures (Vedas), and the saints offer fulsome praise for such benign individuals. One of Camille's personal favourites among Tulsidas' poetry was the following couplet acclaiming benevolence as the essence of religion, devotion and moral conduct.

परहित सरिस धर्म नहिं भाई। पर पीड़ा सम नहिं अधमाई॥
निर्नय सकल पुरान बेद कर। कहेउँ तात जानहिं कोबिद नर॥

Brother! There is no religious duty (dharma) like benevolence, no sin like oppressing others. I have declared to you, dear brother, the verdict of all the Vedas and the Puranas, and the learned also know it. (R. Prasad 1988, p. 713)

These words are inscribed on Camille's memorial statue at St Xavier's College, Ranchi, as a tribute to the missionary who lived by the values of benevolence drawing inspiration from the *Ramcharitmanas*.

Tulsidas believed that nothing was beyond the reach of people with inherent compassion and benevolence. For such benign people, worldly rewards would come easy; yet spiritual progress or salvation too would be always in their grasp. He attached exceptional significance to the virtue of benevolence, and one could find a wonderful continuity in his poetry exalting this attribute. In one of the couplets cited earlier, Tulsidas avers that those who sacrifice their lives for the welfare of others are extolled in the scriptures (Vedas) and the saints praise them. Here, Rama affirms that such people who die for the welfare of others can achieve anything in this world while they attain salvation in the other world.

परहित बस जिन्ह के मन माहीं। तिन्ह कहुँ जग दुर्लभ कछु नाहीं॥
तनु तिज तात जाहु मम धामा। देउँ काह तुम्ह पूरनकामा॥ ॥

There is nothing in this world that is beyond the reach. Nothing is difficult to attain in this world to those who have others' interests at heart. Casting off your body, friend, ascend now to my realm (Ram's divine abode). What more shall I give you, when you have all you desire? (R. Prasad 1988, p. 494)

राम भगत परहित निरत पर दु:ख दुखी दयाल।
भगत सिरोमनि भरत तें जनि डरपहु सुरपाल॥

Sri Ram's devotees are always engrossed in the welfare of others, doing good to others, share the sorrows of others and are compassionate by nature. Bharata is the very crest-jewel of devotees; therefore, be not afraid of him, O ruler of gods. (Tulsidas 2001, p. 389; Bahadur 1994, p. 145)

In the *Ramcharitmanas*, Rama explains the characteristics of a saint, and predictably benevolence, or the concern for the welfare of others, features prominently in this list.

गावहिं सुनहिं सदा मम लीला। हेतु रहित परहित रत सीला॥
मुनि सुनु साधुन्ह के गुन जेते। कहि न सकहिं सादर श्रुति तेते॥ ॥

They are ever engaged in singing or hearing my stories and are intent on
doing good to others without any consideration. In short, O good sage,
the qualities of the saints are so numerous that they cannot be exhausted
even by Sarada (the goddess of speech) nor by the Vedas. (Tulsidas 2001,
p. 505)

Significantly, while narrating the characteristics of a saint, Rama offers a
disclaimer that the saintly qualities are so numerous that even the goddess of
speech and intelligence (Sharada) or the fountainhead of religious knowledge
(the Vedas) fails to provide a comprehensive list. However, Rama assigns
such primacy to benevolence that he mentions it among the two most critical
attributes of a saint. Again, in the *Ramcharitmanas*, Rama explains that
people who work selflessly and without any expectations of rewards are very
dear to him.

सगुन उपासक परहित निरत नीति दृढ़ नेम।
ते नर प्रान समान मम जिन्ह कें द्विज पद प्रेम॥ ॥

Those men who worship my personal form, are engrossed in the welfare
of others, firmly tread the path of righteousness, and are steadfast in
their vow and devoted to the feet of the Brahman are as dear to me as
life. (Tulsidas 2001, p. 564; Bahadur 1994, p. 242)

Rama lists three attributes of his favourite devotees: those who imagine
him as the personal god with form or a divine incarnation in tangible form,
those who steadfastly work for others' welfare and those who revere the
Brahmins. Tulsidas, while describing Rama's reign in Ayodhya (the Ram
Rajya), highlighted people's concern for others' welfare as one of the defining
characteristics of this utopia.[9]

दैहिक दैविक भौतिक तापा। राम राज नहिं काहुहि ब्यापा॥
सब नर करहिं परस्पर प्रीती। चलहिं स्वधर्म निरत श्रुति नीती॥

Nowhere in Rama's realm could one find a person who suffered
from bodily pain, ill fortune or evil circumstance. All the men and

women loved one another, conducted themselves in accordance
with righteousness and were devoted to the injunctions of the Vedas.
(R. Prasad 1988, p. 699)

Tulsidas' description of the utopian social order under Rama's reign reiterated
generosity and concern for others' welfare over and over again.

सब उदार सब पर उपकारी। बिप्र चरन सेवक नर नारी॥

All men and women were generous and charitable and devoted to the
feet of Brahmans. (Ibid., p. 700)

Moreover, for Tulsidas, benevolence is an integral part of saintly behaviour;
the saints happily suffer in order to bring welfare to other people.

नहिं दरिद्र सम दु:ख जग माहीं। संत मिलन सम सुख जग नाहीं॥
पर उपकार बचन मन काया। संत सहज सुभाउ खगराया॥ ॥
संत सहहिं दु:ख पर हित लागी। पर दु:ख हेतु असंत अभागी॥
भूर्ज तरु सम संत कृपाला। पर हित निति सह बिपति बिसाला॥ ॥

There is no misery in this world as terrible as poverty and no blessing
as great as communion with saints. Beneficence in thought, word
and deed is the innate disposition of saints, O king of the birds.
The saints undergo suffering in the interest of others while impious
wretches do so with a view to tormenting others. Tender-hearted
saints, like the birch tree, submit to the greatest torture (even allow
their skin to be peeled off) for the good of others. (Tulsidas 2001,
p. 773)

In his *Vinaya Patrika*, Tulsidas posits that the purpose of human life is to
provide selfless service to fellow human beings without reservations and any
expectations (S. Sahay 1919; Allchin 1966; V. Tripathi 1974; V. Mishra 2015).
As discussed earlier, he claimed that the purpose of human life was to pursue
Rama's devotion and hence seek the spiritual progress of salvation (S. Sahay
1919; B. Mishra 1942; V. Tripathi 1974). The crux of devotion for Tulsidas is to
live like a householder and work for others' welfare; thus, devotion to Rama
and benevolence are the two sides of the same coin. Consider the following
verses.

लाभ कहा मानुष -तनु पाये।
काय, बचन, मन, सपनेहुँ कबहुँक घटत न काज पराये॥

What is the purpose of acquiring the human body if it is not of any good to others even in one's dreams, if the body has never been put to use to help others in their hour of need through the mind, wisdom, speech and deeds to the best? (Chhawchharia 2017, p. 664)

काज कहा नर तनु सारयो।
पर उपकार सार श्रुति को जो धोखेहूँ न विचारयो॥

What great feats have you achieved though this human body if you have not even inadvertently thought of working for the welfare of others, particularly when such benevolence is considered as the essence of all the scriptures and the Vedas? (Ibid., p. 667)

सातैं सप्तधातु-निरमित तनु करिय बिचार। तेहि तनु केर एक फल कीजै पर-उपकार।।

This body is made of seven elements, and one must remember that the only purpose of this human body is to be benevolent, beneficent, compassionate, merciful, helpful and kind to others. (Ibid., p. 676)

जानत हूँ मन बचन करम पर हित किन्हें तरिये।
सो बिपरीत देखि पर सुख, बिनु कारन ही जरिये।।

I know it fully well that by doing good to others in a selfless manner by employing the faculties of my mind as well as with my speech and my deeds. I can cross the ocean symbolised by this mundane, gross and deluding world, but still I act in the opposite manner because I burn with jealousy and envy even without a cause upon seeing the happiness and comfort of others. (Ibid., p. 616)

The basis of devotion to Rama is to consider him omniscient, and a true devotee can never have animosity to any living or non-living being as it would be contradictory to his devotion. The concept of God's universal presence is also mentioned in several Hindu scriptures and sacred texts; following are some specific examples. The *Ishavasyopanishad* is one of the shortest and represents a brief philosophical poem discussing the soul or self (*atman*) and asserts that a wise person sees all the other living or non-living beings as manifestations of the same soul. Thus, it is imperative that a wise person or an enlightened individual should not have any ill feelings towards anything in the world.

यस्तु सर्वाणि भूतानि आत्मन्येवानुपश्यति। सर्वभूतेषु चात्मानं ततो न विजुगुप्सते॥

The wise man who sees the Atman (the Brahman, God) in all beings and that all beings exist in the same Atman has no reason to hate anyone. (Translation by authors)

Similarly, the Bhagavad Gita also proclaims,

यो मां पश्यति सर्वत्र सर्वं च मयि पश्यति।
तस्याहं न प्रणश्यामि स च मे न प्रणश्यति॥

For those who see Me (the Universal Self) present in all beings, and all beings exist within me, they are never lost to me, nor am I ever lost to them. (Translation by authors)

Just as ether exists in the cloud and the cloud in ether, so is God present in every being and every being exists in God. He who realizes this fact is spoken of as seeing God present in all beings and all beings existing in God (Goyandka 2017, p. 294). The *Bhagavata Purana* reiterates the same proclamation.

मामेव सर्वभूतेषु बहिरन्तरपावृतम्।
ईक्षेतात्मनि चात्मानं यथा खममलाशय:॥
इति सर्वाणि भूतानि मद्भावेन महाद्युते।
सभाजयन् मन्यमानो ज्ञानं केवलमाश्रित:॥

He should consider that he visualises me only, manifested in all beings, both internally and externally, like the sky. With a pure, sinless heart he should see me within himself also. In this way, O greatly enlightened Uddhava, he should establish himself in pure knowledge and should consider all created beings as being the God himself and respect them all. (Tagare 1978, p. 2106)

उमा जे राम चरन रत बिगत काम मद क्रोध।
निज प्रभुमय देखहिं जगत् केहि सन करहिं बिरोध॥

[*Shiva while narrating the Rama story to his consort*] O Uma, they who
are devoted to Rama's feet and are free from lust, vanity and anger
look upon the whole word as full of their lord; against whom can they
harbour animosity? (Tulsidas 2001, p. 762)

Unquestionably, benevolence, or concern for others' welfare, is the most
widely referred to in most of Tulsidas' literature. In his *Kavitavali*, he claims
that the ardent devotees of Lord Rama are intrinsically kind, compassionate
and affectionate, and they offer their love to everyone without any
discrimination.

राम के गुलामनि की रीति प्रीति सूधी सब।
सब सों सनेह, सबही को सनमानिए॥

Lord Ram's devotees who surround their Lord are highly noble, polite
and loving. Everyone likes them and their company, and they are
welcome wherever they go. (Chhawchharia 2015b, p. 273)

In his detailed study of Tulsidas' literature, Camille always maintained
that the Indian poet was greatly inspired by the *Adhyatma Ramayana*.
However, he underlined the fact that the major difference between the
Adhyatma Ramayana and the *Ramcharitmanas* is in their formulation of the
devotional approach (C. Bulcke 1996, p. 108). In the *Adhyatma Ramayana*,
Rama defines the nine-fold path of worship and devotion and anoints
wisdom or pursuit of knowledge through contemplation as the final stage. On
the other hand, Tulsidas in his *Ramcharitmanas* portrays the same situation
through Rama's words as follows:

नवम सरल सब सन छलहीना।
मम भरोस हियँ हरष न दीना॥

The ninth form of devotion demands that one should be guileless and
straight in one's dealings with everybody and should in his heart cherish
implicit faith in me without either exultation or depression. (Tulsidas
2001, p. 497)

Camille highlighted that while the *Adhyatma Ramayana* provides a long list of characteristics of saints several times, one will be hard-pressed to find a direct reference to the idea of benevolence, or concern for the welfare of others, as an essential characteristic of devotion or as one of the saintly qualities. Sage Agastya explains to Rama the ideals of a saint in the following verse.

साधवः समचित्ता ये निःस्पृहा विगतैषणाः। दान्ताः प्रशान्तास्त्वद्भक्ता निवृत्ताखिलकामनाः॥
इष्टप्राप्तिविपत्त्योश्च समाः सङ्गविवर्जिताः। संन्यस्ताखिलकर्माणः सर्वदा ब्रह्मतत्पराः॥
यमादिगुणसम्पन्नाः सन्तुष्टा येन केनचित्। सत्सङ्गमो भवेद्यर्हि त्वत्कथाश्रवणे रतिः॥

A Sadhu (a truly holy man) is even-minded towards the most favourable and unfavourable situations and has control over sensory organs, without attachment to or desires about children, wealth and heavenly enjoyment. A placid mind arising from complete self-mastery, with equanimity, sincere devotion, and dedication to the Lord, is devoid of all desires, avarice, and ambitions. Such a mind is not attached to the fruits/results of their actions/endeavours; it abandons evil and selfish actions and has an abiding interest in contemplating the Brahman (the Supreme soul). Such a person upholds the virtues of self-discipline, self-restraint, doing penance and observing austerities and is contented with whatever comes their way. These are the characteristics of pious and holy men; by interacting with such saints, one develops endearment and interest in your [Rama's] divine stories and accounts. (Swami Tapasyananda 2006, p. 130)

Camille underlined the fact that while this list is quite exhaustive, it does not mention benevolence, or concern for the welfare of others, at all. In the *Adhyatma Ramayana*, the ideal seeker is generally indifferent to other people of the world. Camille listed only two instances in the entire text of the *Adhyatama Ramayana* which mention something about offering service to others; however, this benevolence is only available to the devotees of Rama.

एवं मद्भक्तियुक्तानामात्मा सम्यक् प्रकाशते । मद्भक्तेः कारणं किञ्चिद्वक्ष्यामि शृणु तत्त्वतः॥ ॥
मद्भक्तसङ्गो मत्सेवा मद्भक्तानां निरन्तरम् । एकादश्युपवासादि मम पर्वानुमोदनम्॥
मत्कथाश्रवणे पाठे व्याख्याने सर्वदा रतिः । मत्पूजापरिनिष्ठा च मम नामानुकीर्तनम्॥
एवं सततयुक्तानां भक्तिरव्यभिचारिणी । मयि सञ्जायते नित्यं ततः किमवशिष्यते॥ ॥

To those who have devotion to Me, the Atman shines. I shall, therefore, tell you now some of those factors that generate devotion to Me. Association with My devotees, constant service of Me and of My devotees, observance of the vow of Ekadasi and the like, keen interest in listening to, reading and exposition of accounts of, My excellences, adherence to my ceremonial worship, repetition of my name and hymning about my attributes – those who are constantly devoted to these disciplines gain unshakable devotion to Me. (Swami Tapasyananda 2006, p. 136; Nath 1979, p. 71)

Camille argued that the *Adhyatma Ramayana* does not attach any great significance to the virtue of benevolence as part of devotion. The word *parhit* (welfare of others, or benevolence) appears only once as Jatayu[10] praises Rama and says, 'I attain the shelter of lotus-eyed Raghunath, who is served by great souls who do not crave for other's wealth or women; they are always eager to serve others' welfare and find great elation to see virtues and glories in others' (C. Bulcke 1996, p. 113).

परधनपरदारवर्जितानां परगुणभूतिषु तुष्टमानसाम्।
परहितनिरतात्मनां सुसेव्यं रघुवरमाम्बुजलोचनं प्रपधे॥

The one who is fit to be worshipped by those who eschew others' possessions and women, who are ever particular about the welfare of others, and who delight in others' excellences and prosperity – such is the lotus-eyed Rama of Raghu's line in whom I take refuge. (Swami Tapasyananda 2006, p. 159)

To highlight Tulsidas' idea of benevolence as an essential ingredient of devotion, Camille juxtaposed the narration of the same event from the *Adhyatma Ramayana* and the *Ramcharitmanas*. The vulture named Jatayu fought with Ravana to prevent Sita's abduction; however, Jatayu was fatally wounded, gasping for life when Rama and Lakshmana saw him. According to the *Adhyatma Ramayana*, as death approaches, Rama says to a fatally injured Jatayu,

मत्काथार्थं हतोऽसि त्वामतो मे प्रियबान्धवः॥

You were killed for my work. So, you must be a dear brother. (C. Bulcke 1996, p.113)

On the other hand, in his *Ramcharitmanas*, Tulsidas re-narrates and rephrases
this as follows.

जल भरि नयन कहहिं रघुराई। तात कर्म निज तें गति पाई॥ ॥
परहित बस जिन्ह के मन माहीं। तिन्ह कहुँ जग दुर्लभ कछु नाहीं॥

With his eyes full of tears, Raghunatha replied, 'It is your own
meritorious deeds, friend, that have brought you salvation. There
is nothing in the world beyond the reach of those who have others'
interests at heart.' (R. Prasad 1988, pp. 493–494)

In this verse, Tulsidas posits that the quality of serving others and working
for others' welfare is the highest virtue that disrupts the usual process of the
cycle of multiple births. In Hindu cosmology, Jatayu, a vulture, would not be
considered worthy of spiritual progress or salvation. However, through his
selfless service, Jatayu transcends the circumstances of his birth and his life as
an apex predator full of ignorance and violence. As Jatayu lay dying, his head
rests in the lap of Rama and he has no desires left. Moreover, Rama grants
Jatayu a permanent abode in his own realm, taking him beyond the cycles
of birth and death. It is only through offering selfless service that Jatayu
accomplishes the rarest of the rare feats, unimaginable for the most advanced
spiritual seekers and practitioners who spend several lives in its pursuit: not
only having Rama tend to him as he lay dying but also attaining salvation
through Rama.

In the 'Uttarakand' of the *Ramcharitmanas*, Rama, considering the
characteristics of his brothers as saints, says that they also do good to their
enemies and that *parhit* is the best part of religion.

सन्त असन्तन्ह कै असि करनी । तिमि कुठार चन्दन आचरनी॥
काटइ परसु मलय सुनु भाई निज गुन देइ सुगंध बसाई॥

The conduct of saints and the wicked is analogous to that of sandalwood
and the axe, for – mark it brother – the axe cuts down a sandal-tree,
while the fragrant sandal imparts perfume to the very axe that fells it.
(Ibid., p. 711)

Through this dialogue, Tulsidas contrasts the inherent nature of saints and
wicked people; intrinsically, while the wicked people try to harm everyone,

the saints try to help everyone. The inherent nature of sandalwood is to emanate fragrance, while the only use of an axe is to cut trees; both follow their natural behaviour. The sandalwood, like the saints, shares its best assets with the axe which represents the wicked people. One may argue what the purpose is of imparting saintly characteristics to wicked people since an axe with the fragrance of sandalwood would still be used to cut trees. One may argue that forgiveness is a defining characteristic of saints, and, despite suffering enormous damages, they offer their prayers and seek mercy for those who injure them. Also, the saints never stop sharing their uplifting qualities with everyone, and it is up to the receiver whether they accept or reject them. However, it is true that anyone who comes in contact with the saints will definitely be enriched, and it is up to that person whether they embrace and sustain such ennobling interactions.

Even in the 'Aranyakand', Rama does not forget to mention *parhit*, describing to Narada the characteristics of saints.

गावहिं सुनहिं सदा मम लीला। हेतु रहित परहित रत सीला॥
मुनि सुनु साधुन्ह के गुन जेते। कहि न सकहिं सारद श्रुति तेते॥

They are always engaged in singing or hearing my acts and are unselfishly intent on doing good to others. In short, O good sage, the qualities of the saints are so numerous that not even Sharada (the goddess of speech) or the Vedas could narrate them all. (Ibid., p. 505)

Those who follow the path of Tulsidas' devotion do not neglect this world to improve their hereafter. They do not take *sannyasa* (asceticism) to conquer lust and anger. Like Bharata, they consider the observance of duty and the fulfilment of God's orders as their penance and *parhit* (benevolence) – both essential parts of their religious practice.

It will not be too far-fetched to conclude that it was through his reading of Tulsidas' works that Camille discovered the vast philosophical traditions of India, which appealed to his Christian missionary sensibilities. Committed to the idea of serving the Church and Christ, Camille found a spiritual mentor in Tulsidas, who talked about public welfare, morality and personal surrender and devotion to God (Rama) as the path of enlightenment. Tulsidas' devotional texts inspired him enough to think about benevolence and service to humanity by serving God, but he remained steadfast in his commitment to the Christian faith and its beliefs and remained loyal to the path of Christ throughout his life. We discuss the implications and nuances of this encounter further in the next chapter (Chapter 5). One could say that Camille was a Tulsidas *bhakt* (devotee), not a Rama *bhakt*. Reflecting on his devotion to Tulsidas, Camille writes,

> It is due to Tulsidas that I applied myself for so many years to the Ramkatha literature. To promote the welfare of the public is one of the chief characteristics of that great literary tradition, and from that point of view the Rama Legend tradition of Tulsidas is the best representative. In his Ramcharit he has beautifully explained the way of Devotion, and has very much insisted that there is a necessary link between devotion and morality. Devotion to God without morality is, on the one hand, absolutely useless, according to him, and on the other hand, with the help of his devotion to God, man can firmly progress on the path of morality. (C. Bulcke 2010, pp. 137–138)

On Morality

Tulsidas' portrayal of devotion as the confluence of morality and benevolence made Camille his ardent admirer. Camille believed that it was one of the most outstanding accounts of devotion that explained both the concept and its practice in daily life. Tulsidas argued that 'no real bhakti is without good conduct and a determined effort to control one's passions, and that, on the other hand, no one can achieve it without the help of God's grace' (C. Bulcke 2010, p. 148). As a devout Christian, Camille found Tulsidas' emphasis on ethical conduct and moral ideals in the daily lives of ordinary people very similar to his own religious duties as a missionary entrusted to spread these ideals among the common people.

To substantiate his arguments on Tulsidas' conception of morality as devotion, Camille presented the genealogy of the *Ramkatha* tradition since Valmiki and affirmed that the description of the ethical aspects of life in his Ramayana is singled out for special praise from the Indian sources (C. Bulcke 2020 [1950], p. 145). Camille's long list of literature narrating Rama's ideal character includes the non-religious works or the classical literary works considered as part of the genre of *belles-lettres*.[11] The list of notable works on the *Ramkatha* incorporates Kalidas' *Raghuvansham*, King Pravarasen's *Ravanvaha* or *Setubandh*, Kumardas' *Janakiharan*, Bhatti's

Bhattikavya, and Abhinandan's *Ramcharit* (C. Bulcke 2009, p. 64). Rama's story has remained a fertile ground for Sanskrit plays, such as Bhasa' *Pratimanatak*, Bhavbhuti's *Mahavir Charit* and *Uttar Ramcharit*, Mayuraja's *Udatta Raghavam*, Murari's *Anargh Raghav*, Rajshekhar's *Balramayan* and Jayadev's immortal play, *Prasannraghav*.[12] At the beginning of the play *Prasannraghav*, the narrator proclaims, 'The reason so many different poets across different eras eulogise Rama is because he is the perfect abode of all the exalted qualities. Any poetry that does not praise Ram's character is like a tree that would never bear fruits' (Paranjpe and Panse 1894, p. 9; C. Bulcke 2009, p. 64).

With reference to the religious texts, Camille claimed that despite several reiterations and recensions over 2,000 years, the key constituents of promoting public welfare and advocating moral conduct have remained core elements in all the subsequent versions of the *Ramkatha*. Valmiki had depicted Rama not only as a religious, virtuous and godly person but as the embodiment of Dharma, or the Dharma incarnate. However, for Valmiki, Rama's religiosity was not demonstrated through elaborate rituals, ceremonies and paraphernalia; instead, his conduct epitomised morality (C. Bulcke 2009, pp. 66–67). For Valmiki, Rama's personal conduct included four outstanding features: first, he never lies, or he never dishonours his pledge; second, except Sita, he does not even look at other women; third, he obeys every command of his father; and, finally, he is always devoted to bringing welfare to his subjects (ibid.). Camille cited from the *Ananda Ramayana*, where Rama affirms his three rules: 'I never take back any word spoken by me; except Sita every woman is like my mother Kausalya; and I overwhelm my enemies with only one arrow' (ibid.).

Camille also quoted from the 'Jaiminyai Ashvamedha Parva',[13] which proclaims that Rama's character inspires a noble and pious mentality and those who tend to follow Rama's conduct acquire a virtuous mind and heart (C. Bulcke 1996, p. 106). Camille cited some portions from the *Padma Purana*, describing Rama's story.

[W]e meet face to face the rules of Dharma, a woman's fidelity to her husband, deep brotherly affection, and youth's devotedness to the elders. In its verses proper conduct between master and servants is personified and before our eyes, punishment is meted out to the evildoer by the scion of Raghu. (C. Bulcke 2010, p. 145)

From the *Brihaddharm Purana*, Camille cited the following verse.

रामायणं महाकाव्यमादौ वाल्मीकिना कृतम्।
तन्मूलं सर्वकाव्यानाम् इतिहास पुराणयो:।

The Mahakavya (Great Work) known as Ramayana, written by the great Rishi, Valmiki, is the model for all the Puranas and Samhitas. Maharshi Vedavyasa wrote his Mahabharata and the Puranas and Samhitas on the lines of the above book, as did the authors of other great books also. (Banerji 1915, p. 72)

The *Brihaddharm Purana* exalts Valmiki's Ramayana for his description of the life of Rama and for laying down the rules for 'the conduct of women, kings, Brahmans, Kshatriyas, Vaisyas, Sudras, householders and others. He has given a description of the gods and has also dealt with friendship and enmity. All men who are desirous of their well-being should read the Ramayana and try to understand its meaning' (Banerji 1915, p. 78; C. Bulcke 1996, p. 106).

To illustrate Rama as the epitome of ethical conduct and morality, Camille cited the renowned Sanskrit scholar Mahamahopadhyaya Ganganath Jha's Sanskrit verse, giving an exquisite poetic description.[14] In the war with Rama, sensing an imminent defeat Ravana woke up his brother Kumbhakarna and told him that although he had kidnapped Rama's wife, Sita, she did not desire anyone except Rama. Kumbhakarna then asked Ravana that if he could take any form, why he did not take the form of Rama (C. Bulcke 1996, p. 107).

To this, Ravana replies,

सुरुचिरं तालदलश्यामलं रामांकं भजतो ममापि कलुषों भावो नसंजायते

Many times, I have assumed the graceful form of Rama, but my sinful intellect is destroyed as soon as I assume his form. (Ibid.)

Rama is depicted as the embodiment of righteousness and is considered as one who 'adds lustre to virtue and prosperity' and has a deep regard for truth, is free from envy and jealousy, and his disposition is excellent (H. Shastri 1952, p. 154). Thus, it is impossible for anyone who tries to imitate Rama, even as an impostor, to not lose all their defects, sinful thoughts, conduct and aspirations.

To highlight morality as the highest ideal of life, Camille cited from the *Dharmasutras*, some of the oldest sacred texts describing the ethical approach to life. As *Gautama Dharmasutra* states, '[E]ven if someone has had these forty sacraments administered to himself, but lacks the eight virtues of the soul, one does not attain *sayujya mukti*, i.e., the highest kind of liberation' (Buckle 2010, p. 147). The eight virtues of the soul include 'compassion for all creatures, forbearance, freedom from anger, purity, quietism, auspiciousness, freedom from avarice, and freedom from covetousness' (Buhler 1879, p. 215). Camille also cited from *Vashistha Dharmsutra* that declares, 'The study of the Vedas, along with its six auxiliary branches, will not sanctify a man without good conduct' (C. Bulcke 2010, p. 147).

Camille highlighted that Tulsidas followed this long tradition of the *Ramkatha* and placed morality as one of the prerequisites for devotion. For Tulsidas, while no genuine devotion is possible without morality, one could not achieve such ethical conduct without the help of God's grace. Tulsidas described his *Ramkatha* as a pious lake that only focuses on moral, ethical and righteous conduct (C. Bulcke 1996, p. 110). Camille highlighted that in the introduction of the *Ramcharitmanas*, Tulsidas wrote,

सब बिधि पुरी मनोहर जानी। सकल सिद्धिप्रद मंगल खानी॥
बिमल कथा कर कीन्ह अरंभा। सुनत नसाहिं काम मद दंभा॥
रामचरितमानस एहि नामा। सुनत श्रवन पाइअ बिश्रामा॥
मन करि विषय अनल बन जरई। होइ सुखी जौ एहिं सर परई॥

I have here (at Ayodhya) begun this sacred story that destroys all lust and pride and hypocrisy in him who hears it. Its name is The Holy Lake of Rama's Acts, and those who listen to it are refreshed; a soul that burns with the fever of worldly desire, like an elephant in a forest fire, is happy if it plunges into this lake. It puts an end to wicked ways and all the sin of the Kaliyuga. (C. Bulcke 2010, p. 148)

During Tulsidas' time, a branch of Krishna *bhakti* (Sakhi Sampraday) had emerged as very popular; it focused on the romantic, sensual and erotic aspects of the relationship between Krishna and his female companions (the Gopis). Even within Rama *bhakti*, the influence of Sakhi Sampraday was visible, and like the Krishna *bhakti* followers, they too focused only on the sensual and erotic elements in the *Ramkatha* (C. Bulcke 1977a, p. 73). Camille claimed that Tulsidas was aware of these campaigns to eroticise the *Ramkatha* while obliterating its message of public welfare through ethical and moral behaviour. Camille referred to the specific verses in which Tulsidas described people who sought to debase Rama's story 'as villainous, lustful and miserable wretches' (C. Bulcke 2010, p. 148).

अति खल जे बिषई बग कागा। एहि सर निकट न जाहिं अभागा॥
संबुक भेक सेवार समाना। इहाँ न बिषय कथा रस नाना॥
तेहि कारन आवत हियँ हारे। कामी काक बलाक बिचारे॥
आवत ऐहिं सर अति कठिनाई। राम कृपा बिनु आइ न जाई॥

Sensual wretches are like accursed cranes and crows who come not near the lake. For here are no prurient and seductive stories like snails, frogs and scum. That is why the lustful crows and cranes lack the heart to visit this place. For there is so much difficulty in approaching this lake, and it is not possible to reach it without the grace of Rama. (R. Prasad 1988, p. 33)

Camille highlighted that one of the most outstanding features of the *Ramcharitmanas* is the sense of decorum and dignity that Tulsidas maintained throughout this vast text. One cannot find even a single reference to vulgarity; rather, Tulsidas refrained from invoking colourful descriptions of romantic or erotic love. One of the illustrative examples of sublimation of romantic love is Tulsidas' description of the conjugal life of the newlywed Lord Shiva and Parvati.

जगत मातु पितु संभु भवानी। तेही सिंगारु न कहउँ बखानी॥

Shambhu (Lord Shiva) and Bhavani (Goddess Parvati) are the parents of the universe; hence, I refrain from portraying their amorous dalliance. (R. Prasad 1988, p. 76)

In another instance, narrating the first meeting of Lord Rama and Sita in the *pushp vatika* (flower garden), Tulsidas says that at very first sight, both are enchanted seeing each other's supernatural beauty. However, as Camille underlined in his description, Tulsidas maintains the dignity, decorum and the sacred nature of the *Ramkatha*, and there is no trace of sensualising the divine nature of this love at first sight between Rama and Sita (C. Bulcke 2009, p. 59). Narrating Sita's beauty through Rama's eyes, Tulsidas wrote,

देखि सीय सोभा सुखु पावा। हृदयँ सराहत बचनु न आवा॥
जनु बिरंचि सब निज निपुनाई। बिरचि बिस्व कहँ प्रगटि देखाई॥

सुंदरता कहुँ सुंदर करई। छबिगृहँ दीपसिखा जनु बरई॥
सब उपमा कबि रहे जुठारी। केहिं पटतरौं बिदेहकुमारी॥

When Rama saw Sita's beauty, he was filled with rapture; he admired
it in his heart, but utterance failed him. He felt as though Brahma the
Creator had put forth all his creative skill in visible form and revealed
it to the world. 'She lends charm to charm itself,' he said to himself,
'and looks as if a flame of light is burning in the house of loveliness.
The similes already employed by the poets are all stale and hackneyed;
to whom shall I liken Videha's daughter?' (R. Prasad 1988, pp. 157–158)

Likewise, describing Rama's beauty through Sita's eyes, Tulsidas wrote,

देखि रूप लोचन ललचाने। हरषे जनु निज निधि पहिचाने॥
थके नयन रघुपति छबि देखें। पलकन्हिहूँ परिहरीं निमेषें॥
अधिक सनेहँ देह भै भोरी। सरद ससिहि जनु चितव चकोरी॥
लोचन मग रामहि उर आनी। दीन्हे पलक कपाट सयानी॥

Beholding the beauty of Sri Rama, her eyes were filled with greed;
they rejoiced as if they had discovered their long-lost treasure. The eyes
became motionless at the sight of Sri Rama's loveliness; the eyelids too
forgot to fall. Due to the excessive love, Her body-consciousness began
to fail; it looked as if a Chakora bird were gazing at the autumnal moon.
Receiving Sri Rama into the heart through the passage of the eyes, she
cleverly shut Him up there by closing the doors of her eyelids. (Ibid.)

Camille praised Tulsidas for dexterously portraying a very sensitive scene
with exceptional beauty and with so much dignity and decorum. Similarly,
renowned Hindi littérateur Acharya Ramchandra Shukla highlighted the
flower garden incident as an epitome of Tulsidas' poetic genius in propagating
the etiquettes and norms of social propriety and high moral values (Shukla 1935,
p. 66). While Sita's heart was filled with love for Rama and vice versa, both soon
realised that their union could only happen once Rama fulfils the unassailable
vow of Sita's father, of stringing or breaking Lord Shiva's immovable bow.

जानि कठिन सिवचाप बिसूरति। चली राखि उर स्यामल मूरति॥
प्रभु जब जात जानकी जानी। सुख सनेह सोभा गुन खानी॥
परम प्रेममय मृदु मसि कीन्ही। चारु चित भीतीं लिख लीन्ही॥

Considering how hard it is to break the (unyielding) bow of Shiva, she proceeded sobbing silently on her way with the image of the swarthy form in her heart. When the Lord saw Janaka's daughter going, that fountain of bliss and affection and grace and virtue – then, with gentle ink of supreme love, he traced her infinite beauty on the tablet of his soul. (R. Prasad 1988, p. 160)

Shukla says in this portrayal of mutual love that Tulsidas expertly shows the discipline of upholding the societal norms and the etiquette of those times. Not once did Sita think that regardless of her father's vow, she would only marry Rama; nor did Rama think that regardless of who breaks Shiva's bow, only he would marry Sita (Shukla 1935, p. 66). Transgressions were not looked at favourably, and Tulsidas upheld the conservative social norms in his rendering of the *Ramkatha*.

Camille underlined the fact that apart from education and enlightenment, in his *Ramcharitmanas*, Tulsidas portrayed such characters who are vivid examples of moral ideals and ethical conduct. In this way, he provides moral strength and values to millions of common people – the ordinary householders and not the renunciates (C. Bulcke 1977a, p. 74). For Tulsidas, an ideal devotee is someone who performs all the worldly duties and always behaves according to the prevailing moral and ethical framework. To highlight the portrayal of major protagonists in the *Ramkatha* as exemplary characters, Camille cited the following verse from the *Ramcharitmanas*.

सुनु सीता तव नाम सुमिरि नारि पतिब्रत करहिं।
तोहि प्रानप्रिय राम कहिउँ कथा संसार हित॥

Anusuya then blessed Sita saying: 'You shall be the ideal of womanhood and your name shall be taken by all women who aspire for highest fidelity to their husbands.' Lord Rama is dear to you as your own life; I narrate these stories of your virtuous conduct for the benefit of the world. (Bahadur 1994, p. 176)

Camille always claimed that Tulsidas narrated the *Ramkatha* to present higher standards of moral and ethical conduct for the common people. In fact, those words of Anasuya could also apply to Tulsidas – that he narrated these stories of the virtuous conduct of Rama and Sita for the benefit of the world (C. Bulcke 1977a, p. 74). We want to emphasise here that Camille's own sense of puritanical Christian morality (specific to Europe in the early nineteenth and twentieth centuries) was validated through Tulsidas' conservative morality of his era, where there was little acceptance of transgressions of established social norms and etiquette. The *Ramcharitmanas* is an example of great lyrical artistry, sublime textual beauty and supreme devotional composition, while at the same time upholding the conservative hierarchical social order of its times by superimposing prevailing moral values onto the lead characters of Rama, Sita, Lakshmana, Hanuman and others who could do no wrong, and whose virtues transcended time itself. Even today, various renditions of the *Ramkatha* and especially the *Ramcharitmanas*, and also the enactment of the *Ramleela*,[15] emphasise moral conduct and ethical living and differences between good and evil to keep society anchored in traditional values. The popularity of the Ramayana has been timeless because it offers insights into human behaviour and is a blueprint of morality that should be the guiding principles for every society across time and space. Even today, the *Ramkatha* narrations take place, providing a moral anchor to society and are still very popular.

On Self-Surrender and Humility

For Camille, the essence of Tulsidas' *bhakti marg* (devotional path) 'consists of a humble acknowledgement of one's sinfulness, a serious and persistent endeavour to fulfil God's will and a trustful surrender to God' (C. Bulcke 2010, p. 146). As a devout Christian and a missionary, Camille found major similarities between his own and Tulsidas' idea of devotion. Camille explained that the essence of Christianity is love – love for God and love for his creation; this love for God is complete surrender to him, not following our will but his, and the recognition of one's sinfulness and wickedness (D. Prasad 2002, p. 68). Tulsidas defines this surrender as devotion to achieve salvation.

सेवक सेब्य भाव बिनु भव न तरिअ उरगारि।
भजहु राम पद पंकज अस सिद्धांत बिचारि॥

'I am the servant, and the Lord Rama is my master' – without this relationship, Garuda, it is not possible to cross the ocean of birth and death. Holding to this established doctrine, worship the lotus feet of Sri Rama. (R. Prasad 1988, p. 778)

The devotion that Tulsidas has propounded is *dasya bhakti*, or surrendering oneself in the service of the God who is worthy of being served and serving with all the sense organs and feeling a hearty sense of elation in offering such service. Camille highlighted the passage from the *Ramcharitmanas* in which Tulsidas presented Bharata as the ideal devotee. Bharata goes to the forest to call the exiled Rama back and return the kingdom to him; however, when Rama asks Bharata to take the final decision, Bharata says humbly,

सहज सनेहँ स्वामि सेवकाई। स्वारथ छल फल चारि बिहाई॥
अग्या सम न सुसाहिब सेवा। सो प्रसादु जन पावै देवा॥

It is to serve my master with guileless and spontaneous affection forgetting my own interests and neglecting the four ends of human existence. There is no better way to serve a good master than by obeying his command. (C. Bulcke 2010, p. 147)

Camille argued that in this verse, Tulsidas reiterates what has been the essence of all the scriptures from all the religions. Tulsidas posits that complete surrender is a form of devotion in which the devotee feels that the Lord is ready to do whatever the devotee wants. Yet the true devotee like Bharata says to God, 'Thy will be done' (C. Bulcke 2009, p. 39). Tulsidas used Bharata as an example to illustrate that devotion is not just sentimentality; instead, the genuine welfare of man lies in accepting God's law and fulfilling his desire (ibid.). To illustrate Tulsidas' description of a true devotee, Camille cited from the *Ramcharitmanas*: 'It is impossible for any creature to be happy while it is hostile to the Lord' (C. Bulcke 1996, p. 171).

Camille claimed that apart from the *Ramcharitmanas*, it is the *Kavitavali* and the *Vinaya Patrika* in which Tulsidas has expounded self-surrender to the Lord in the most profound and poetic expressions (C. Bulcke 1977a, p. 69). He emphasised that the *Vinaya Patrika* is one of the foremost among the best works of devotional literature across the world and for the ages (ibid.). Towards the end of the *Vinaya Patrika*, Tulsidas says that he has inscribed the feelings of his heart in it and he entreated the Lord, his Father, to accept his humble plea (V. Mishra 2015).

विनय पत्रिका दीन की बापू आप ही बांचो।
हिये हेरि तुलसी लिखी, सो सुभाय सही परि, बहुरि पूँछिये पाँचो॥

Oh! my Father, please be kind to read yourself this humble petition of this poor fellow (Tulsidas) which he is presenting to you in the form of this composition called 'Vinay Patrika'. Tulsidas has searched his heart and poured out whatever was inside it, and therefore whatever is written in it is true and honest, and without deceit and pretensions. So, oh Lord, remember your merciful nature and take pity on Tulsidas to first put your signature on it as a token of your approval and only then you may consult your company of advisors later. (Chhawchharia 2017, p. 897)

In his essay 'Why Is Ramkatha My Research Interest?' Camille underlined the fact that several critics may find Tulsidas' humility detrimental to one's worldly and also spiritual progress. Debunking this proposition, Camille argued that 'a man rises high only when he accepts his humility by bowing before the Lord, recognizing the reality of his condition' (C. Bulcke 2009, p. 16). Explaining his lifelong fixation with Tulsidas and his *Ramkatha*, Camille affirmed that it is Tulsidas' humility and self-effacement that impressed him the most (ibid.).

हौंहु कहावत सबु कहत राम सहत उपहास।
साहिब सीतानाथ सो सेवक तुलसीदास॥

Everybody calls me a servant of the Lord and I myself claim to be one; and Sri Rama puts up with the scoffing remark that a master like Sita's Lord has a servant like Tulsidas. (Tulsidas 2001, p. 56)

On several occasions, Camille reiterated that the focus on public welfare of the *Ramkatha* and Tulsidas' affirmation of his sinfulness and the complete surrender to his chosen deity Rama had compelled him (Camille) to devote his life to research on Rama. In his comprehensive overview of Tulsidas' writings, Camille highlighted several parts that show Tulsidas' complete surrender and unwavering devotion only to Rama. Camille cited the following verse from Tulsidas's *Dohavali*.

एक भरोसो, एक बल, एक आस विश्वास। एक राम घनस्याम हित, चातक तुलसीदास॥

Tulsidas says that he has only one source of reliance, only one source of strength, only one source of hope, and only one belief or faith (and it is in Lord Rama). Verily, Tulsidas has become like the bird 'Chatak' for the sake of the dark rain-bearing cloud in the form of Lord Rama. (Chhawchharia 2015a, p. 286)

Camille also quoted one of the verses from Tulsidas' *Kavitavali*, proudly proclaiming Lord Rama as his solitary deity.

जानत जहानु, मन मेरेहूँ गुमान बड़ो, मान्यो मैं न दूसरो, न मानत, न मानिहौं।

The world knows and I am also proud of the fact that I recognise no one else except you – hadn't till date, and shall never in future. (Chhawchharia 2017, p. 159)

Similarly, in the *Vinaya Patrika*, propounding singular and unflinching devotion to Rama, Tulsidas says,

जाउँ कहाँ तजि चरन तिहारे। काको नाम पतितपावन जग, केहि अति दीन पियारे॥

Oh Lord! Where else should I go except at your holy feet? Who else is called the purifier of sinners and who else dearly loves the wretched, the poor, the distressed, the humble, the hapless and the helpless creatures more than you? (Ibid., p. 341)

श्रवननि और कथा नहिं सुनिहौं, रसना और न गेहौं।
रोकिहौं नयन बिलोकत औरहिं, सीस ईस ही नेहौं

I will not listen to anything else, will not talk about anyone else, will prevent my eyes from wandering anywhere else in this world seeking any better source for my happiness and peace, and I will bow my head to the Lord alone and no one else. (Ibid., p. 349)

Apart from his complete and unreserved surrender to his deity, Tulsidas saw himself as a sinner and sought Rama's compassion to forgive his wretchedness. This sentiment was also expressed by other poets during the Bhakti movement, and prominent among them was Surdas, who appealed to the impartial Krishna to not pay attention to his sins and grant him salvation: 'हमारे प्रभु, अवगुण चित न धरौ। समदरसी है नाम तुहारौ, सोई पार करौ॥' As a devout Christian, Camille related to these acknowledgements of one's own sinfulness and seeking God's mercy to overcome one's impiety. From

Tulsidas' *Vinaya Patrika*, Camile found the following verse as one of his most beautiful prayers.

तू दयालु, दीन हौ । तू दानी, हौ भिखारी ॥ हौ प्रसिद्ध पातकी। तू पाप-पुंज हारी॥
ज्यों-त्यों तुलसी कृपालु! चरन-शरन पावै॥

Thou art compassionate and I am wretched. Thou art generous and I, a beggar. I am a well-known sinner, thou the remover of all sin. O Merciful one: may Tulsidas find refuge at thy feet. (C. Bulcke 2010, p. 147)

From the *Vinaya Patrika*, Camille cited another verse where Tulsidas epitomises the Lord's infinite kindness and his own wickedness. These ideas of God's infinite kindness and an individual's wickedness are very close to the core tenets of Christianity. It is no wonder that Camille was drawn to so many ideas of Tulsidas since they resonated with his Christian beliefs.

कह्यो न परत, बिनु कहे न रह्यो परत,बड़ो सुख कहत बड़े साँ, बलि दीनता।
प्रभु की बड़ाई बड़ी, आपनी छोटाई छोटी, प्रभु की पुनीतता, आपनी पाप-पीनता॥

(Oh Lord, I am in a dilemma.) It is not possible to say anything, but equally difficult to keep quiet. I invoke your gracious and merciful nature to gather enough courage to humbly submit before you that though it is true that a person feels very glad and relieved when he narrates his tale of woes, miseries, sufferings and problems in front of his able superiors, but still I feel hesitant to do so when on the one hand I consider the Lord's greatness and, on the other hand, the inconsequential nature of my complaints, as well as my impertinence and meanness in approaching the Lord who is so holy and pure while I am so sinful, lowly and pervert. (Chhawchharia 2017, p. 857)

The concept of sin is one of the fundamental features of Christianity. One of its core beliefs is the belief that humans are sinners. This sin of humankind is a legacy of the original sin of Adam and Eve, from which the incarnation of Christ took place to redeem mankind. Along with humility and meekness, there is also a sense of guilt or sinfulness in Tulsidas. His mention of his own culpability reminded Camille of a psalm of David found in the Old

Testament of the Bible. Tulsidas does not hide his faults and always reveals his inferiority. He says in the *Vinaya Patrika*,

तुलसीदास प्रभु! कृपा करहु अब, मैं निज दोष कछु नहीं गोयो॥

Oh, Lord of Tulsidas! I have come out clean and have not concealed even a single of my countless faults and shortcomings from you. Hence (and since I am truthful – and this is a virtue – so), show your mercy, grace and kindness on me now. (Ibid., p. 796)

To this, Camille said,

Reading this line of his reminds me of the Psalms of David, especially Psalm 51, in which he says: 'Know about my wrongs, and I can't forget my sin. You are the only one I have sinned against; I have done what you say is wrong. You are right when you speak and fair when you judge. I was brought into this world in sin.' (Nelson 2006)

Explaining this verse, Camille argued that the recognition of one's sinfulness is associated with the dawn of the divine light of God on that individual. He posited that 'just as the dust particles floating in the air of a room are not visible until the rays of the sun illuminate them, similarly in the absence of divine light the common man remains ignorant of his actual sinfulness' (C. Bulcke 1977a, p. 71). By the grace of the Lord, if a seeker is blessed with that divine light, then he speaks with Tulsidas.

माधव! मो समान जग माहीं। सब बिधि हीन, मलीन, दीन अति, लीन-बिषय कोउ नाहीं॥

Oh Lord Madhava! There is no one in this world who is like me, there is none who is worse-off than me for lack of resources, someone who is a greater sinner, more humble, lowly, downtrodden, helpless and hapless than me, and someone who is engrossed more in the pleasures of the senses and the desire to gratify them, and who is more attracted to the materialistic world as compared to me. (Chhawchharia 2017, p. 373)

This recognition of one's shortcomings and defects is considered the first step towards self-improvement, and Tulsidas implores his deity Rama to help him overcome these faults.

लोभ-मोह-काम-कोह-दोश-कोसु-मोसो कौन? कलिहूँ जो सीखि लई मेरियै मलीनता।
एकु ही भरोसो राम! रावरो कहावत हौं, रावरे दयालु दीनबंधु! मेरी दीनता॥

Who else is a treasury of such negative traits as greed, avarice, attachments, delusions, passions, desires, lust and anger like me? It appears that Kaliyug (the present era which is considered to be most corrupt, sinful and full of negativity) has learnt all its dark and demeaning qualities from me. 'Yes, I have only one hope (of salvation), and that is, "I call myself yours (Lord Rama's)." You (Sri Rama) are a friend of the wretched, the downtrodden and the distressed. You are full of kindness, and I am extremely humble (so, live up to your reputation, and protect and save me!)' (Chhawchharia 2015b, p. 159)

Camille argued that the critics may find these statements as hyperbole or exaggeration, only because such erudite people lack this divine light. One day Saint Francis of Assisi went out to visit the city with a companion. On the way he saw that some soldiers were taking a murderer to be hanged. Saint Francis said to his companion, 'If I had not received God's grace in abundance, I would have become a greater sinner than that murderer' (C. Bulcke 1977a, p. 71). Camille claimed that a genuine spiritual seeker would acknowledge his sinfulness and would see it as a path to seek divine intervention.

तुलसी राम कृपालु सों कहि सुनाउ गुन दोष। होय दूबरी दीनता परम पीन संतोष॥

Tulsidas advises that one should make an honest, sincere, truthful and full confession to Lord Rama about one's virtues and faults. By doing this, one will have twofold benefit – one, his sense of misery, depression and dejection as well as of guilt would be diminished, and second, he will have a lot of peace of mind and enjoy renewed confidence in himself because now he is assured of the Lord's protection and benevolence as he has made an honest confession and has hidden nothing from the Lord. This results in his self-confidence, his sense of contentedness and fulfilment that comes with being upright, truthful and honest to be fortified and to become stronger and more robust. (Chhawchharia 2015a, p. 90)

Camille went on to claim that despite all this, Tulsidas is fully convinced that he will ultimately be victorious over the world because he has discovered sincere faith in Rama (C. Bulcke 1977a, p. 72).

मैं तोहिं अब जान्यो, संसार। बाँधि न सकहिं मोहिं हरि के बल, प्रगट कपट-आगार॥

Oh (you delusory) World! Now I have realised your true (evil) nature and (cunning) form. You are an obvious abode of deceit, pretentions, falsehood, treachery, cunning, trickery and cheating, but remember that now I have the support and strength of Lord Sri Rama with me, and so you will not be able to trap and pillory me in your web or net of deceit, fraud and falsehood. (Chhawchharia 2015a, p. 620)

Tulsidas' faith on overcoming worldly delusions is based on his belief that his deity, Rama, has finally taken him under his wings.

तुलसी जहाँ मातु पिता न सखा नहि कोउ कहूँ अवलंब देवैया॥
तहाँ बिनु कारन राम कृपाल बिसाल भुजा गहि काढ़ि लेवैया॥

Describing the horrors of the Vaitarni River, literally the river which flows in hell and drowns the sinners, Tulsidas says – there is no one to help; there are no parents, friends and other kin to give any kind of support. Only Lord Rama shows mercy and kindness without cause, and only he can extend his long arms to pick you up from drowning and will be there to save you from the horrors of this river. (Ibid., pp. 153–154)

Tulsidas posits that any person without any special religious, spiritual or yogic training and with all the earthly desires and faults can strive for spiritual progress through devotion. For Tulsidas, devotion is not an esoteric, philosophical, doctrinal discourse; instead, it arises from practising complete self-surrender to the deity. Rama is the embodiment of the supreme consciousness, or Brahma, for Tulsidas, and he believes that complete self-surrender to the lotus feet of his chosen deity is the way to proper conduct in the world and for salvation hereafter. The other major theme of Tulsidas' devotion is the self-recognition of his faults and then seeking mercy and guidance from the chosen deity to overcome these obstacles. The two themes resonated with Camille's personal approach to religiosity and spiritual progress, and no wonder Camille saw Tulsidas as his spiritual mentor and guide.

Tulsidas' Staunchest Votary

Starting as an aficionado of Tulsidas' poetic style, Camille became an ardent devotee of the Indian poet and stayed his most loyal defender. He underlined that even in his old age, while composing the *Kavitavali*, Tulsidas remembered his misfortune of being an orphan and bemoaned his ill fate.

मातु पिता जग जाय तज्यो विधि हू न लिखी कछु भाल भलाई।
नीच निरादर भाजन कादर कूकर टूकनि लागि ललाई।

> My parents abandoned me at birth; providence wrote nothing auspicious on my forehead. I was wretched, an object of contempt, helpless and hungering for the titbits thrown before the dogs. (C. Bulcke 2010, p. 153)

However, Camille always asserted that despite all the misfortunes and deprivations in his early childhood, Tulsidas not only overcame all these challenges but carved such a lofty pedestal for himself that few in the world would imagine. In order to promote the popularity of Hindi, the Government of India and some of its affiliated organisations decided to hold a major event under the banner of the World Hindi Conference in 1975. Camille, with his eminence among the Hindi literary world, was invited to address this gathering, and it was here during his speech that probably for the only time he countered his favourite poet and argued, 'Whatever may have been the distress of his childhood days, we cannot agree that providence wrote nothing auspicious on his forehead' (ibid., p. 153). Camille underlined that the fact that such a grand ceremony would commemorate Tulsidas on such an occasion contradicts the great Indian poet's lament. Obviously, no one during Tulsidas' lifetime would have imagined that with the advent of the printing press, this frail old poet from the Assi Ghat of Varanasi would attain unprecedented popularity (C. Bulcke 2009, p. 36). Who would have thought that millions of copies of Tulsidas' compositions would be sold after the printing system was established in India? During the same conference, the organisers celebrated the fourth centenary of the

Ramcharitmanas and, to mark the event, asked Camille to unveil the statue of Tulsidas.

In his address, Camille underlined that the celebration of the composition of the *Ramcharitmanas* in independent India was a testament to the enduring relevance and reverence of Tulsidas (ibid.). He often cited renowned historian Vincent A. Smith's tribute to Tulsidas.

> It is a relief to turn from the triviality and impurity of most of the versifiers in Persian to the virile, pure work of a great Hindu – the tallest tree in the 'magic garden' of medieval Hindu poetry. His name will not be found in the Ain-i Akbari, or in the pages of any Muslim annalist, or in the books by European authors based on the narratives of the Persian historians. Yet that Hindu was the greatest man of his age in India – greater even than Akbar himself, in as much as the conquest of the hearts and minds of millions of men and women effected by the poet was an achievement infinitely more lasting and important than any or all of the victories gained in war by the monarch. (Smith 1917, p. 417)

The high acclaim of Tulsidas and his total absence in the writings of the Mughal court historians surprised Smith and several other colonial-era scholars and historians. Remarkably, not only did Smith find Tulsidas' poetry exceptional, but he also placed his depiction of theology equal to that of Christianity such that 'many passages might be applied to Christian uses by simply substituting the name of Jesus for that of Ram' (ibid., p. 419). Camille also mentioned George Grierson's famous acclaim for Tulsidas as 'the greatest of Indian authors of modern times' and his *Ramcharitmanas* as 'worthy of the greatest poet of any age' (Grierson 1893, p. 260). In several of the analytical writings on Indian literature, European scholars like Grierson acclaimed the greatness of Tulsidas as the epitome of Indian literary achievements (Grierson 1903, 1977; Keay 1920). It should come as no surprise that with his Christian theological training, Camille found great affinity with Tulsidas' devotional approaches.

Camille was not just an ardent admirer of Tulsidas, but also a self-appointed attorney defending his idol on different occasions and at different forums. He was aware of the emerging trends of scholarship and literary criticism and saw that Tulsidas attracted severe criticism from different sections. He was sometimes judged too harshly without any acknowledgement and appreciation of the prevalent social and cultural milieu. Along with

Dineshwar Prasad, Camille published an abridged version of Tulsidas'
Ramcharitmanas as *Manas Kaumudi* (An Exposition of the *Ramcharitmanas*),
and in his introduction to this compilation, he explained his purpose of writing
this book.

> The reasons for the decline in popularity of the Manas in contemporary
> times, especially among the educated class may be attributed to its
> voluminous text and the lack of knowledge of Awadhi and Braj among
> the elite sections. However, the most important factor is that the
> educated Indians consider it a representative text of the medieval era
> and obsolete values. These elite Indians claim that Ramcharitmanas
> only glorifies *varnashrama* order, propagates misogyny and promotes
> superstitions and thus does not offer any inspiration for the modern
> times. Our aim in preparing this book, the *Manas Kaumudi*, is to remove
> such misconceptions about Tulsidas' Ramcharitmanas. (C. Bulcke and
> Prasad 1979, p. 1)

In the modern era, Tulsidas' depiction of the social order has come into
sharp criticism; even during Camille's lifetime, modern critics censured
the Indian poet for propagating medieval ideas. Camille, as a discerning
Tulsidas devotee, was one of the few scholars who acknowledged in the light
of such strident, out-of-context and unjust criticism that he was obliged to
address these critiques (C. Bulcke 1977a, p. 60). In his interactions at various
events to commemorate the great Indian Bhakti poet, he had heard several
complaints from the students and intellectuals on the approbatory portrayal
of archaic traditions in Tulsidas' literature. Camille underlined that two of
the most common themes of this criticism focus on Tulsidas' propagation
of the archaic caste-based social order of the *varnashrama dharma*, or the
social organisation based on birth, and his uncomplimentary or disrespectful
references to women. We discuss these in the next two sections to provide the
context for Camille's defence of Tulsidas.

On Caste and Varnashrama Dharma

Varnashrama dharma is composed of two words: *varna*, which refers to colour
or an individual's social category, and *ashrama*, which refers to the stages of
life. In the Vedic era, *varna* represented social stratification as the hierarchical
structure of the four *varnas* (Basham 1989, p. 105). The social order of the

four *varna*s included the Brahmins, the priestly class; the Kshatriyas, the warriors and rulers; the Vaishyas, the traders and skilled craftsmen; and the Shudras, the labourers and serfs (ibid., pp. 28–29). *Ashrama* is also divided into four stages: *brahmacharya*, the student life; *grihastha*, the householder's life; *vanaprastha*, the retired householder; and *sanyasa*, when an individual renounces worldly pursuit and dedicates their life to spiritual pursuits (Svami 2022, p. 42). The *varna* division was not hereditary; one person could transcend this classification through their own conduct and accomplishments (Radhakrishnan 1927, p. 112). In the Mahabharata, the three most important teachers of Dharma are all Shudra *varna* by birth: Vidura, Sanjaya and Vyasa (Vanita 2022, p. 53). The Mahabharata also narrates the story of a Shudra from the hunter-butcher community working as a meat seller who becomes a Dharma teacher to the Brahmin sage Kaushika (ibid., p. 205). Gradually, with the rise of different occupations, the *varna* system led to hereditary *jati*s, or the caste system. Unlike the *varna* system, the *jati* (caste) system does not allow the transcendence of one's caste. Camille argued that Tulsidas did not see reforming the prevalent social order as one of his primary aims in life, and thus he was not part of a social or political campaign to challenge the *varnashrama* system (ibid.). Indeed, Tulsidas was an adherent of the social order sanctioned by the ancient texts including the Vedas, the Puranas and the Smritis (Shukla 1935, p. 40). From his various writings, it is easy to surmise that he was distraught at the rapid changes in the social and political order of his times, particularly the decline of the traditional *varnashrama* system (U. Singh 1966, p. 230). Camille believed that Tulsidas drew inspiration from the Bhagavad Gita that equated the *varnashrama dharma* to the law of God.

चातुर्वर्ण्यं मया सृष्टं गुणकर्मविभागशः

The four divisions of human order were created by Me according to the differences in qualities, activities and aptitude. (Goyandka 2017, p. 214)

It is our understanding that Camille did not engage deeply with the Gita, which has a much more nuanced understanding of the *varna* system and does not attribute *varna* on the basis of birth, but on *karma* (a concept of action, work, or deed and its effect or consequences) and *guna* (qualities). This discussion is beyond the scope of this book, but we want to acknowledge that

Camille was driven by the desire to defend Tulsidas, and he may not have fully grasped the complex history of the *varna* system and its place in Hindu theology and philosophy.

While Tulsidas never intended to write a commentary on the social and political situation of his times, the collapse of the traditional social order deeply pained him. It is significant to note that while he does not offer a detailed exposition on the configuration and the functioning of the *varnashrama dharma*, he takes cognisance of the breakdown of the prevalent and traditional social order (U. Singh 1966, p. 209). There are numerous references in his copious writings where he complained about the disintegration of the *varnashrama dharma*.

Tulsidas was critical of the collapse of the traditional social order and critiqued both the scope and speed of these changes. He considered these changes as detrimental, which brought chaos and disorder by challenging the existing order. Tulsidas argued that this defiance of the traditions and customs took people away from the established norms and opened doors to depraved, degraded and decadent behaviour by sanctioning heresy, pretensions, deception and heterodoxy (Chhawchharia 2017, p. 457).

In the *Kavitavali*, Tulsidas says,

आश्रम - बरन - धरम - बिरहित जग, लोक - बेद - मरजाद गई है।
प्रजा पतित, पाखंड - पापरत, अपने अपने रंग रई हैं॥

All regulations envisioned for the proper, smooth and cordial functioning of the society with respect to the four 'Varnas' (i.e. the four sections of the society such as the Brahmins, Kshatriyas, Vaishyas and Sudras) and the four 'Ashrams' (i.e. the four divisions or phases in the lifespan of a person, such as Brahmacharya, Grihastha, Sanyas and Vanaprastha) have vanished or been obliterated. The sanctity of the Vedas and established norms of the world have been completely lost. The people of the world have fallen from their path, becoming morally depraved, degraded and decadent. They do what suits them irrespective of the propriety, probity and correctness of their actions and deeds. (Ibid., pp. 457–458)

Similarly, in the *Ramcharitmanas*, Tulsidas laments the collapse of the *varnashrama dharma*.

बरन धर्म नहिं आश्रम चारी। श्रुति बिरोध रत सब नर नारी।

There is no *dharma* of the four classes or the life stages, and all men and women are bent on defying the Veda (Lutgendorf 2023, p. 209). In this couplet, the four classes refer to the four *varna*s or 'the transactional social orders (priests, warriors, farmers and merchants, and peasants), and to the concept of the ideal stages in the male life cycle (student, householder, contemplative retiree and total renunciate) as codified in the authoritative Sanskrit texts'. (Ibid., pp. 323–324)

सब लोग बियोग बिसोक हुए। बरनाश्रम धर्म अचार गए।।

People are all smitten with bereavement and profound sorrow. The duties and rules of conduct prescribed for the four orders of society and stages in life are neglected. (Ibid., p. 1075)

Again, in the *Kavitavali*, Tulsidas writes,

बरन-धरमु गयो, आश्रम निवासु तज्यो,
त्रासन चकित सो परावनो परो-सो है।

During these dire times, the regulations and rules of behaviour, known as *varna dharma* that regulates the life and conduct of the members of the four principal castes of society have become extinct or gone awry. (Chhawchharia 2015b, p. 175)

As Camille argued, Tulsidas considered the *varnashrama dharma* an ideal social system. His description of the Ram Rajya, or the ideal rule of Lord Rama, was that the king exalts the conduct of his people along with the prescribed *varnashrama dharma*.

बरनाश्रम निज निज धरम निरत बेद पथ लोग।
चलहिं सदा पावहिं सुखहि नहिं भय सोक न रोग॥

Devoted to duty each according to his own caste and stage of life, the people trod the path of the Vedas and enjoyed happiness. They knew no fear, nor sorrow nor disease. (Tulsidas 2001, p.995)

Tulsidas in his *Gitavali* also describes the Ram Rajya as an exemplar of every individual observing the *varnashrama dharma* – that is, following their duties and obeying the rules of life as sanctioned by the scriptures (Bahadur 1996, p. 138; Chhawchharia 2016, p. 713). For his reverence for the traditional social order, some critics label Tulsidas as 'the maximum champion of a conservative interpretation of *varnashrama dharma*' (Lorenzen 1995, p. 14).

However, Camille underlined that Tulsidas was not blind to the defects of the *varnashrama dharma* and acclaimed those who could defy the rigid caste hierarchy (C. Bulcke 1977a, p. 60).

जाति पाँति धनु धरमु बड़ाई। प्रिय परिवार सदन सुखदाई॥
सब तजि तुम्हहि रहइ उर लाई। तेहि के हृदयँ रहहु रघुराई॥

He who, renounces his caste and kinsmen, wealth, duty and glory, his dear kinsfolk and happy home, and treasures yourself alone – in his heart, O Lord of Raghus, take up your abode. (R. Prasad 1988, p. 332)

Tulsidas says that the place of Rama's abode is the hearts of those with no place for caste, religion, pride, wealth and other worldly possessions and preoccupations. A person who is confined within the rigid boundaries of religion, caste, creed and wealth cannot afford to host Lord Rama; by overcoming such narrow-mindedness can one create a suitable place for the Lord. In other words, Tulsidas is telling Rama that there is no place for him around anyone obsessed with caste, creed, pride and wealth (V. Mishra 2015, p. 37).

We do not see this verse as a censure of the caste system and would argue that Tulsidas was referring here to caste as identity and attachment like wealth, fame, and so on. So even though he may have favoured the caste-based social order, he did believe that freeing oneself from any identity and privilege was the only way to realise God.

Camille also picked several verses from various writings to highlight that Tulsidas had made a strident critique of the Brahmins who claim these privileges without following the requisite regulations of learning, conduct and etiquettes (C. Bulcke 1977a, p. 61). Camille argued that despite defending the traditional social order and the *varnashrama* system, Tulsidas was not advocating caste-based privileges for those who did not uphold their *dharma*, or the prescribed duties.

सोचिअ बिप्र जो बेद बिहीना। तजि निज धरमु बिषय लयलीना॥

Pity rather the Brahman who is ignorant of the Vedas, and who has abandoned his religious duty and is engrossed in the pleasures of senses. (R. Prasad 1988, p. 358)

बिप्र निरच्छर लोलुप कामी। निराचार सठ बृषली स्वामी॥

As for the Brahmans, they are unlettered, grasping, lascivious, reprobate and stupid and the husbands of lewd outcastes. (Ibid., p. 755)

द्विज श्रुति बेचक भूप प्रजासन। कोउ नहिं मान निगम अनुसासन॥

The Brahmans sell the Vedas; the kings bleed their subjects; no one respects the injunction of the Vedas. (Tulsidas 2001, p. 1070)

Camille argued that Tulsidas considered caste, clan, lineage, pride, prosperity, dexterity and astuteness as superfluous attributes of his devotional path (*bhakti marg*). In his address to Sabari, an old tribal lady, who had acquired fame for her piety and devotion, Tulsidas writes that Rama underscored that devotion is above all these external markers and material acquisitions, including wealth, fame and family (Ibid., p. 497).

कह रघुपति सुनु भामिनि बाता। मानउँ एक भगति कर नाता॥
जाति पाँति कुल धरम बड़ाई। धन बल परिजन गुन चतुराई॥
भगति हीन नर सोहइ कैसा। बिनु जल बारिद देखिअ जैसा॥

Answered the Lord of the Raghus: 'Listen, O good lady, to my words I recognise no other kinship except that of Devotion. Despite caste, kinship, lineage, piety, reputation, wealth, physical strength, the numerical strength of his family, accomplishments and ability, a man lacking in devotion is of no more worth than a cloud without water'. (Ibid., p. 496)

In his *Kavitavali*, Tulsidas laments that the people are more concerned about a person's caste, clan and class rather than their devotion and love for Rama. He says that being born in a high-caste, large, famous, illustrious, learned and wealthy family, acquiring great knowledge of the scriptures, and all such worldly or scholarly achievements are futile. Tulsidas claims that while he has never attained glorious feats that 'a man usually yearns for, he still considers himself highly successful and fulfilled because he has sincere and abiding devotion and love for Lord Rama' (Chhawchharia 2015b, p. 196).

> मेरें जाति-पाँति न चहौं काहू की जाति-पाँति, मेरे कोऊ काम को न हौं काहू के काम को।
> लोकु परलोकु रघुनाथ ही के हाथ सब, भारी है भरोसो तुलसी के एक नाम को॥
> अति ही अयाने उपखानो नहि बूझैं लोग, 'साह ही को गोतु गोतु होत है गुलाम को।

I have no caste and neither do I wish to find out about the caste of others. No one is of any use to me and neither do I wish to be of any use to others. My entire destiny and existence are in the hands of Lord Rama. Tulsidas has the only reliance and succour in the name of Sri Rama. The people are utterly foolish – they do not understand that the 'Gotra' of the servant is the same as that of his master. (Ibid.)

Camille argued that Tulsidas was against the practice of untouchability, and in his depiction of the Ram Rajya there was no scope for such social ills (C. Bulcke 1977a, p. 61).

> राजघाट सब बिधि सुंदर बर। मज्जहिं तहाँ बरन चारिउ नर॥
> तीर तीर देवन्ह के मंदिर। चहुँ दिसि तिन्ह के उपबन सुंदर॥

The best and most beautiful in every way was the royal ghat, where men of all four castes could bathe. All along the bank stood temples sacred to the gods and surrounded by lovely groves. (Tulsidas 2001, p. 1003)

In his detailed response to the modern critics who accuse Tulsidas of medieval ideas, especially the glorification of the Brahmins, Camille argued,

It seems to me they read too much in some of those expressions. Besides our poet seems to have forestalled the criticisms in his introduction to the *Ramcharitmanas*: 'When the poet contemplates the Lake of Rama's Acts, his heart is filled with bliss and ecstasy and swells with a flood of love and happiness, and then the beauteous stream of poetry flows out, filled with the water of Rama's stainless glory. Social and scriptural doctrines are its fair banks' (loka beda mata mañjula kūla: I, 39). It is as he wanted to stress the fact that he exposes his vision of Rāmabhakti, according to the existing social opinions (lokamata) and the teachings of the Veda (bedamata). It was never his intention to introduce changes in the political and social structure of his time. (C. Bulcke 2010, pp. 152–153)

Tulsidas envisioned an ideal social order with infinite happiness and prosperity, structured along the traditional norms of society, or the *varnashrama dharma*. He was an adherent of the order of four *varna*s and the four stages of life; conversely, for him, the breakdown of the *varnashrama dharma* would lead to social disorder and cultural chaos.

On Women

Even before Camille arrived in India, Tulsidas had already come under severe criticism for his unsympathetic or harsh portrayal of women. In his most renowned work, the *Ramcharitmanas*, there are numerous instances where Tulsidas, either himself or through the characters, has made deprecatory comments about women, particularly about their physical weakness and lack of discretion (C. Bulcke 1977a, p. 61). Camille admitted that if any female character commits any mistake anywhere, then Tulsidas is quick to censure all of womenfolk; conversely, no matter how many crimes the male character commits, all of menfolk never receive the same sweeping condemnation (ibid.). Camille's claim that Tulsidas generalised individual defects or shortcomings of one woman as those of the entire womenfolk found acceptance with his PhD supervisor and noted Hindi scholar Mataprasad Gupt's explanation on the same issue (M. Gupta 1942, p. 299). To substantiate his claim, Camille cited that despite critiquing the demon king Ravana's depravity, Tulsidas never extrapolated these vices to the entire male population (ibid.).

Camille was one of the few scholars who genuinely revered Tulsidas the poet, understanding and appreciating his sublime poetry and the intense devotional sentiment behind it. Yet he was also one of the few forthright intellectuals who did not try to exonerate Tulsidas' insensitive depiction of women. Camille dared to disagree even with some of the most eminent Hindi scholars who believed that Tulsidas' harsh words about women were a ploy to keep the focus on spiritual practice (where liaisons with women were considered distractions). Tulsidas depicted women as a symbol of lust and depravity and, thus, a major hindrance for spiritual seekers to regulate their spiritual practice. He referred to women as the manifested form of illusion (*maya*), more painful than lust, anger, pride, attachment and covetousness and one that destroys chanting, rules, restraint and penance (U. Pandey 2018, p. 158).

It is significant to underline the fact that several writers have tried to exonerate Tulsidas of the insensitive portrayal of women on the grounds that he was trying to stipulate strict physical and mental discipline for spiritual seekers. As Acharya Ramchandra Shukla posits, Tulsidas used harsh words about women to reinforce the rigid discipline for spiritual practice since it was impossible for a person seeking carnal pleasures to pursue the lofty spiritual path (Shukla 1935, p. 47). Contrary to Shukla's arguments, Camille claimed that most of Tulsidas' writings are for common householders seeking God and their spiritual progress, not for renunciates or hermits. Moreover, Tulsidas was such an evolved spiritual seeker that he would not be afraid of getting distracted by such temptations himself (C. Bulcke 1997a, p. 62).

Some Hindi littérateurs, such as Mataprasad Gupt, were puzzled by Tulsidas' harsh portrayal of women. Gupt acknowledged that 'in different eras, artists are often sympathetic and liberal in depicting women, Tulsidas comes out as illiberal. Although the reason for his disdain is a mystery, but his animosity toward women is a fact that cannot be denied' (M. Gupta 1942, p. 299). Unlike his PhD advisor, Camille explored some of the reasons that may have triggered such harshness about women in an otherwise very sensitive, kind and generous Tulsidas. Camille believed that as an adherent of the social traditions, conventions and customs, Tulsidas' views were shaped by his reverence for the ancient texts and his deference to the prevalent social order. Camille posited that Tulsidas' harsh statements for women are borrowed from ancient literature or the local proverbs and idioms (C. Bulcke 1977a, p. 62). To substantiate his argument, Camille cited some of the verses from the *Ramcharitmanas*, which disparage women, but he believed they are nothing more than rephrasing some of the ancient texts. In the *Ramcharitmanas*, Tulsidas says,

ढोल गवाँर सूद्र पसु नारी। सकल ताड़ना के अधिकारी॥

A drum, a rustic, a Shudra, a beast and a woman – these are fit subjects for beating. (R. Prasad 1988, p. 575)

This half-verse from the *Ramcharitmanas* is one of the most cited parts criticising Tulsidas for his conservatism, casteism and misogyny. While the verse is often touted as representative of his literary corpus, it is often quoted without any reference to the context. To reach Lanka, Rama had to cross the ocean with his army. Rama pleaded with the ocean for three days to show him the way, but the ocean ignored these requests. Eventually, Rama lost his temper and threatened to dry the ocean. The ocean then appeared in human form and sought Rama's forgiveness, claiming to be dim-witted and thus deserving of punishment (beating). Several scholars have deployed the context of place, time, character and situation in the narrative to rationalise this statement or to claim that the statement from a character in a text does not reflect its author's belief system. However, Philip Lutgendorf argues that 'it is clear enough that words on a page do not oppress people – people oppress people – but it should be as clear by now that no scripture, least of all the [*Ramcharitmanas*], is simply "words on a page"' (Lutgendorf 1991, p. 405).

Several commentators have explained the verse by exploring the different meanings of the verb *tadana*, which means 'to punish, to beat, to chide, to admonish – thus, one "beats" a drum but merely "rebukes" a (wayward) villager, low-caste peasant, or woman' (Lutgendorf 2020, p.346). Mahatma Gandhi, who revered the *Ramcharitmanas*, also tried to offer his rationale to address this controversial verse. Gandhi suggested one should discern a text's meaning in a *shastra* and 'should not stick to its letter, but try to understand its spirit, its meaning in the total context' (Gandhi 1968, p. 318). Explaining his interpretation of the verse, Gandhi wrote,

> Ramayana is one of the greatest works because its spirit is that of purity, compassion and devotion to God. An evil fate awaits one who beats his wife [just] because Tulsidas has said in his work that a Sudra, a dull-witted person, a beast and a woman merit chastisement. Rama not only never raised his hand against Sita, he did not even displease her at any time. Tulsidas merely stated a common belief. He could never have thought that there would be brutes who might beat their wives and justify their action by reference to his verse. (Ibid.)

Camille listed some of the quotations and references from several other textual sources to claim that Tulsidas must have drawn inspiration from them. He cited the following verse from the *Garuda Purana*.

दुर्जनाः शिल्पिनो दासा दुष्टाश्च पटहाः स्त्रियः।
ताडिता मार्दवं यान्ति न ते सत्कारभाजनम्॥

Wicked persons, artisans, slaves, defiled ones, drums and women are softened by being beaten; they do not deserve gentle handling. (J. Shastri 1957, p. 333)

Similarly, Camille explained that the following verse from the *Ramcharitmanas* was inspired by another verse from one of the Sanskrit proverbs.

भ्राता पिता पुत्र उरगारी। पुरुष मनोहर निरखत नारी॥
होइ बिकल सक मनहि न रोकी। जिमि रबिमनि द्रव रबिहि बिलोकी॥

At the very sight of a handsome man, be he her own brother, father or son, O Garuda, a (wanton) woman gets excited and cannot check her passion, like the sunstone that melts at the sight of the sun. (R. Prasad 1988, p. 478)

This is a contradiction in itself given how women have always been considered objects of sexual desire and distractions for men in the quest for spiritual pursuits. Here, there is recognition of women's own desires but in an incestuous and derogatory way.

Camille claimed that the insensitive portrayal of women in some places in the *Ramcharitmanas* reflects the prevalent social norms and public opinion more than Tulsidas' personal opinions. In order to deflect the criticism of Tulsidas, Camille argued that one should blame the Indian traditions, ancient Indian texts or even the entire world literature, which are full of such negative portrayals of women (C. Bulcke 1977a, p. 62). As an example, Camille cited a verse from the Bhagavad Gita.

मां हि पार्थ व्यपाश्रित्य येऽपि स्युः पापयोनयः।
स्त्रियो वैश्यास्तथा शूद्रास्तेऽपि यान्ति परां गतिम्॥

Lord Krishna says, 'Arjuna, women, Vaisyas (members of the trading and agriculturist classes), Shudras (those belonging to the labouring and artisan classes), as well as those of impious birth (such as the pariah), whomever they may be, taking refuge in Me, they too attain the supreme goal'. (Goyandka 2017, p. 467)

We do not interpret this *shloka* (a Sanskrit verse) in the Bhagavad Gita as being derogatory or demeaning to women, but a discussion of that is beyond the scope of this book. Suffice to say, Camille was willing to attribute the responsibility of Tulsidas' derogatory comments on women to one or the other Hindu text, prevailing social milieu or patriarchal traditions that were deeply entrenched in Indian society.

However, despite offering such a spirited defence of Tulsidas based on the reading of the prevalent religious, social and literary traditions, Camille himself was not always convinced of these explanations. Thus, he questioned: 'Why did a great soul like Tulsidas just repeat those words?' (C. Bulcke 1977a, p. 62). He then undertook a psychological analysis of Tulsidas, an orphan since childhood, and compared Tulsidas' childhood to his own in Belgium. Camille asserts that had Tulsidas received the tender love, affection and care of a doting mother like his own, he would have never described any woman with any negative attributes (Saxena 2015, p. 157). Adopting his own unique approach, Camille stated that being deprived of the love and care of an affectionate mother had deprived Tulsidas of experiencing the unconditional, selfless and infinite love of a woman and led him to reiterate those harsh statements about women either from old texts or prevalent proverbs.

Critical works on Tulsidas' views regarding women are available in the public domain as Camille himself suggested.[16] It is not our mandate in this book to analyse and offer any more critique of Tulsidas' writings, which more knowledgeable people have undertaken. Here, we are interested in Camille's empathetic reading of Tulsidas and his justification of Tulsidas' unflattering and even problematic views about women. That Tulsidas was a product of his life experiences and circumstances and was writing at a certain time in history is sufficient to locate him in that context. We have accorded that same respect and courtesy to Camille himself, learning from him that criticism of anyone whose contributions are otherwise extraordinary must take into account their context, without superimposing modern vocabularies and sensitivities onto them.

Tulsidas *Bhakti,* Not Rama *Bhakti*

Camille always maintained that he was a devotee of Tulsidas and not of Rama (R. Tripathi 2015, p. 258). From a religious and denominational perspective, as a devout Christian, he was an ardent devotee of Jesus Christ. Yet he could seek inspiration from Tulsidas' devotion to Rama and tried to emulate such single-minded and unwavering devotion to Christ. In his address on the occasion of the unveiling of Tulsidas' statue, Camille rephrased a verse from one of the greatest devotional poets, Kabirdas, as his tribute.

हे तुलसी !
सब धरती कागद करूँ लेखनि सब वनराय।
सात समुद की मसि करूँ, तब गुन लिखा न जाय॥

Hey Tulsi! Even if I convert the entire earth into paper, turn the whole forests into pens and make ink from the seven seas, I shall still not be able to describe your great qualities. (C. Bulcke 2009, p. 41)[17]

As a devout Christian, Camille's reverence for Tulsidas was exceptional; inspired by one of Tulsidas' verses, he devoted his entire life working on the *Ramkatha*, yet he left this world with two unfulfilled wishes. He wished to complete the Hindi translation of the Old Testament and then write a book on Tulsidas. Even on his sickbed, and through his last days, he only had two books that he sought solace from: the Holy Bible and the *Ramcharitmanas*. He always said, 'On reaching the other world, the first person I will seek would be Tulsidas' (Saxena 2017, p. 78). Indeed, Tulsidas remained the destination of Camille's journey here and in the hereafter.

Camille's affection and devotion to Tulsidas led him to not just learn Hindi but also seek a deeper understanding of Indian literature, particularly those related to the *Ramkatha*. He obtained such outstanding proficiency that he emerged as an authority on the language and its literature, and also as a renowned Indologist. He remained an ardent admirer and devotee of Tulsidas, and this unwavering devotion led him to create some of the most brilliant literary and lexicographical works that have inspired subsequent generations interested in both the *Ramkatha* and Indology. In the next chapter, we will evaluate his contributions to Indology in some detail.

Notes

1. Annie Besant, née Annie Wood, born in 1847 in London to Irish parents, emerged as a proponent of the rights of trade unions, national education, women's right to vote and birth control in England. She embraced Theosophy, a religious movement founded in 1875, and later became the leader of the

Theosophical Society. She came to India in 1893, emerged as a prominent face in the Indian nationalist movement and was also a leading member of the Indian National Congress. She died in 1933 in Madras (present-day Chennai), India. Sister Nivedita was born Margaret Elizabeth Noble in 1867 in Dungannon, Ireland. She was a schoolteacher and an innovative educator. She became a follower of the Indian spiritual leader, Swami Vivekananda, and moved to India. She emerged as an influential leader in the Indian independence struggle and offered support to nationalists, including Aurobindo. She died in 1911 in Darjeeling, India. The 'Mother' was born Mirra Alfassa in 1878 in Paris and became an accomplished artist; she developed an interest in spiritual development. In 1914, she came to India and met Aurobindo, who is considered her inner spiritual guide. She had to leave India during the First World War, and upon her return to India in 1920, she stayed in Pondicherry and founded Sri Aurobindo Ashram in 1926. Aurobindo entrusted the full material and spiritual charge of the ashram to her; she led the ashram for nearly 50 years. In 1952, she established the Sri Aurobindo International Centre of Education and, in 1968, an international township, Auroville. She died in 1973 in Pondicherry. Mirabehn was born Madeleine Slade in 1892 in Surrey, England, in an English aristocratic family. She read the French novelist Romain Rolland's biography of Mahatma Gandhi and decided to come to India and live in Gandhi's ashram. Gandhi gave her the nickname Mirabehn (Sister Mira), and she often accompanied Gandhi on his tours and became one of Gandhi's confidants and an ardent champion internationally for India's freedom from British rule. Mirabehn decided to stay in India after its independence and the assassination of Gandhi. However, she returned to England in 1959 and a year later moved to Vienna, where she died in 1982.

2. See the previous chapter (Chapter 3) for a discussion on Constant Lievens.

3. *Lokasangraha* (also *lokasamgraha*) is a term formed by two words: *loka* (world) and *sangraha* (holding together). The term's literal meaning is 'holding all people with a unitary principle of service aimed at the well-being of every person in society'. It is the welfare of all and selfless service with a compassionate heart.

4. In his translation of the verse, Camille replaced 'Rama's votary' with 'God's votary'. The literal translation of the verse is 'Only that woman is a mother in this world who has a son devoted to Raghunatha' (R. Prasad 1988, p. 296).

5. Jnaneswar was a thirteenth-century Bhakti poet and saint from Maharashtra.

6. This is the English translation of the *Ramcharitmanas* published by Gita Press, Gorakhpur. It does not attribute the translation to any person(s); hence, the cited source is attributed to Tulsidas.

7. The Prakrits were Middle Indo-Aryan languages spoken between 500 BCE and 500 CE. The name Prakrit (*prākṛta*) means 'derived', a name contrasting with Sanskrit (*saṃskṛta*), meaning 'complete' or 'perfected', reflecting the fact that the Prakrit languages were considered historically secondary to and less prestigious than Sanskrit.

8. Some traditions identify Vedavyasa as the author of the *Adhyatma Ramayana* and link it to the *Brahmanda Purana*, while others link it to the fourteenth or fifteenth century CE, with the author unknown. The *Adhyatma Ramayana* is the portrayal of a conversation between Lord Shiva and Goddess Parvati on the divinity of Rama. It is this work that provided Tulsidas with the inspiration to compose his immortal work, the *Ramcharitmanas*.

9. The reign of Rama was called the Ram Rajya, the reign of righteousness and truth. The Ram Rajya was marked by peace, prosperity and harmony, where the king served the people and ensured their well-being and happiness before those of his own.

10. Jatayu, an old vulture, hears Sita's helpless cry when she is abducted by Ravana. Despite his old age, the bird fights the 10-headed mighty demon. The vulture is no match to the force of the demon. The latter leaves Jatayu in a pool of blood by cutting its wings. In search of Sita, Rama, with his brother Lakshmana, reaches there and sees the poor injured bird. Jatayu relates to him the whole story and breathes his last, after which Rama performs the necessary funeral rites for the bird.

11. *Belles-lettres*, the 'French term for "fine writing", [was] originally used (as in "fine art") to distinguish artistic literature from scientific or philosophical writing.... A category of elegant essay-writing and lightweight literary chatter, of which much was published in Britain in the late nineteenth and early twentieth centuries' (Baldick 2015, p. 38).

12. *Raghuvansham* (The Genealogy of Raghus) is a celebrated classical poem by Kalidas, which describes the genealogy of the Raghu clan. *Setubandh* (Building a Bridge) is a Prakrit poem by Pravarasena II and depicts the epic story of Rama, from his advance against Ravana and the building of a bridge of stone to Lanka to his return to Ayodhya after the extermination of the demon king. *Bhattikavya*, originally called *Ravana Vadh* (The Slaying of Ravana), is a classical Sanskrit poem of Bhatti, which depicts the lives of Rama and Sita. *Janakiharan* (The Abduction of Sita) is an epic poem in

Sanskrit by the Sinhalese poet Kumaradasa and describes Rama and Sita's life. *Ramcharit* (Rama's Conduct) is an epic poem in Sanskrit by the poet Abhinandan and depicts Rama's search for Sita, his victory over the demon king Ravana and his coronation in Ayodhya. *Pratimanatak* is a Sanskrit play by the poet Bhasa and depicts the story of the Ramayana. *Pratima* means 'statue' and *nataka* means 'drama' or 'play'. The theme of the play comes to light in the third act when Bharata enters the hall of statues situated outside Ayodhya after Rama's exile. *Mahavir Charit* is a Sanskrit play written by Bhavabhuti; the title translates to mean 'the exploits of the great hero', and the story revolves around Rama, the hero of the Ramayana. *Uttar Ramcharit* is another Sanskrit play written by Bhavabhuti. The title translates to 'the concluding book of Rama's story', and the story describes Sita's abandonment, her residence at the hermitage of Valmiki, the birth of Kusa and Lava and, finally, Rama and Sita's union. *Udatta Raghavam* (The Illustrious Raghava [Rama]) is a Sanskrit play by Mayuraja, and the story is based on Rama's life. *Anargh Raghav* (Inestimable Raghav) is a Sanskrit drama by Murari Misra, which revolves around the life events of Rama, the descendant of Raghu. *Balramayan* (The Childhood of Rama) is a Sanskrit play by Rajashekhar; it dramatically describes the *Ramkatha* from Rama and Sita's marriage to their return to Ayodhya. *Prasannraghav* (Gracious Raghav) is a Sanskrit play by the poet Jayadeva. The story offers an account of the various vicissitudes in the life of Rama, the hero of the Ramayana, commencing with his marriage to Sita and ending with his final victory over the demon king, Ravana.

13. The 'Jaiminyai Ashvamedha Parva' is sage Jaimini's description of the Ashvamedha *yajna*. The Ashvamedha *yajna*, or horse sacrifice, was performed by autocrats to establish their supreme sovereignty. The horse was let out to roam about all countries; those who opposed the sovereignty of the king could stop the horse and tie it. Then the king had to defeat him before conducting the horse sacrifice. The text of the 'Jaiminyai Ashvamedha Parva' narrates the story of Rama resuming his kingship of Ayodhya after his return from Lanka and then an expectant Sita's exile on account of public doubt over her character. Sita had two sons, Kusa and Lava, who captured Rama's ceremonial horse for this sacrifice and fought Rama's army, leading to the reconciliation of Rama and Sita. This happy ending of Rama's story is very similar to the narrative of the *Padma Purana*'s 'Patalakanda' (C. Bulcke 2020 [1950], p. 140).

14. *Mahamahopadhyaya* means a very great preceptor, and it also refers to a title given to learned men and reputed scholars. In ancient India, a scholar who

wrote works based on topics related to the Shastras was granted the title Mahopadhyaya. The title Mahamahopadhyaya was bestowed on the best amongst the Mahopadhyaya scholars. Ganganath Jha (1871–1941) was a renowned scholar of Sanskrit, Indian philosophy and Buddhist philosophy. He has written original texts of high quality on philosophical subjects in Hindi, English and Maithili languages. His biggest contribution has been the translation of important ancient Sanskrit texts into English. This work of his provided an opportunity for Western scholars to become familiar with the ancient knowledge of India. He taught Sanskrit at the University of Allahabad and then became the principal of Banaras Sanskrit College. His son, Amarnath Jha, was the vice chancellor of the University of Allahabad, who allowed Camille to submit his PhD dissertation in Hindi.

15. *Ramleela* is the dramatic performance of the story of Rama, mostly enacted by folk artists.

16. We also discuss this in the last chapter (Chapter 6).

17. The original verse by Kabirdas says, 'Even if I convert the entire earth into paper, turn the whole forests into pens and make ink from the seven seas, I shall still not be able to describe the great qualities of my guru [teacher]'.

5

⊰⊱

Contributions to Indology
and Scholarly Legacy

As mentioned in the earlier chapters, Camille's evolution as a Christian priest and a scholar of Indian traditions and his knowledge were shaped at the Calcutta School of Indology – an umbrella institution, which made a genuine, rational and scientific approach to explore, examine and explain Indology to its members, to the wider Indian scholarly community and to the entire world. One must recognise the fundamental ethos of the Calcutta School of Indology as reflected in Camille's body of work. Not only did he produce some of the most extraordinary works on ancient and medieval Indian literature, philosophy and theology, but he also undertook the herculean and exceptional campaign to indigenise Christian sacred texts, philosophy and theology for ordinary Indians.

Camille's most renowned contribution to the field of Indology is his study of the *Ramkatha*; his doctoral thesis was turned into a celebrated book titled *Ramkatha: Utpatti Aur Vikas*. Right from its publication, this book was considered a tour de force, and as Dineshwar Prasad argues, Camille's work on the *Ramkatha* is the first of its kind that 'compiled the narrative from various Indian and foreign sources and analysed each and every fact and meaning of it through a systematic, scientific and conclusive research' (D. Prasad 2002, p. 22). Camille explored the Ramayana literature beyond Sanskrit and Hindi and studied 'Tamil, Telegu, Malayalam, Kannada, Bengali, Kashmiri and Sinhalese' versions of the story (D. Verma 1950, p. 6). The renowned Hindi littérateur Dhirendra Verma[1] called this book an 'encyclopaedia of the Ramkatha narrative' that includes 'the Rama-Story found abroad and in this connection information available from Tibet, Khotan, Indonesia, Indo-China [Laos, Cambodia, Vietnam], Siam [Thailand], Burma [Myanmar]' (ibid.). The details and scholarly analysis highlight that 'its range is simply astounding and kaleidoscopic' (ibid.).

Camille's book is a testament to the broad sphere of Indian civilisational influence around South-East Asia based on the popularity of the *Ramkatha*. The story of Rama (*Ramkatha*) remained his lifelong passion, and apart from revising this book, he also wrote several research essays in Hindi, English, French and Flemish on this theme. The multiple variations of the Ramayana narrative is pursued in several scholarly studies. Some of the prominent ones include A. K. Ramanujan's 'Three Hundred Ramayanas' in Paula Richman's edited volume *Many Ramayanas: The Diversity of a Narrative Tradition*. Other representative works on the same theme are Srinivas Iyengar's *Asian Variations in Ramayana*, V. Raghavan's *The Ramayana Tradition in Asia*, Yogendra Pratap Singh's *Ram Sahitya Kosh* and A. A. Manavalan's *Ramayana: A Comparative Study of Ramkathas*. While several volumes exploring the diversity in the *Ramkatha* narrative have appeared in the last few years, each of them owes a debt of gratitude to Camile's monumental work on this theme.

Camille recognised that most of the Christian priests lacked an adequate vocabulary in Hindi and felt the need of an authentic and efficient English–Hindi dictionary (C. Bulcke 1968). Camille took up the arduous task of compiling the technical glossary and later an exhaustive English–Hindi dictionary to help develop the Hindi language and to adapt the religious sermons to suit the local cultural milieu. He translated several sacred Christian texts into Hindi so that the true spirit, genuine meaning and philosophical insights from these texts could be communicated to the local people in a simple yet authentic way. His translation of the Holy Bible into Hindi as *Pavitra Bible*, published posthumously, is considered the most authentic rendition of the text for north Indian audiences. He also translated *The Saviour: The Four Gospels in One Narrative*, the *Sermon on the Mount* and *St. Luke's Gospel*. Apart from these, Camille translated numerous hymns, litany, prayers and songs into Hindi, as well as the details and processes of several Christian religious rituals.

Camille's devotion to Hindi is well known and seen as one of his most outstanding services to the ordinary Hindi speakers. He made notable contributions to the body of knowledge in Hindi as a lexicographer, and as a dedicated Hindi protagonist made scholarly exposition on the competence of the language. As a lexicographer, Camille is peerless, producing one of the most authentic English-to-Hindi dictionaries, serving both preliminary learners and proficient linguaphiles. The lack of an authentic dictionary for non-Hindi speakers compelled Camille to prepare an expedient and abridged but highly effective dictionary titled *A Technical English–Hindi Glossary* in 1955. He intended to prepare a working dictionary for the Christian priests so that they could explain the accurate Hindi equivalents of the Christian philosophical–theological words and rituals. However, his little experiment as a lexicographer turned out to be highly successful, and he compiled a full-fledged English–Hindi dictionary.

Camille's English–Hindi dictionary provides the apt Hindi equivalents of English words and their standard pronunciation in the Devanagari script. It is deemed the best encyclopaedia of words and phrases to provide authentic knowledge of Hindi to Hindi-speaking Indians in English and to Indians and non-Indians learning Hindi through English. The dictionary has achieved unrivalled fame as the most reliable and bona fide reference for students, professionals, government officers, translators and littérateurs. His scholarly and evidence-based analysis to foreground Hindi as the language for bureaucratic, academic, legal, business and modern science and technology work is widely acclaimed.

Apart from these outstanding literary contributions, Camille's work on comparative religion and his writings on several significant issues of his era are also part of his repertoire. His exposition on some of the basic tenets of both Christianity and Hinduism provide an erudite explanation of the two belief systems, their similarities and differences. His outstanding humanitarian values, magnetic personality and generosity exalted him to the position of a sagely figure, and he began to be called 'Baba Bulcke' by most of the people he came across (Ghosh 2015, p. 132).

One may use a broad classification to discuss Camille's copious works under four main categories.

1. *Ramkatha* and Valmiki
2. Christian texts in Hindi
3. Hindi and dictionary work
4. Comparative religious studies

Ramkatha and Valmiki

It is hard to pin down a polymath and polyglot as prolific as Camille Bulcke to the narrow confines of one specific scholarly theme or academic discipline.

However, he achieved eternal fame and global recognition for his works related to the *Ramkatha*; his thesis published as the book *Ramkatha: Utpatti Aur Vikas* is considered as one of the most innovative, authoritative and comprehensive accounts of the Ramayana story. The exceptional popularity of his book was matched by Camille's lifelong pursuit of exploring new material and revising the book. Camille first published the book in 1950 and witnessed three editions in his lifetime, and before his death, he included some newly discovered material in the manuscript of the fourth edition. Despite his preoccupation with other responsibilities, such as that of a lexicographer, translator, public intellectual and mentor to numerous students, the *Ramkatha* remained his abiding passion, leading to prolific research and writing on the subject throughout his life. Apart from continually refining his masterwork, Camille also wrote some of the most original and enlightening pieces on different characters of the *Ramkatha*. He highlighted the poignant and vivid depiction of human emotions, the ethical framework for moral conduct and steadfast devotion expressed in *Ramkatha* literature, especially Tulsidas' *Ramcharitmanas*.

As we have indicated earlier, Camille's lifelong fascination with the *Ramkatha* started fortuitously, which he referred to as divinely ordained or predestined. One may trace this journey to Camille's affection for Guido Gezelle's mellifluous poetry, a chance encounter with the German translation of one of the profound verses of the *Ramcharitmanas* and his admiration for Constant Lieven's missionary work in India. Camille did not come to India with a clear plan to work on the *Ramkatha*; it was indeed accidental that he found himself in a country which brought back the harsh memories of the linguistic colonisation against Flemish, his own mother tongue, during his childhood and adolescence. As part of his struggle against linguistic colonisation, he laboured to learn Hindi, and in the course of it, he rediscovered Tulsidas, which changed the course of his life. When Dhirendra Verma, the head of the department, asked Camille, after he completed his MA degree in Hindi at the University of Allahabad, if he would like to pursue further research on the renowned poet, Surdas, Camille politely declined. Verma realised almost instantaneously that his prodigious student was dedicated to Tulsidas, and thus, nothing else would ignite the passion and nothing contrary would interest him.

Camille used to cite a short story – not to undervalue Surdas against Tulsidas on the grounds of creativity or poetic aesthetics but to contrast the essence of their writings. The story goes like this: Once a person went to Tulsidas and asked whether his or those of Surdas' compositions could be considered poetry. Tulsidas replied unhesitatingly, 'Sur's composition is poetry.' The man then went to Surdas and asked, 'You tell me whether Tulsi's composition is poetry or yours.' Surdas was engrossed in thoughts and after some time said, 'Indeed, my composition is poetry, but Tulsi's writing is a mantra. If you want to enjoy poetry, come to me and if you want to achieve salvation [*mukti*], go to Tulsi' (C. Bulcke cited in Kalsi 1987, p. 162). It was not just the beauty of Tulsidas' poetry and writings that attracted him, but the promises of devotional purity and surrender to the supreme God to attain salvation, as preached by Tulsidas, which inspired Camille all his life.

Camille was right to claim that his association with the *Ramkatha* was preordained; as a religious man devoted to a life full of piety, poetry, literature, philosophy and theology, he was destined to encounter Tulsidas, one of the finest proponents of devotional poetry. Moreover, once he decided to live and serve the people in the Hindi-speaking areas, he had to come across and then marvel at the phenomenon aptly described by him as 'the wonder that is Tulsidas' (C. Bulcke 2010, p. 144). As Philip Lutgendorf argues, 'Anyone interested in the religion and culture of Northern India sooner or later encounters a reference to the epic poem *Ramcharitmanas* and its remarkable popularity' (Lutgendorf 1991, p. 1). Tulsidas' *Ramcharitmanas* has been acclaimed as 'the Bible of Northern India', as 'the best and most trustworthy guide to the popular living faith of the Hindu race at the present day', 'as something like a living sum of Indian culture' and as 'defining work of Indian Culture' (Macfie 1930, p. vii; Growse 1891, p. i; R. Prasad 1988, p. xii; Lutgendorf 2016, p. vii). The text has gained extraordinary popularity even in the south of India and is part of ritual singing and chanting across the country. Most *Ramkatha vachak*s (those who narrate the story of the Ramayana) consider this book as the basis of their discourses about Dharma, Indian culture and moral conduct that epitomises the essence of all the sacred Hindu texts.

Another fortuitous development relates to Camille's PhD journey; he did not choose to work on the genesis of *Ramkatha* but, by accident, ended up producing his most celebrated work. Camille was assigned to work under Mataprasad Gupt, a renowned expert on Tulsidas. He then prepared a detailed outline of his research with the help of his supervisor and registered his thesis under the title 'Tulsi's Devotion to Rama' (C. Bulcke 2015 [1976], p. 334). Camille, the diligent, meticulous and methodical researcher, started to gather material for the introductory chapter titled 'Development of *Ramkatha*'. Soon he was overwhelmed with the volume of information on the genesis and development of the Rama story; the popular text of Valmiki's Ramayana only had three versions with significant differences in events, protagonists and their interactions (ibid.). The more Camille endeavoured to find one master narrative, the more competing narratives he discovered; it seemed as if the entire Indian literature was *Ram–may*, or replete with Rama (C. Bulcke 2009, p. 14). Camille found that the popularity of the *Ramkatha* was manifested not only in Sanskrit literature but also in vernacular literature within India; the literature of South-East Asia also had abundant material on the *Ramkatha* (ibid.). Having spent an entire year exploring, collating and analysing the material for the *Ramkatha*, he suddenly realised that he had not even finished half of the first chapter. However, his guide found the collected material so comprehensive and the analysis so innovative that he asked Camille to write about the development of different episodes of the *Ramkatha*. Once Camille started writing, the introduction itself turned out to be so extensive and so original that he was allowed to submit his dissertation titled 'Ramkatha: Origin and Development' (ibid.).

Camille explained at the very beginning of his book that the objective of his research was not to explore Rama *bhakti*, or the devotion to Rama; instead, he intended to explore the sources and development of the *Ramkatha* in the literary traditions of India and its extended neighbourhood. This is a significant point that must be kept in mind while referring to his most celebrated work; Camille removed any sacred, religious, divine sanctity and cultural significance to Rama, the chief protagonist of the *Ramkatha* in the Hindu traditions. His focus was only on *Ramkatha* literature and how this literature has evolved and progressed to such wide acclaim and popularity. Indeed, his research on the *Ramkatha* literature forged new grounds and discovered some unexplored territories through a systematic, meticulous and conclusive research process.

In order to collate the enormous and diverse mass of information into a coherent, logical and lucid exposition, Camille segregated the material into four different sections: ancient *Ramkatha* literature; the genesis of the *Ramkatha*; an overview of post-Valmiki *Ramkatha* literature; and, finally, the different stages of the development of the *Ramkatha*. Within each section, Camille catalogued the extensive references and source material followed by his analysis, arguments and inferences from the available information. While the source material of his thesis was always available, Camille's ingenuity and meticulous research brought such precious but scattered and often unnoticed knowledge into one repository. Apart from compiling so much information, Camille interpreted every text and verified the facts and the meanings of the text from different traditions and in different languages. Indeed, Camille's work on the *Ramkatha* forged a new method and an innovative approach to how the Rama story is interpreted (D. Prasad 2002). We highlight further some of the most significant discoveries made in Camille's groundbreaking research.

Given the centrality of the *Ramkatha* to Indian literary traditions, it is not unusual to imagine that the story has its origins in ancient times and existed in the Vedic period because the names of many of its main characters are found in Vedic literature. Accordingly, Camille began his inquiry about the origin of the *Ramkatha* in the Vedas and found menions of 'Ikshvaku',[2] 'Dasharatha',[3] and 'Rama' in the Vedic texts. Camille asserted that while the *Rigveda* mentions Ikshvaku and Dasharatha in different contexts, it does not offer any evidence or reference to the relationship between the two (C. Bulcke 2020 [1950], p. 3). He claimed, with reference to Ikshvaku and Dasharatha, that 'their mutual relation is not impossible, but there is no indication of it; moreover, these names are not mentioned anywhere else in the Vedic literature' (ibid., p. 8). The name Rama appears in Vedic literature as a king in the *Rigveda*, along with three other references – as a Brahmin teacher, Rama Margaveya; as a sage, Rama Aupatasvini; and as a philosopher and teacher, Rama Kratujateya. Camille argued that in the Vedic times the name Rama was prevalent among both kings and Brahmins. While the historicity of the name is beyond doubt, these people do not seem to have any relation with the Rama of the Ramayana (ibid., p. 3).

The other names of the Ramayana story that feature in Vedic literature include Sita, the name of Rama's wife, and Janaka, the father of Sita. Camille provided a detailed list of such references and claimed that Vedic literature refers to two Sitas: Sita Savitri[4] and Sita, the presiding deity of agriculture. The number of references related to Sita, the goddess of agriculture, is much more than those related to Sita Savitri. However, according to Camille's interpretations, the Sita in Vedic literature is not the character mentioned in the Ramayana because instead of referring to an actual historical person, the Vedic Sita is a personification of the term which is synonymous with the method of ploughing (ibid., pp. 6–10). Similarly, Camille catalogued the number of references to Janaka, as a learned philosopher named Janaka

Videha, who guided the sages about the proper rites in the conduct of Agnihotra (pouring oblations into the fire). From the available information in Vedic literature, Camille deduced that while the Ramayana links Vedic Kanaka with Janaka, the father of Sita, one cannot find any proof of this link in the Vedic texts (ibid., p. 19). Similarly, despite the repeated references to Janaka and Sita in Vedic literature, the text does not make any specific or categorical statement on the father–daughter relationship between the two (ibid.).

Camille concluded that while some of the names from the Ramayana appear in Vedic literature, none of these characters depict the kinship and associations claimed in the Ramayana. He argued that the only tenable claim is the presence of some historical persons mentioned in the Vedic literature who shared the name with characters in the Ramayana, and no other association can be made between Vedic texts and the *Ramkatha*.

Camille then explored the genesis of the *Ramkatha* and debunked the two dominant perspectives on the origin myth of the Rama story propagated by two renowned Indologists, Albrecht Weber and Hermann Jacobi. Weber posited that the original narrative of the Rama story is borrowed from the Buddhist text *Dasharatha Jataka*,[5] while the story of Sita's abduction is borrowed from Homer's Iliad, which describes Helen's abduction (Weber 1873; Telang 1873). Through his detailed analysis, Camille claimed that the Rama story in the *Dasharatha Jataka* is a distorted form of the Valmiki Ramayana and some parts are from the ancient *Ramkatha* narratives from before the Valmiki compositions (C. Bulcke 2020 [1950], p. 72). Camille argued that there could be no tenable connection between the Iliad and the Ramayana, given that ships are of great importance in Homer's work, while the Ramayana talks of building a bridge to cross the sea instead of using ships (ibid., p. 79). Jacobi proposed that the Ramayana was created by assembling two distinct and independent parts: the first part describing Rama's childhood and youth in Ayodhya is historical, while his exile and his battles against the demons are fictional (Jacobi 1893). Camille suggested that the differences in tone and tenor between the two parts of the narrative are possible given the different contexts of a prince living with his clan in the kingdom and facing dire situations in exile. However, he argued that it is a usual literary device to deploy exaggerations to represent a valiant and upright hero fighting against a wicked villain (C. Bulcke 2020 [1950], p. 86). The difference in language and poetic style does not mean that the two distinct parts were somehow amalgamated later (ibid.).

Based on his extensive research of the various Buddhist, Jain and Hindu sources, Camille asserted that the *Ramkatha* is neither an imaginary or allegorical story nor a combination of material available in various sources. Its characters and events are real from the past, and its historicity is proven in the Buddhist, Jain and ancient Hindu texts. The Buddhists acknowledged the popularity of *Ramkatha* and acclaimed Rama as Bodhisattva,[6] while the Jains tried to adapt Valmiki's Rama to fit their belief system (ibid., p. 116). From his study of the Buddhist Tripitaka, the Mahabharata and the Ramayana, Camille claimed that the *Ramkatha*, the narrative poetry, originated after the Vedic period in the fourth century BCE (ibid., p. 25). Valmiki is the first poet who arranged this narrative poetry into a proper composition, acknowledging so in the concluding sections of his own Ramayana; the renowned Sanskrit poet Kalidasa also refers to Valmiki as the *adikavi* (the first poet) (ibid., p. 106). Camille, thus, considered Valmiki a poetic genius who first compiled the narrative poems of the *Ramkatha* into one integral literary work around 300 BCE (ibid., p. 108).

In his research, Camille came across four persons named Valmiki: the grammarian Valmiki, Suparna Valmiki, the *maharishi* (great sage) Valmiki and the *adikavi* (first poet) Valmiki. In the Ramayana, Valmiki the first poet and Valmiki the *maharishi* are depicted as the same person, who learns the *Ramkatha* from the sage Narada, thereby establishing the existence of the narrative poetry before Valmiki's compilation (ibid., p. 35). Valmiki is shown as contemporaneous with the Ramayana's events and as the one person who offers Sita shelter after Rama abandons her (ibid.). In the Mahabharata and some Puranas, Valmiki is mentioned as a Brahmin and the same as the sage Chyavana Bhargava[7] (ibid., pp. 28–29). Several texts including the Mahabharata also describe Valmiki as a dacoit who became an ascetic. He followed strict austerities and went into such deep meditation that his entire body was covered in a termite hill; etymologically, the name Valmiki is derived from 'termite hill' (ibid.).

These references related to Valmiki are so varied and different from each other that it is impossible to find the personality of the great poet. Camille suggested that while there is no doubt that the first complete Ramayana was composed by Valmiki, 'there is a complete lack of authentic material regarding the biography of this great poet' (ibid., p. 25). However, based on his analysis of the available material, he posited that Valmiki had some highly skilled *kusilavas* (rhapsodes) as his disciples who travelled around reciting his poetry. In the 'Uttarakanda' of the Ramayana, Valmiki instructed his two disciples to recite the poem in the sacred enclosures of the *rishis* (sages) and the dwellings of the Brahmins, along the roads and highways and around the palaces of kings (ibid., p. 109). Thus, it can be deduced that the Ramayana was disseminated orally, and the itinerant professional singers or rhapsodes used to recite it and make a living through their singing. It also implies that the Ramayana did not exist as a book or a written text, and the rhapsodes kept the poem alive by memorising it and passing it onto the next generations. However, these rhapsodes would be obliged to cater to the preferences and expectations of their audience and, thus, make changes to the poem to suit their audiences. This autonomy to expand the narratives to suit their audience drove the popularity of the Ramayana, but it also introduced several interpolations to the original poem (ibid., p. 110).

Camille argued that given the absence of one master copy of the first poet Valmiki's original rendition, as a book or text, the autonomy of the itinerant singers led to several different versions (recensions) of the Ramayana. The different recensions of the Valmiki Ramayana have several interpolations, leading to confusion and contradiction among different versions of the text. The Oriental Institute, Baroda, took on the task of compiling a critical edition to standardise the original text, by verifying various manuscripts available from various parts of India. Given his eminence as a *Ramkatha* scholar and his profound knowledge of the development of the *Ramkatha*, Camille was invited to be a member of the board of referees for this endeavour.

The popularity of the Valmiki Ramayana across India was brought by itinerant singers who learned the poem by heart and performed it in public. However, these singers also introduced several alterations and variations to the original poem to suit their audience or to produce dramatic impact by exaggerating certain descriptions. Sheldon Pollock argues that 'by the twentieth century more than two thousand manuscripts of the poem, in whole or in part, are known to exist' (Pollock 1984, p. 82). Among the different versions of the Valmiki Ramayana, there are two popular recensions: one from northern and the other from southern India. The northern recension is further classified into two variants: one is from north-western India, while the other is popular in Bengal and is referred to as the Gaudiya version. Pollock argues that the 'manuscripts of the northern recension come from: Gujarat, Rajasthan, Kashmir, Nepal, Bihar, and Bengal; those of the southern recension from: Kerala, Andhra Pradesh, and Tamil Nadu' (ibid.).

Camille listed three popular recensions of the Valmiki Ramayana.

1. Southern recension: The Gujarati Printing Press (Mumbai), Nirnaya Sagar Press (Mumbai) and the southern editions. This version is comparatively more popular and widespread.
2. Gaudiya recension: Edited by G. Gorresio (Paris) and Calcutta Sanskrit Series editions.
3. North-western recension: Dayananda College (Lahore)'s edition, which is available these days from Sadhu Ashram, Hoshiarpur (Punjab). (C. Bulcke 2020 [1950], pp. 20–21)

In each recension, many *shloka*s are found in one that do not occur in the other, and the substantial differences among the recensions have attracted the attention of many scholars (Brockington 1998, pp. 345–348). To underline the method of identifying differences among the recensions, Camille deployed Jacobi's[8] classification.

1. Each recension has a good number of verses, even longer passages and entire cantos, which are not to be found in one or, at times, even both of the others. Comparing the southern and Bengal recensions, we find that one-third of the verses are common in each recension.
2. Each recension differs from one or, at times, even from both of the others in the common verses; the southern recension is usually considered as much closer to the original text.
3. The sequence of the verses is often different, even in all three recensions.

Camille argued that while the differences under the first heading may be considered as additions or omissions, the differences 'under Nos. 2 and 3 prove that the recensions were independently written down on the basis of a text, differing in its oral transmission' (C. Bulcke 2010, pp. 43–44). As one of the examples, he showed that against the southern recension's 1,303 verses, the Bengal recension had 1,228 verses and only 748 were common to both (ibid.). However, he argued that despite the substantial numerical differences, 'an examination of the subject-matter shows that, in reality, the narrative has changed very little' (ibid.). Camille's substantial argument is that the essence of the narrative remains similar across all the recensions, and it has sustained across time and space, which can be witnessed in the literature of different eras, cultures, languages and regions.

Camille suggested that both the size and narrative of Valmiki's initial version of the Ramayana underwent extensive expansion due to the interpolations inserted by the itinerant professional singers. They broadened the narrative of popular portions to address the curiosity of their listeners primarily by reiterating certain dramatic events, repetitions of emotional passages and adding spectacular and preternatural happenings (ibid., p. 27). Camille argued that Valmiki's original composition had only five books, while the contemporary version of Valmiki's Ramayana, which he referred to as the vulgate Valmiki Ramayana, has seven different books. Each book is referred to as *kanda* (a major section or segment, which is sometimes translated into English as canto) (Debroy 2017, p. xv). The popular version of the Valmiki Ramayana consists of around 24,000 *shloka*s and is distributed across seven *kandas*: 'Balakanda' (Book about Youth), 'Ayodhyakanda' (Book about Ayodhya), 'Aranyakanda' (Book about the Forest), 'Kishkindhakanda' (Book about Kishkindha), 'Sundarakanda' (Book about Beauty), 'Yuddhakanda' (Book about the War) and 'Uttarakanda' (Book about the Sequel) (ibid.).

Table 5.1 *Kanda*s in the original Valmiki Ramayana and the vulgate Valmiki Ramayana

Original Valmiki Ramayana	Vulgate Valmiki Ramayana
	1. Balakanda
1. Ayodhyakanda	2. Ayodhyakanda
2. Aranyakanda	3. Aranyakanda
3. Kishkindhakanda	4. Kishkindhakanda
4. Sunderkanda	5. Sunderkanda
5. Yuddhakanda	6. Yuddhakanda
	7. Uttarakanda

Source: Collated by the authors based on information presented in C. Bulcke (2020 [1950]), pp. 95–96.

Camille believed that the 'Balakanda' was introduced to provide details on the origin stories, the childhood and youth of the lead protagonists such as Rama, Sita and others, while the 'Uttarkanda' was introduced to exalt Rama as an avatar or incarnation of God or Lord Vishnu. To rationalise his arguments about the books of 'Balakanda' and 'Uttarkanda' as interpolations,

Camille posited that the itinerant singers might have prefixed some introduction to Valmiki's poem. As the poem gained popularity and attracted a bigger audience, people would have inquired about Rama and Sita's earlier history, birth, upbringing, youth, marriage, and so on. The answer to all these inquiries emerged 'as the first nucleus of Balakanda' (C. Bulcke 2010, p. 28). Further, Camille argued that the idea of Rama as an incarnation of Vishnu or attributing the avatar-hood to Rama must have emerged close to the time when the composition of the 'Balakanda' neared its completion. Camille believed that to address this new development, the 'Balakanda' refers to Rama as Vishnu in two places: 'in the *putrestiyajna* [sacrifice to obtain a son] and in the encounter with Parasurama' (C. Bulcke 2020 [1950], p. 229).

Camille also posited that the entire book of the 'Uttarakanda' is nothing but interpolation – later additions to construct the narrative of the divinity of Rama (ibid., p. 484). While the concept of avatar is found in the Vedic literature, their worship or imagining of Vishnu as an avatar was not present in these texts; the advent of the Krishna avatar inspired a new impetus on asserting avatar-hood for the chosen deity. Initially, Vasudeva Krishna, the presiding deity of the Bhagavatas, was not seen as an avatar, but in later developments around the third century BCE, he was represented as the incarnation of Vishnu (ibid., p. 114). Soon, Vishnu Narayana emerged as the most important deity, and all the earlier avatars described in Vedic literature were also shown as incarnations of Vishnu (ibid.).

Camille believed that the ascription of avatar-hood to Rama was an inexorable development or almost a natural process. Given that the bards had sung Rama's praises for several centuries, Valmiki 'transformed the old story into an epic which idealised Rama further'. Moreover, the old idea of 'God becoming manifest on earth in various forms had received great impetus ever since Krishna had been identified with Vishnu' (C. Bulcke 2010, p. 28). As Camille argued, it was almost inevitable that Rama would be divinised as an avatar of Vishnu, and this inevitability and its widespread recognition is established once we see that the Buddhists revered Rama as Bodhisattva and the Jains deified Rama as one of the eight Baldevas[9] (C. Bulcke 2020 [1950], p. 116). Camille also argued that the bards created the 'Uttarkanda' for the same reasons that led to the creation of the 'Balakanda': 'to satisfy the very natural curiosity of their listeners as to the further history of Rama and Sita' (C. Bulcke 2010, p. 28).

To substantiate his claim that both the 'Balakanda' and the 'Uttarkanda' are later interpolations, Camille cited the addition of extraneous narratives, contradictory information and the differences in writing styles and poetic expressions in these two from the other parts of Valmiki's composition. He argued that the Ramayana's first table of contents (the first canto), did not list any of the subject matter described in the 'Balakanda'. In order to accommodate the later interpolations, a new table of contents was introduced to combine the new narratives. Similarly, the 'Uttarakanda' was never part of the original composition (C. Bulcke 2020 [1950], pp. 95–96). Moreover, Camille underlined that the style of composition of the 'Uttarakanda' is entirely different from that of the other authentic cantos (ibid.). The lack of discussion on avatar-hood in all the original five books and the pervasiveness of avatar-hood in the 'Uttarakanda' prove this part was added later to the composition.

Camille insisted that the entire 'Balakanda' and the 'Uttarakanda' are interpolations based on the major linguistic and stylistic differences from the rest of the text. However, he did not consider several other sources claiming that some parts of the 'Balakanda' and the 'Uttarkanda' are part of the original core (Goldman 1984, p. 15). Even Jacobi (1893) considered some portions of the 'Balakanda' to be a part of Valmiki's work; otherwise, this composition 'has an abrupt beginning, which is contrary to the narrative technique of India' (Guruge 1960, p. 32). Moreover, despite the different poetic styles, the 'Uttarkanda is considered an integral part of Ramayana because it contains the story of Ravana, the villain of the epic' (Kibe 1947, p. 55) Some scholars argue that the nucleus of the 'Uttarakanda' was Valmiki's original composition because 'the history and greatness of Ravana required to be detailed somewhere, for without them the poem would have been incomplete and the greatness of Rama without a strong relief' (Vaidya 1901, pp. 47–48). Furthermore, the painful sequel of the poem, which narrates 'the disappearance of Sita has so beautifully been conceived that even if the incidents were supposed to be imaginary none but the great poet himself could have conceived them' (ibid.).

Apart from the detailed work on the genesis and origins of the *Ramkatha*, Camille's other notable contribution is tracing the evolutionary process through different developmental stages of the Rama story. In his work on the development of the *Ramkatha*, like an expert cartographer, Camille prepared a detailed map of the *Ramkatha*'s dissemination, adaptations and evolution within India and its extended neighbourhood. While some work on the development of the *Ramkatha* had already existed, most of it remained inaccessible to a wider audience for lack of awareness, geographical remoteness and linguistic barriers. By compiling several of these works along with the more popular texts, Camille produced an all-inclusive, insightful and enlightening encyclopaedia at one place. This is one of his consummate contributions to Indology. Anyone who goes through his work on the *Ramkatha* will not remain where they started because their outlook would expand with a deep understanding of the much broader interlinguistic and international context (D. Prasad 2002, p. 49).

In his research, Camille included practically all the available material on the *Ramkatha* from the Vedic period until his time and in all languages from India, its neighbourhood and South-East Asia. His meticulous research of tracing almost every significant episode or notable event in various renditions and traditions makes his research one of the most insightful works. His overall assessment of the popularity of the *Ramkatha* is its adaptation to local factors, customs and preferences; basically, the *Ramkatha* travelled along with the legend of Rama and became localised in the process. This assimilation of local, social, cultural, religious and customary practices enabled the *Ramkatha* to gain unprecedented popularity and acclaim. It is easy to compare this analysis and the line of arguments reflected in several subsequent works, such as Ramanujan's 'Three Hundred Ramayanas', Iyengar's *Asian Variations in Ramayana*, and Manavalan's *Ramayana: A Comparative Study of Ramkathas*.

Another aspect of Camille's numerous essays on the evolutionary nature of the *Ramkatha* is his detailed analysis of the character development of some of its major protagonists through tracing the historical narratives from different traditions and languages. One of his major contributions to such analysis is the inclusion of the non-mainstream folk traditions regarding the birth stories of the characters such as Sita and Hanuman. Camille argued that there have been so many depictions of the characters from the Valmiki Ramayana, along with their birth stories, interactions with other actors and activities, that one can never establish a stable, final, fixed narrative for these characters. Time, space and circumstances, as well as the personal preferences and experiences of the narrators, have caused many alterations to the narratives. Camille argued that for most of the characters in *Ramkatha*, one must remember that literary representation preceded the devotional aspects. Therefore, it is critical to acknowledge that despite the reverence associated with devotion, all these characters have undergone a long development process and that evolutionary aspects need due recognition and proper understanding. Camille's essays carry significant knowledge for those who wish to take these characters out of the limits of a particular creation and see them in a larger temporal context and understand their representation from different social, cultural and religious perspectives.

In his detailed study of the *Ramkatha*, Camille, while accepting so many changes to the depiction of its events and characters, affirmed that despite all the regional differences and changes, the fundamental unity of Valmiki's narrative has remained intact to date. Acclaiming the genius of Valmiki, Camille declared that 'no poet in the history of world literature can rival the profound influence the Adikavi from India exerts on the later literature' (C. Bulcke 2020 [1950], p. 579).

Bible and Christian Theology

In 1940, Father Ivan Extross[10] met Camille, a young and enthusiastic Christian missionary in Allahabad, while he was inquiring about the possibilities of getting admission into the MA programme in Hindi at the famous University of Allahabad. Extross recalled that at that time hardly any Catholic priests were interested in the in-depth study of Hindi, for they could get by with a superficial knowledge of Hindi and mostly colloquial expressions in their daily interaction beyond the seminaries (Extross 1987, pp. 70–71). English was the language for conducting all the official work and the only medium used in religious services. Extross also recalled that Camille's commendable and celebrated achievements in Hindi inspired several Christian priests to pursue formal qualifications in Hindi and engage with its literature. Apparently, Camille's oft-quoted phrase 'English only addresses the intellect, whereas Hindi addresses the heart' was the new mantra. Soon, the religious services were performed in Hindi, and as Extross said, 'Now we Christians often do our worship in Hindi, and the credit for translating the prayers and hymns goes to Father Bulcke (ibid.).

It is hard to cite one specific incident or date when Camille realised the exigent need for an authentic and lucid translation of the Christian sacred texts, prayers, hymns and other devotional songs into Hindi. On the first day of his arrival in Ranchi, he observed the hegemony of English over the local population, and he recognised the prevalent European etiquettes and modes of interaction among the clergy at Manresa House, the missionary residence in Ranchi. It is not that the Christian missionaries in India did not make concerted efforts to translate the holy books and the church services into the local Indian languages. Nevertheless, these translations never captured the imagination of the local Christians. As already explained in earlier chapters, within the first few days of his arrival, Camille resolved to learn Hindi and restore it to its rightful honourable place in India. For Camille, Hindi's rightful honourable place was not just in the worldly affairs of commerce, administration and academia but also in the devotional and ecclesiastical circles. It is worth reiterating that Camille landed in India in 1935 and immediately started learning Hindi. In 1942, he published the four Gospels from the Bible as *The Saviour: The Four Gospels in One Narrative* in English and its translation as *Muktidata* in Hindi. Dineshwar Prasad highlights that *Muktidata*, Camille's first Hindi translation, is a testament to how quickly he had gained such proficiency in Hindi (D. Prasad 2002, p. 14). It is also a testament to his ardour and pledge to translate the sacred Christian texts and prayers into Hindi from the very early stages of his priestly training. Camille found the lack of adequate language skills and vocabulary in Hindi among the Christian priests as a major shortcoming. He realised that the language barrier was preventing the clergy from creating a strong bond with the local people who were not proficient in English.

During his time in India, Camille came across the earlier translations of the Holy Bible, and with his profound knowledge of both Hindi and the Bible, he was disappointed because of the language, the style and the inappropriate meanings attributed to the religious and philosophical terms. He identified that these translations were not in accordance with the nature of the Hindi language or with the sensibilities and temperament of Hindi speakers; the language seemed artificial, tedious and, in many places, incoherent. The lack of a high-class Hindi translation of the Bible must have aggrieved Camille the linguaphile given that he knew of so many brilliant translations of the Bible in European languages. In several instances, the translation of the Bible turned out to be the first literary work in those languages, and its outstanding quality made them an epitome of lucid writing and expressions. Camille argued that the Hindi translations of the Bible used a stilted language which lacked sincerity, coherence and clarity – essential characteristics for a captivating and informative book. Camille explained the rationale behind his endeavour to translate the Bible as follows.

> Several translations of the Bible have been published in Hindi, presently more translations are in the process of publication. However, I had decided to undertake the translation of the Bible a long time ago, because the Hindi translations that came before me were indifferent to

the finer nuances of the language and the subtleties of its idioms and proverbs. The language was such that the reader would develop disgust towards Christianity. (C. Bulcke 2015 [1976], p. 339)

It is imperative to have a quick overview of the earlier attempts to translate Christian holy books into local Indian languages. Given the paucity of missionaries with sufficient linguistic proficiency, one would find some translation of small portions from the Bible into Hindi, Hindustani and Urdu – starting with John Jeshua Kettler's book *Lingua Hindostanica* (Hindustani Grammar) in 1698, Benjamin Schultz's *Grammatica Hundustanica* in 1741 and Casiano Baligati's *Alphabetum Brammhanicum* in 1771 (Vechoor 1987, p. 169). All these books contained translations of some portions from the Bible: Kettler translated the Lord's Prayer; Schultz translated David's Psalms and the Gospels of Luke, Mark and John, while Baligati included the translation of the Lord's Prayer (D. Prasad 2002, p. 75). Kettler's and Schultz's translations were only in the Roman script, while some parts of Baligati's translations included the Devanagari (Hindi) script (ibid.).

William Carey holds the credit of translating the entire text of the New Testament into Hindi, published in 1811, while Henry Martyn published the first Urdu version of the New Testament in 1815 (Vechoor 1987, p. 172).[11] These two versions were considered the prototype and highly reliable in all the subsequent attempts made by William Bowley, John Chamberlain, John Thompson, William Yachts, Leslie Parson, F. E. Schneider and William Hooper (Fernando 2019, p. 127). Most of the earlier translations were carried out by the Protestants, and despite their large numbers in India, the Catholics were late in taking to the Hindi translation of the Holy Bible. Most of the time, the Roman Catholics relied on an Urdu translation known as the Hartman's version, published in 1864 (ibid.). In 1958, Father R. P. Sah published the first complete translation of the New Testament in Hindi, followed by Father Stanislaus Wald's Hindi translation of the Old Testament in 1965 (Vechoor 1987, p. 172). These translations by Sah and Wald were the prevalent versions of the two parts of the Holy Bible among the Catholics in India.

The most sacred books of Christians are the two parts of the Bible: the Old Testament and the New Testament; the former is the scripture of the Jews, and the latter of the Christians. The Old Testament is considered the historical–ideological foundation of the Christian faith because the coming of the Prophet is repeatedly mentioned in the Old Testament, which according to the Christians is Jesus Christ. The Old Testament contains the 'Five Scrolls'[12] believed to exist since the twelfth century BCE. The Protestants consider the number of books in the Old Testament to be 39, while the Catholics believe the number to be 45. However, both concur that the New Testament comprises 27 books written by several authors in Koine Greek[13] between 50 and 120 CE.

The New Testament can be divided into four parts: Gospels, Acts of the Apostles, Epistles and Apocalypse. There are four Gospels: Matthew, Mark, Luke and John; these narrate the stories of Jesus' life, ministry and death. Acts of the Apostles, composed by Luke, describes the spread of the Christian church from the death of Jesus to the death of the apostle Paul (Ehrman 2016, p. 3).

The Bible was not composed in a single language; the greater part of the Old Testament used ancient Hebrew or Aramaic. In the New Testament, one would find Aramaic, standard Greek and Koine or colloquial Greek. The tradition of the Greek translation of the Old Testament dates back to before the Christian era, and it continued till the third century CE. However, in the fourth century CE, Saint Jerome authentically translated the Bible into Latin. This Latin translation is referred to as the Vulgate Bible and is universally recognised and revered throughout the Christian world. Given the use of so many different languages, it is clear that the translation of the original Bible required an authentic knowledge of four ancient languages: Hebrew, Aramaic, Greek and Latin. Most of the earlier Bible translators into Hindi had very limited or no knowledge of multiple languages; moreover, several of them relied on the English translation of the Bible as their source document. However, one must remember that all these earlier translations of the Bible into Hindi, despite their imperfections, created the groundwork for Camille to produce his brilliant work.

A significant point worth mentioning here is that Camille did not suddenly take up the Holy Bible's translation; instead, it was a gradual and long-drawn intellectual pursuit. This an intellectual journey started with the publication of *Muktidata*, the translation of *The Saviour*, in 1942, and continued for the next 40 years until his death in 1982. As a perfectionist, Camille was never satisfied with his translation and continued to refine the text leading to three successive editions of *Muktidata* in 1950, 1956 and 1967. Indeed, his first brush with the translation from the Bible taught him several valuable lessons that honed his skills and sharpened his sensibilities as a translator. More importantly, his first partial translation from the Bible into Hindi also brought him face to face with enormous challenges all his predecessors must have grappled with during their translation work. The biggest challenge in the Bible's translation into Hindi is to find appropriate synonyms for the Biblical terms and the specific cultural, ideological and philosophical vocabulary. Like his predecessors and even peers among the clergy, Camille too faced these issues during his first translation and spent considerable energy to prepare *A Technical English–Hindi Glossary*, which was published in 1955 (C. Bulcke 2015 [1976], p. 338).

Enthused with the success of translating *The Saviour* as *Muktidata* and assisted by his handy glossary, Camille started working through other parts of the New Testament. In 1959, he published the Hindi translation of his favourite work, the Sermon on the Mount, titled *Parvat Pravachan*. The rapid success of this translated work and wider appreciation from the missionaries, clergy and other Hindi-speaking Christians inspired Camille to take on more significant translations. He published the translation of the Gospel according to Saint Luke in 1963, which he described as an experiment to test his own competence as a translator of the Bible. In his interview with Dineshwar Pasad, he said,

> I first translated the Gospel of St. Luke as an experiment to see the response from others that would determine my future of Bible translations. Soon after its publication, there was a request from the Bishops to translate the entire Bible. Dr Dhirendra Verma wrote a letter asking why I did not translate the Bible. (C. Bulcke 2015 [1976], p. 339)

This request from the bishops was like the official sanction or mandate from the Jesuit authorities, while the appreciation and query from Verma was the seal of approval from one of the most eminent linguists of his times. He translated the four Gospels into Hindi from the New Testament under the title *Chaaron Susamachaar* in 1970 and the Acts of the Apostles as *Prerit Charitra* in 1973. He completed the Hindi translation of the New Testament in 1977, published as *Hindi Bible: New Testament* and the second edition in 1979 as *Naya Vidhaan: New Testament*. This translation gained wide popularity among Christian clerics, Bible experts and Christian and non-Christian Hindi speakers. The lucid language, simple expressions and textual purity were so impressive that Camille's translation of the New Testament was considered equal to his magnum opus *Ramkatha: Utpatti Aur Vikas* (D. Prasad 2002, p. 78).

The remarkable aspect of Camille's commitment to indigenise Christianity is not restricted to highbrow academic work alone. Along with his translation of the New Testament, one would find that he undertook the translation of a large volume of prayers and hymns for church service. Starting with *Maria Sangat Sahachar* (A Companion to the Congregation of Mary) in 1954, Camille published the prayers in Hindi for the Holy Week (the week between Palm Sunday and Easter, including the mass for Easter Sunday) as *Punya Saptaah* in 1957. Other translations included a book on church by-laws titled *Upvidhiyan* in 1955 and the translation of the priestly ordination process titled *Purohit Abhishek Ki Dharmvidhi* (The Religious Ceremony of Priestly Ordination) in 1969. He also published the Hindi translation of the Psalms in three different volumes titled *Paath Sangrah*, the Psalms for the Sunday service titled *Ravivareey Paath Sangrah* (A Collection of Sunday Prayers) and the evening prayers titled *Ratri Vandana* (Night Prayers). In these collections, Camille used the relevant sections from both the Old Testament and the New Testament; he published another collection of Psalms under the title *The Hindi Psalter of the Breviary* in 1980.

The unprecedented popularity of Camille's translation of the New Testament prompted the Catholic bishops to urge him to undertake the translation of the Old Testament (Vechoor 1987, p. 173). Camille had not planned to translate the whole text of the Old Testament as a standalone book, though he had already done partial translation of the text into several of his collections of the Psalms. Given that the volume of the Old Testament was three and a half times as large as the New Testament, and with his failing health, Camille did not feel confident enough to undertake such an arduous task of an independent translation from scratch. Therefore, he planned to revisit Stanislaus Wald's Hindi translation of the Old Testament and make necessary improvements. To start this process, Camille followed Wald's translation of the five books (Torah), the book of Tobit and the other historical texts, and the book of Jeremiah from chapters 1 to 26 (D. Prasad 2002, p. 79). For his revision and improvements of the existing Hindi text by Wald, Camille used several Hebrew, Latin and Greek texts and English, French and Dutch translations.

Once Camille finished his meticulous and thorough amendments to Wald's translation, the revisions were more like a completely new translation. It had no resemblance to the earlier versions. However, Camille found this process of revising Wald's translation extremely gruelling and tedious, so he decided to do the rest of the translation independently. He continued with the translation of the remainder of the Old Testament; having completed 930 pages, he only had another 150 pages to complete this assignment. However, his health deteriorated severely; he died before completing the remaining translations, including of Jeremiah's books (chapters 27–52), Ezekiel, Lamentations and the Song of Solomon. The Bishop's Council requested Dineshwar Prasad and William Dwyer[14] to complete this work. Camille's translation of the Old Testament and the New Testament was published in 1986 and titled *Pavitra Bible*. Even after so many decades and reprints, Camille's translation of the Holy Bible is still regarded as one of the finest among the Bible translations anywhere in the world.

Apart from his meticulous translation of the Holy Bible, in 1958 Camille also translated Maurice Maeterlinck's famous French play *The Bluebird* into Hindi as *Neel Panchhi* on the request of the Bihar Rashtrabhasha Parishad (C. Bulcke 1958). The translation of the Christian theological works was extremely important to him to bring the message of Christ to his followers in India and to make the prayers and rituals accessible to common people in their own language. However, translation for him was not merely a way to propagate his faith; it was also a scholarly enterprise in which he was deeply invested all his life.

The Art of Translation

Camille always maintained that as a language, Hindi has the vocabulary and expression to explain the most complex concepts and complicated philosophies in simple, lucid and logical way. However, to do so, one needs to clearly understand the subject matter they wish to explain in Hindi or, for that matter, in any other language (C. Bulcke 1987). Reading Camille's translation of the Bible and his other translations of the prayers and hymns, two things are obvious; first, he had the most profound understanding of the Bible and other Christian texts; second, he had an exceptional grasp of Hindi (D. Prasad 2002, p. 84). His translations are like individual pieces of creative writing, not a simple conversion of the literal meanings from the original text to Hindi. He was very vigilant in not just retaining the form of the source but also reconstructing the character, individuality and temperament of the original text according to the nature of the language (A. Singh 1987, p. 182). For Camille, translation was a creative literary process where he captured those inherent vibrations of the composition in the original language. These vibrations are not in a single word or line but pervade the whole composition, and which cannot be captured by relying on the literal meaning of the words. The artistic mind of the translator should receive this flowing vitality of the subject matter from the source language and then be able to reproduce it in the target language, while observing the linguistic guidelines and conventions of the target language (ibid.).

In the case of the translation of the Bible, capturing the sensitivity of the original text and preserving it in the translated text demands superior intellectual capabilities of a polyglot with excellent proficiency in maintaining linguistic integrity across multiple languages. Camille was mindful of these concerns, and the preface to his translation of the New Testament says, 'Unlike other translation works, the Bible's translator must be very vigilant in preserving the original spirit of the text' (C. Bulcke 1977b, p. 1). For the most part, the original language of the New Testament is Greek, and unlike earlier Hindi translators who relied on English translations, Camille used the original Greek text and other authentic translations in several of the European languages. In fact, Camille used the original Greek texts for most of his translations. In the introduction to the translation of the Acts of the Apostles, published as *Prerit Charitra*, he wrote, 'Taking inspirations from the modern French, English and Dutch translations I have translated the original Greek text and have presented it in a simple, natural, popular and standard Khari Boli Hindi' (C. Bulcke 1973, pp. 6–7). Similarly, in the English preface to the Hindi psalter, Camille mentioned using three best French translations (of Dhorme, of Hosty and the *Traduction œcuménique de la Bible* [Ecumenical Translation of the Bible]) (cited in D. Prasad 2002, p. 79). To ensure the authenticity of the translation, Camille relied on the renowned German dictionary of the Bible which lists the frequency of each word of the scripture and the contextual differences (C. Bulcke 1980).

In all the translations of the Biblical texts, Camille decided to use standard yet simple and lucid Hindi. In the preface to the translation of the New Testament, he wrote, 'I have attempted to present a simple, natural translation of the original Greek text in standard Hindi' (C. Bulcke 1977b, p. xi). Camille argued that the language of the original Bible is also simple, natural and lucid because its purpose is to convey its message to the masses. He used the same principle for the quick and easy understanding of his translations of the Bible for his general readership or untrained audience. When asked to explain the distinctive features of his translations of the Bible from others, Camille asserted,

My claim regarding my translation is that even a middle [school] pass person can understand it. Christians who have read it say they did not understand the Bible before but do so now. I have adopted a strategy to keep testing the simplicity of my translation. I narrate my translation to ordinary assistant brothers, and when they say that there is no difficulty in understanding it, then only I am satisfied with my Hindi. Following this principle, I have translated St. Paul's or Paul's letters, which are considered difficult even in their original form. I have worked for hours on them to present their expressions in popular language. I sometimes have considered many options to determine the correct and straightforward synonyms of each sentence, idiom, phrase or word. I am satisfied that these letters are as intelligible to people as the Gospels. (C. Bulcke 2015 [1976], p. 339)

Camille undertook the translation of the Bible after examining the merits and demerits of the efforts of several generations of its Hindi translators. When evaluated from the point of view of an adaptation of the original and the naturalness of the language and easy communicability, it is far superior to the earlier translations of the Bible. He believed that 'the speciality of a successful translation should be that it should not appear to be a translation' (C. Bulcke 1977b, p. xi). His translation of the Bible into Hindi is not merely an invaluable document; it is also a great creative work on its own.

The Diligence of the Lexicographer

Camille's proficiency in different European languages epitomised his exceptional language skills, a competence that hastened his Hindi learning. However, while learning Hindi, he also realised the challenges a new learner would face in this process.

After completing the [PhD] research, I thought about how best to serve Hindi literature. I knew my limits – I could not serve my beloved language by writing poems, stories or novels. I realised the lack of a reliable English–Hindi dictionary; hence I started to think in this direction. I also recognised that most of the Christian priests had a rudimentary vocabulary. Given their deficient vocabulary and the lack of a functional knowledge of Hindi, I prepared a small dictionary titled

A Technical English–Hindi Glossary to help the Christian priests. This glossary was so well received that it inspired me to toil for the next five years to create the English–Hindi Dictionary. (C. Bulcke 2015 [1976], p. 338)

Clearly, Camille's idea of working in Hindi was not to strive for timeless classics or produce world-renowned literature; his focus was on making functional, handy and pragmatic interventions to facilitate language learning. There are two connected yet distinct aspects of Camille's work for Hindi; as a lexicographer, he produced an outstanding dictionary, and as a litterateur, he produced several scholarly commentaries to promote Hindi.

Camille's English–Hindi dictionary is considered one of India's most popular reference books across academia, administration, media and business. Camille never planned to create a dictionary; had he known the torment of compiling it, he probably would have stayed clear of it. As he explained through an old Dutch poem – should a judge decide to decree extreme torture to a criminal, he should not sentence him to hard labour or solitary confinement but order him to compile a dictionary; the criminal would then undergo the concurrent punishment of all these sentences! (C. Bulcke 2009, p. 131). He joked that a lexicographer must have created this poem because, like the pain of childbirth, one has to undergo the pain of compiling a dictionary. In the most celebrated English dictionary of Samuel Johnson, the word 'lexicographer' is defined as 'a harmless drudge', which refers either to an indefatigable workhorse or a fool. Clearly, Johnson implied the first meaning since he did not consider himself a fool. From his experience, Camille could vouch that compiling a dictionary is back-breaking work (ibid.). The Hindi counterpart for 'harmless drudge' is *kolhu ka bael*, or the bull used to power the cold-press oil-extraction unit by walking around in circles all day!

Camille had experienced the exertion in compiling his technical English–Hindi glossary and had pledged never to take up the work of a lexicographer. After the publication of the dictionary in 1955, he stuck to this resolution for many years. However, during his other writing tasks, he started to make notes of the translation of specific words. Gradually, he accumulated such an impressive list that he was forced to renege on his pledge, and he started work on building a complete English–Hindi dictionary. He recalled that dictionary-making is such an onerous and mentally exhausting work that there is no time left to take an interest in other subjects; consequently, solitude becomes an integral part of the intellectual life of a lexicographer. He complained that while he was immersed in preparing his dictionary for the next five to six years, he had no opportunity to read a single book on any of his favourite subjects, such as the *Ramkatha*, Tulsidas and any sacred Christian texts. He used to quickly flip through all the new books on the *Ramkatha* that he received during these times and then stash them inside a cupboard. Given the lack of time, he used to decline all requests to write articles, dispose of all the visitors rather quickly and defer all letter writing to a later date!

Working on a dictionary not only takes over the lexicographer's life, but it also gradually takes possession of his whole mind. Amid several conversations, Camille would suddenly hear some Hindi words and become lost in thought while looking for the best English synonym. Likewise, if he heard some English word, he would be lost in the search for its appropriate Hindi translation, totally oblivious to the ongoing conversation. His visitors, though surprised at Camille's conduct, would make a hasty retreat thinking that 'Father is immersed in some spiritual meditation' (ibid., p. 132). Like his favourite poet, Tulsidas – who saw the entire world full of his presiding deities, Rama and Sita – a lexicographer, in Camille's view, also sees the whole world full of words and their meanings. Camille was so consumed with lexicography that the letter he wrote to his father each month was full of the progress of the dictionary. Camille's father once wrote to him saying, 'Son, please come soon; I have reached "z", the last letter of my life's alphabet' (ibid.). Camille published his English–Hindi dictionary in 1968. To fulfil his father's longstanding desire, he travelled to Belgium in 1970 and spent four months with him. This was their last meeting, as Camille lost his father in 1975 but could not be with him in his final days (C. Bulcke 2015 [1976], p. 345).

Camille used to visit another famous Hindi lexicographer, Ramchandra Verma, in Varanasi. The two would not even mention the most sensational news or significant events of the times; however, they would engage in hours-long discussions exclusively on dictionary-making progress and pitfalls. Verma led the creation of the encyclopaedic work on *Manak Hindi Kosh*, or the Standard Hindi Dictionary of 1962. To express his lifelong fixation with words, Verma used one of the couplets of poet Kabirdas: 'Sabd ki chot lagi more man mein, bhedhi gaya tan saara' (As words have wounded my heart, it is my whole body that is pierced) (R. Verma 1968). Similarly, Camille cited the example of Professor Turner,[15] who would shut himself inside his study room without food or water, totally engrossed in dictionary-making. His wife had to make every effort, including loudly knocking on his door, to offer him food. Camille had no family and, thus, without any such welcome interruptions; he would agonise over different shades of the synonyms of a word well past midnight without food on several occasions (C. Bulcke 2009, p. 132).

Dictionary-making is onerous, turning its creator into a recluse and requiring constant exertion in solitude. After a few months, the third meaning of the drudge work dawns. That is, like the bull in cold-press oil extraction, the lexicographer is plodding around in circles the whole day and yet staying at the same place. The lexicographer's work is tedious, exhausting and boring; they would often be tempted to burn all the papers and destroy all the work (ibid.). Camille was on the verge of giving up, but then he realised that all his cherished friends were aware that he was compiling a dictionary. It also dawned on him that should he quit this project midway, he might need help to face his friends in Allahabad. Finally, he requested the publisher to start printing before the entire manuscript was finished so that he would be left with no other way but to complete the work (ibid., p. 133). This was his way of keeping himself inspired and motivated.

Despite facing so many obstacles and putting in so much hard labour in dictionary-making, the lexicographer in Camille still defended this occupation (or, perhaps, vocation for him), declaring that the most tedious and frustrating job for him was proofreading. He complained that his eyes suffered the most while proofreading, and he had to seek help from an ophthalmologist. He also found some exciting aspects in his work as a lexicographer, particularly the pursuit of the exact and coherent meaning of English words to fit with the milieu and contexts of Hindi speakers. Like solving a very complex puzzle, he found this quest challenging and intellectually stimulating. He often quoted Patanjali, an ancient Sanskrit exegete who wrote a commentary on Panini's Sanskrit grammar (ibid., p. 134). Contrasting the formation of new words with other objects of daily use, Patanjali wrote, for instance, that he who uses a pot goes to the potter's house and says, 'Make a pot; I have to use it.' But no one similarly goes to the house of a grammarian and says, 'Coin words; I shall make use of them' (Sastri 1944, p. 58).[16]

Following Patanjali's dictum, Camille argued that as a lexicographer, it was not his mandate to create new words; instead, his job was to include the prevalent words in the dictionary. However, he encountered several practical issues in enforcing the rigid approach of not coining new words as a lexicographer in preparing a dictionary for Hindi speakers. He explained that during the reign of the sultans and Mughals, the official language was Persian. It was also when the learning of science and other fields of knowledge was considered unimportant (C. Bulcke 2009, p. 134). Similarly, during British rule, the official language and the medium of educational instruction was English. Until Indian independence, Hindi was a language for *belles-lettres*; only in post-independent India did Hindi emerge as a language for official, educational and other formal interactions. Therefore, as a language, Hindi needed a rich vocabulary to cater to modern knowledge and scientific, technical and administrative terminologies.

Given the dearth of apt Hindi synonyms for scientific and technical terms, Camille believed that a lexicographer must take on the mantle of a wordsmith. While the various government committees provided valuable service by incorporating or inventing appropriate terms in Hindi, Camille explained, 'I had to sit in my room and create many new words based on Sanskrit. I have taken great care that the new words I create should be as simple and understandable as possible' (ibid.). He admitted that some artificiality and unnecessary complexity might have crept in at some places.

After six years of hard labour, Camille finished the dictionary in 1968 and thought he had reclaimed his life and would get to sleep comfortably. The elation was short-lived because after a month or so, he had to prepare for the second edition of the dictionary, which kept him occupied for another two to three years. There is no rest for a lexicographer as dictionaries need constant revisions and expansion. Camille was planning to make substantial amendments to the next edition. He wished to do justice to the richness of Hindi's vocabulary and, thus, expand the existing edition of 900 pages into a 1,200-page edition (C. Bulcke 2015 [1976], p. 338).

While there have been several eminent lexicographers who have produced outstanding English–Hindi dictionaries before Camille's work, the vast popularity of the 'Bulcke dictionary' had to do with some of its unique features. The creator himself was the most distinctive feature; he was not only a lexicographer but also a prolific polyglot, littérateur, linguist, translator and a teacher of Hindi and Sanskrit. Camille's dictionary is considered the most scientific work on this subject and is the most authentic and functional reference for translation (D. Prasad 2002, p. 85). The lack of a simple, pragmatic and yet comprehensive English–Hindi dictionary compelled Camille to undertake this task. Therefore, the dictionary has been prepared from the perspective of a learner, a translator and a commoner; no wonder it has a ubiquitous presence across ordinary homes, educational institutions, government offices, administrative units and media outlets.

Among the other bilingual dictionaries, one of the most distinctive features of Camille's dictionary is the excellent care and discretion in listing words that feature in our daily, regular and routine conversations. Most of the words listed in the dictionary are popular, handy, functional and straightforward, unlike other more sophisticated dictionaries that tend to include all the words, even the archaic ones. The large dictionaries are truly encyclopaedic as they list all the complex and complicated words, which also end up confusing the new learner. Camille only tried to accommodate those words that were in contemporary usage and their meanings in the current context. The exceptions to these broad guidelines are the scientific and technical terms, which have either become a part of the common language, or their definition and meaning are necessary to acquire primary knowledge about modern science and technology (ibid., p. 86).

Another distinguishing feature of Camille's dictionary is the Devanagari transliteration of the standard pronunciation of English words. The phonetic transliteration of the English words in the Devanagari script and the explanation of pronunciation through the vowel–consonant list in the Devanagari symbols for the appropriate pronunciation of Roman alphabets is intelligible, simple and scientific (ibid., pp. 86–87). The different sounds of the vowels in Hindi are explained with the necessary instructions, and the consistency across all of these transliterations makes it very easy to understand the pronunciation pattern. These instructions on the correct pronunciation of English words in Hindi and Devanagari transliteration of each English word are very valuable for people who are fluent in English. Camille followed the popular and prevalent British pronunciation at the time of the publication of this dictionary.

An advantageous aspect of Camille's dictionary is how he associates the English word with several different meanings with subtle variations. In the long developmental process of any language, even though the words of the language may be monosemic in the beginning, with the passage of time and its demographical spread, various meanings are associated with the words. The older the language, the larger is the presence of polysemy, and this applies to English as well as to Hindi. While creating the dictionary, Camille faced this challenge of polysemy and resolved it as follows.

Many words in English seem simple, but their meanings are completely different in the numerous Hindi synonyms. For example, there were eighteen Hindi equivalents of the English word 'close' and I was satisfied only when I made it clear with the help of parentheses, which equivalent should be used in what context.... There is no difficulty in writing fifteen-twenty synonyms of the English word 'strong', but it takes a lot of time to indicate which meaning is used in which context. (C. Bulcke 2009, p. 133)

Services to Hindi

The other part of Camille's service to Hindi was his tireless campaign in promoting this language to the forefront of administrative, academic and legal work and producing modern knowledge in it. Camille's support for Hindi exemplified his struggle against cultural colonisation and language imposition; in his youth, he fought against French imposition over the Flemish-speaking population in his homeland, Belgium. Upon reaching India, he again witnessed the supremacy of the colonial language over the language of the ordinary people, and he resolved to fight for the prestige of Hindi. Camille reached India in 1935, coinciding with the surge of the Indian independence struggle under Gandhi's leadership. One of the major aims of this movement was the opposition to English and the promotion of Hindi as the link language of the nation (D. Prasad 2002, p. 91). Although English was the dominant language in the Christian missions, some missionaries considered English a hindrance to their proselytisation efforts and wanted to use the local languages. However, there was lack of a concrete plan or any tangible action to promote the use of local languages in the functioning of the missions.

Camille's affection for Hindi was not simply an emotive issue; his rationale for adopting Hindi as the official language was based on historical, linguistic, cultural and political factors. According to him, among all the Indian languages, Hindi had acquired national eminence and international spread. He claimed that Hindi was one of the early pre-modern Indian languages, demographically the largest and linguistically the most accomplished among other alternatives. Accordingly, Camille believed that Hindi was the most viable indigenous alternative for English, the colonial language, to carry forward the nation-building process. To establish his case for Hindi as the language for the whole of India, Camille presented a strong linguistic rationale.

Most people associate the birth of modern literary Hindi to the year 1803 when the dialect around Delhi 'was given the distinctive nomenclature viz, Khari Boli (Standard Dialect)' (C. Bulcke 2010, pp. 205–206). Camille maintained that while 'some people trace the origin of Khari Boli to Urdu', on the contrary, both Urdu and Hindi are the offshoots of 'self-same old Khari Boli' (ibid.). He asserted that the history of Khari Boli is as old as that of any other Aryan language of medieval India, which, like Awadhi, Rajasthani and other languages of these regions, sprung up from Apabhramsha in the tenth century CE. Amir Khusrau, a renowned Indian poet from the fourteenth century CE, wrote beautiful poetry in a language he referred to as Hindavi, Hindi and Dehalavi, and equated its vocabulary and other linguistic constructs with Arabic and Persian. Camille argued 'that the grace and polish in Amir Khusrau's extant Hindi compositions' is proof of a much longer and richer tradition of creative literature in this language (ibid.). He believed that while the outstanding poetry flourished in Khari Boli, it 'did not get the deserved recognition due to its proximity to the Braj region and the extraordinary literary attainment of Awadhi and Braj of the time' (ibid.).

Camille argued that Khari Boli has the largest presence in terms of demographic density and territorial spread. The language was already a link language in northern India and some parts of southern regions, where a distinct version of Hindi, known as Dakkhini, began to flourish (ibid., pp. 206–207). The decline of the imperial authority in Delhi did not prevent its rapid progress across different regions as the trading classes took it with them. While prose literature was not popular in Khari Boli, since the beginning of the nineteenth century it has emerged as an important genre of writing. He highlighted the contribution of Bhartendu Harishchandra and Mahavir Prasad Dwivedi in developing a grammatically correct style of Hindi which has emerged as the literary language of the whole of the Hindi region (ibid.).

Camille had no interest in politics or politicking; however, he recognised the importance of Hindi in propagating and sustaining India's political unity as a community, society and nation. He was also aware of how the language-based politicking by different regions might pose a challenge to both India's hard-earned political independence and its territorial integrity. He claimed that like Gandhi, every self-respecting citizen of India realises 'the imperative need for an Indian language as the official language for the country and the link language between intellectuals' (ibid., pp. 207–208). He quoted Gandhi's statement in which the latter had said that *swarajya* (self-government) for the common people meant that only Hindi should be the link language of the country. Gandhi had insisted that 'the medium of instruction would not be a foreign language' and had proposed 'Hindi as the common language of contact between the sections of the population speaking different languages' (ibid.). Moreover, Gandhi suggested that to build the edifice of emotional integration of the country, English was unacceptable as the official language of the sovereign democratic republic of India (ibid.). Camille believed that Hindi was the cultural language of 200 million Indians and was also ranked as 'third in the world from the point of view of the numerical strength of the people who speak and understand it' (ibid.).

Apart from the political significance of Hindi as a language, several inherent qualities of Hindi, such as flexibility, expressiveness, richness and intelligibility, make it an ideal choice to be the link language. According to Camille, Hindi has come into contact with different cultures and 'has passed through many vicissitudes and it has developed the art of adjusting itself to the changed circumstances' (ibid.). This long-term interaction with other languages endowed Hindi with 'remarkable flexibility and expressiveness, an ability to coin new words and the dynamic capacity to accept and absorb words from other languages' (ibid.). He argued that no developed language in the world could rival Hindi's simplicity, and unlike English, there is a perfect correspondence between spelling and pronunciation in Hindi. Unlike German and French, Hindi follows simple and intuitive rules for pluralisation and conjugation. He argued that it would add to the popularity of original literature in Hindi and minimise the inconvenience of non-Hindi readers.

One of Camille's lifelong missions was to establish a standard version of Hindi (Khari Boli) as the common language for all the regions that used a dialect close to Hindi (particularly in the northern and central parts of India). He urged the intellectuals and scholars in the Hindi-speaking states to sponsor a movement to use correct standard Hindi (Khari Boli) in their teaching, writing and even daily use. His support for Hindi also meant promoting this standard Hindi to facilitate its congruence by effecting standard rules, regulations and specific guidelines to bring in some of the basic conventions in the usage of the language, its vocabulary, spelling and grammar. He urged teachers in schools and universities to adopt Khari Boli as Hindi and evaluate students on their proficiency in the language. He stated that the school syllabus of Hindi includes extracts from Dingal,[17] Maithili, Brij, Awadhi and other such dialects, where the word can have several forms that appear proximate but have different meanings. This makes the students believe that Hindi allows multiple spellings as a language and there is no need to follow any spelling rule. To counter this misperception, Camille proposed that the high school syllabi should include text written 'in correct Khari Boli only and the prescribed Hindi textbooks should provide glimpses of the life and achievements of the great literary masters of Hindi, Sanskrit and other Indian languages' (ibid., p. 216). His proposal had wide support among the linguists, and he believed that the time had come to accept and implement these suggestions.

To usher in some systems in place and enforce discipline in teaching and learning standard Hindi across the country, Camille was keen to adopt Khari Boli as the ideal. However, while his ideas had definite merits, he seemed to be driven by the narrative of European modernity and the rationality of the European civilising missions. He argued that in the dictionaries of the developed languages of Europe, only authentic, pure and well-defined words from the language are found. In contrast, the Hindi dictionaries were full of words from Awadhi, Brij and other such dialects (C. Bulcke 2009, p. 122). He believed that the time had come for only the words of well-defined Khari Boli to be included in the dictionaries of modern Hindi. He was aware of the potential resistance to his proposal by the protagonists of the local dialects and stressed that Europe is an excellent example of how embracing a standard language for teaching and learning does not obliterate the dialects (ibid.). He further stated,

> While the natural beauty of the forest, the greenery of the fields, and the playfulness of the rainy rivers will continue to exist, the development of civilisation demands that roads be constructed through the forest, gardens be built, and canals are dug. Similarly, the creation of idealised literary languages while having dialects is essential for the development of culture. (Ibid., p. 122)

While he never claimed that 'original belles-lettres in Hindi are superior to those in other Indian languages, from the point of view of the number of textbooks for higher education, Hindi is unquestionably far ahead of the other languages' (C. Bulcke 2010, p. 211). He insisted that Khari Boli should be accorded the pre-eminent position among all the other dialects of Hindi to foster linguistic unity of the Hindi provinces. As an example, he cited that while each province in France, Germany and Italy had its own dialect to facilitate 'cultural progress, the richness of their literature and the emotional integration of their country', they all have adopted 'standard French, German, Italian or the like as the medium of instruction and the vehicle of all social and public life' (ibid.). Tracing the genealogy of the languages in north India, he claimed that despite the linguistic diversity, only one language had occupied the prime position. As the preferred medium of cultural and literary expression after Sanskrit, Prakrit, Apabhramsha, Brij and Awadhi, Khari Boli now held that proud position (ibid.).

According to him, 'various dialects in the countries of Europe are still alive and dynamic despite the unchallenged monopoly of a standard language; similarly, the dialects of the Hindi-speaking states are not doomed to oblivion' (ibid., pp. 216–217). In order to ensure the preservation of various regional languages and the dialects of Hindi, Camille stated that 'their regional ascendancy will never cease to exist and they will continue to enrich standard Khari Boli' (ibid.). He believed that attaching undue importance to the dialects or elevating them 'to the status of the medium of secondary education' might lead to a lack of linguistic unity in northern India, which would eventually prove detrimental to the progress of Hindi (ibid). To substantiate his argument for accepting Khari Boli as the primary language, he stressed that while regional languages such as 'Bengali, Marathi and the like too have several dialects, none proposes to divide their region based on these dialects' (ibid.).

Camille identified anglomania, or 'the excessive adoration of English which afflicts the majority of the intellectuals and the higher classes of society', as the biggest impediment to elevating Hindi to its rightful place in India (ibid., p. 217). He believed this anglomania to be a relic of India's erstwhile political bondage, which not only brought disrepute to India in other countries but also relegated Hindi to an inferior position. In one of his most cited statements, Camille deployed a gendered analogy that 'Sanskrit is the Empress (Maharani), Hindi the queen of the house (Bahurani) while English is the maid (Naukarani)' (D. Prasad 2002, p. 17). In 1966, addressing a literary event in Ranchi, he said, 'In India, Hindi is the mistress of the house, while English can only be a housemaid. However, regrettably, despite India's self-rule, we are not prepared to put English into its place, which is subordinate to Hindi' (cited in Shrivastava 1973, p. 183).

He firmly believed that to promote Hindi and to allow its evolution into a pan-Indian language, English needed to be banished from the social and public life in the Hindi states. However, his idea of banishment was not to remove all the Hindi words that seemed to have English origins or to stop learning English altogether. His idea was that while one must acquire proficiency in such a versatile and developed language as English, one must also respect the languages of their own country and use them for educational purposes. Camille highlighted that several educationists have proven that 'there is an intimate relationship between the mother tongue and the natural development of intelligence' (C. Bulcke 2010, pp. 217–218). Thus, the anglomaniacs' arguments for linking the quality of educational standards with English are against solid scientific evidence. A student trained in their own language would quickly 'learn any foreign languages because of the mature development of his mind' (ibid.). Camille associated the rise of Hindi as the national, official link language with Indian self-respect and democracy and argued that gradually the slim majority made up of the disciples of Macaulay would lose to the more significant majority of Hindi speakers.

He was aware of the growing reservations among the non-Hindi speakers about the imposition of Hindi, or Hindi imperialism. He identified that the reason behind the anxiety towards Hindi was 'based on the assumption that the interests of Hindi are at variance with those of the other regional languages' (ibid.). However, he stated that such fear was without any basis because 'even in the distant future Hindi cannot replace Gujarati, Marathi, Bengali, Tamil and the like' (ibid.). Hindi, according to Camille, 'will subsist in those states only as a link language in the same way English is the link language for the educated people of various provinces nowadays' (ibid.). He urged all Hindi speakers to invest in strengthening and popularising Hindi so that it becomes 'the key to Indian culture such that the non-Hindi speaking people will like to learn Hindi'. He cited the example of the adoption of Arabic, a language spoken by around 100 million people, as the sixth language of the United Nations Organization, with the 19 Arab countries joining forces to steer this resolution to success at the world body. Similarly, according to Camille, if Indians wished to elevate their language Hindi, a language spoken by around 200 million people, to an exalted position, they would have to first honour it in their country. The whole world would honour it then, and Hindi would earn the proud status of an international language.

As the head of the Department of Hindi and Sanskrit at St Xavier's College, Ranchi, Camille was concerned about the lack of quality in the academic research of Hindi. He argued that several students in postgraduate studies and research scholars lacked fundamental skills in the language and could not write in correct and standard Hindi (C. Bulcke 2009, p. 136). To improve the quality of scholarly research in Hindi, he asserted that only the most talented researchers must be retained and get the best of the facilities. However, more than the quality of research scholars, he held the university professors, research supervisors and guides responsible for decline in the quality of academic research in Hindi and demanded that the examiners impose the most exacting criteria to evaluate the worthiness of the PhD dissertations (ibid.). He insisted that PhD examiners follow the king Janaka, who placed the most formidable challenge of stringing Lord Shiva's bow as the eligibility criteria for winning the hand of his daughter, Sita, in marriage (ibid.). What he left unsaid was that Rama, who easily overcame such an arduous task, was also trained by the sages Vasishtha and Vishwamitra, two of the most accomplished teachers. Thus, he placed the onus of enhancing the quality of academic research in Hindi on the teachers and academicians.

Camille's intention was noble: to make Hindi the link language of a large number of Indians, especially in north India, and to bring an end to the hegemony of English in post-colonial India. However, it is clear that his insistence on homogenising Hindi, by freeing it of influences of the various dialects, and propagating it as the main language of communication in India would have met with stiff resistance in contemporary times. In a multilingual and diverse country such as India, his campaign for Hindi would find few takers today, except among those interested in a narrow religious and linguistic nationalism.

Comparative Studies of Christianity and Hinduism

As a devout Christian missionary, Camille spent significant time studying, analysing and writing on subjects related to Christianity. He insisted that while philosophy, or even Christian philosophy, could not capture his interest, he was greatly inspired by the sermons of Jesus and the preaching of Christianity (C. Bulcke 2015 [1976], p. 340). He wrote several analytical articles comparing some of the fundamental tenets of Christianity and

Hinduism. His training with some of the eminent Indology specialists from the Calcutta School of Indology – Joseph Bayart and Jules Volckaert – and his own intellectual pursuits enabled him to undertake comparative studies of the two religions. His most substantial work on comparative religious studies centres on the concept of *avataravada*[18] and incarnation in Hinduism and Christianity. His renowned works on these themes include three essays titled 'Ethics and Avataravada', 'Avatara and Incarnation' and 'Tulsidas and Incarnation'. He made a clear distinction between *avatara* as 'descent', as in descent of God on earth in Hinduism, and the concept of incarnation, which has a different meaning in Christianity (ibid.).

For the sake of convenience and ease of understanding, one may divide Camille's analysis of *avataravada* in Hinduism into two parts.

1. Evolution of *avataravada* in Hinduism
2. Comparison between the Christian idea of incarnation and the avatars in Hinduism

Hindu Avatars

Camille claimed that the first mention of the idea of an avatar in Hinduism occurs in 1000 BCE in the *Shatapatha Brahmana*,[19] which assigns three different avatars of a fish, a tortoise and a boar to Prajapati, the monistic creator. Vishnu's avatar as a dwarf (Vamana) is also mentioned in the same *Shatapatha Brahmana*, while the *Aranyaka*[20] mentions Vishnu as a man-lion (Narasimha) avatar. Based on this evidence, he posited that the idea of avatar emerged in the late Vedic period and that the idea of avatar is not limited to only one god (ibid.). He claimed that the concept of the avatar was not prevalent in Hinduism, but it was only in the third century BCE that Vasudeva Krishna was depicted as an incarnation of Vishnu. This led to the advent of avatarhood as a religion devised by 'the Brahmanical religion to stop the people from becoming Jains and Buddhists; from this identification was born Vaishnavism' (C. Bulcke 2010, p. 169; C. Bulcke 2020 [1950], p. 114). This change elevated Vishnu as the most important deity, and all the preceding and subsequent avatars were attributed to Vishnu. Camille backed his arguments about Krishna's avatarhood and the Brahaminical attempts to preserve their Hindu adherents from crossing over to Buddhists and Jains, citing three specific sources (Raychaudhuri 1920, p. 63; Monier-Williams 1875, p. 317; Vaidya 1906, p. 25). Indeed, all three sources agree that the avatarhood of Krishna was a later development, and so was the idea of Vaishnavism. However, only Monier-Williams offered a very feeble defence to support the notion of deploying avatarhood or using the two epics of the Ramayana and the Mahabharata to prevent Hindus from becoming Buddhists. In the following quote, Monier-Williams appears far more reticent vis-à-vis Camille's bold assertion: 'Possibly, too, they may have hoped to turn them into important engines for arresting the progress of Buddhistic rationalism. Accordingly, I conjecture that in the fourth century B.C., they commenced re-constructing and remodelling the two great Epics' (Monier-Williams 1895, p. 317).

Camille claimed that *avataravada* found scriptural endorsement in the Bhagavad Gita, which affirmed Vasudeva Krishna as the only deity endowed with taking different avatars and explaining the ethical purposes behind these avatars.

यदा यदा हि धर्मस्य ग्लानिर्भवति भारत।
अभ्युत्थानमधर्मस्य तदात्मानं सृजाम्यहम्॥
परित्राणाय साधूनां विनाशाय च दुष्कृताम्।
धर्मसंस्थापनार्थाय सम्भवामि युगे युगे॥

For the protection of the virtuous, for the extirpation of evil-doers and for establishing Dharma (righteousness) on a firm footing, I manifest Myself from age to age. (Goyandka 2017, pp. 306–307)

In his analysis of the ethics and *avataravada* in the context of Krishna, Camille argued that contrary to the Gita's proclamation, in several instances Krishna's conduct was neither ethical nor within the parameters of morality. Evidently, he was ambiguous about the representation of Krishna, referring to him as a Kshatriya, or a warrior-prince, a fearless Kshatriya in some places, while also calling him a Yadava prince in other places (C. Bulcke 2010, p. 182). Camille mentioned the same source, Vyasa's Mahabharata, to substantiate his claims. He suggested that the *Bhagavata Purana* introduced a new dimension to Krishna's personality, adding new erotic elements through the description of the *rasalila*, or the autumnal dance with the *gopi*s (milkmaids) (ibid., p. 184).[21] Camille's description of the *rasalila* merely as erotic elements shows his lack of understanding of Vaishnava ideas of worship and devotion.

The *rasalila* is not just Krishna's dance with the *gopi*s; instead, it is depicted as a dance of pure, spiritual love and devotion, symbolising the eternal love between the individual soul (*atma*) and the divine (*paramatma*). In offering a very Christian interpretation, Swami Vivekananda suggested that these *gopis* saw 'Krishna only as the Krishna of Vrindavan. He, the leader of the hosts, the King of kings, to them was the shepherd, and the shepherd for ever' (Vivekananda 1964, p. 258). To Krishna, every Gopi pleaded: 'I do not want wealth, nor many people, nor do I want learning; no, not even do I want to go to heaven. Let me be born again and again, but Lord, grant me this, that I may have love for thee, and that for love's sake' (ibid.) Based on the narrative of the *rasalila*, Jayadeva, a medieval Indian poet, composed *Gita Govind* (Song of Govinda), referred to as the 'Indian Song of Songs' by some Western scholars (Arnold 1875; Pope 1977). The *rasalila* has been honoured as 'the crown-jewel of all acts of God by several Vaishnava traditions' very much like 'the Song of Solomon has been elevated to the highest status above all other biblical books by many Jewish and Christian mystics, and thus has become known as the "Song of Songs"' (Schweig 2005, p. 8).

Camille referred to the *Bhagavata Purana* and other Puranas that show 'Krishna as a child whose cult was expressed as tender devotion' to claim that 'historically it is possible that the late cult of Krishna in the arms of the Madonna was borrowed from Christianity' (C. Bulcke 2010, p. 170). Camille's claim about the Krishna legend as a derivative discourse borrowed from Christianity should be seen as a continuation of a historical narrative building. Since the middle of the nineteenth century, several European scholars have asserted that 'the legends relating to Krishna have been taken from the life of Jesus Christ' (Robertson 1900, p. 137). Even in the eighteenth century, several European Christian missionaries avowed that the name Krishna was nothing but 'a corruption of the very name of the Saviour Christ, whose deeds had been impiously debased by inexpressibly wicked impostors' (ibid.) Indeed, this desire to impose Christian beliefs on other faiths comes from 'the distinctive Christo-centric worldview' and the principle that in dealing with inter-religious dialogues, 'the Christian must take into account the normativity of Christ as a crucial yardstick' (Praturi 2021, p. 407).

Quite remarkably, Camille posited that while the 'first account of the life of Krishna is found in the Mahabharata, whether the original form of this epic made mention of Krishna at all must remain an open question' (C. Bulcke 2010, p. 182). Similarly, he asserted that Krishna's 'teachings are codified in the Bhagavad Gita, in which he is deified and appears as Lord Krishna'; however, he also suggested that the Gita is now a part of the Mahabharata, clearly implying that the two texts were created separately at different times (ibid., p. 188). In the Gita, Krishna is portrayed as 'the upholder of moral order and teacher of a completely ethical system of Bhakti' and epitomises the spirit of *lokasangraha*, or the welfare of the world (ibid.).

Camille referred to several instances from the Mahabharata, the *Bhagavata Purana* and several later Puranas to claim that Krishna's conduct violated the ethical and moral conduct of the Dharma he vowed to uphold. He described Krishna's unethical conduct 'as a blot on his escutcheon' and 'unworthy of a Kshatriya and downright against the accepted code of war' (ibid, p. 187). He argues that Krishna did not adhere to the ideals of *lokasangraha*: 'the ethical teaching of the Gita stands in sharp contrast with the casuistry wherewith the warrior Krishna defends his unchivalrous behaviour' (ibid.). Camille cited *rasalila* as a major infraction in his behaviour; there is 'not only a complete absence of asceticism and restraint, but he acts openly against the accepted moral code in his dealings with the gopis' (ibid., p. 188). Having analysed the various interpretations and justifications of the *rasalila*, Camille concluded that while all Vaishnavas consider it to be historical, they are also 'fully aware of its moral implications and [have] tried in various ways, though not always successfully, to meet this challenge' (ibid., p. 193).

Rama is the other critical and widely popular avatar. In his comprehensive work on the *Ramkatha*, Camille claimed that Valmiki depicted Rama as an ordinary human in his Ramayana. He posited that all the portions of the Ramayana that show Rama as an avatar of Vishnu or as an incarnation of the Supreme are interpolations (ibid., pp. 170–171). He asserted that while the story of Rama was popular in India around 400 BCE, it is a historical fact that several centuries elapsed before the religion of Rama was developed (ibid.). He suggested that only in the twelfth century, Rama was envisioned as the incarnation of the Supreme, with Sita as the incarnation of God's *shakti*, or *mula prakriti*.[22] He argued that after this time, all the modern Indian languages produced 'a rich Ramayana literature where the devotion to Rama as the incarnation of the Supreme is the rule' (ibid.).

Tulsidas reiterated his belief in the dual aspect of Brahma (the Supreme): the unmanifested, unqualified form (*nirguna*) and the manifested, qualified form (*saguna*) (ibid., p. 195). He asserts that there is no essential difference between the two aspects of the Supreme.

सगुनहि अगुनहि नहिं कछु भेदा। गावहिं मुनि पुरान बुध बेदा॥
अगुन अरूप अलख अज जोई। भगत प्रेम बस सगुन सो होई॥

There is no difference whatever between saguna and aguna (nirguna). So say the sages, the Purānas, wise men and the Vedas. The aguna, formless, invisible and unborn, becomes saguna for the love of the devotees (bhaktas). (Ibid., p. 195)

However, Tulsidas also states that while the two aspects represent the same Supreme, the manifested, visible, tangible form is much harder to understand since the human form and deeds of the Supreme as an ordinary human being generate confusion even among the learned and the wise.

निर्गुन रूप सुलभ अति सगुन जान नहिं कोई।
सुगम अगम नाना चरित सुनि मुनि मन भ्रम होई॥

The nirguna form is easy to understand but no one understands the saguna form. Even sages are perplexed when they hear of his various acts, some simple, some mysterious. (Ibid., p. 196)

In the *Ramcharitmanas*, in order to remove perplexities about the human deeds of Rama, Tulsidas deployed his 'docetic theory of incarnation, which is explicitly stated on various occasions. The body of Rama is not a real human body as that of other people' (ibid., p. 200).

बिप्र धेनु सुर संत हित लीन्ह मनुज अवतार।
निज इच्छा निर्मित तनु माया गुन गो पार॥

For the sake of Brahmans and cows and gods and saints, he came down to earth as a man, in a body formed of his own will, which transcends illusion, the elements of nature and the senses. (Ibid.)

Based on this formulation, Tulsidas claims that 'not only is the body of Rama not that of a human being, but the sorrow, the fatigue and the ignorance he exhibits are assumed, like those of an actor on the stage' (ibid.).

Remarkably, despite his professed veneration for Tulsidas, Camille could not bring himself to subscribe to the idea of Rama as the incarnation of the Supreme. One of his contemporaries, Reverend A. G Atkins, acclaimed the description of Rama as the incarnate of Lord Vishnu by Tulsidas, who then established a relationship with Rama, the Supreme conceived in the Personal (Atkins 1954, p. ix). Similarly, Frank Whaling argues that Tulsidas uses the word 'Rama' in the sense of 'God'. Moreover, 'the usual comparison has been between Rama and Christ, but perhaps an apter comparison is between Rama and the Christian God, for in terms of Ramology, Rama is equivalent to God the Father, Son and Holy Spirit' (Whaling 1980, p. 324). On the other hand, Camille denied any historicity to Tulsidas' idea of Rama as an incarnation; he cited certain verses from the *Ramcharitmanas* that describe the innumerable incarnations of Rama that have led to divergent narratives (C. Bulcke 2010, p. 202).

रामकथा कै मिति जग नाहीं। असि प्रतीति तिन्ह के मन माहीं॥
नाना भाँति राम अवतारा। रामायन सत कोटि अपारा॥
कलपभेद हरिचरित सुहाए। भाँति अनेक मुनीसन्ह गाए॥
करिअ न संसय अस उर आनी। सुनिअ कथा सारद रति मानी॥

There is no limit to the stories of Rama in the world. The wise are convinced in their hearts that Rama has, in various forms, become incarnate and that the Ramayana, though consisting of a thousand million verses, is yet measureless. Great sages have sung the charming stories of Hari in different kalpas (aeons) and various ways. Bearing this in mind, do not entertain any doubt and hear this narrative with reverence and love. (R. Prasad 1988, p. 29)

Camille then went on to assert that Tulsidas never claimed to be writing a historical narrative, and thus his text cannot be interpreted as an authentic account of history.

We may conclude from this that Tulsidas himself did not consider his Ramacharitamānas as a strictly historical narrative but as an illustration of the infinite mercy of the Supreme, who became manifest for the sake of his devotees. The King of Thailand, Rama I, wrote the Thai version of the Rama-story, Ramakien, in 1797. At the end, he adds a conclusion, wherein he says, 'One should not believe all these words, for this is a story for entertainment and good example.' (R.A. Olsson, Rāmakien, P. 424. Bangkok, 1968). Tulsidas might very well have agreed. He seems to have no objection if somebody prefers to treat the Rama-story as an allegory and he has hinted at this interpretation when he clearly states the allegorical nature of Rama's struggle against Ravana. (C. Buclke 2010, pp. 202–203)

From this statement, Camille was depriving Tulsidas and his entire corpus of devotional literature of any semblance of historicity by projecting the whole idea of Rama and his divinity as fiction. Camille was influenced by the positivist vision of the European concept of history and the British colonial arguments that relegated Indians outside of history. As James Mill asserted, 'no historical composition existed in the literature of the Hindus; they had not reached that point of intellectual maturity' (Mill 1840, p. 67). The primary inspiration of this objective and scientific approach to history writing was to bring the whole world under the Western order of 'world-history' (Guha 2002, p. 72). As Ranajit Guha argues, Indian *itihasa*, based on the renditions of the Ramayana and the Mahabharata, follows traditional storytelling where each subsequent rendition is never a replica of the earlier (ibid.). The construction of 'world-history' is a statist project where the Western idea of history supersedes the Indian notion of *itihasa*, such that 'the story, as history, was dislodged from civil society and relocated in the state' (ibid.). From the world-history standpoint, the Ramayana and the Mahabharata are myths, but from the Indian *itihasa* perspective, both are epics based on great historical events.

Camille's claim that the *Ramcharitmanas* is nothing more than an allegory deprives the text and its narrative of any authenticity, historicity and religious sanctity. Moreover, he is contravening his favourite poet, Tulsidas, who, in the first verses of the *Ramcharitmanas*, the 'Mangalacharan' (Invocation), declares the historical sources of this composition.

नानापुराणनिगमागमसम्मतं यद् रामायणे निगदितं क्वचिदन्यतोऽपि।
स्वान्तःसुखाय तुलसी रघुनाथगाथा–भाषानिबन्धमतिमञ्जुलमातनोति॥

In accordance with many Puranas, Vedic texts, and sacred treatises, and with what is recounted in the Ramayana and in other places, too. Tulsidas, for his own inner joy, extends the saga of the lord of Raghus as a most delightful composition set in common speech. (Lutgendorf 2016, p. 6)

Camille's proposition that Tulsidas himself was not convinced of one definitive narrative on Rama is based on selective interpretation of the *Ramcharitmanas*. He left out some of the most significant verses where Tulsidas affirmed that Lord Vishnu took the human form as the son of Dasharatha and his wife Kaushalya, the royal couple of Ayodhya.

जनि डरपहु मुनि सिद्ध सुरेसा। तुम्हहि लागि धरिहउँ नर बेसा॥
अंसन्ह सहित मनुज अवतारा। लेहउँ दिनकर बंस उदारा॥
कस्यप अदिति महातप कीन्हा। तिन्ह कहुँ मैं पूरब बर दीन्हा॥
ते दसरथ कौसल्या रूपा। कोसलपुरीं प्रगट नर भूपा॥
तिन्ह कें गृह अवतरिहउँ जाई। रघुकुल तिलक सो चारिउ भाई॥

Fear not, O sages, adepts, Indra (the chief of gods)! For your sake I shall assume the form of a man with every element of my divinity incarnate in the glorious Solar race [clan]. The Sage Kashyapa and his wife Aditi practised severe penance; to them I have already granted a boon. They have taken birth in the city of Ayodhya as Dasharatha and Kaushalya, a royal pair. In their house I shall become incarnate as four brothers, the pride of the house of Raghus. (R. Prasad 1988, p. 129)

Camille made some sweeping generalisations in considering every portion of the Valmiki Ramayana that considers Rama as the incarnation of Vishnu as an interpolation. His criteria of considering some parts as interpolations while others as authentic have come in for criticism for its arbitrariness (Swami Karpatri 2019, pp. 199–207). The Eurocentric formulation of history denies any historicity to the Indian myths, legends, Itihasas and Puranas. The objectivist criteria of authentic history mandate factuality, impartiality, strict adherence to chronology and causality (or attributing events to justification) (Kaul 2018, pp. 17–20). In such a positivist formulation of historiography, most Indian literary and historical traditions and narratives are considered fictive and, thus, inferior to 'the Greco-Roman or the Judeo-Christian counterparts' (ibid.). The historian Shonaleeka Kaul, writing about Kalhana's *Rajatarangini*,[23] argues that in order to exalt this composition from a fictive literary text to an authentic historical narrative, European scholars indeed applied the positivist, objectivist criteria of facticity, objectivity and scientific method (ibid., p. 19). However, these scholars also tend to disown or ignore the parts of the *Rajatarangini* that either rely on epics, Puranas and myths or engage with poetic figuration that contravene the scientific rational and empiricist approaches (ibid.).

One can conclude that Valmiki's Ramayana or Tulsidas' *Ramcharitmanas*, too, could be claimed as authentic histories if the empiricist and positivist criteria are applied with the same flexibility. The political thinker and noted post-colonial scholar Ashis Nandy writes, 'Traditional India not only lacks the Enlightenment's concept of history; it is doubtful that it finds objective, hard history a reliable, ethical, or reasonable way of constructing the past' (Nandy 1995, p. 63). The modern objectivist notion of history in the nineteenth century made a clear distinction between 'factual' (true) history and 'fictive' (false) literature, thereby abrogating the practice that considered fine literature as history 'with no prejudice to its truth values' (Kaul 2018, p. 18). Trained in European Enlightenment, Camille was also invested in that problematic separation of fictive text from actual history when it came to the Ramayana.

Incarnation and Avatar

The other part of Camille's work on comparative religions is the study of the avatar-hood of Hindus with the idea of incarnation among the Christians. Listing the similarities between the two concepts of incarnation and avatar, Camille argued that 'both imply a free entry of God into this world' and that 'God does not thereby lose his Transcendence and Omnipotence. His divinity remains unimpaired' (C. Bulcke 2010, p. 176). The other major similarity is 'the aim of Incarnation ("proper nos homines et proper nostram salutem") and Avatar (the establishment of Dharma in this world and release of the devotees)' (ibid., p. 177). Camille highlighted how the two religions emphasise 'the loving, compassionate nature of God, coming to the rescue of man and making Salvation not only possible, but easy. God becomes the comforter, the friend and companion of man' (ibid.). In such a description of God, man develops 'a loving devotion (Bhakti) to the Incarnate, a total surrender to God so merciful and compassionate' (ibid.).

Having established some equivalences between the idea of the Hindu avatar and the Christian incarnation, Camille made his substantial arguments to highlight the differences between the two systems. His first major point of divergence between the two is the reality of human nature, or the difference between incarnation versus theophany (ibid., p. 177). He argued that 'Jesus Christ is true God and true man; the second person of the Holy Trinity hypothetically unites two natures. The human nature, consisting of a genuine human body and soul, is subject to real suffering and limitations' (ibid., p. 177). On the contrary, the avatar (such as Rama or Krishna) is not a human body; instead, it 'is made of purely spiritual matter and is consequently not bound by the laws of nature – no effort, no suffering, no death. He is not a real man' (ibid.). All his worldly actions, including 'the powerlessness, the limitations, the sufferings are not real, but a play on the part of the Avatar.

Tulsidas also very often stresses the point that Rama is not really suffering, but manifests feelings and utters words as an actor on the stage' (ibid.).

Camille stated that while the Hindus claim that 'a suffering God, the deity with a crown of thorns cannot satisfy the religious soul', the Christians aver that 'a suffering God does appeal to the religious soul; twenty centuries of Christianity bear witness to this fact' (ibid., p. 178). Camille asserted that 'Christian devotion finds more inspiration in the Cross than in the miracles of Christ' and that 'the love of God is revealed more clearly in the Incarnation, where God loves and suffers death on the Cross for sinful man' (ibid.). He also asserted that on the contrary, the avatars of Hindus do not suffer for sinful man.

> Krishna ... has never borne on his shoulders the guilt of the world and the consequences of sin. Our salvation has cost him nothing. We do not see Krishna on a cross, and yet the cross is the symbol of that love that loves itself away.... The Indian ideal of self-sacrificing love even in God thus finds its consummation in Christ alone. (Ibid.)

Camille highlighted differences in the nature of redemption as one of the major differences between Christian incarnation and Hindu avatars. He argued that for the Christians, 'Christ has redeemed the world once for all and at the end of time all things will be restored in Christ. He is the consummation of human history' (ibid., p. 179). Conversely, for the Hindus, there is no beginning and end, and while 'avatars will keep on appearing in different ages', only some souls will escape the cycle of rebirth and not the entire world (ibid.). For Camille, the differences in the ethical conduct upon assuming the human form between Christ's incarnation and Hindu avatars are indeed significant. He underlined that 'Christ assumed a real human nature with its limitations and obligations.... He was moreover an Incarnation of a Holy God and could not possibly sin. He was sinless both by choice and by nature' (ibid.). On the other hand, Camille claimed that in the avatar system, the God incarnate does not uphold the rigid standards of ethical or moral behaviour (ibid.). The other major difference for Camille was religiosity; he claimed that Christ is a man of religiosity of his own and 'in his religious life he is an inspiration and an example for us' (ibid., p. 180). While 'the avatar, not being really human, cannot possibly have a spiritual life (sadhana) and is, therefore, neither morally nor religiously, an example for our own spirituality' (ibid.).

Camille's comparative analysis of theological differences between Hindus and Christians on avatar and incarnation is inadequate and manifestly Christocentric. Avatar, a word in Sanskrit, literally means descent into visible form or incarnation and refers to the revelation of the godhead in humanity. For Hindus, avatarhood is the descent of the divine into the world, in a human or non-human form, to lead people to higher stages of perfection. The avatar as the descent of God in a human form is not imaginary or illusory as Camille argued; instead, it represents the Hindu cosmology and the understanding of the human, divine and universal self. As Sri Aurobindo explained, 'the eternal and universal self of every human being is God; even his personal self is a part of the Godhead' (Aurobindo 1997, p. 158). Camille's proposition that avatars do not suffer for sinful man is untenable under the Hindu philosophy and theology because every human is the manifestation of 'a partial consciousness of the one Consciousness, a partial power of the one Power, a partial enjoyment of world-being by the one and universal Delight of being, and therefore in manifestation or, as we say, in Nature a limited and finite being of the one infinite and illimitable Being' (ibid.). The real difference between humans and avatars is that 'in ordinary human birth, the Nature-aspect of the universal Divine assuming humanity prevails; in the incarnation, the God-aspect of the same phenomenon takes its place' (ibid., p. 159).

In the Hindu understanding, time is cyclic, and no avatar is final, whereas in Christianity, 'the Incarnation of the Son comes only once' (Michael 2016, p. 339). The Hindu cyclic worldview and the idea of rebirth imagines multiple avatars and even parallel avatars. In the Christian understanding, the incarnation of Christ has radically changed the world process and history 'definitively oriented towards a transcendent destiny' (ibid.). Therefore, 'in the absence of such a decisive intervention', the Hindu avatars, have to come into the world over and over again, 'unlike his once-for-all action in the Incarnation of Christ for the redemption of the world' (ibid., p. 340).

Camille's understanding that avatar is not human and is not bound by human limitations is flawed. 'The Avatar is not supposed to act in a non-human way – he takes up human action and uses human methods with the human consciousness in front and the Divine behind' (Aurobindo 2012, p. 473). If these restrictions do not bind the avatar, then 'his taking a human body would have no meaning and would be of no use to anybody. He could just as well have stayed above and done things from there' (ibid.). However, descent to the earth does not mean 'an entire absence of the use of supernormal powers such as Christ's so-called miracles of healing' (Aurobindo, 1997, p. 165).

Rama and Krishna had to act like normal humans, take upon themselves the burden of humanity and struggle with different challenges throughout their time on earth. As Aurobindo explained:

> The Divine does not need to suffer or struggle for himself; if he takes on these things it is in order to bear the world-burden and help the world and men; and if the sufferings and struggles are to be of any help, they must be real. A sham or falsehood cannot help. They must be as real as the struggles and sufferings of men themselves – the Divine bears them and at the same time shows the way out of them. Otherwise his assumption of human nature has no meaning and no utility and no value. (Ibid., p. 472)

For Camille, one of the most significant differences between Christ's incarnation and the different avatars of Hinduism is the historicity. He argued that 'Christ is a strictly historical figure and the Gospels relate historical facts. The enemies of Christ have unsuccessfully tried to reduce Christ to a myth in order to condemn Christianity' (C. Bulcke 2010, p. 180). However, he asserted that 'the stories about the avatars are myths. Parashurama, Rāma, and Krishna are not strictly speaking historical figures' (ibid.). Moreover, he claimed that in the absence of a central authority and the strictly historical sense, like the apocryphal Gospels, the Hindus may have invented additional stories to glorify the hypothetical existence of some personalities that were seen as avatars (ibid.).

Having presented an elaborate set of arguments debunking the authenticity, historicity and sanctity of the Hindu avatar system, Camille embraced the standard approach of a civilising mission. He claimed that 'for more than two thousand years religious-minded people of India have cherished the idea that God came down on earth to help man in acquiring Salvation' (ibid., p. 181). However, Camille equated this cherishing of God with the longing for Christ and, as a Christian missionary, believed he was obliged to bring Christ to them. His missionary zeal took over, despite his deep knowledge of Indian traditions, philosophy and religious beliefs.

> This desire, this instinct, this trust in God, is not wrong; they were right in expecting a descent of God on earth. Even their myths are not wholly wrong; they have been realised in Jesus Christ.... It is up to us to show

with great humility and genuine sympathy that we have found Christ, the reality behind their dreams. (Ibid.)

It is important to underline that Camille was a devout Christian missionary devoted to spreading the gospel he could respect other religious traditions but could not accept their fundamental beliefs. In that sense, he was a devout Christian who believed that only Christianity offered the path to salvation. He noted that the modern educated Hindus embrace agnosticism and 'are partly responsible for religious indifference prevalent in India' (ibid., p. 162). He believed that such agnostic Hindus might have an attachment to the scriptural traditions but are uninformed about the fundamental tenets of their religion. Camille would have mostly interacted with a class of Hindus who were university-educated, modernists and avowedly secular during the Nehruvian era. As per the prevalent trend, these people always felt uncomfortable identifying themselves with their religion and made all efforts to either downplay or totally disown any religious association. During this time, it was a norm for many Indians to appear modern, progressive, liberal and cosmopolitan, which included shunning any discussion or deriding Hindu religiosity in scholarly and academic discussions.

> All religions are equally good; all are rivers flowing into the sea, and every discussion on religion ends on this note. I have often tried to make them realise their responsibility towards the truth by saying, 'You believe in rebirth; I believe that there is no rebirth, one of us is wrong.' When they hear this, they are shocked, shake their head and answer: 'It is not as simple as all that'. In spite of this agnosticism, they are attached to the spiritual treasures contained in their traditions and will never forsake them. Just as I would take along with me the Bhagavad Gita and the Ramayana, if ever I were obliged to leave India. (Ibid.)

Therefore, despite his reverence for the Gita and Tulsidas' *bhakti marg*, it was impossible for Camille to accept Rama or Krishna as the avatar of God. On several occasions, Camille stated that he greatly admired Tulsidas' devotional approach and literary genius, but he was not a devotee of Rama. For him, unlike Hinduism, Christianity had a detailed historical account and irrefutable testimony of Christ and his life, and the canonisation procedure represented an exact, scientific and definite process based on substantial and incontrovertible evidence. During their conversations on rebirth and reincarnation, Camille was surprised to find that, like millions of Indians, his dear friend Raghuvansh, too, believed in this phenomenon.

In their discussions on the lives of Christian saints, Camille was astounded to find that Raghuvansh equated the spiritual accomplishments and historicity of Hindu saints with the Christian saints. A surprised Camille asked if Raghuvansh really believed in the folklore, myth and legends of the Hindu saints. Since the canonisation of Christian saints required long and rigorous research and a thorough process to evaluate the evidence, this entire process was supervised by the office of a cardinal in Rome (Raghuvansh 1961, pp. 218–222). Raghuvansh replied that the lack of such a formal process does not mean that all the Hindu saints are mere imaginations. He argued that given that both Hindu and Christian saints achieve the same level of piety, devotion and spiritual advancement, both should be accorded the same level of divinity. Camille disagreed with his friend and said, 'Raghuvansh, we cannot believe that this is also true and that is also true; like claiming that truth is also true, and falsehood is also true. There will be only one truth, if one thing is true, then its opposite thing will be false. Your rationale that this may be true, and this may also be true, is only a state of doubt' (ibid.). A startled Raghuvansh then tried to explain that he did not believe in absolute truism contained within only one path, tradition and system. Instead, he believed that man is neither wholly constrained nor infinitely liberated, and thus, while man cannot envision the entire truth, he is still capable of comprehending an aspect of the truth. Hence, Raghuvansh claimed that 'it is not difficult for me to accept that my belief is based on truth and also to accept that the belief of another, which seems to be contrary to mine, is also based on truth' (ibid.).

Raghuvansh was also anxious that he might have caused distress to his dear friend Camille. Yet he recognised that the biggest tragedy of the human race, whether in religion, politics, society or philosophy, was the complete faith in seeing only one truth – that is, truth from only one point of view. It is very hard to overcome such cognitive biases ingrained through training, education and culture for all, not just for householders, but also monks (ibid.). He might not have been able to say this directly to Camille, but it was evident to Raghuvansh that Camille's sagacity and deep knowledge of different traditions were not enough for him to accept multiple truths and pathways towards God realisation. Deep down, Camille remained steadfastly bound to his religious training and monotheistic beliefs that made him reject historicity, avatar-hood and other more eclectic and spiritual beliefs of the Hindus. He could not overcome the idea of Christian superiority over the polytheistic beliefs of the people in the country he had adopted as his home. In that, his knowledge and wisdom did not make him question the fundamental aspects of his own beliefs and training, and he remained true to his missionary spirit all his life.

Keeping Politics at Bay?

As an individual, despite his large circle of friends and acquaintances, Camille was generally a loner and reticent who would listen more and speak just enough. The renowned Hindi writer and linguist Prabhakar Machave[24] recalled that Camille was an individual who used to speak less and was never engaged in any gossip or slander of his contemporaries, a usual practice among the littérateurs of Hindi (Machave 1987, p. 165). Camille always tried to be non-partisan and non-aligned and was indifferent to high praise or sharp criticism (ibid.). Evidently, this disinterest in political games in interpersonal relations also shaped much of his conduct in every other sphere. He was cautious to stay clear of any political campaigns and, thus, would avoid any association with such activism that had any covert or declared political implications. Despite his fervent, persistent and vocal activism for the promotion of Hindi as the official language, he always clarified that he did not represent the political or legal campaign; instead, his participation was from a cultural perspective (C. Bulcke 2009, p. 118).

Camille was great friends with Radhakrishna, a famous Hindi author from Ranchi; both were members of the working committee of the Bihar Rashtrabhasha Samiti (National Language Council, Bihar). In some of the meetings of the committee, to resolve some intractable situations, Camille would often say, 'Leave it alone, while some people drive their political agenda, we are here to serve Hindi' (Karan 1987, p. 119). During 1974–1975, Bihar became the epicentre of a massive student movement against the then central and state governments of the Congress Party.[25] His friend Radhakrishna was the leader of this protest movement in Ranchi, and he had invited Camille to join the movement. Camille declined to participate in the political agitation and even advised his friend Radhakrishna that littérateurs should abstain from such political activities. He believed that one day this student movement would be hijacked by political leaders to become a tool for serving the political agenda of the leaders (ibid.).

On another occasion, the renowned revolutionary leader and littérateur Prafulla Chandra Patnaik refused to accept a literary award from the Bihar state government, citing the lack of due recognition to tribal writers. Patnaik recalls that on being asked for his reaction to this incident by some journalists, Camille reportedly said 'that such action may stir political confusion' (Patnaik 1987, p. 95). Patnaik believed that as a fellow writer based in Ranchi and as a part of the tribal region, Camille should have openly supported him. However, he also realised that as a missionary confined within the disciplinary boundaries of an organisation with foreign connections, Camille did not have as much autonomy as other laypeople did (ibid.). Camille never made any public statement on this issue; he was keen to separate literary activism from political activism even if his silence invited criticism.

Similarly, Camille's old friend from his university days in Allahabad, Bishan Narayan Tandon, who went on to become a senior bureaucrat with the prime minister's office in the 1970s, recalled an incident that shows Camille's reluctance to get caught up with political campaigns. To overcome the growing political instability, Indira Gandhi, the then Indian prime minister, declared an internal emergency, imposing severe restrictions on several fundamental rights of the citizens between June 1975 and March 1977. During this period, on 30 April 1976, Tandon received a letter from Camille, who had sought his bureaucrat friend's advice. The renowned social worker Acharya Vinoba Bhave had invited Camille to participate in a scholarly conference in June 1976. Camille had written,

> I am in a dilemma; I have always stayed away from politics, and I suspect there are some political motives behind organising this conference. I aways stand with any campaign that is for the welfare of the country. However, on this occasion, I am uncertain whether I should participate in this event. Please advise. (Tandon 2015, p. 95)

Given the sensitive position Tandon held in the Indian bureaucracy and given the volatile political situation, he did not send any reply to Camille. However, he did talk to Camille after a few days, and the conference itself was postponed. Camille, like several other prominent and pragmatic people, stayed away from this movement to avoid any unpleasantness from the then Indian government. It was a practical decision to avoid provoking the Indian state into taking any punitive action against him. Moreover, in those times, the Christian missions were careful not to appear confrontational or be seen indulging in anti-government activities.

Camille's disinterest in political campaigns did not imply that he was bereft of political consciousness; on the contrary, he was a keen observer of the social and political developments of his time and expressed his opinions on several issues. His views on the role of Christians in India's social and cultural development offer important insights into the community's work and contributions towards nation-building, while his idea of Indian-ness is the manifesto of a politically conscious and conscientious Indian citizen. We discuss these in the next sections.

Views on Christianity and Indian Secularism

Camille wrote some insightful pieces on the role of Christians in the nation-building of India and the specific characteristics of Indian secularism. Writing on the history and evolution of Christianity in India, he argued that although the Hindu and Christian religions have different historical, cultural and ideological foundations, they share many similarities. He also noted that since the status of Christianity witnessed a surge with the arrival of the Europeans in India, the religion itself is presented as 'foreign'. However, he claimed that history tells that this religion entered India even before Europe; the Christians in south India firmly believed one of the 12 Apostles of Christ, Saint Thomas, had preached Christianity there (C. Bulcke 2009, pp. 109–111). Camille admitted that while no authentic argument can be presented against this traditional belief, there are historical arguments for the existence of Christianity in south India in the fourth century CE (ibid.). As a religion, Christianity developed in India for centuries and was eventually absorbed into the daily life of ordinary people, adapting to local customs and traditions.

He underlined the fact that numerically the Christians formed a tiny minority, yet they played a significant role in the country's culture, education and social development. Jesuit missionaries drew the attention of Europe towards the Sanskrit language and Indian philosophy, due to which these began to be studied in the universities there. Similarly, the Christian missionaries prepared the first dictionaries and grammar of all the Aryan, non-Aryan, developed and underdeveloped Indian languages (ibid.). At the beginning of the nineteenth century, the first translation of the Bible appeared in Hindi, followed by the publication of a large number of books in Hindi. This campaign eventually led to the development of Khari Boli[26] as the standard form of Hindi. The Christian missionaries were pioneers in establishing modern educational institutions, including co-educational institutions, and founded Asia's first women's college in Lucknow in 1895 (ibid.). India's first agricultural college was established by Christian missionaries in Naini. They also established leprosy hospitals, orphanages and general hospitals in other places (ibid.).

Given such a long historical association and the prolific contribution to India's nation-building and cultural development, Camille believed it was unjust to see Christians as outsiders or to label them as anti-India and anti-Indian (D. Prasad 2002, p. 105). He narrated an old folktale from south India to illustrate the sense of selfless service to the nation and fellow human beings among the Christians.

> Having learnt about the miracles of Saint Thomas, the King of Malabar asked him to build a luxurious palace within three months. Once the stipulated three months had lapsed, and no palace was in sight, the King asked Saint Thomas, 'Where is the palace that you had promised to build for me?' St. Thomas calmly pointed to a group of new Christians and said, 'Sir! Look at these people; they are your palace, which is more permanent than the palace of marbles. These people are religious, hardworking and loyal. Any king can be proud of such subjects.' (C. Bulcke 2009, pp. 110–111)

Camille affirmed that Christians are taught patriotism and that they cannot be honest with God without being honest with their country (ibid.). Rephrasing Saint Thomas' accreditation of the first Indian Christians, Camille proclaimed that, like the Christians of Malabar, other Christians also strive to be able citizens by developing the qualities of righteousness, hard work and patriotism. 'As Christians, we want to brighten the future of our country by standing shoulder to shoulder with our brothers so that Mother India can be proud of her Christian subjects' (ibid.). He believed that Christianity and Indian-ness could coexist in harmony, guided by patriotism and love for fellow human beings.

In all his works though, there was little discussion on why conversions were important and why the Church continued to attract foreign missionaries, whose aim was to bring people into the Christian faith. His own country, Belgium, has had a brutal history of colonial conquests in Africa in which

Christian missionaries played a significant role, and surely Camille was aware of that during his times. Aggressive and large-scale conversions organised under various missions; conflicts between Christians and non-Christians; the homecoming, or 'ghar wapasi', campaigns by some right-wing groups to bring the Christians back to their Hindu roots; and anti-conversion legislations have dominated India's political and social landscape, especially in recent times. They have especially been points of friction in Camille's home state of Jharkhand, where he spent his life among the tribals. While he painted a harmonious picture of coexistence and was an enlightened soul, interested in more than his own faith, his ideas would have sat uncomfortably with contemporary India. Despite his anti-colonial language politics, his silence on some of these pertinent issues perhaps tells us that he wanted to stay away from more controversial subjects which would distract him from his mandate of missionary work and his own self-inspired scholarly pursuits.

Writing about India's secular constitution, Camille underlined the apparent paradox. On the one hand, India is a deeply religious country and is the birthplace of many religions and sects, but the constitution declares this country not as a theocratic polity but as a secular republic. Indian secularism means *sarva dharma sama bhava*, which means equal respect for all religions. No discerning person would equate Indian secularism with the absence of religion in society. However, it proclaims and stipulates that the government of India does not discriminate between citizens on the basis of religion or sect and does not give any privilege to any one religion (C. Bulcke 1996, p. 237). Camille reiterated that the Indian constitution builders placed four separate articles to protect the religious freedom of minorities, in which, apart from the secularism of the government and the right of the citizens to follow and propagate their religion, all religious communities have been given the right to govern their institutions (ibid.). These protections are enshrined in the constitution to make minorities feel safe and facilitate the country's emotional unity (ibid.).

He highlighted three interrelated factors that would help India's secularism remain strong and sustain the country's religious amity and cultural unity (ibid., pp. 239–240). First, one must understand that religion itself is not the cause of communalism; the reason for it is the fanaticism of the followers. He believed that no matter which religion one follows, a religious person does not fight with the followers of other religions. Spirituality binds humans in the thread of unity, while rituals separate them, and therefore one should give less importance to rituals and more importance to righteousness and ethical conduct (ibid.). The second important factor, according to Camille, is for people to learn more about religions other than their own. Studying other religions would lead to a better understanding and knowledge about their context, perspectives and practices; this would promote healthy reverence for all religions. Camille's third point is for the minorities; he suggested that the Indian citizens belonging to the minority communities have no other country of their own except India. Therefore, as citizens of this great country, it is appropriate for them to get a little insight into India's glorious past and history, its culture spanning centuries, the epics and the rich ancient literature. In this way, by considering themselves as the natural children of the soil of India, they would feel integrated with the national mainstream of India.

Camille believed that while the Indian constitution guaranteed legislative and legal protection to the country's rich diversity, the real force behind Indian secularism is not only the constitution but also the Indian culture that has shaped the liberal and inclusive social psyche. His essay titled 'Bharteeyata Meri Pehchaan' (Indian-ness as My Identity) provides the essence of his lifelong association with Indian history, culture and literature. For him, Indian-ness meant the general characteristics of the Indian culture that have existed and evolved for centuries, and the elements and values, that can rise above the particular community and can be beneficial and inspiring for all Indian citizens (ibid., p. 231). This Indian culture, the basis of Indian-ness, is very receptive and liberal; its living values are not confined to Hindu ideals but are universal and non-conflictual.

Camille claimed that Indian-ness is not an abstract concept, but it is a site for ongoing and live human interactions and also lived experiences. He argued that no discussion on Indian-ness can ignore the fact that Indian culture is syncretic and liberal by nature, and it is so diverse that it has a place for every religion. He stated,

> I believe that there is so much generosity in traditional Indian beliefs that Christianity can become one of them. In my own way, I myself am a small example of the congruence between Christianity and Indianness. Several friends remind me that too frequently I am more Indian than them. (C. Bulcke 2015 [1976], p. 342)

To highlight Indian-ness as a lived experience, he reminisced about his days as a student at the University of Allahabad, when he watched millions of pilgrims gathering at the banks of the Ganga River for a holy dip. This reminded him of a quotation in the Bible: 'For here we have no lasting city, but we seek the city that is to come' (C. Bulcke 1996, p. 235). He defined the essence of his Indian-ness through a verse from the *Vinaya Patrika* of Tulsidas.

राम सनेही सों तैं न सनेह कियो।
अगम जो अमरनि हूँ सो तनु तोहिं दियो॥
यह भरतखंड, समीप सुरसरि, थल भलो, संगति भली।

Oh, you creature! You did not develop affection towards Lord Sri Rama, who has been kind, affectionate and graceful to you, because he has given you a human body which is rare and most difficult even for the Gods to obtain. One is blessed for being born in a land known as Bharat which is regarded as a holy land, and where the holy river Ganges is nearby. To cap it all, there is the added advantage of having the company of saints and the opportunity of communion with sages and seers, where spiritual guidance and divine discourses are given, and good things are discussed in a routine manner. (Chhawchharia 2017, pp. 423–424)

The same Indian-ness in expressed in Tulsidas' *Kavitavali* too.

भलि भारत भूमि, भले कुल जन्म, समाज सरीर भला लहिकै।
जौ भजै भगवान सयान सोई तुलसी हठ चातक ज्यों गहिकै।

You have taken birth in the holy land of Bharat [India], in an exalted clan, and have found a good society and body. Tulsidas says that one who always worships Lord Rama with concerted and focused devotion, like the Chatak bird, is considered wise and clever. (Chhawchharia 2015b, p. 144)

Camille always thanked God from the bottom of his heart for sending him to this religious country and blessing him with the 'good company' of devotional Indian people. He always expressed the desire to be sensible and serve India and keep being inspired by the country's cultural values (C. Bulcke 1996, p. 236). He received his Indian citizenship on 24 January 1950 deservingly, and an honour that few 'foreigners' have achieved; he was also conferred the third highest civilian award, the Padma Bhushan, in 1974 (Ponette 1991, p. 292).

Reflecting on his life spent in India, Camille stated,

> Most of my life was spent in India. Thinking about this, a feeling of gratitude arises in my heart – thanks to God, who has sent me to India and thanks to India, which has received me with such love! I left a small country, and a great country accepted me. That's why I consider myself lucky God has sent me to India, so if I leave for the other world from India, God will definitely welcome me. (C. Bulcke 2015 [1976], p. 345)

Camille's contributions are enormous, but not without problems, contestations and inconsistencies, as we have indicated in this chapter. It is possible both to see the direct impact of his extraordinary scholarship and his legacy and to tease out nuances of his strategic silences and often simplistic and perhaps overtly optimistic readings of the important issues at stake. He was always keen to protect the uniqueness and superiority of Christianity as a faith and tradition, but that did not stop him from respectfully engaging with other traditions and forms of knowledges, learning from them and critiquing them. In his methods alone, there is a lesson for us all.

Notes

1. Dhirendra Verma was the head of the Department of Hindi at the University of Allahabad and the man responsible for getting Camille into the MA programme of the university.
2. Ikshvaku was the founder of the royal dynasty in which Rama was born.
3. Dasharatha was the father of Rama.
4. Sita Savitri was one of the two daughters of Prajapati, who was later married to King Soma. The other Sita is the deity of abundance and nourishment through the earth.
5. *Jataka* refers to birth history. It is a genre of Buddhist literature that narrates the previous births of the historical Buddha (Siddhartha Gautama). The *Dasharatha Jataka* depicts Rama's life as the son of Dasharatha.
6. Bodhisattva refers to one who has awakened himself and then awakens others; he who necessarily will become Buddha is called Bodhisattva. Bodhi

is the wisdom of the saint who has destroyed the impurities. The person born from this wisdom, protected by the sages and served by the sages, is called Bodhisattva.

7. Chyavana was a great sage, the son of sage Bhrigu. He performed penance for many centuries. So long did that penance last that an anthill had grown around him. He is referred to as Valmiki or Chyavana Bhargava.

8. One of the most important European Indologists, Hermann Jacobi (1850–1937), was a pioneering scholar and a major figure in Jain studies. He demonstrated that Jainism had been separate from Buddhism. He produced numerous editions of Jain texts in Sanskrit, Prakrit and Apabhramsha and also several works of translation.

9. In the Jain cosmology, an illustrious or worthy person is referred to as *shalakpurush*, and there are 63 such illustrious beings. Rama is seen as a *shalakpurush*, and Rama and Lakshmana are the eighth Baldev and Vasudeva.

10. Ivan A. Extross was living in St Joseph's Seminary, Allahabad; Camille stayed at the same seminary during his stay in Allahabad. On Camille's first visit to the university when he met Dhirendra Verma in the Hindi department, Extross had accompanied him.

11. William Carey (1761–1834) was an English Baptist missionary, educator and translator. He translated the Bible into Bengali, Oriya, Marathi, Hindi, Assamese and Sanskrit. Henry Martyn (1781–1812) was ordained a priest in the Church of England and became a chaplain for the British East India Company. He translated the New Testament and the Book of Common Prayer, into Urdu and supervised the translation of the New Testament into Arabic and the Persian language, Farsi.

12. The Five Scrolls are the five shortest books of the Hebrew scriptures. They are the Books of Esther, Lamentations and Ruth, the Ecclesiastes, and the Song of Songs.

13. Koine was the Hellenistic Greek spoken and written from the fourth century BCE until the time of the Byzantine emperor Justinian (mid-sixth century CE) in Greece, Macedonia and parts of Africa and the Middle East.

14. William (Bill) Dwyer held the position of the principal of St Xavier's School, Hazaribagh, Jharkhand, in 1978. His proficiency in Hindi made him the most suitable candidate to complete the remaining translation of the Holy Bible.

15. Ralph Lilley Turner is credited with compiling the first Nepali–English dictionary. A comparative and etymological dictionary of the Nepali language was published in 1931 in London.

16. 'तद्यथा घटेन कार्यं करिष्यन् कुम्भकारकुलं गत्वा आह कुरु घटं कार्यमनेन करिष्यामीति, न तद्वत् शब्दान् प्रयोक्ष्यमाणो वैयाकरणकुलं गत्वा आह कुरु शब्दान् प्रयोक्ष्ये इति' (Tadyatha ghaten karyam karishyan kumbhakarakulam gatva aah kuru ghatam karyamanen karishyamiti, na tadthvat shabdaan prayokshmano vayakarankulam gatva aah kuru shabdaan prayokshaye iti).

17. Dingal was the mediaeval poetic language of the bards of Rajasthan.

18. *Avatara* means 'descent' and refers to the descent of God on earth; *avataravada* refers to the system itself (C. Bulcke 2010, p. 168).

19. The Brahmanas are prose commentaries attached to the Vedas, the earliest writings of Hinduism. They explain the significance of the ritual sacrifices and the symbolic import of the priests' actions. The *Yajurveda*, one of the four Vedas, has two divisions: the 'Shukla (White) Yajurveda' and the 'Krishna (Black) Yajurveda'. The *Shatapatha Brahmana* (Of 100 Paths), consisting of 100 lessons, belongs to the 'Shukla Yajurveda'.

20. The Brahmanas as part of the Vedic literature are further divided into two parts: the Aranayakas (Book of the Wilderness), which contain esoteric doctrines meant to be studied by the initiated in the forest or some other remote place, and the Upanishads, which speculate about the ontological connection between humanity and the cosmos. The Upanishads constitute the concluding portions of the Vedas, they are called 'Vedanta' (the conclusion of the Vedas), and they serve as the foundational texts in the theological discourses of many Hindu traditions.

21. *Rasalila* is described briefly in the *Vishnu Purana* and the *Harivamsha Purana*, and it is described in detail in the *Bhagavata Purana*. It is derived from the Sanskrit word *ras*, which means 'nectar', 'emotion' or 'sweet taste'; *lila* stands for 'act', 'play' or 'dance'. *Rasalila* refers to Krishna dancing with the *gopis*.

22. *Mula prakriti* is the root (basic) energy from which all things are formed – the divine *prakriti*, or energy of God. Mula Prakriti (or Maya) and Para Brahman (or Purusha) are the eternal entities in perfect union.

23. *Rajatarangini* (River of Kings) is a Sanskrit poem in eight cantos. Each canto is called a *taranga*, or wave.

24. Prabhakar Machave (1917–1991) was a prolific writer and linguist and an authority on Indian literature. A gifted and creative writer, he wrote many plays and poems and over 100 books. He was also an artist and painter. His sketches are compiled in a book titled *Shabd Rekha* (Sketches of Eminent Personalities).

25. Jayaprakash Narayan (1902–1979) was a renowned Indian socialist leader who also participated in the Indian independence movement against British

colonial rule. In the 1960s, he retired from active politics but, in 1974, returned to lead a non-violent protest of the students against high inflation, high unemployment and a shortage of supplies and necessities in the state of Gujarat. The movement soon spread to Narayan's home state of Bihar, to be called the JP Movement or the Bihar Movement and also as Sampoorna Kranti (Total Revolution). The then Indian prime minister, Indira Gandhi, declared an internal emergency, suspended the Indian constitution and jailed most of the agitators, including Narayan. Several prominent and pragmatic people stayed away from this movement to preclude any unpleasantness of the then Indian government.

26. Khari Boli was an early dialect of Hindi, which originated in Delhi and an adjacent region within the Ganges–Yamuna *doab* (interfluve) during the Mughal period (in the early sixteenth to mid-eighteenth centuries).

6

⊰⊱

The Man and His Mission

A Critical Appraisal

A Different Kind of 'Ghar Wapasi'[1]

In March 2018, a significant event occurred in Ranchi that provided the much-needed inspiration to work on this biography. Father Camille Bulcke's remains were brought from Delhi's Nicholson Cemetery and reburied on the premises of Ranchi's St Xavier's College, located on Camille Bulcke Path, named after him. The reburial of his skeletal remains was announced as part of the tribal tradition of *hadgadi*, where the remains of ancestors are carried as a blessing and reburied as the tribes move from one village to another. The exhumation of dead bodies and remains is also a known practice among Catholics, especially for beatification and canonisation purposes. In several contexts and for various reasons, the family members of the dead can also make personal requests to the Church and local administration to allow them to rebury their loved ones elsewhere. It is not uncommon to witness the exhumation of remains of a family grave at various times when a new member is to be buried at the same site (Parashar 2018).

The Jesuit Society of Jharkhand worked closely with their Delhi counterparts and had to cross several bureaucratic hurdles to bring back the remains of Father Bulcke. They received help from Father Ranjit Tigga, the head of the Department of Tribal Studies at the Indian Social Institute, New Delhi, who oversaw the digging of the grave in Delhi, the exhumation of the remains and the logistical arrangements to transport them to Ranchi, where the casket was received in a traditional tribal ceremonial welcome. In the past, another Belgian priest, Father Constant Lievens (1856–1893), known to have officially 'converted' a large number of Chhota Nagpur tribals to Catholicism, had his ashes transferred from Belgium and interred at St Mary's Cathedral in Ranchi in 1993. Efforts towards the canonisation of Father Lievens were ongoing, even as we were working on this manuscript.

Speakers at the reburial and commemoration event included Father Bulcke's close associates, noted littérateurs, former students and members of the Jesuit Society who reflected on his life and contributions – ranging from original commentaries on religious texts and high-quality translations to arguably the best English-to-Hindi *shabdkosh* (dictionary) still found in most Indian homes and offices. His generosity was remembered by many to whom he lent books from his personal library even though they were strangers. His interactions with women students who also benefitted from his library and his mentorship, when women were not allowed into classes at St Xavier's College during the 1960s, were fondly remembered. The stories and anecdotes shared also suggested that he had an extraordinary influence over a large number of people from different fields. His students had various memories of interactions with him; his Jesuit colleagues had their own views; his literary friends and critics had their carefully crafted thoughts on his contributions and on his strengths and weaknesses; and then there were people who had imagined him through the stories they had heard of him.

The prayers at the event were conducted by the Christian clergy, and it was uniquely moving to see them reciting Sanskrit verses and *doha*s and *chaupai*s from the *Ramcharitmanas*.[2] Cardinal Telesphore Toppo of the Ranchi diocese, who passed away on 4 October 2023, mentioned that it might have been preordained that Father Bulcke, born in Ramskapelle in Belgium, would find his intellectual and spiritual moorings in the Rama of Tulsidas, despite being a devout Catholic. In casual conversations, people also reflected on the remarkable similarities between Father Bulcke (or Baba Bulcke) and his spiritual inspiration, the author of the *Ramcharitmanas*, Goswami Tulsidas. Both tried to capture the wisdom and devotion of religious texts, the Ramayana and the Bible, into common peoples' languages, Awadhi and Hindi; both made the core values of humanism the focal point of the retelling of these texts, and the stories were not more important than the messages they carried; both perhaps believed in the superiority or effectiveness of the *bhakti* yoga over *gyan* yoga; and both suffered immense physical pain towards the end of their lives.

Camille was accustomed to physical suffering; his hearing had worsened over the years, and chronic asthma made him often seek medical attention. During the months of June and July of 1982, a blood clot was found in an artery of his right leg, and he was admitted to different hospitals in Patna, Mandar, Delhi and, finally, at the All India Institute of Medical Sciences (AIIMS) in Delhi. The treatment was worse than the ailment as three of his toes were amputated to prevent the spread of gangrene (Goswami 1987, p. 20). He bore all these painful amputations with exceptional fortitude and would say that he did not need toes to write (Ponette 1991, p. 122). Once the disease set in, all the other ailments – 'asthma, a weakened heart, his affected lungs, his damaged kidneys, an ulcerous stomach, and gangrene – conspired to strain his heart beyond endurance, and it gave way several times before it stopped for good' (ibid.). Camille had the inkling of the approaching end, and he had asked to see Father Provincial a day earlier. In complete serenity, with eyes closed and hands folded on his chest, Camille told Father Provincial, 'I wholeheartedly accept God's will, and I am ready to meet Him. I am no longer worried about the completion of my translation. The Lord calls me: here I am!' (ibid.). His exact words in Hindi were 'Main prastut hun'.

After weeks of physical suffering and pain, on 17 August 1982, Camille left this world, embracing his fate as the will of God. He was buried at the Nicholson Cemetery, in Kashmere Gate in Delhi, before his remains were brought to Ranchi and reburied in March 2018. His spiritual mentor, Tulsidas, was also afflicted with physical ailments towards the end of his life as pus-filled boils, rashes and lesions appeared all over his body. He tried various medicines and traditional healing methods, but his pain did not subside. It is said that Tulsidas alleviated his physical suffering by immersing himself in the worship of Lord Hanuman and composing the *Hanuman Bahuk* (The Arm of Hanuman)[3] during this period. Historians vary on the year of this composition, but it is assumed to be in the early part of the seventeenth century.

In an India where religious conversion has always been a highly sensitive and contentious issue and anti-conversion laws have been introduced by various state governments in the last few years, where conflict simmers between Christian and non-Christian tribals, between Hindus and Muslims, between Christians and Hindus and between Christians and Muslims, people of all religions attended the ceremonial reburial of Father Bulcke's remains to mark his final resting place in his *karma bhumi* (workplace), Ranchi in Jharkhand, 35 years after his death. We attended this reburial and commemoration event and felt an urgent need to tell the story of this remarkable personality from Ranchi, where he first arrived from Belgium and later worked as a missionary and teacher. In conclusion, we would like to reflect on how Camille's life and his scholarship might appear to different constituencies, who were either direct beneficiaries of his work or had a close association with him.

To Jharkhand and Adivasis

Father Bulcke's 'ghar wapasi' (return to his original home) as part of the reburial ceremony has restored a sense of pride to various communities in Jharkhand, and there is great admiration for his work and what he achieved living in what was then really the small city of Ranchi (Parashar 2018). The city's premier educational institute, St Xavier's College, is home to the Father Camille Bulcke Research Centre, and at the entrance stands his bust with a quote from the *Ramcharitmanas*. It is at this college that he first founded and then taught at the Hindi and Sanskrit departments. Manresa House, the Jesuit headquarters next door, and Camille's erstwhile 'home' which was the hub of intellectual activities during his times, has many memories of his stay; a huge statue of its most illustrious resident and patron greets the visitors, on its premises. If there was a 'home' away from home (Belgium), it was Ranchi, where Camille spent many years of his life in the service of the Church and the common people, especially students whom he taught with great commitment and affection.

Jharkhand was carved out of the erstwhile state of Bihar in the year 2000, after a long period of resistance and demand for a separate state for the Adivasis (tribals), who comprised 26 per cent of the total population of Bihar (Tillin 2013, p. 73). Since its formation, the state has been the site of several political and social contestations and resistance movements, especially those related to the marginalisation of tribal life and culture (Xaxa 2018; Basu 2024). In this context, it must be acknowledged that Camille was not an overt champion of tribal rights or culture, and his struggles, priorities and concerns were different. His emphasis on Hindi as the national and unifying post-colonial language of India could be seen as part of the Hindi hegemonic campaign that has been central to the language wars in independent India. He worked tirelessly for Hindi and Sanskrit and had little to say about the development of tribal languages and cultural communication tools. His European linguistic and cultural sensibilities, in a post–Second World War context, had a homogenising and nationalistic impulse and did not equip him sufficiently to understand the multilingual context and the immeasurable diversity of India's people, culture, traditions and languages. Hindi has still not found acceptance as the 'national' language of India, and efforts to impose it have been resisted, even violently sometimes.

On occasion, especially with respect to the uniformity and standardisation of language, he held unflattering views about people who did not embrace European modernity as the only successful model of development (C. Bulcke 1996, p. 256). In fact, he saw Europe as the beacon of enlightenment for territorial consolidation through language and for the trajectory of development. Although critical of British colonialism, he had nothing to say about the indigenous rights of peoples anywhere, especially in Africa, where his own country of birth, Belgium, was engaged in a brutal colonial conquest. Our hope was to avoid a hagiographical account of Camille Bulcke, and it is here that we struggled to make sense of the baffling silence around other colonialism projects and the rights of colonised peoples in places that he was familiar with. As a scholar-activist who had lived his adult life in Europe and was deeply engaged in resisting French cultural imposition in his native Flanders, it is hard to imagine that he was completely unaware of the European colonial project, and the complicity of the Church and early Christian missions, and with that Belgium's own violent colonial rule, especially in the Congo (erstwhile Zaire), Rwanda and Burundi. We found no reference to these topics in any of his writings.

As we indicate in Chapter 4, on various political issues that emerged during his times in India, Camille chose to remain silent or non-committal; taking political sides made him uncomfortable, and he avoided that path. If he did not understand the issues at stake or what his own position ought to be, he consulted his politically astute friends for advice. It is our view that his missionary commitment towards strengthening the Christian church and its activities in India and assisting Christian integration into the post-colonial Indian republic, which had witnessed unprecedented levels of communal violence at the dawn of independence from British rule, remained his major objectives. It made him less inclined to engage in political activism, especially for tribal cultural and political autonomy, which would put him in direct confrontation with the state and various governments. Missionaries who came to India before him, during colonial times, such as Constant Lievens, had concerned themselves with tribal lives and causes in Jharkhand, treating the local landlords, moneylenders, middlemen and other agents as a common enemy. However, their mandate was to appeal to the masses and spread the gospel among them; converting a large number of people to Christianity was an important agenda.

Camille carved a different mission for himself: to understand India and Indian religious and literary traditions better, and to situate his Christian values and teachings within the larger context of the Indian civilization and secularism of the Indian constitution. He did not strictly follow the path of his missionary predecessors and went beyond the mandate of his mission, which led to unease within and sometimes even quiet resistance from the ecclesiastical community. This tension was not helped by his scholarly pursuits which earned him many non-Christian friends; his worsening hearing disability turned him into a recluse, especially among those who did not care to understand or appreciate his work and passion.

To the Ecclesiastical Community

We have emphasised that Camille did not deviate from his original mission and calling, which was to serve the Christian church and to spread the message of Jesus Christ. As a devout Christian, his faith in Christianity was unshakeable – even to the extent of proving its superiority to other existing faiths, especially Hinduism for which he developed a deep and abiding scholarly interest. At various places in his own writings and in his exchanges with his friends, especially with Raghuvansh, he entered into uncomfortable conversations where he even tried to (unsuccessfully) prove that Christianity as the organised religion was the only way to redeem oneself, that it was based on compassion and centrality of ideas and laced with historical evidence of the 'son of God' being the savior of humanity. His Tulsi *bhakti* was also in line with his thinking of serving Christ with the same devotion as Tulsidas had served Lord Rama, although several people mistakenly assumed that he became a devotee of Rama.

One of his friends, the Hindi writer, Lallan Prasad Vyas, asked him, 'Bulcke ji, given that you have studied Rama's story in such great and minuscule detail, do you also believe in the divinity of Lord Rama? To which Bulcke replied – I am just a devotee of Tulsidas ji' (Vyas 2015, p. 98). Camille's answer intrigued Vyas, who could not comprehend how an avowed devotee of Tulsidas could not be a devotee of Rama when Tulsidas himself claimed to be in the service of his Lord Rama. However, with time, Vyas came to appreciate the fact that 'as a Christian priest, Father Bulcke could become a devotee of Tulsidas but not of Lord Rama, who we [Hindus] exalt as God' (ibid.). In a similar vein, Bishan Tandon, a friend from university days in Allahabad, asked

Camille how he could find so much reverence for the *Ramakatha* and Tulsidas given that most Christian preachers do not hesitate to mock Hindu gods and goddesses for the promotion of their religion (Tandon 2015, pp. 94–95). An offended and sad Camille replied, 'Bishanji, I am as proud to be an Indian as I am to be a Christian. There is so much liberality in the traditional ideas of India that Christianity cannot face any kind of crisis here, but the sad thing is that the followers of the Christian religion, mainly the Christian preachers, did not try to understand this' (ibid.). India and Hinduism appealed to his spiritual and religious sensibilities, but it did not clash with his Christian missionary identity. He remained a steadfast and staunch Christian, an icon among the few missionaries who wanted to indigenise Christianity for Indian believers.

Namrata Chaturvedi argues, 'In Hindi studies, there is scholarly attention given to figures like Father Camille Bulcke, which reveal a tendency to highlight Hinduized Christianity as acceptable and worthy of inter-cultural explorations' (Chaturvedi 2021, p. 173). While this attention to Camille might be the result of his works on Tulsidas and the *Ramkatha*, to reduce him to a 'Hinduised Christian' is both unfair and a misreading of his life and contributions. He never wavered from his Christian faith and remained committed to the path of Christ all his life; he considered it the best path for attaining salvation and realising the purpose of human life. He was deeply inspired by the Bhakti literary traditions of India and the vast spiritual and philosophical insights of Hinduism, but it was the method that attracted him more than the visible manifestations of beliefs and rituals. He wished to learn from and apply that method – that is, the *bhakti*, or personal devotion, to God – in the service of Christ and the Church.

It is worth reflecting that in the current political and social milieu, no 'foreign' Christian monk would find easy acceptance among his own brethren if he tried to extoll the virtues of the Ramayana and the *Ramkatha*. They would reject his scholarly pursuits as blaspheming against his own faith and pandering to the current populism of the Hindu nationalists. His language activism for the supremacy of Hindi would also be considered an appeasement of populist sentiments. Was it any different during Camille's lifetime? Father Pierre Ponette, Camille's contemporary at Manresa House, in his obituary to Camille throws important light on the latter's fraught relationship with his own Christian brethren during his times. It supports our view that the ecclesiastical community was less enthusiastic about Camille's intellectual pursuits than is known or acknowledged; he remained an enigma to his own

Christian brothers who were completely taken by surprise at the outpouring of grief and the sense of loss among the Indian public after Camille's death. 'The image he had projected outside had hardly been noticed by those who lived with him' (Ponette 1991, p. 121). It was believed that Camille was more at home with his Hindu friends than with his Christian brethren, and the former admired his 'simplicity, sense of humour, charm, unaffected warmth and great openness' (ibid.).

Ponette believes that Camille's health problems, his hearing disability and his scholarly pursuits on the Ramayana left little space for him to interact with the other Jesuits. He had already annoyed his clergy colleagues at Manresa House when he turned up in a saffron cassock after receiving his doctoral degree from the University of Allahabad. Outwardly, they applauded him, but he had 'raised the hackles of some' (ibid.); and that relationship was never fully mended although Camille kept trying, by having quiet one-to-one conversations with people. However, 'soon enough the cacophony of the loud conversations of others grated so much on his eardrum that he had to withdraw' (ibid.). His social nature found expression in his interactions with his students and his scholarly friends in the Hindi world, but to his Christian clergy colleagues, he appeared reticent and inhibited. His insistence on using the pure Hindi language for speaking and in publications also got him into disagreements with his fellow clergymen, and he appeared uncompromising at times (ibid.).

Camille worked hard to promote the spiritual growth of his co-religionists, and this is evident from his focus on Christian texts rather than other Hindi publications, but in the views of the Church, he perhaps fell short of the missionary target. Ponette's insights are a valuable assessment of Camille the clergyman: 'He did not reap a harvest of conversions, but he brought nearer to God all those who contacted him' (ibid.). Camille had his own sense of what was right for him, and he was not interested in other people's appreciation or endorsement.

> His spiritual life was like a closed book which he kept firmly shut. We could only see its cover. Thus, his fidelity to daily Mass, even when travelling and at what trouble, his faithful recitation of the breviary and his deep devotion to Our Lady. Besides his whole apostolate was an act of piety, a life of service and concern for his fellow-Christians and the Hindu community at large. His was not a run of the mill ministry, yet was nonetheless motivated by his keen awareness of a mission to

accomplish. He opened doors, cleared away prejudices, paved the way for dialogue. The Allahabad clergy in particular gratefully acknowledge that it is Camille who broke down the barrier that kept them away from the town's intelligentsia. (Ibid.)

A nagging question for the Church will always be whether they were too slow to recognise Camille's contributions, precisely because he dared to traverse the missionary mandate. On the other hand, while it may seem that he enjoyed greater acceptance and camaraderie among his Hindu friends and acquaintances during his lifetime, hard-line Hindu nationalists today would mock his interests and reduce his appeal and influence to mere demagoguery to serve the missionary zeal of his Christian faith. Some would even question his 'knowledge' and motives and accuse him of appropriation to further preach and propagate the gospel. Very few on either side (the ecclesiastical community and the Hindu nationalists or Hindutva followers) would be willing to understand and appreciate the complex world that this European Christian priest, with a scholarly and human interest in India and Indian literary traditions, lived through and navigated with ease as well as discomfort.

To His Critics and Friends

In the previous chapters, we highlighted Camille's scholarly contributions, but there was a greater humane side to him that we were only able to capture in glimpses. Despite his busy schedule and rigorous scholarly work, Camille always found time for his favourite hobbies and little pleasures. Right from childhood, he loved cycling. Even in Ranchi, people remember him on a bicycle; after his coffee at 3 p.m., he would venture out cycling to the rural areas, meeting people, only to return after dusk. He called cycling an entertaining exercise that filled him with energy and enthusiasm for his scholarly pursuits in the evening. His other interests were solving crossword puzzles in the daily newspapers with Father Clarysse, playing a weekly game of bridge in the seminary and reading detective novels (ibid.). It is in the course of these hobbies, other mundane activities, his travels and his scholarly pursuits that he encountered so many people with whom he had remarkable exchanges which had a transformative impact on his life.

An important aspect of his personality was that Camille did not discuss Christianity and Christian beliefs in public or in private with his non-Christian friends and visitors unless it was brought up by them. He kept his Christian preachings to his church services and for the Christian community; with Hindus, he exchanged thoughts on the Ramayana and Tulsidas (ibid.). Camille was an ardent admirer of Tulsidas and considered him a guide for the character-building of people. He tirelessly explained the moral values of Tulsidas at the many meetings of religious Hindus and to millions of people. Camille's affection for Tulsidas was akin to his love for God; he was asked to officiate at the unveiling of the statue of Tulsidas on 14 January 1975 as part of the first World Hindi Conference in 1975. Camille said, 'While Tulsi says Lord Rama makes everyone dance, in my case, it is Lord Tulsi who makes me dance. To disseminate Tulsi's message, I run around to different parts of the country' (D. Prasad 2002, p. 15). He was invited as the main speaker to many Tulsidas Jayanti events (birth anniversary commemorations of Tulsidas), and every year received more invitations than he could accept from all over the country. He expounded the virtues of the *Ramcharitmanas* and Tulsi's portrayal of human values in the characters of the Ramayana, in his chaste and simple Hindi and with his endearing sense of humour and devotion (Ponette 1991). He did so in his full Christian monk attire, invoking awe and adoration – not the sloganeering, threat and criticism he would have possibly received in present times. He believed that 'as a priest, it was his sacred and important duty to help people live the most virtuous and moral lives within the limits of their traditions' (Extross 1987, p. 71).

Camille found it very hard to tolerate any criticism of Tulsidas, for he considered his favourite poet an epitome of his unflinching devotion and unblemished conduct. On one occasion, the Ranchi College organised a seminar to celebrate Tulsidas Jayanti, and one of the speakers levelled many allegations of elite atrocities against Tulsidas. Camille found a novel way to show his displeasure at the conclusion of the event. He covered both his ears and exclaimed with disdain, 'Blessed is this building where such a speech was heard!' (K. Kumar 2015, p. 118)

Camille's life was an open book, and he regularly received visitors; if he got tired of them, he would pick up his pen and start writing as a way to convey to the visitor that it was time for them to take leave (Ponette 1991). The door to his abode at Manresa House was never locked, and if he had to leave his house, he would hang a placard on the door on which a sentence to this effect was written: 'I will return in a short while. Till then, please sit' (Ghosh

2015, pp. 132–133). As soon as he returned, he would collect the placard and start talking to the visitor; these placards conveyed that Camille was always waiting for someone. The wait for 'Father's visitors was never tedious since his room was always full of magazines and books from most scholarly periodicals, and academic journals to the latest literary and professional magazines' (ibid.).

Most of his associates and contemporaries remember him for his art of making conversations with others. He was always sympathetic, and given that he was a very emotional and sensitive person himself, he was afraid of offending anyone. With great calmness and dexterity, he would find such words for his guests that – no matter what class they belonged to – made them feel comfortable and at ease. People thronged to him to have a conversation or to borrow a few books from his library, and very often these alone were enough to solve their problems. One can only surmise what mysterious inspiration gave him so much peace amidst so many different tasks and while bearing the burdens of others. The fact that 'he was a monk and had immense faith in God was his biggest strength. God dwelt in his heart and gave him the strength to help everyone' (Ponette 1987, p. 69).

Often missionaries or priests have limited social life and remain in their own environment, but this was not the case for Camille, who was so sensitive and social that he was always ready to offer selfless service and help to the people around him. One of his best friends in Ranchi, the renowned Hindi writer Radhakrishna, was suffering from asthma. Camille was also suffering from asthma, and he used to get inhalers from Belgium. Every time he received inhalers, he would visit Radhakrishna to share them with his friend. Later 'Camille started to get medicines from Germany, and he would always give half of the medicines to Radhakrishna ji and kept the other half himself' (Karan 1987, pp. 118). If the medicine supplies ran low, Radhakrishna used to get anxious, and then 'Camille would console him – "Don't worry, God will do everything on time" and after a week, the father would personally go to their house and deliver the medicine' (ibid.).

Camille's physician, Siddharth Mukherjee, was impressed not only by his patient's extraordinary scholarship, but also by his humility, openness, generosity and humaneness (Mukherjee 2015, p. 128). Mukherjee remembers that whenever Father Bulcke visited him for consultation, 'he would sit at the back and even after my request, he would not allow me to examine him until I had seen the patients who had come before him' (ibid.). As Camille used to wait for the doctor, he would always inquire about the well-being of each of the patients, console them and take leave of everyone before returning. It seems that sharing the scarcest medicines was Camille's usual behaviour as Mukherjee narrates,

> Father Bulcke can give his medicine to others even when he is in trouble. He was a chronic patient of asthma, and his friends used to send medicines for it from Belgium. Often, these medicines were available only with Father Bulcke in Ranchi. It happened once that he himself was suffering from severe asthma, and when he came to see me, I told him that another patient, Mr. Sahi, was in dire need of the medicine (Ventolin) as he had run out of the medicines. When Father Bulcke heard this, he returned straight to Manresa House and shortly afterwards returned with the medicines. On enquiry, it was found that this was the last Ventolin he had brought. When I refused to take the medicine, seeing his condition, he said – 'Sahi ji's need is greater than mine, and I have got used to bearing this disease.' With this small example, the creation of his inner self can be understood very well. (Ibid.)

Camille was always very friendly and used to mingle with all classes of people as if they were members of his family. He was welcomed in the homes of all eminent intellectuals, government officials, middle-class families and the poor. However, he was very careful to stay off the snares of politics and never provided any opportunity for political people or groups to exploit him (Extross 1987, p. 71). He had close contact with several politicians such as Ram Manohar Lohia, Ganga Sharan Singh, Karan Singh, and Shankar Dayal Singh, among others, but he avoided the traps of any kind of political deceit. During the days of the Hindi movement, it was quite possible that Camille too would have become a political crusader for Hindi, much like his involvement in the Flemish language movement, but he kept himself away from such political projects. He was not unfamiliar with the fact that often the outcome of political movements becomes a means of fulfilling personal interests. Therefore, he kept himself away from any kind of political shenanigans (Rituparna 2015, p. 47).

One of his most public displays of political activism could be seen during the Chinese invasion of India in 1962, and that too as a literary figure offering his wisdom and thought during a conference in Allahabad organised by Mahadevi Verma (Ghosh 2015, p. 133). Though not a political person, Camille managed to successfully diffuse a potentially divisive issue that might have led to a political crisis, unrest or even open conflict. Towards the end of the decade of the 1950s, there was a dispute between Jains and Hindus over two chapters in the *Jain Ramayana* in the state of Madhya Pradesh, and it seemed a major face-off was imminent in Raipur. Some of the sensible people invited Camille, a renowned scholar of the *Ramkatha*, to visit Raipur and help resolve this dispute. In those days, Father Steve van Winkle used to live with Camille at Manresa House, and he recounts,

> I advised Dr Bulcke not to get involved in the controversy since we did not know how the situation would turn out. However, an ardent devotee like Dr Camille Bulcke had no fear in his mind and said – 'No, I must go. Nothing will happen to me. Who knows, this dispute will stop with the grace of Tulsi.' He received a hearty welcome on his arrival in Raipur, and it was publicized that he would give speeches about Rama's poems for three days. He made speeches in an open field and did not even touch the controversy. Rather, based on his extensive knowledge, he kept speaking only on the greatness of Ramakatha and its message. It had a deep impact on the people. Rather, the Hindi knowledge of a foreign priest and his factual speeches on Ramkatha erased that controversy. (van Winkle 2015, p. 31)

Camille's reverence for Hindi was incomparable; he mentioned, 'My God doesn't like prayer in English, so I pray in Hindi or Latin' (Tandon 2015, p. 92). He never used any English word while speaking in Hindi and used to take offence should anyone else use an English word while conversing with him. One of Camille's students, Neelam Pandey, was working with him, and all of a sudden, unannounced, her maternal uncle turned up to take her home. Camille asked the guest for his introduction, and the visitor replied that he was Neelam's uncle. Instead of using the appropriate Hindi synonym, the visitor used the English word 'uncle' to describe himself. Neelam recalls that she had never seen Father Bulcke so angry as he said tersely, 'Uncle? What is the meaning of uncle? Please tell me. Are you her paternal uncle (*chacha*), maternal uncle (*mama*), maternal aunt's husband (*mousa*) or paternal aunt's husband (*phoopha*)? My maternal uncle's head was bowed down in shame. I was also feeling ashamed of the hollowness of Hindi speakers like my maternal uncle, who considered it necessary to add English words after every four words' (N. Pandey 2015, p. 168). On another occasion, he 'indignantly refused to lend books to an M.A. girl student who had addressed him in English' (Ponette 1991). This trend continues today, and Camille would have been appalled at the degradation of Hindi language and the widespread popularity and usage of English in contemporary India.

Once a senior bureaucrat and an old student from St Xavier's College, Ranchi, accompanied author-politician Shankar Dayal Singh to meet Camille. As usual, Camille spoke in Hindi, while Singh's companion chose to converse only in English. After a few sentences, an exasperated Camille asked,

> You don't know Hindi? That gentleman again replied in English. Father Bulcke got even more irritated and said I must have taught you Hindi, and when I, being a foreigner, am talking to you in Hindi, then why don't you talk in your mother tongue and national language? It's a shame. Singh's companion was so embarrassed with Camille's reprimand that he started scratching the ground with his toes; his bowed forehead did not rise again. (S. Singh 2015, p. 106)

Siddharth Mukherjee, Camille's physician in Ranchi, fondly remembered the latter's infinite love for Hindi that used to embarrass Anglophile Indians like him. He narrates that on the occasion of the World Health Day, the Indian Medical Association, Ranchi, organised a seminar on high blood pressure and invited physicians and patients as speakers (Mukherjee 2015, p. 129). While all doctors spoke in English, Father Bulcke delivered his speech in Hindi. Addressing the seminar, Camille said,

> Although I can speak in English very easily, I will not speak in it; instead, I will speak in Hindi. I do not understand the purpose of studying all subjects through English medium in India, while most of the people here do not know English but can understand Hindi. How surprising it is that the doctors here write prescriptions in English for their patients who do not know even a single letter of this language. Should the doctors write prescriptions in Hindi, the patients will be greatly benefitted, and their treatment will also be facilitated. (Ibid.)

Camille's persistence that Indians must embrace Hindi in daily lives made an immediate impact on Mukherjee, and some others in the medical fraternity started writing prescriptions in Hindi (ibid.). Clearly, he was a language purist whose love for Hindi was not just professed but practised.

Camille was part of a wider network of Hindi writers since his university days in Allahabad and had an illustrious list of friends such as Mahadevi Verma, Dharmavir Bharati, Raghuvansh, Vishnu Prabhakar, Sarveshwar Dayal Saxena, Sachchidananda Hirananda Vatsyayan (popularly known as Agyeya), Harivansh Rai Bachchan and Sumitranandan Pant, among others. He was well respected, and he engaged in productive conversations with many of them. That was an era in which differences in thoughts and approaches were never impediments to long-lasting friendships. While some of the more robust and hard-hitting critique of Camille's works came directly from Hindu theologians such as Swami Karpatri, his friends greatly respected his scholastic mission and at the same time offered very sophisticated and nuanced critiques of what they perceived as his simplistic understanding or misreading of Hindu philosophy, literary traditions, myths and practices. His belief that the Christian ethical worldview was universal, historical and superior as compared to the Indian or Hindu belief systems that lacked both historicity, centrality of tenets and universal ethics was rarely challenged by his friends. The most profound and yet gentle rebuke came from one of his closest associates and friends, Raghuvansh, who pointed out that Camille wanted him (Raghuvansh) to write the story of Christ with his (Camille's) approval so that it adhered to the religious sensibilities of those who practised the Christian faith and that his fixation with a singular 'truth' (that of Christianity as the answer to the human spiritual quest) was problematic and limited in its vision (Raghuvansh 1961, pp. 220–221).

It is our reading that on certain issues Camille's Christian missionary training and his own fastidiousness did not enable a space where he could question his own theological certitudes and embrace more diverse and dynamic interpretations of the human quest for truth and spiritual knowledge. The Indian idea of *bhakti*, or devotion, fascinated him, but his missionary robe prevented him from the kind of scholarly and spiritual transgressions that would have further enriched his works, free of all constraints. His friends, luminaries of the Hindi literary world, understood his limitations and yet admired his diligent work to unpack some of the complex Indian literary traditions and acquire proficiency in both Hindi and Sanskrit. Many of his critics and friends saw him as an inquisitive foreigner, a benign white European scholar who wanted to understand India. While this in itself was not a new phenomenon given the number of European Indologists who had contributed towards knowledge creation about India during the colonial era, what set Camille apart was his devotion to India and the people of India, ultimately embedding himself within the Indian ethos.

To the Idea of India and Indian-ness

India and the larger South Asia have witnessed disturbing levels of communal polarisation and vigilante justice and frequent incidents of religious mob violence in recent times. We have seen the targeting of religious minorities across the region and the bullying and silencing of several scholars and activists who have tried to critically engage with their own faiths and traditions or those of communities that they may not belong to – prominent cases being the Indologist Wendy Doniger, Malayalam writer M. M. Basheer, Santhal author Hansda Sowvendra Shekhar, Bangladeshi writer Taslima Nasrin, Indian-origin novelist Salman Rushdie and many others. The Taliban regime in Afghanistan has banned women's education and attacked women's public presence in many ways, even going to the extent of killing women who have spoken out. Amidst these militarised, masculinist and extremist worldviews are lost many an opportunity to experience empathy, collective and comparative wisdom and shared humanism of religious and philosophical traditions that have stood the test of time. Where diversity of thoughts, beliefs and practices have always existed, these traditions now appear to be hard-line, impermeable and exclusivist beyond recognition.

A parallel process is visible in contemporary India where 'Indic' civilisational values are being revived and debated with great passion and vigour, to which Father Camille Bulcke actually contributed in significant ways. In fact, Camille's legacy could be selectively appropriated in different and perhaps polarising ways. For the majoritarian Hindu nationalists, his idea of Hindi as the link language and his interest in the *Ramkatha* as the moral and inspirational source would be extremely appealing, while he could also appear as the ideal 'secular' Christian priest for those who are invested in challenging hard-line majoritarian positions. In other words, he could sit comfortably in both the right-wing and the left-liberal camps in contemporary India.

For Camille, India was his only home, and he could never think of leaving. One of his students, Scholastica Kujur, recalls that she had seen Father Bulcke cry only twice: the first time was upon learning about the death of his mother and the second when he heard that there was a move to ask foreign-born priests to leave India (Kujur 2015, p. 163). Camille said, 'I can't go anywhere except you people now. I want to die in India, among you all.' Kujur narrates that 'later, this proposal to repatriate the foreign-born missionaries was dropped, and a much-relieved Father Bulcke said that he would be able to complete his mortal journey in India. Both of us started to cry with happiness' (ibid.). In March 2018, at the reburial commemorative meet in Ranchi, one of his associates recalled that Father Bulcke was an Indian citizen and resented being labelled a 'foreigner' in any context. He never imagined himself as anything but Indian and took great pride in being known as an Indian. He was overwhelmed by the warmth and generosity of this country that had accepted him. On one occasion, he had said, 'Thank God, who has sent me to India and thanks to India, who has received me with so much love!' Some called him more Indian than Indians, and others conferred the title of 'Bhumiputra' (son of the soil) to honour his relationship with Jharkhand.

On several occasions, Camille underlined that it was Tulsidas from whom he derived his 'complete Indian-ness', reflecting human perfection and totality (Lodha 1987, pp. 81–82). Camille believed that 'human perfection lies only in the complete immersion with the vast and universal consciousness of life. Where an individual rises above his narrow, self-centred existence and crosses the Lakshmana rekha[4] or defies the confines of time and space and succeeds in merging with the universal consciousness, the immense ocean of unbounded love and affection' (ibid.). He not only considered Tulsidas as one of the greatest poets of the world but also considered his devotion to God as an ideal for human beings (D. Prasad 1987, p. 11). He considered 'Tulsidas's devotion as the nectar which liberates an individual from fear and enables the person to rise above the worldly bondages and attain the supreme yoga or *Sayujya* with *Isht Devta*, that is, the union of the devotee with his or her personal deity' (Lodha 1987, pp. 81–82). This was Camille's vision of life, and he believed such devotion would make a person 'a complete human being, a complete Indian and one who is united with the spirit of Tulsi' (ibid.).

Indian-ness was not just an esoteric concept for Camille; he had imbibed Indian values and used to think like a native Indian from the Hindi-speaking region. In his everyday interactions with his friends and colleagues, he used to express himself in proverbs and metaphors that would make an expert native Hindi scholar proud. Raghav Prasad Pandey, his long-time colleague in the Department of Hindi at St Xavier's College, Ranchi, recounts one such incident where Camille expressed himself in such a way that locals would understand.

Within two or three years of his joining the college, the teaching of Sanskrit also started in the college, and Father Bulcke was assigned to head the new Sanskrit department. In 1961, with the appointment of a new professor in the Department of Hindi, Father Bulcke felt that if he wanted, he could devote his entire time to research and writing instead of teaching. While Father Bulcke was relieved of teaching, he was to remain the head of the Hindi-Sanskrit department. Informing his colleagues, Father Bulcke said, 'I have enough daughters-in-law (*bahus*) in my family who are capable of running the household, and I wish that the mother-in-law (*saas*) should be allowed to have a relaxed life and thus be relieved from teaching.' (R. Pandey 1987, p. 115)

Indeed, only someone immersed in the customs and norms of an Indian family system and affinities would be able to superimpose such intricate and delicate relations between a mother-in-law and her daughter-in-law. Camille was proud of the Indian citizenship that he acquired later and was also honoured with the Padma Bhushan, the third highest civilian award, by the government of India in 1974 for his extraordinary literary achievements and his contribution to education. He was a worthy recipient of these honours and adapted to Indian-ness and Indian values with great sensitivity and emotional and spiritual connect. His outward and inward journeys in India enriched him immensely, and in turn, he gave a lot to India as a scholar, educationist, spiritual mentor and quintessential humanitarian invested in social welfare.

To Us Who Tell His Story

Camille was a staunch constitutionalist, who offered a model of social and political integration where every community, including minorities, had rights as well as obligations. He strongly believed that Christianity thrived in India because there was an existing assimilative Indic ethos that enabled coexistence and curiosity. He was a strong advocate of religious learning where it was obligatory to learn about other faiths and their beliefs and practices to develop respect and understanding, and his own life exemplified his beliefs. That said, we do not think his relationship with the Church or with the non-Christians, and especially Hindus in India, was complete on its own. His works and views, at times, sat uneasily with his audiences and his belongingness was always enabled by productive transgressions. He was a better Christian in

India because he chose to learn about and from other Indian traditions and made Christianity accessible and appealing to the local milieu and in the language of the people. He enjoyed respect from non-Christians and Hindus because he never belittled or passed harsh judgements on their beliefs, traditions and practices. On the contrary, he admired many things he learned from them and kept his engagements scholarly and respectful. Hence, he enjoyed great legitimacy and respect as the narrator of the Ramayana story, among his Hindu admirers. They found no contradiction those days in a cassock-wearing foreign priest narrating to them the virtues and teachings of the *Ramcharitmanas* and the profound legacy of its author, Tulsidas.

If only the followers of all persuasions understood or cared for the lessons in humanism that Father Camille Bulcke left as an enduring legacy of an India, where intellectual curiosity and the search for everyday human values meant constantly crossing boundaries, including those put in place by one's own religious training and inherited dogmatism. If only building bridges was the mission instead of building walls everywhere! It is in that spirit that we offer this first-ever biography of Father Camille Bulcke in English to our readers, a modest attempt to capture certain elements of his life and works, and to contribute to existing and future debates on the post-colonial condition, the 'white man's burden' and Christian missionaries in the service of the 'Empire' and beyond. This book is an attempt to understand Camille's complex contributions to the syncretic traditions of India, avoiding the trappings of a hagiographical account. As we have indicated, Camille's devout Christian mission and unwavering faith in Christ, on the one hand, and his understanding of *Ramkatha* and Hinduism, on the other, sat uneasily with each other. Nevertheless, his human endeavour to mitigate rather than amplify differences, to continuously strive for spiritual perfection, and his spirit of lifelong learning and service to humanity can serve as a source of learning and inspiration.

While it may be de rigueur to refer to a multidisciplinary approach in contemporary times, it is inescapable when documenting the biography of a man as multifarious as Camille. His life and works transcended every rigid boundary based on religion, race, denomination, organisation and traditions, and he combined theology, linguistics, Indology, history, lexicography and translation effortlessly in his scholarly and spiritual pursuits. A coherent account of the different yet interconnected aspects of Camille's life was difficult, and what we have offered here is an overview of his life story and his scholarly legacy instead of exploring each theme independently. Camille

Bulcke was not perfect, and neither is this biographical account, where our biases and our lack of erudition might be evident. Our hope is that it is a conversation starter and more such stories will be told in the future.

It is befitting that the plaque installed below his beautifully sculpted bust at St Xavier's College, Ranchi, is engraved with the following *doha* from the *Ramcharitmanas* of Tulsidas.

> *Parhit saris dharam nahin bhai*
> *Par peera sam nahin adhmai*

There is no better *dharma* (religious duty) than benevolence; nothing more sinful than malevolence towards others.

Thus commemorated with the words of his spiritual mentor, Tulsidas, at his final resting place, Reverend Father Doctor Camille Bulcke, SJ would have smiled approvingly.

Notes

1. We use *ghar wapasi* (return to original home) as a pun here. *Ghar wapasi* became a popular political term for the reconversion of Christians and Muslims back to the faith of their ancestors by Hindu nationalists. We mean here that Father Camille Bulcke had a different kind of *ghar wapasi* when his remains were brought from Delhi and reburied in his hometown of Ranchi.
2. A *doha* is a typical Hindi poetic metre, a self-contained rhyming couplet in poetry. A *chaupai* is a quatrain verse of Indian poetry, especially medieval Hindi poetry, that uses a metre of four syllables.
3. Tulsidas wrote this poetic composition as a petition to Hanuman when he was suffering from intolerable pain in his arm.
4. The Ramayana narrates that during the exile of Rama, Sita and Lakshmana in the forest, Lakshmana, Rama's younger brother, drew a protective line around their hut, asking Sita to stay within the line for her safety while he left to see if Rama was in any trouble and help him get back home safely. That line which Lakshmana drew to safeguard Sita is called Lakshmana *rekha*. Ravana was unable to cross this line to abduct Sita, and hence he tricked her into crossing it.

Glossary

Adhyatma Ramayana   lit., 'Spiritual Ramayana'; a Sanskrit rendition of the story of Rama from the Advaita, or non-dualist, school of philosophy. This composition presents Rama as the manifestation of the supreme Vishnu. It is one of the sources of the *Ramcharitmanas* of Tulsidas.

Ananda Ramayana   lit., 'Blissful Ramayana'; a Sanskrit epic including several events from a later period. Some unsubstantiated claims attribute the authorship of this work to sage Valmiki. However, literal and historical analysis suggests that it was composed in the fourteenth or fifteenth century.

Anusuya   lit., 'free from envy and jealousy'; the wife of sage Atri. She was very pious and always practised austerities and devotion, which allowed her to attain miraculous powers. She explained the *stridharmarahasya*, or secrets of the *dharma* of women, to Sita.

Apabhramsha   a medieval Indo-Aryan vernacular language of northern and western India, used by the Jains and others for extensive literary and religious compositions

Awadhi   a dialect of Hindi spoken in parts of eastern Uttar Pradesh in India

Bhagavata Purana	one of the most popular and influential of all Hindu texts, also known as the *Bhagavata*. It is a Vaishnava work produced in south India in the ninth or early tenth century CE.
bhakti	a generic term for a complex of religious attitudes and practices predicated on total devotion to a supreme deity with whom the devotee (*bhakta*) has a personal relationship. Through that deity's grace, such devotion becomes the principal or exclusive means of salvation.
Brihaddharm Purana	one of the several minor, or *upa*, Puranas. It aims to reconcile the three main forms of Hindu worship: Shaiva, Vaishnava and Tantra (worship of God in the form of Kali, Durga, and other female Gods).
Brij Bhasha (also Braj Bhasha)	a dialect of Hindi spoken in the Braj region (Uttar Pradesh and Rajasthan in India); a language in which much medieval Vaishnava *bhakti* literature, such as the chronicles of the Vallabha sect and the poetry of Surdas, exists. Awadhi and Brij Bhasha are considered two predominant literary languages in north and central India before the switch to Khari Boli in the nineteenth century.
chakora	a type of partridge; a legendary bird described in Hindu mythology that feeds only on the moon's beams. Indian literature has traditionally used this bird as a metaphor to depict deep devotion and love.
chatak	a type of cuckoo known to drink drops of rain that fall during *swati nakshatra* (a specific temporal moment).
chaupai	lit., 'four feet'; a quatrain verse of Indian poetry, especially medieval Hindi poetry. It comprises two lines, each containing 32 beats, and hence has a total of 64 beats.
Dakkhini (Deccani)	a variety of Hindi–Urdu spoken in Andhra Pradesh, Telangana and other southern states

of India. The history of Dakkhini begins after the decision of Muhammad bin Tughlaq to move his capital from Delhi to Daulatabad (or Deogiri) around 1327 CE.

Dasharatha Jataka
Jataka literally means 'birth history' that depicts the Buddha in his infinite earlier births. The *Dasharatha Jataka* is a Buddhist tale narrating the Ramayana with a view to explain Buddhist doctrines.

Devanagari
Sanskrit character or alphabet; a script used as a literary hand for various modern languages of India

dharma
a polysemic term, the more precise meanings of which depend upon the context in which it is used. Less precise meanings range from 'truth' and 'order' (both cosmic and social) to 'law' (both universal and particular), 'teaching', 'duty', 'virtuous behaviour' and 'religion'. It is not the same as religion in the Western understanding; instead, it denotes cosmological, ethical, social and legal principles for the proper conduct of individuals, groups, society and the universe.

Dingal
the literary language of Rajasthan mixed with Apabhramsha. Like Dingal, Rajasthani poets coined the name 'Pingal'. An admixture of inter-regional languages with regional dialects became an all-India language known as Braj Bhasha or simply Bhasha in Hindi.

doha
a typical Hindi poetic metre; a self-contained rhyming couplet in poetry. It consists of rhyming couplets of 24 syllables each. The simple form of the *doha*, which conveys an image or idea in two verses, has made it especially useful for describing devotional, sensual and spiritual states.

Dohavali
a poetic composition by Tulsidas that is an anthology of verses on morality based

on *dharma*. To construct the discourse on morality, Tulsidas draws from the life and deeds of Rama as the foundations of *dharma*.

Gautama Dharmasutra   classified Vedanga (and therefore as Smriti) texts dealing with *dharma* – in this context, less the question of civil law than the ritual, moral and social questions of how people should conduct themselves in relation to *varna* and *ashrama* in the light of Vedic injunction and customary practice. *Gautama Dharmasutra* is considered one of the oldest in this genre and contains a series of rules and duties for different classes of people in ancient Vedic society.

Gitavali   an anthology of 330 songs by Tulsidas based on the deeds of Rama narrated in the *Ramcharitmanas*

hadgadi   the reburial of skeletal remains as part of the Adivasi tradition in India, where the remains of the ancestors are carried as a blessing and reburied as tribes move from one village to another

Hanuman Bahuk   lit. 'The Arm of Hanuman'. In the last years of his life, Tulsidas suffered severe pain in one arm due to lesions and boils. He could not get any relief from medications and prayers, so he invoked Lord Hanuman and composed the *Hanuman Bahuk*, which contains forty-four verses and is considered his last substantial composition.

Ishavasyopanishad   part of the 40th chapter of the 'Shukla Yajurveda'. In the category of 108 Upanishads, it has the first place. In this Upanishad, God's qualities, self, renunciation of unrighteousness, and so on, are described.

isht devta   composed of the words *isht* (desired, liked, cherished) and *devata* (godhead, divinity, tutelary deity) or *deva* (deity). The root of devotion (*bhakti*) is good action (*satkarma*) and

	the worship of one's own favourite deity, or *isht devta*.
Itihasa	a term for narrative texts widely regarded within the tradition as true and therefore, in the widest sense, historical stories, although Western sources usually classify them as 'mythical'. The two epics, the Mahabharata and the Ramayana, along with the Puranas, refer to the corpus of authoritative narrative material.
'Jaiminyai Ashvamedha Parva'	Sage Jaimini was a scholar, poet, philosopher and astrologer. It is believed that he also composed the Mahabharata – much more extensive in comparison to the Mahabharata composed by Vyasa. However, most of his Mahabharata is lost except the 'Ashvamedha Parva', which gives a vivid description of the Ashvamedha *yajna* (homa or sacrifice) performed by Yudhisthira.
Jain Ramayana	The Jain scholars composed their religious literary texts incorporating Rama's story. The sources of the Buddhist Ramayanas are written in the Pali language. The Jains, on the other hand, have composed texts connected to Rama's story in Prakrit, Apabhramsha and Sanskrit.
Jatayu	a character in the Ramayana; the king of vultures and a friend of Rama's father, Dasharatha. He fought Ravana to foil the abduction of Sita and was fatally wounded. He survived long enough to point Rama and Lakshmana in the right direction. They conducted his funeral rites and saw him ascend to heaven in a chariot of fire.
Kaliyuga	a term used to designate the last in sequence and most degenerate of the four world ages, or *yuga*s. The current period is called Kaliyuga, and it is characterized by a shorter lifespan and a general decay of moral and spiritual capacity.

Kavitavali	an anthology of 325 poems by Tulsidas drawn from Rama's deeds and his glorious qualities. It presents the human aspects of the divine incarnation and reflects the divinity's concern for human beings.
Khari Boli	the standard Hindi language that originated in and around Delhi within the Ganga–Yamuna *doab* (interfluve) region in present-day Uttar Pradesh in India. During the Mughal period, Khari Boli absorbed numerous Persian words and became a lingua franca throughout the empire. The Hindus used the script (Devanagari) and vocabulary mainly from Sanskrit.
Maithili	a language of the Mithila region, the land of Sita's father, King Janaka. It is spoken in the eastern and northern regions of Bihar in India and the south-eastern plains, known as *tarai* (foothills) of Nepal.
'Mangalacharan'	benedictory verses that are a staple feature of Sanskrit treatises; they are statements of reverence for a principle deity (*isht devta*) or a revered teacher placed at the forefront of the texts. While they are ostensibly composed in order to remove obstacles to the full composition of texts, they are included in the texts as auspicious introductions and for pedagogical purposes.
Marathi	an Indo-Aryan language spoken by the Marathi people of western India (Maharashtrians). Along with Bengali, Marathi is the oldest of the regional literatures in Indo-Aryan languages and derives its grammar and syntax from Pali and Prakrit.
nirguna	the transcendence of all qualities (*guna*), properties or predicates by the absolute Brahman (God); the conceptualisation and worship of God as transcending all mundane categories

Puranas	a huge body of narrative texts, originally mostly in Sanskrit verse, purporting to deal with an ancient past. Along with Itihasas (the epics), the Puranas embody the tradition (Smriti), which informs theistic Hinduism.
Rajatarangini	lit., 'River of Kings'; a historical chronicle of early India, written in Sanskrit verse by the Kashmiri poet Kalhana in the twelfth century. It is considered the best and the most authentic work of its kind. It covers the entire span of history in the Kashmir region from the earliest times to the date of its composition.
Ramcharitmanas	lit., 'Lake of Rama's Deeds'; a poetic retelling by Tulsidas of Valmiki's Ramayana, along with several other sources in the eastern dialect of Hindi, known as Awadhi. Tulsidas narrated the life story of Rama in a full-fledged Bhakti text, which quickly became the most widely disseminated, popular and influential version of the story in northern India.
Ramleela (or Ramlila)	annual north Indian festivals that celebrate and perform the 'play' (*lila*) – that is, the story – of Rama and Sita. Based on the sixteenth-century Awadhi version in Tulsidas' *Ramcharitmanas*, the sequence of performances may last up to a week.
saguna	possessing attributes, qualities (*guna*) or form. It is most frequently applied to the embodied or anthropomorphic deity worshipped in Bhakti traditions. The Brahma is envisioned as a personal deity and the object of devotion.
Sakhi Sampraday	a sub-sect within Krishna *bhakti*; also known as the Haridasi Sampradaya of Vrindavan. It is named after the musician-saint Haridas. The devotee must aim to become one of the companions or attendants (*sakhi* or *sahacari*) who watch and promote the love play with Krishna.

Sanatana Dharma	the eternal *dharma* of all, regarded by Hindus as the true religion – a 'pure' Veda-based form of Hinduism. It has become a synonym for the 'eternal' truth and teachings of Hinduism.
shakti	divine power or energy, personified as a feminine principle and therefore either as a male god's consort (his active and immanent power) or as the ultimately independent female absolute – the Goddess, or Devi (also known as Sakti or Shakti)
Srimad Bhagavad Gita	a part of Vyasa's Mahabharata. It is in the form of a dialogue between Arjuna (one of the five Pandava princes) and Krishna (an avatar or incarnation of the god Vishnu). The Gita has always been cherished by Hindus for its spiritual guidance and is one of the most popular religious texts of Hinduism.
Sharada	the goddess of speech, art, learning and intelligence, also known as goddess Saraswati
Urdu	a version of Khari Boli popular in some north Indian regions and among the Muslim community. It is grammatically identical to Hindi, but draws much of its vocabulary from Persian and Arabic and is written in the Perso-Arabic script.
varnashrama dharma	*Varnashrama* is composed of two words: *varna*, which refers to the grade or colour of an individual's social category, and *ashrama*, which refers to the stages of life. It refers to the traditional social order (priests, warriors, farmers and merchants, and peasants) and the ideal stages in the life cycle (student, householder, retiree and renunciate).
Vinaya Patrika	lit., 'A Letter of Imploration'. Tulsidas wrote *Vinaya Patrika* towards the later stages of his life. It comprises 279 hymns in the form of a 'plaint for mercy'.

Upanishads

Vedic literature is composed of four components: *Samhita* (mantras and benedictions), *Brahmana* (treatise on various rites for sacrificial ceremony), *Aranyaka* (forest texts, or writings meant for the forest-dwelling hermit) and *Upanishad* (text on philosophical and spiritual significance of Vedic rituals). Upanishads are also referred to as Vedanta – the conclusion, essence or culmination of the Veda.

Bibliography

Aldrich, R., and A. Stucki (2022). *The Colonial World: A History of European Empires, 1780s to the Present*. New York: Bloomsbury Publishing.

Aleaz, K. P. (1979). The theological writings of Brahmabandhav Upadhyaya re-examined. *Indian Journal of Theology* 28(2): 55–77.

Allchin, F. R. (1964). *Kavitāvalī of Tulsidas*. London: Allen & Unwin.

——— (1966). *The Petition to Rām: Hindi Devotional Hymns of the Seventeenth Century*. London: Allen & Unwin.

Amaladass, A. (1988). *Jesuit Presence in Indian History: Commemorative Volume on the Occasion of the 150th Anniversary of the New Madurai Mission, 1838–1988*. Anand: Gujarat Sahitya Prakash.

Amaladass, A., and F. X. Clooney (2000). *Preaching Wisdom to the Wise: Three Treatises by Roberto de Nobili*. St. Louis, MO: Institute for Jesuit Sources.

Anderson, C. (2007). *The Indian Uprising of 1857–8: Prisons, Prisoners and Rebellion*. London: Anthem Press.

Animananda, B. R. (1946). *The Blade: Life and Work of Brahmabandhab Upadhyay*. Calcutta: Roy & Sons.

Arnold, E. (1875). *The Indian Song of Songs: From the Sanskrit of the Gita Govinda of Jayadeva*. London: Trubner & Co.

Atkins, A. G. (1954). *The Ramayana: Rendered into English Verse*, vol. 1. New Delhi: Hindustan Times.

Aurobindo. (1997). *Essays on the Gita*. Pondicherry: Sri Aurobindo Ashram.

——— (2012). *Letters on Yoga: The Complete Works of Sri Aurobindo*, vol 28. Pondicherry: Sri Aurobindo Ashram.

Bahadur, S. P. (1994). *Complete Works of Goswami Tulsidas*, vol. 1: *Ramcharitmanasa*. New Delhi: Munshiram Manoharlal Publishers.

———— (1995). *Complete Works of Goswami Tulsidas*, vol. 2: *Vinay Patrika*. New Delhi: Munshiram Manoharlal Publishers.

———— (1996). *Complete Works of Goswami Tulsidas*, vol. 3: *Gitavali*. New Delhi: Munshiram Manoharlal Publishers.

———— (1997a). *Complete Works of Goswami Tulsidas*, vol. 5: *Kavitavali*. New Delhi: Munshiram Manoharlal Publishers.

————(1997b). *Complete Works of Goswami Tulsidas*, vol. 6: *Dohavali*. New Delhi: Munshiram Manoharlal Publishers.

Baldick, C. (2015). *The Oxford Dictionary of Literary Terms*. Oxford: Oxford University Press.

Banerji, S. C. (1915). *The Brihad-Dharma Purana*. Lucknow: Indian Commercial Press.

Bara, P. (1987). Father Bulcke ki Hindi shiksha ki pratham pathshala. In *Dr Bulcke Smriti Granth*, edited by D. Prasad and S. K. Goswami, p. 91. Ranchi: Dr Bulcke Smriti Granth Samiti.

Basham, A. L. (1989). *The Origins and Developments of Classical Hinduism*. Boston, MA: Beacon Books.

Basu, I. (2024). *Reclaiming Indigeneity and Democracy in India's Jharkhand*. London: Oxford University Press.

Bauman, C. M., and M. Voss Roberts (2021). *The Routledge Handbook of Hindu–Christian Relations*. London and New York: Routledge.

Beltramini, E. (2016). Hinduism in the Roman Catholic imagination between the two world wars. *Asiatische Studien/Études Asiatiques* 70(2): 333–345.

Bharati, D. (1987). Bhor kee puja. In *Dr Bulcke Smriti Granth*, edited by D. Prasad and S. K. Goswami, pp. 57–60. Ranchi: Dr Bulcke Smriti Granth Samiti.

Brockington, J. (1998). *The Sanskrit Epics*. Leiden: Brill.

Brown, L. W. (1982). *The Indian Christians of St. Thomas: An Account of the Ancient Syrian Church of Malabar*. Cambridge, MA: Cambridge University Press.

Buhler, G. (1879). *Sacred Laws of the Aryas: As Taught in the Schools of Apastamba, Gautama, Vasishtha and Baudhayana*. London: Clarendon Press.

Bulcke, C. (1942a). *The Saviour: The Four Gospels in One Narrative*. Ranchi: Catholic Press.

———— (1942b). *Muktidata: Hindi Translation of 'The Saviour': The Four Gospels in One Narrative*. Ranchi: Catholic Press.

———— (1947). *The Theism of Nyaya–Vaisesika: Its Origin and Early Development*. Delhi: Motilal Banarasidass.

———— (1955). *A Technical English–Hindi Glossary*. Ranchi: Dharmik Sahitya Samiti.

———— (1958). *Neel Pancchi* (Hindi translation of Maurice Maeterlinck's French play). Patna: Bihar Rashtrabhasha Parishad.

———— (1968). *Angreji–Hindi Kosh*. Ranchi: Catholic Press.

———— (1973). *Prerit Charitra*. Ranchi: Catholic Press.

———— (1977a). *Ramkatha Aur Tulsidas*. Allahabad: Hindustani Academy.

———— (1977b). *Hindi Bible: New Testament*. Ranchi: Catholic Press.

———— (1980). *The Hindi Psalter of the Breviary*. Ranchi: Catholic Press.

———— (1987). Mera gaon. In *Dr Bulcke Samriti Granth*, edited by D. Prasad and S. K. Goswami, pp. 15–18. Ranchi: Dr Bulcke Smriti Granth Samiti.

———— (ed.) (1996). *Manthan: Father Camille Bulcke Ke Nibandhon Ka Sangrah*. Patna: Bihar Granth Academy.

———— (ed.) (2009). *Ek Isai Ki Aastha: Ramkatha Aur Hindi*. New Delhi: Prakashan Sansthaan.

———— (2010). *Ramkatha and Other Essays*. New Delhi: Vani Prakashan.

———— (2015 [1976]). 'Father Camille Bulcke: Ek antarang sakshahkar' by Dineshwar Prasad. In *Father Camille Bulcke: Bharteeyata Ke Prakash Punj*, edited by S. Rituparna, pp. 323–345. New Delhi: Indian Council for Cultural Relations.

————. (2020 [1950]). *Ramkatha: Utpatti Aur Vikas*. Prayag: Hindi Parishad Prakasan, University of Allahabad.

Bulcke, C., and D. Prasad (1979). *Manas Kaumudi*. Patna: Anupam Prakashan.

Bulcke, J. (1987). Bhai ke sansmaran. In *Dr Bulcke Smriti Granth*, edited by D. Prasad and S. K. Goswami, pp. 65–66. Ranchi: Dr Bulcke Smriti Granth Samiti.

Callewaert, W. M. (1987). Louvain vishwavidayalay. In *Dr Bulcke Smriti Granth*, edited by D. Prasad and S. K. Goswami, pp. 197–198. Ranchi: Dr Bulcke Smriti Granth Samiti.

Casanova, J., and T. F. Banchoff (2016). *The Jesuits and Globalization: Historical Legacies and Contemporary Challenges*. Washington, DC: Georgetown University Press.

Chandra, U. (2016). Flaming fields and forest fires: Agrarian transformations and the making of Birsa Munda's rebellion. *Indian Economic and Social History Review* 53(1): 69–98. https://doi.org/10.1177/0019464615619540.

Chaturvedi, N. (2021). Masihi kavya: Reading Christian devotional literary expression in Hindi. *Sambhāṣaṇ* 2(1–2): 167–182.

Chhawchharia, A. K. (2015a). *Dohavali Ramayan of Goswami Tulsidas*. Ayodhya: n.p.

———— (2015b). *Kavitavali Ramayan of Goswami Tulsidas*. Ayodhya: n.p.

——— (2016). *Gitavali Ramayan of Goswami Tulsidas*. Ayodhya: n.p.

——— (2017). *Vinaya-Patrikā: A Book of Supplication & True Love for God*. Ayodhya: n.p.

Clarysse, L. (1985). *Father Constant Lievens, S. J.* Ranchi: Satya Bharati.

——— (1987). Lissewege. In *Dr Bulcke Smriti Granth*, edited D. Prasad and S. K. Goswami, pp. 194–196. Ranchi: Dr Bulcke Smriti Granth Samiti.

Clooney, F. X. (2009). From apologetics to Indology: A case study in the scholarship of Roberto de Nobili, SJ. *Toronto Journal of Theology* 25(1): 41–56. https://doi.org/10.3138/tjt.25.1.41.

——— (2017). *Future of Hindu–Christian Studies: A Theological Inquiry*. London and New York: Routledge.

——— (2018). Alienation, xenophilia, and coming home: William Wallace, SJ's from Evangelical to Catholic by way of the East. *Common Knowledge* 24(2): 280–290.

——— (2020). *Western Jesuit Scholars in India: Tracing Their Paths, Reassessing Their Goals*. Leiden: Brill. https://doi.org/10.1163/9789004424746.

——— (2021). Hindu–Jesuist encounters. In *The Routledge Handbook of Hindu–Christian Relations*, edited by C. M. Bauman and M. V. Roberts, pp. 79–89. London and New York: Routledge. https://doi.org/10.1163/9789004424746 _002.

Coleridge, H. J. (1872). *The Life and Letters of St. Francis Xavier*, vols. 1–2. London: Burns & Oates.

Copland, I. (2006). Christianity as an arm of empire: The ambiguous case of India under the Company, c. 1813–1858. *Historical Journal* 49(4): 1025–1054. https://doi.org/10.1017/S0018246X06005723.

Couttenier, P. (1998). National imagery in 19th century Flemish literature. In *Nationalism in Belgium*, edited by K. Deprez and L. Vos, pp. 51–60. London: Palgrave Macmillan.

——— (2016). Introduction. In *Poems of Guido Gezelle: A Bilingual Anthology*, edited by P. Vincent, pp. 1–8. London: UCL Press. https://doi.org/10.14324/ 111.9781910634943.

Coward, H. (1993). *Hindu–Christian Dialogue: Perspectives and Encounters*. New Delhi: Motilal Banarsidass.

Cronin, V. (1959). *A Pearl to India: The Life of Roberto di Nobili*. London: Rupert Hart-Davis.

Debroy, B. (2017). *The Valmiki Ramayana*. Gurugram: Penguin Random House India.

Deleu, J. (1999). Guido Gezelle, a limpid singer. *Low Countries* 7: 100–107.

Deprez, K., and L. Vos (1998). *Nationalism in Belgium: Shifting Identities, 1780–1995*. London: Palgrave Macmillan.

Devriendt, K. L. (1987). Louvain mein Father Bulcke. In *Dr Bulcke Smriti Granth*, edited by D. Prasad and S. K. Goswami, pp. 77–80. Ranchi: Dr Bulcke Smriti Granth Samiti.

Doyle, S. (2006). *Synthesizing the Vedanta: The Theology of Pierre Johanns, SJ.* Oxford: Peter Lang.

Dugdale, J. (2015). Should biographers be on first-name terms with their subjects? *The Guardian*, 20 February. https://www.theguardian.com/books/booksblog/2015/feb/20/biographer-on-first-name-terms. Accessed 20 March 2023.

Ehrman, B. D. (2016). *A Brief Introduction to the New Testament*. New York, NY: Oxford University Press.

Extross, I. A. (1987). Father Camille Bulcke S.J. ke sansmaran. In *Dr Bulcke Smriti Granth*, edited by D. Prasad and S. K. Goswami, pp. 70–71. Ranchi: Dr Bulcke Smriti Granth Samiti.

'Father Constant Lievens (1856–1893)'. Ranchi Jesuits. https://www.ranjesu.org/biographypub/view/6. Accessed 25 April 2024.

Fernando, L. (2014). Jesuits and India. In *Oxford Handbook Topics in Religion*. Oxford: Oxford University Press.

———— (2019). North India. In *Claiming India: French Scholars and the Preoccupation with India in the Nineteenth Century*, edited by J. Mohan, pp. 119–130. New Delhi: Sage Publications.

Feys, J. (1988). Fr. Bulcke: The Indologist. In *Jesuit Presence in Indian History*, edited by A. Amaladass, pp. 205–222. Anand: Gujarat Sahitya Prakash.

Firth, C. B. (1998). *An Introduction to Indian Church History*. New Delhi: Indian Society for Promoting Christian Knowledge.

Fitzgerald, J. (1943). Father Constant Lievens, S.J. (1856–93). *Irish Monthly* 71(845): 454–458.

Frick, H. (1926). Is a conviction of the superiority of His message essential to the missionary? *International Review of Mission* 15(60): 625–646.

Froerer, P. (2018). *Religious Division and Social Conflict: The Emergence of Hindu Nationalism in Rural India*. London and New York: Routledge. ·

Frykenberg, R. E. (ed.) (2003). *Christians and Missionaries in India: Cross-Cultural Communication since 1500 with Special Reference to Caste, Conversion, and Colonialism*. London: Routledge.

———— (2008). *Christianity in India: From Beginnings to the Present*. Oxford: Oxford University Press.

Fujitani, J. (2016). Penance in the Jesuit mission to Japan, 1549–1562. *Journal of Ecclesiastical History* 67(2): 306–324.

Gallien, C. (2021). From one empire to the next: The reconfigurations of 'Indian' literatures from Persian to English translations. *Translation Studies* 14(2): 225–241. https://doi.org/10.1080/14781700.2019.1678069.

Gandhi, M. K. (1968). *The Collected Works of Mahatma Gandhi*, vol. 28, New Delhi: Publications Division, Ministry of Information and Broadcasting, Government of India.

Ganeri, M. (2007). Catholic encounter with Hindus in the twentieth century. *New Blackfriars* 88(1016): 410–432.

Ghosh, S. S. (2015). Baba 'Bulcke'. In *Father Camille Bulcke: Bharteeyata Ke Prakash Punj*, edited by S. Rituparna, pp. 132–135. New Delhi: Indian Council for Cultural Relations.

Gispert-Sauch, G. (ed.) (1973). *God's Word among Men: Theological Essays in Honour of Joseph Putz SJ*. New Delhi: Vidyajyoti.

Glenn Hinson, E. (1996). *The Early Church: Origins to the Dawn of the Middle Ages*. Nashville, TN: Abingdon Press.

Goldman, R. P. (1984). *The Ramayana of Valmiki: An Epic of Ancient India*, vol. 1: *Balakanda*. Princeton, NJ: Princeton University Press.

Gopal, S. (1989). *Radhakrishnan: A Biography*. New Delhi: Oxford University Press.

Goswami, S. K. (1987). Unhe chaar sou ghanton ke mohlat chhahiye thi. In *Dr Bulcke Smriti Granth*, edited by D. Prasad and S. K. Goswami, pp. 20–22. Ranchi: Dr Bulcke Smriti Granth Samiti.

Goyandka, J. (2017). *Shreemad Bhagvad Gita: Tatva Vivecani (with Translation into English and Commentary)*. Gorakhpur: Gita Press.

Grierson, G. (1893). Notes on Tulsi Das. *Indian Antiquity* 22: 89–274.

———. (1903). Tulasi Dasa, poet and religious reformer. *Journal of the Royal Asiatic Society* 11: 447–466.

——— (1977). Tulasidasa, the great poet of medieval India. In *Tulasidasa: His Mind and Art*, edited by Nagendra, pp. 1–6. New Delhi: National Publishing House.

Growse, F. S. (1891). *The Ramayana of Tulsidas*. Cawnpore: E. Samuel.

Guha, R. (2002). *History at the Limit of World-History*: New York, NY: Columbia University Press.

Guillén Preckler, F. (2017). *History of the Church in Asia: A Historical Survey*. Rome: Urbaniana University Press.

Gupt, M. (1912). *Bharat-Bharati*. Chirgaon, Jhansi: Sahitya Sadan.

Gupta, J. (1987). Father Bulcke: Mere guru-bhai. In *Dr Bulcke Smriti Granth*, edited by D. Prasad and S. K. Goswami, pp. 61–64. Ranchi: Dr Bulcke Smriti Granth Samiti.

Gupta, M. (1942). *Tulsidas: Ek Samaalochanatmak Adhyyan*. Prayag: India Prayag Vishvadiyalay Hindi Parishad.

Guruge, A. (1960). *The Society of Ramayana*. Colombo: Samran Press.

Halbfass, W. (1989). *India and Europe: An Essay in Philosophical Understanding*. Albany, NY: SUNY Press.

Henn, A. (2014). *Hindu–Catholic Encounters in Goa: Religion, Colonialism, and Modernity*. Bloomington, IN: Indiana University Press.

Holder, R. D., and S. Mitton (2013). *Georges Lemaître: Life, Science and Legacy*. Springer-Verlag.

Inden, R. B. (1986). Orientalist constructions of India. *Modern Asian Studies* 20(3): 401–446.

Israel, H. (2010). Protestant translations of the Bible in Indian languages. *Religion Compass* 4(2): 86–98. https://doi.org/10.1111/j.1749-8171.2009.00201.x.

Iyengar, K. R. S. (1983). *Asian Variations in Ramayana*. New Delhi: Sahitya Akademi.

Jacobi, H. (1893). *Das Ramayana*. Bonn: Verlag von Friedrich Cohen.

Jeyaraj, D. (2019). South India. In *Christianity in South and Central Asia*, edited by D. Jeyaraj, T. M. Johnson, and K. R. Ross, pp. 143–155. Edinburgh: Edinburgh University Press.

Kalsi, B. (1987). Ramkatha ke purodha: Baba Camille Bulcke. In *Dr Bulcke Samriti Granth*, edited by D. Prasad and S. K. Goswami, pp. 159–164. Ranchi: Dr Bulcke Samriti Granth Samiti.

Kanakappally, B. (2020). The Catholic church's encounter and engagement with Hinduism: Evolving attitudes and perceptions. In *The Handbook of Hinduism in Europe*, vols. 1–2, edited by K. A. Jacobsen and F. Sardella, pp. 55–77. Leiden: Brill.

Karan, C. (1987). Radhakrishna aur Father Camille Bulcke. In *Dr Bulcke Smriti Granth*, edited by D. Prasad and S. K. Goswami, pp. 117–119. Ranchi: Dr Bulcke Smriti Granth Samiti.

Kaul, S. (2018). *The Making of Early Kashmir: Landscape and Indentity in the Rajtarangini*. New Delhi: Oxford University Press.

Kavunkal, J. (2008). The mystery of god in and through Hinduism. In *Christian Theology in Asia*, edited by S. C. H. Kim, pp. 22–40. Cambridge (UK) and New York: Cambridge University Press.

Kaye, J. W. (1896). *A History of Sepoy War in India 1857–1858*. London: W. H. Allen & Co.

Keay, F. E. (1920). *A History of Hindī Literature*. Calcutta: Association Press.

Kibe P. V. (1947). *Location of Lanka*. Poona: Manohar Granthmala.

Kujur, S. (2015). Mere pitaji. In *Ek Chikitsak Ke Sansmaran*, edited by S. Rituparn, pp. 162–166. New Delhi: Indian Council for Cultural Relations.

Kumar, K. (2015). Ram sanehi na mare. In *Father Camille Bulcke: Bharteeyata Ke Prakash Punj*, edited by S. Rituparna, pp. 115–121. New Delhi: Indian Council for Cultural Relations.

Kumar, S. (1990). Christianisation among the Oraons of Chotanagpur. *Proceedings of the Indian History Congress* 51: 434–439.

Lambert, D., K. A. van Bibber, L. Ampleman and P. J. E. Peebles (2015). *The Atom of the Universe: The Life and Work of Georges Lemaitre*. Kraków: Copernicus Center Press.

Lipner, J. J. (2001). *Brahmabandhab Upadhyay: The Life and Thought of a Revolutionary*. New Delhi: Oxford University Press.

Lodha, K. (1987). Father Camille Bulcke: Ek deeksha. In *Dr Bulcke Smriti Granth*, edited by D. Prasad and S. K. Goswami, pp. 81–82. Ranchi: Dr Bulcke Smriti Granth Samiti. https://doi.org/10.1007/bf00202951.

Lorenzen, D. (1995). The historical vicissitudes of Bhakti religion. In *Bhakti Religion in North India: Community Identity and Political Action*, edited by David N. Lorenzen, pp. 1–34. Albany, NY: SUNY Press.

Lutgendorf, P. (1991). *The Life of a Text: Performing the Rāmcaritmānas of Tulsidas*. Berkeley, CA: University of California Press.

———. (2016). *The Epic of Ram*, vol. 1. Cambridge, MA: Harvard University Press.

———. (2020). *The Epic of Ram*, vol. 5. Cambridge, MA: Harvard University Press.

———. (2023). *The Epic of Ram*, vol. 7. Cambridge, MA: Harvard University Press.

Macfie, J. M. (1930). *The Ramayan of Tulsidas or the Bible of Northern India*. Edinburgh: T. & T. Clark.

Machave, P. (1987). Hindi premi vidvaan loshkar: Dr Bulcke. In *Dr Bulcke Smriti Granth*, edited by D. Prasad and S. K. Goswami, pp. 165–167. Ranchi: Dr Bulcke Smriti Granth Samiti.

Manavalan, A. A. (2022). *Ramayana: A Comparative Study of Ramakathas*. New Delhi: Vitasta Publishing Private Limited.

Mattam, J. (1974). Interpreting Christ to India today: The Calcutta School. *Indian Journal of Theology* 23: 191–205.

McRae, K. D. (1983). *Conflict and Compromise in Multilingual Societies*. Waterloo, Ontario: Wilfrid Laurier University Press.

Michael, P. (2016). 'Avatar' and incarnation: Gita spirituality and ignatian spirituality at the crossroads. *Gregorianum* 97(2): 323–342.

Mill, J. (1840). *The History of British India*. London: James Madden & Co.

Mishra, B. P. (1942). *Tulsi Drashan*. Prayag: Hindi Sahitya Sammelan.

Mishra, V. S. (2015). *Vinay-Patrika Mein Prapattivaad*. New Delhi: Swakshar Prakashan.

Moffett, S. H. (2005a). *A History of Christianity in Asia*, vol. 1: *Beginnings to 1500*. Maruknoll, NY: Orbis Books.

——— (2005b). *A History of Christianity in Asia*, vol. 2: *1500–1900*. Maruknoll, NY: Orbis Books.

Monier-Williams, M. (1875). *Indian Wisdom: On Examples of the Religious, Philosophical, and Ethical Doctrines of the Hindus*. London: W. H. Allen & Co.

Mukherjee, S. (2015). Ram sanehi na mare. In *Ek Chikitsak Ke Sansmaran*, edited by S. Rituparna, pp. 127–129. New Delhi: Indian Council for Cultural Relations.

Namboodiry, U. (1995). *St Xavier's: The Making of a Calcutta Institution*. New Delhi: Viking Press.

Nandy, A. (1995). History's forgotten doubles. *History and Theory* 34(2): 44–66. https://doi.org/10.2307/2505434.

Nath, B. (1979). *The Adhyatama Ramayana*. New Delhi: Munshilal Manoharlal Pubishers Pvt Ltd.

Nehru, J. (1962). *Glimpses of World History*. New York: John Day Company.

Neill, S. (1954). The indigenous church in self-governing countries. *East and West Review*: 35–42.

——— (1984a). *A History of Christianity in India: 1707–1858*. Cambridge, UK: Cambridge University Press. https://doi.org/DOI: 10.1017/CBO97805 115 20556.

——— (1984b). *A History of Christianity in India: The Beginnings to AD 1707*. Cambridge, UK: Cambridge University Press. https://doi.org/DOI: 10.1017/CBO9780511520556.

Nelson, T. (2006). *The Holy Bible: New Century Version*. Nashville, TN: Thomas Nelson Inc.

Nuytten, D. (2005). Architectural research of the former abbey barn of Ter Doest. *Bulletin van de Kon. Ned. Oudheidkundige Bond* 104(2–3): 58–64.

Pandey, N. (2015). Father Camille Bulcke: Mere maanas pita. In *Ek Chikitsak Ke Sansmaran*, edited by S. Rituparna, pp. 167–169. New Delhi: Indian Council for Cultural Relations.

Pandey, R. P. (1987). Father Camille Bulcke: Saint Xavier's College, Ranchi ke Hindi–Sanskrit vibhagadhyaksh ke roop mein. In *Dr Bulcke Smriti Granth*, edited by D. Prasad and S. K. Goswami, pp. 113–116. Ranchi: Dr Bulcke Smriti Granth Samiti. https://doi.org/10.1007/bf00202951.

Pandey, U. (2018). Naari bhavna. In *Tulsi: Radhkrishna Muluakan-Mala*, 11th ed., edited by U. Singh, pp. 151–161. New Delhi: Radhakrishna Prakashan.

Paranjpe, S. M., and N. S. Panse (1894). *Prasanna Raghava by Jayadeva*. Poona: Shiralkar & Co.

Parashar, S. (2016). The Belgian Jesuit who submitted the first-ever Hindi research project to an Indian university. *Scroll.in*, 19 September. https://scroll.in/magazine/815925/the-belgian-jesuit-who-submitted-the-first-ever-hindi-research-project-to-an-indian-university. Accessed 19 April 2023.

———. (2018). The 'gharwapasi' of Padma Bhushan Father Camille Bulcke. *Indian Express*, 17 March.

Patnaik, P. C. (1987). Punyashlok sant Camille Bulcke. In *Dr Bulcke Smriti Granth*, edited by D. Prasad and S. K. Goswami, pp. 92–95. Ranchi: Dr Bulcke Smriti Granth Samiti.

Pollock, S. (1984). The Ramayana text and the critical edition. In *The Ramayana of Valmiki: An Epic of Ancient India*, vol. 1: *Balakanda*, edited by R. P. Goldman, pp. 82–93. Princeton, NJ: Princeton University Press.

Ponette, P. (1987). Father Bulcke: Kuchh amit smritiyan. In *Dr Bulcke Smriti Granth*, edited by D. Prasad and S. K. Goswami, pp. 67–69. Ranchi: Dr Bulcke Smriti Granth Samiti. https://doi.org/10.1007/bf00202951.

——— (1991). Fr. Camille Bulcke, S.J. (1909–1982): A Hindi scholar. In *To Chotanagpur with Love and Service: Pioneers in the Ranchi Jesuit Province*, edited by P. Tete, pp. 117–123. Ranchi: Ranchi Jesuit Society.

Pope, M. H. (1977). *Song of Songs: A New Translation with Introduction and Commentary*. Garden City, NY: Doubleday.

Prasad, D. (1987). Dr Camille Bulcke: Jeevan rekhayen. In *Dr Bulcke Smriti Granth*, edited by D. Prasad and S. K. Goswami, pp. 3–14. Ranchi: Dr Bulcke Smriti Granth Samiti.

———— (1989). Ek punya smaran. In *Father Camille Bulcke: Ek Sant-Sahityakar Kee Yaad*, edited by S. D. Singh, pp. 23–29. Patna: Muktkanth.

———— (2002). *Father Camille Bulcke*. New Delhi: Sahitya Academy.

Prasad, D., and S. K. Goswami (eds.) (1987). *Dr Bulcke Smriti Granth*. Ranchi: Dr Bulcke Samriti Granth Samiti.

Prasad, R. C. (1988). *Ramacharitamanasa*. New Delhi: Motilal Banarasidass.

Praturi, A. (2021). Playing straight into God's hands: A comparative study of the Hindu and christian understandings of play. *Christian Scholar's Review* 50(4): 403–421.

Priolkar, A. K. (1961). *The Goa Inquisition: Being a Quatercentenary Commemoration Study of the Inquisition in India*. Bombay: Bombay University Press.

Qualben, L. P. (1933). *A History of the Christian Church*. New York: Thomas Nelson & Sons.

Quiren, F. (1987). Guido Gezelle. In *Dr Bulcke Smriti Granth*, edited by D. Prasad and S. K. Goswami, pp. 211–215. Ranchi: Dr Bulcke Smriti Granth Samiti.

Radhakrishnan, S. (1927). *The Hindu View of Life*. London: Macmillan Publishers.

Raghavan, V. (1980). *The Ramayana Tradition in Asia*. New Delhi: Sahitya Akademi.

Raghuvansh (1961). *Hari Ghati: Yatra-Diary-Sansmaran*. Kashi: Bharteey Gyanpeeth.

———— (1987). Ek atmeey. In *Dr Bulcke Smriti Granth*, edited by D. Prasad and S. K. Goswami, pp. 55–56. Ranchi: Dr Bulcke Smriti Granth Samiti.

Rajya Sabha TV (2017). 'Father Camille Bulcke - Baba Bulcke - Christian Hindi Scholar: Virasat'. YouTube. https://www.youtube.com/watch?v=1UGU6Bb5NqQ. Accessed 25 March 2024.

Ramanujan, A. K. (1991). Three hundred Ramayanas: Five examples and three thoughts on translation. In *Many Ramayanas: The Diversity of a Narrative Tradition in South Asia*, edited by Paula Richman, pp. 22–49. Berkley, CA: University of California Press.

Raychaudhuri, H. C. (1920). *Materials for the Study of the Early History of the Vaishnava Sect*. Calcutta: R. N. Bhattacharya.

Richman, P. (1991). *Many Ramayanas: The Diversity of a Narrative Tradition in South Asia*. Berkley, CA: University of California Press.

Richter, J. (1908). *A History of Missions in India*. New York, NY: Fleminh H. Ravell Co.

Rituparna, S. (ed.) (2015). *Father Camille Bulcke: Bharteeyata Ke Prakash Punj*. New Delhi: Indian Council for Cultural Relations.

Robertson, J. M. (1900). *Christianity and Mythology*. London: Watts & Co.

Robinson, B. (2004). *Christians Meeting Hindus: An Analysis and Theological Critique of the Hindu–Christian Encounter in India*. Milton Keynes, UK: Regnum Books.

Roosbroeck, G. L. v. (1919). *Guido Gezelle, the Mystic Poet of Flanders*. Vinton, IA: Kruse Publishing Co.

Ross, A. C. (2019). Alessandro Valignano: The Jesuits and culture in the East. In *The Jesuits: Cultures, Sciences, and the Arts, 1540–1773*, edited by John W. O'Malley, Gauvin Alexander Bailey, Steven J. Harris and T. Frank Kennedy, pp. 336–351. Toronto: University of Toronto Press (74th edition).

Rubiés, J. P. (2000). *Travel and Ethnology in the Renaissance: South India through European Eyes, 1250–1625*. Cambridge, UK: Cambridge University Press.

——— (2005). The concept of cultural dialogue and the jesuit method of accommodation: Between idolatry and civilization. *Archivum Historicum Societatis Iesu* 74(147): 237–280.

Rukmani, T. S. (2003). Dr. Richard De Smet and Sankaras Advaita. *Journal of Hindu-Christian Studies* 16(1): 12–21.

Sahay, K. N. (1968). Impact of Christianity on the Uraon of the Chainpur Belt in Chotanagpur: An analysis of its cultural processes. *American Anthropologist* 70(5): 923–942.

Sahay, S. (1919). *Goswami Tulsidas*. Patna, India: Bihar Rashtrabhasha Parishad.

Saran, M., and V. C. Khanna (2018). Camille Bulcke's 'Ramakatha: Utpatti Aur Vikas': An important reference work for scholars in the field of Ramayana studies. In *Cultural and Civilisational Links between India and Southeast Asia: Historical and Contemporary Dimensions*, edited by S. Saran, pp. 225–237. Singapore: Springer. https://doi.org/10.1007/978-981-10-7317-5_13.

Sastri, P. S. S. (1936). The Ramayana. In Krishnaswami Aiyangar Commemoration Volume, edited by V. Rangacharya, C. S. Srinivasachari and V. R. Rarnachandra Dikshitar, pp. 231–233. Madras: Dr. S. Krishnaswami Aiyangar Commemoration Committee.

———. (1944). *Lectures on Patanjali Mahabhshya*, vol. 1. Annamalainagar: Annamalai University.

Saxena, S. (2015). Father Bulcke: Mere guru. In *Father Camille Bulcke: Bharteeyata Ke Prakash Punj*, edited by S. Rituparna, pp. 151–161. New Delhi: Indian Council for Cultural Relations.

——— (2017). *Father Camille Bulcke: Bharteey Sanskriti Ke Anveshak*. New Delhi: Priya Sahitya Sadan.

Schouten, J. P. (2018). A foreign culture baptised: Roberto de Nobili and the Jesuits. *Exchange* 47(2): 183–198. https://doi.org/10.1163/1572543X-12341477.

Schweig, G. M. (2005). *Dance of Divine Love: The Rāsa Līlā of Krishan from the Bhāgavatapurāṇa, India's Classic Sacred Love Story.* Princeton, NJ: Princeton University Press.

Selwyn, J. D. (2016). *A Paradise Inhabited by Devils: The Jesuits' Civilizing Mission in Early Modern Naples.* London and New York: Routledge.

Sharan, A. (ed.) (1950). *Manas Piyush*, vols. 1–7. Gorakhpur: Gita Press.

Sharma, K. (1987). *Bhakti and the Bhakti Movement: A New Perspective.* New Delhi: Munshiram Manoharlal Publishers.

Shastri, H. P. (1952). *The Ramayana of Valmiki.* London: Shanti Sadan.

Shastri, J. L. (ed.) (1957). *The Garuda Purana.* New Delhi: Motilal Banarsidass.

Shore, P. (2020). The years of Jesuit suppression, 1773–1814: Survival, setbacks, and transformation. *Brill Research Perspectives in Jesuit Studies* 2(1): 1–117. https://doi.org/https://doi.org/10.1163/25897454-12340005.

Shrivastava, M. (1973). *Hindi Ke Europeey Vidvaan: Vyaktitva Aur Krititva.* Patna: Bīhar Hindi Grantha Akadami.

Shukla, R. (1929). *Hindi Sahitya Ka Itihas.* Varanasi: Kashi Naagri Pracharini Sabha.

———. (1935). *Goswami Tulsidas.* Allahabad: Kashi Naagri Pracharini Sabha.

Singh, A. K. (1987). Dr Camille Bulcke ka rachna sansaar. In *Father Camille Bulcke: Bharteeyata Ke Prakash Punj*, edited by D. Prasad and S. K. Goswami, pp. 181–187. Ranchi: Dr Bulcke Smriti Granth Samiti.

Singh, S. D. (1982). *Father Camille Bulcke: Ek Sant-Sahityakar Kee Yaad.* Patna: Muktkanth.

——— (2015). Ek sant sahityakaar kee yaad. In *Ek Chikitsak Ke Sansmaran*, edited by S. Rituparna, pp. 102–107. New Delhi: Indian Council for Cultural Relations.

Singh, U. (1966). *Tulsi-Kavya-Mimansa.* New Delhi: Radhakrishna Prakashan.

Singh, Y. P. (2014). *Ram Sahitya Kosh.* New Delhi: Rajkamal Prakashan.

Smith, V. A. (1917). *Akbar: The Great Mogul 1542–1605.* London: Clarendon Press.

Sri Aurobindo (1997). *Essays on the Gita.* Pondicherry: Sri Aurobindo Ashram.

——— (2012). *Letters on Yoga: The Complete Works of Sri Aurobindo*, vol. 28, Pondicherry: Sri Aurobindo Ashram.

Stanard, M. (2019). *The Leopard, the Lion, and the Cock: Colonial Memories and Monuments in Belgium.* Leuven: Universitaire Pers Leuven. https://doi.org/10.1353/book.65135.

Standaert, N. (2019). Jesuit corporate culture as shaped by the Chinese. In *The Jesuits: Cultures, Sciences, and the Arts, 1540–1773*, edited by J. W. O' Malley, G. A. Bailey, S. J. Harris and T. F. Kennedy, pp. 352–363. Toronto: University of Toronto Press. https://doi.org/doi:10.3138/97814426 81569 -020.

Strakhovsky, L. I. (1939). The Louvain concept of a university. *Catholic Historical Review* 25(2): 179–183.

Subrahmanyam, S. (1998). *The Career and Legend of Vasco da Gama*. Cambridge, UK: Cambridge University Press.

Svami, C. S. (2022). *Hindu Dharma: The Universal Way of Life*. Mumbai: Bhartiya Vidya Bhavan.

Swami Karpatri (2019). *Ramayana Mimansa*. Vrindavan: Radhakrishna Dhanuka Prakashan Sansthaan.

Swami Tapasyananda (2006). *Adhyatama Ramayana (Sanskrit Verse with English Translation)*. Kolkata: Advaita Press.

Tagare, G. V. (1978). *Bhagavata Purana*, vols. 1–5. New Delhi: Motilal Banarsidass.

Tandon, B. N. (2015). Father Camille Bulcke: Kuchh yaden. In *Father Camille Bulcke: Bharteeyata Ke Prakash Punj*, edited by S. Rituparna, pp. 87–96. New Delhi: Indian Council for Cultural Relations.

Telang, K. T. (1976 [1873]). Was the Ramayana copied from Homer? A reply to Professor Weber. *Students' Literary and Scientific Society Bombay*. Bombay: Bombay Publishers Parlour.

Tete, P. (1984). *A Missionary Social Worker in India: JB Hoffmann, the Chota Nagpur Tenancy Act and the Catholic Co-Operatives, 1893–1928*. Rome: Gregorian Biblical BookShop.

——— (ed.) (1993). *Constant Lievens and the History of the Catholic Church in Chotanagpur*. Ranchi: Archbishop's House.

Tillin, L. (2013). *Remapping India: New States and Their Political Origins*. Oxford: Oxford University Press. https://doi.org/10.1093/acprof: oso/9780199336036.001.0001.

Tisdall, W. S. C. (1901). *India: Its History, Darkness and Dawn*. London: Student Volunteer Missionary Union.

Tiwari, U. N. (1987). Shubhashansa. In *Dr Bulcke Smriti Granth*, edited by D. Prasad and S. K. Goswami, pp. 36–37. Ranchi: Dr Bulcke Smriti Granth Samiti.

Tripathi, R. (2015). Ramkatha ke vyakhyata Baba Camille Bulcke. In *Father Camille Bulcke: Bharteeyata Ke Prakash Punj*, edited by S. Rituparna, pp. 256–258. New Delhi: Indian Council for Cultural Relations.

Tripathi, V. (1974). *Lokvadi Tulsidas*. New Delhi: Radhakrishna Prakashan.

Tulsidas. (2001). *Śrī Rāmacaritamānasa (with Hindi Text and English Transliteration)*. Gorakhpur: Gita Press.

Turner, R. L. (1931). *A Comparative and Etymological Dictionary of the Nepali Language*. London: K. Paul, Trench, Trubner & Co.

United Nations Alliance of Civilizations (UNAOC) (2006). *Alliance of Civilizations: Report of the High-Level Group*. New York: United Nations.

Vaidya, C. V. (1901). *The Riddle of the Ramayana*. Poona: Manohar Granthmala.

van Acker, J. (2021). Ter Doest Abbey. Mmmonk.be. https://www.mmmonk. be/en/discover/history-of-the-collections/history-abbeys/history-doest. Accessed 10 March 2022.

van Exem, A. (1988). Jesuit impact on Chotanagpur. In *Jesuit Presence in Indian History: Commemorative Volume on the Occasion of the 150th Anniversary of the New Madurai Mission; 1838–1988*, edited by A. Amaladass, pp. 78–98. Anand: Gujarat Sahitya Prakash.

van Winkle, S. (2015). Sahas kee murti: Dr Bulcke. In *Ek Chikitsak ke Sansmaran*, edited by S. Rituparna, pp. 31–32. New Delhi: Indian Council for Cultural Relations.

Vanita, R. (2022). *The Dharma of Justice in the Sanskrit Epics: Debates on Gender, Varna, and Species*. Oxford and New York (NY): Oxford University Press. DOI: 10.1093/oso/9780192859822.001.0001.

Vanthemsche, G. (2012). *Belgium and the Congo, 1885–1980*. Cambridge, UK: Cambridge University Press.

Vanthemsche, G., and R. D. Peuter (2023). *A Concise History of Belgium*. Cambridge, UK: Cambridge University Press.

Vechoor, M. (1987). Bible ke Hindi anuvadak aur Dr Camille Bulcke. In *Dr Bulcke Smriti Granth*, edited by D. Prasad and S. K. Goswami, pp. 169–180. Ranchi: Dr Bulcke Smriti Granth Samiti.

Verma, D. (1950). Introduction. In *Ramkatha: Utpatti Aur Vikas*, 3rd ed., edited by C. Bulcke, pp. 5–6. Prayag: Hindi Parisfiad Prakasan.

Verma, M. (1987). Ek shabd-chitra. In *Dr Bulcke Smriti Granth*, edited D. Prasad and S. K. Goswami, pp. 31–32. Ranchi: Dr Bulcke Smriti Granth Samiti.

———. (2021). *My Family (English Translation of Mera Parivar)*. New Delhi: Penguin Hamish Hamilton.

Verma, R. (ed.) (1962). *Manak Hindi Kosh (in 5 Volumes)*. Prayag: Hindi Sahitya Sammelan.

———(1968). *Shabdharth Darshan*. Allahabad: Rachna Prakashan.

Vincent, P. (2016). *Poems of Guido Gezelle: A Bilingual Anthology*. London: UCL Press. https://doi.org/10.14324/111.9781910634943.

Vivekananda (1964). *The Complete Works of Swami Vivekananda*, vol. 3. Calcutta: Advaita Ashrama.

Vu Thanh, H. (2019). The Jesuits in Asia under the Portuguese Padroado: India, China, and Japan (sixteenth to seventeenth centuries). In *The Oxford Handbook of the Jesuits*, edited by I. G. Županov, pp. 400–426. Oxford: Oxford University Press.

Vyas, L. P. (2015). Soumya sant Bulcke jee. In *Father Camille Bulcke: Bharteeyata Ke Prakash Punj*, edited by S. Rituparna, pp. 97–98. New Delhi: Indian Council for Cultural Relations.

Wagner, K. A. (2017). *The Skull of Alum Bheg: The Life and Death of a Rebel of 1857*. New York: Oxford University Press.

Weber, A. (1873). *On the Ramayana*. Bombay: Thacker, Vining & Co.

Whaling, F. (1980). *The Rise of the Religious Significance of Rama*. New Delhi: Motilal Banarsidass.

Witte, E., J. Craeybeckx and A. Meynen (2009). *Political History of Belgium: From 1830 Onwards*. Brussels: Belgium Academic and Scientific Publishers.

Woitrin, M. (1998). Louvain-Ia-Neuve: A new city for an old university. In *The Urban University and Its Identity: Roots, Location, Roles*, edited by H. van D. Wusten, pp. 71–86. Dordrecht: Springer.

Xavier, Â. B., and I. G. Županov (2015). *Catholic Orientalism: Portuguese Empire, Indian Knowledge (16th–18th Centuries)*. New Delhi: Oxford University Press.

Xaxa, V. (2018). Isolation, inclusion and exclusion: The case of Adivasis in India. In *Adivasi Rights and Exclusion in India*, edited by V. S. Rao, pp. 27–40. New Delhi: Routledge.

Young, R. F. (1989). Francis Xavier in the perspective of the Saivite Brahmins of Tiruchendur temple. In *Hindu–Christian Dialogue: Perspectives and Encounters*, edited by H. G. Coward, pp. 64–79.

Županov, I. G. (2001). *Disputed Mission: Jesuit Experiments and Brahmanical Knowledge in Seventeenth-Century India*. New Delhi: Oxford University Press.

——— (2005a). *Missionary Tropics: The Catholic Frontier in India, 16th–17th Centuries*. Ann Arbor, MI: University of Michigan Press.

——— (2005b). 'One civility, but multiple religions': Jesuit mission among St. Thomas Christians in India (16th–17th centuries). *Journal of Early Modern History* 9(3): 284–325. https://doi.org/10.1163/157006505775008473.

Index